THE MUSIC OF
JAMES TENNEY

THE MUSIC OF
JAMES TENNEY

VOLUME 1

Contexts and Paradigms

ROBERT WANNAMAKER

**UNIVERSITY OF
ILLINOIS PRESS**
Urbana, Chicago, and Springfield

Publication supported by grants from the AMS 75 PAYS
Endowment of the American Musicological Society, supported
in part by the National Endowment for the Humanities and the
Andrew W. Mellon Foundation; the Henry and Edna Binkele
Classical Music Fund; and the California Institute for the Arts.

Frontispiece: Untitled pencil sketch by Carolee Schneemann
(1956). ©2020 The Carolee Schneemann Foundation / Artists
Rights Society (ARS), New York.

Library of Congress Cataloging-in-Publication Data
Names: Wannamaker, Rob, author.
Title: The music of James Tenney / Robert Wannamaker.
Description: Urbana : University of Illinois Press, 2021. | Includes
    bibliographical references and index. | Contents: Volume 1.
    Contexts and paradigms — volume 2. A handbook to the pieces.
Identifiers: LCCN 2021010713 (print) | LCCN 2021010714 (ebook)
    | ISBN 9780252043673 (v. 1 ; hardcover) | ISBN 9780252043680
    (v. 2 ; hardcover) | ISBN 9780252052569 (v. 1 ; ebook) | ISBN
    9780252052576 (v. 2 ; ebook)
Subjects: LCSH: Tenney, James—Criticism and interpretation. |
    Music—20th century—History and criticism.
Classification: LCC ML410.T3215 W36 2021 (print) | LCC ML410
    .T3215 (ebook) | DDC 780.92—dc23
LC record available at https://lccn.loc.gov/2021010713
LC ebook record available at https://lccn.loc.gov/2021010714

for Karen

Contents

Preface   xi

Conventions and Abbreviations   xv

1. Introduction   **1**

1.1. A Summary Chronology   3

1.2. Aesthetic and Methodological Bases: Music in Sound   10

2. Early Works and Influences (1934–59)   **18**

2.1. Stan Brakhage and *Interim* (1952)   19

2.2. Manhattan and Meeting Carolee Schneemann   21

2.3. Lionel Nowak, Carl Ruggles, and Charles Ives's *Concord* Sonata   23

2.4. *Seeds* (1956/1961)   25

3. Tape Music and "Meta/Hodos" (1959–61)   **31**

3.1. Lejaren Hiller and Harry Partch   31

3.2. The University of Illinois Electronic Music Studio   32

3.3. *Collage #1 ("Blue Suede")* (1961)   34

3.4. "Meta/Hodos" (1961)   41

4. Computer Music and Ergodicity (1961–64) 48

4.1. Edgard Varèse, D'Arcy Thompson, and "Growth to Form" 51

4.2. John Cage, Variety, and Ergodicity 54

4.3. Max Mathews and MUSIC 59

4.4. The Acoustic Correlates of Timbre 62

4.5. Algorithmic Composition 63

4.6. *Analog #1 (Noise Study)* (1961) 68

4.7. *Phases* (1963) 76

5. Performance and the Social (1964–68) 83

5.1. Downtown in the 1960s 83

5.2. Tone Roads and an American Experimental Tradition 86

5.3. Fluxus and Friends 89

5.4. Carolee Schneemann, Antonin Artaud, Wilhelm Reich 93

5.5. *Choreogram* (1964) 97

5.6. *Fabric for Che* (1967) 101

6. Process and Continuity (1969–71) 110

6.1. Gradual Processes 112

6.2. *For Ann (rising)* (1969) 118

6.3. *Postal Pieces* (1965–71) 124

7. Interlude: Harmonic Theory 135

7.1. The Meaning of *Harmony* 137

7.2. The Harmonic Series 140

7.3. Interval Tolerance and "The Language of Ratios" 144

7.4. A History of *Consonance* and *Dissonance* 147

7.5. Roughness and Beating (CDC-5) 148

7.6. Toneness and Harmonicity (CDC-2) 149

7.7. Harmonic Space (CDC-1) 155

7.8. Harmonic Measures and Their Applications 165

8. Canons and the Harmonic Series (1972–79) 169

8.1. The Harmonic-Series Music   170

8.2. *Clang* (1972)   172

8.3. *Spectral CANON for CONLON Nancarrow* (1974)   176

8.4. *Harmonium #1* (1976)   183

8.5. *Three Indigenous Songs* (1979)   189

9. Harmonic Spaces (1980–85)   193

9.1. The Harmonic-Space Music   193

9.2. *Harmonium #3* (1980)   195

9.3. *Bridge* (1984)   199

9.4. *Koan for String Quartet* (1984)   216

10. Transition and Tradition (1986–94)   224

10.1. *Critical Band* (1988)   225

10.2. *Flocking* (1993)   231

11. Spectra and Diaphony (1994–2006)   237

11.1. Dissonant Counterpoint and Statistical Feedback   237

11.2. *In a Large, . . .* (1994–95)   241

11.3. *Diaphonic Study* (1997)   246

11.4. *Arbor Vitae* (2006)   250

12. A Tradition of Experimentation   259

Appendix A. Acoustics, Sensation, and Logarithmic Models   261

Appendix B. Spectrographic Analysis   265

Notes   271

References   301

Index   315

Preface

In the 1950s, while still an undergraduate student, James Tenney boldly under-took to perform the colossal *Concord* Sonata for piano by Charles Ives. Regarding his motivation, he later remarked, "My performance of other people's music has always been motivated by my desire to understand that music better. . . . I wanted to hear into it" (Tenney 2005a). The same primary motivation has continually underlain my own analytical project: I have wanted to expand and sharpen both my experience and my understanding of Tenney's music as heard. It is my hope that this book will also enrich the engagement of other listeners with Tenney's music while supporting future scholarly and creative responses to his work.

This text is thus intended first as a contribution to the literature on music analysis, and I supply analyses for all of Tenney's mature compositions. My perspective is that of a composer, so I have been concerned with the relation-ship between Tenney's ideas and techniques and the experiences prospectively afforded by his music. With respect to the latter, my analyses frequently offer aural heuristics in response to a notable paucity of such perceptually grounded approaches in the literature surrounding experimental music.

I have included substantial supporting consideration of Tenney's theoretical work, intellectual contexts, and early biography because these motivated and are reflected in his music to an extraordinary degree. In particular, much of Tenney's compositional production—like that of Henry Cowell, Harry Partch, and Milton Babbitt—must be understood in relation to theoretical investigations undertaken in tandem with it. Therefore, although this book is not intended to provide an exhaustive account of Tenney's theoretical work, it supplies reasonably detailed condensations of his formal, timbral, and harmonic theories that may furnish useful springboards to the primary sources in *From Scratch: Writings in Music Theory* (Tenney 2015). With respect to his harmonic theories in particular, I have significantly augmented the information available in published sources with insights derived from unpublished archival materials. I hope that historical musicologists will find topics of interest in the biographical and aesthetic contexts discussed in the early chapters and that these will encourage further research and commentary.

The book is divided into two volumes, each of which is organized chronologically and with the same periodization. Volume 1, *Contexts and Paradigms*, furnishes a general survey of Tenney's creative development and output. Most chapters—especially the early ones—begin with one or more sections providing biographical and technical context that supports understanding of his music in the associated period. In each case, this is followed by analyses of a small number of pieces that were selected in order to illuminate concerns, characteristics, and techniques that emerged in his music around that time. Thus the works analyzed in volume 1 were chosen primarily for their capacity to illustrate particular topics, and many major works are not included among them (but instead appear in volume 2).

Volume 2, *A Handbook to the Pieces*, is conceived as a reference work. It supplies analyses of all of Tenney's significant experimental works created after 1959 that were not included in volume 1. It is intended to serve readers interested in particular pieces or particular periods or who want to explore beyond the conspectus provided in the first volume. Curious readers will discover a profusion of unique compositional ideas, with striking new ones often appearing serially from one work to the next. For the most part I have taken Tenney's earliest works, occasional pieces in popular styles, and arrangements of works by other composers to reside outside the scope of this project, but I have briefly listed them for reference in dedicated chapters.

In most cases, the reader needn't have a score at hand in order to digest my analysis of a particular composition. Although many of Tenney's scores contain unique and elegant notational aspects worth studying, I have often included score excerpts or relevant discussion in such instances. Like that of an architect, Tenney's compositional process typically proceeded top-down—from large-scale features to local details—and he joked that he consequently used more graph paper than staff paper (Tenney 2008, 84). Accordingly, important formal and structural features in his music are often more lucidly captured by a graph or diagram than by a score, and this book contains many such figures. These sometimes supply an outline in time that can be instructively compared with the unfolding music, much like a graphical score or score excerpt. In any case, readers should be alerted that figures herein often bear considerable autonomous expository significance and thus warrant dedicated examination apart from the text.

Although access by the reader to a work's score may not be obligatory, access to an audio recording of the music is usually indispensable. I have not included a discography, since extensive, searchable, and continually updated discographic websites are freely available online. In instances where no commercially released recording of a particular work is available, there remains that resource to which most composers turn today in order to keep abreast of musical developments, even if not all will admit it: YouTube (with SoundCloud as a second resort). If the reader has a recording available, I recommend that they audition it in an audio editor or, better yet, use spectrographic analysis software such as the freeware Sonic Visualiser (appendix B, note 1). Such software permits a listener to practice *hearing* in the same manner that a professional musician practices *execution*: by repeating particular excerpts. The reader is encouraged to adopt a critical attitude toward the analyses herein by shuttling continually between the text and the music so that no assertion is allowed to pass without being immediately compared to the corresponding musical passage as heard.

A fanning of these pages will confirm that Tenney's work sometimes involved theoretical and technical aspects and that I have not shied away from detailing them. I have aimed, however, to introduce most requisite technical concepts within the text itself and to make the exposition accessible to any musically literate reader who is prepared to reread the occasional passage. Perhaps more than would be the case with some composers, I believe readers will find that these technical and theoretical considerations illuminate Tenney's broader thought and attitudes, invite creative adaptations and extensions, and possess an appealing elegance of their own. Most importantly, they elucidate and enrich the listening experience because they are very intimately grounded in it. As Tenney himself remarked in connection with his harmonic-space models, "An abstraction is only of interest to me if I feel I can connect it back to experience."[1] Accordingly, the importance of listening closely to Tenney's music in conjunction with any analysis of it cannot be overstated. To borrow a phrase: just as a computer model of a thunderstorm will not get you wet, no analysis abstracted from Tenney's music can ultimately capture the sensuous experience of hearing it.[2]

• • •

My debts as author are many. Lauren Pratt, executor of the Tenney Estate, has been extraordinarily generous and helpful in providing me with access to materials, answering my many questions, and reading this entire text. I count myself privileged to have spent two days in August 2017 interviewing artist Carolee Schneemann (1939–2019) at the 1750 stone Huguenot house that she and Tenney restored and shared in the 1960s along the Wallkill River in Springtown, New York. Later, Schneemann helpfully read and commented on various sections of my manuscript. Artists Alison Knowles and Hannah Higgins also generously granted to me a 2018 interview regarding Knowles's interactions and collaboration with Tenney.

Archivists Anna St. Onge and Julia Holland at the Clara Thomas Archives and Special Collections at York University in Toronto, Canada, were immensely helpful during my delves into the James Tenney Fonds housed there. In the library at the California Institute of the Arts, Susan Lowenberg and Lavinia Busch were tirelessly accommodating in the face of my many requests, and archivist Kathy Carbone assisted me in the CalArts Institute Archives. At various times, I was aided in obtaining particular materials or information by Daniel Corral, Cassia Streb, Tashi Wada, Michael Winter, and Gayle Young.

I am deeply grateful to director Laurie Matheson and to all of the staff at the University of Illinois Press for their enthusiasm and support while bringing this complex project to publication. The manuscript was much enhanced by valuable and timely advice from reviewer Kyle Gann and an anonymous reviewer. I am also grateful to Tom Erbe, who provided me with comments regarding various passages.

Funding from the California Institute of the Arts Faculty Development Fund and from the Herb Alpert School of Music at CalArts has facilitated travel, research, and publication of this project. I would especially like to thank David Rosenboom, who, as dean of the Herb Alpert School of Music at CalArts, provided his steady support and encouragement.

Musical scores and excerpts thereof by James Tenney appearing herein that date from 1985 and earlier are copyrighted by Sonic Art Editions and used by permission of Smith Publications, 54 Lent Road, Sharon, Vermont. Tenney's scores and excerpts thereof that date from 1986 and later are copyrighted by and used by permission of the Estate of James Tenney and are distributed by the Canadian Music Centre. Substantially revised and augmented excerpts from "The Spectral Music of James Tenney" (Wannamaker 2008b) have been absorbed into two chapters of the current project, and Chapter 7 of the current volume expands upon my contribution to *The Oxford Handbook of Spectral Music* (forthcoming).

Throughout the completion of this book project, I have been grateful for the patience and love of my marvelous family: Karen, Aidan, and Emily. Any typographical errors are entirely the responsibility of our two tabbies, Leo and Oscar.

Conventions and Abbreviations

In this book, the following abbreviations are sometimes used. Nomenclature and operations pertaining to pitch classes and tone rows are consistent with *Introduction to Post-tonal Theory* (Straus 2016).

JTF	James Tenney Fonds (Inventory #F0428), Clara Thomas Archives and Special Collections, York University, Toronto, ON, Canada

nTET	n-tone equal temperament (e.g., 12TET)
pc	pitch class
pcset	pitch-class set
i	ordered pitch-class interval
ic	unordered pitch-class interval (interval class)
sc	set class
T_i	pitch-class transposition through ordered pitch-class interval i
T_iI	pitch-class inversion with index of inversion i
R	retrogression

GCD	greatest common divisor
LCM	least common multiple

BW	bandwidth
CF	center frequency
IAD	interattack duration
cent	one one-hundredth of a semitone in 12TET

Unless otherwise stated, the following conventions are observed.

- The pitch A_4 corresponds to a frequency of 440 Hz.
- The adjective *tempered* refers to 12TET.

- Tempered pitch classes are sometimes numbered 0, 1, 2, 3, 4, 5, 6, 7, 8, 9, A, B, so that the single characters A and B correspond to the decimal numbers 10 and 11, respectively.
- pc0 corresponds to the note letter name C, pc1 to C-sharp/D-flat, and so forth.
- A set class may be designated by either its prime form or its Forte number.

THE MUSIC OF
JAMES TENNEY

CHAPTER 1

Introduction

When asked in 1989, "Had you been born 60 years later, . . . who would you study with today?" John Cage immediately replied, "I think I would study with James Tenney" (Cage and Nancarrow 1989).

Whereas in the 1960s Cage had been a mentor and aesthetic lodestone for the young Tenney, near the end of his life it was Cage who suggested that there was much for young artists to learn from his former protégé. Musicologist Bob Gilmore in turn described Tenney as "the composer who is in a way Cage's natural successor in the next generation" (2014, 25). Among composers, further expressions of regard for Tenney and his work are not difficult to find. Late in life, Edgard Varèse pronounced Tenney his "only musical heir" (Brakhage 1982).[1] According to composer Anne LeBaron, György Ligeti described Tenney as one of the "greatest American composers living today, in the company of Ives, Partch, and Nancarrow" (2006). For Larry Polansky, "Jim Tenney was the most important and brilliant composer/theorist of the second half of the twentieth century" (2007, 10). John Luther Adams has remarked, "I shudder to think what might have become of me had I not had the extreme good fortune to study with Jim [Tenney], one of the great composers of the twentieth century. . . . He was one of the most brilliant people I have ever known" (2013). Appreciations of Tenney and his work have furnished the content of four separate Festschriften (Garland 1984; Polansky and Rosenboom 1987; Dibelius et al. 1990; Hasegawa 2008).

Yet although Tenney had been producing significant work since the late 1950s, before 1983 the number of his compositions that had been commercially recorded was a total of two (and those were on obscure out-of-print compilation recordings). In the words of composer and writer Kyle Gann, "No other composer is so revered by fellow composers, and so unknown to the public at large" (1997, 167). In the 1990s, however, the situation began to change. Broader recognition of Tenney's work first began to grow in Europe after John Cage—following an absence of more than three decades—brought Tenney with him when he returned to teach at the Darmstadt International Summer Courses for New Music in Germany. In the following years, Tenney received a steady stream of commissions from European ensembles. In the late 1990s and into the 2000s, recordings of his work began to proliferate and, since the year 2000, North American programming of Tenney's music both new and old has become common. Among adventurous emerging performers and composers, an enthusiasm for Tenney's work is today widespread, and rock, techno, and ambient musicians have covered or remixed his music.

As composer, theorist, writer, performer, and educator, Tenney contributed to an extraordinary number of areas in twentieth-century musical culture. His compositions of the early 1960s include significant harbingers of sampling culture and plunderphonics, the first substantial musical applications of computerized sound synthesis, and some of the earliest applications of computer algorithms in the composition of both electronic and instrumental music. He has been described as a Zelig-like figure in 1960s American experimentalism because he seemed to appear in an uncannily far-flung array of contexts not only within but also outside of the domain of music. Tenney's minimalist process pieces of the early 1970s are some of the most rigorous, elemental, and oft-performed pieces of their sort. His subsequent music of that decade invoked the harmonic series in ways that paralleled, anticipated, or contrasted with the development in Europe of a major style now known as *spectral music*. Tenney's harmonic-series pieces were joined in the 1980s by complex large-scale works in nonstandard tuning systems that were concerned with a general renovation of harmonic practice. Although Tenney asserted that "I am first of all a composer and only secondarily and occasionally a theorist" ([1993c/2003] 2015, 380), in conjunction with his compositional work he produced influential original theories concerning the perception of musical form, timbre, and harmony. Finally, his complementary activities as performer, writer, and educator did much to consolidate the influential concept of a particular American experimental music tradition.

I have found that individuals with specific musical interests often know certain facets of Tenney's wide-ranging work and history but are quite surprised to discover others. With this in mind, the next section optionally furnishes readers with a greatly condensed overview of his history, to be expanded in the coming chapters. It doubles as an outline of volume 1. This is followed in section 1.2 by an orientation to certain fundamental aesthetic and methodological premises that underlie Tenney's mature music.

1.1 A Summary Chronology

During the first half of his career, significant developments in Tenney's musical concerns and style roughly correlated with his movements. Changes in his milieu and resources seem to have occasioned new directions or creative renewals. The first of these was a simple change of high school in Denver, Colorado, that brought Tenney into contact with artistically minded peers, including an aspiring poet named Stan Brakhage. Brakhage, tacking from poetry toward film, would eventually become the most celebrated experimental filmmaker of the second half of the twentieth century. In a fateful move, Brakhage in 1951 recruited Tenney, a promising pianist, to score his first film (section 2.1). This project seems to have crystallized Tenney's identity as a composer, although he would not commit professionally for another two years. Especially during the first decade of their friendship, impassioned dialogue and correspondence between Brakhage and Tenney did much to fortify their artistic identities. They would remain close friends until Brakhage's death in 2003.

Tenney moved from Colorado to New York in the autumn of 1954 to study piano at the Juilliard School. At this time he made initial acquaintance with the two composers whose music would most influence his own: Edgard Varèse and John Cage. Perhaps the most consequential event in his life during that period, however, was the commencement of a thirteen-year relationship with artist Carolee Schneemann (section 2.2). Still a student at the time, in the coming years she would make groundbreaking and enormously influential contributions to assemblage, performance art, experimental film, multimedia, and feminist art (Filippone 2011). Throughout their partnership, Tenney and Schneemann would live and create closely together, each of them significantly affecting and participating in the other's work and development (sections 3.3, 4.1, 5.4–5.5; volume 2, sections 4.5–4.6).

Soon abandoning formal piano instruction, Tenney devoted himself to the study of composition—at first privately in New York, subsequently at Bennington College in Vermont, and informally with Varèse until his death in 1965 (sections 2.2–2.3). The primary antecedents that Tenney was digesting in the mid- to late 1950s were those of Anton Webern's aphoristic nonserial music circa 1910, the music of Varèse, and Cage's *Sonatas and Interludes* (1948) for prepared piano. An emphasis in all of these upon the sensuous qualities of timbre would have a powerful and lasting influence on Tenney's own sensibility. Moreover, Varèse's deemphasis of thematic working in favor of a process-like accretion of musical materials would have a durable impact on Tenney's approach to form, while the emphatically dissonant textures of Webern and Varèse would reflect clearly in Tenney's early music (and again in his late music). Tenney's unique consolidation of these influences is represented by the pithy suite *Seeds* (1956/1961; section

2.4), which he considered to be both his earliest mature work and a harbinger of his compositional concerns in years to come (especially in its close attention to timbre).

Concurrently with his undergraduate studies in Vermont (1956–58), Tenney befriended and undertook informal private study nearby with another composer of resolutely dissonant music: Carl Ruggles (section 2.3). The intensely expressive chromatic polyphony of Ruggles's small but refined oeuvre is representative of an American twentieth-century atonal style that is sometimes referred to as *dissonant counterpoint* and that is also associated with certain works by composers Henry Cowell and Ruth Crawford, among others. While the immediate influence of his studies with Ruggles would be relatively short-lived, aspects of dissonant counterpoint would unexpectedly resurface in Tenney's music of the 1990s (section 11.1).

In the 1930s, Varèse had already foretold many of the ways in which technology would in future permit the realization of new musical possibilities with respect to pitch, timbre, rhythm, dynamics, and spatialization. Deeply excited by Varèse's vision, in 1959 Tenney enrolled in a new master's program at the University of Illinois, this being the first academic program in the United States focused on electronic music composition (chapter 3). The program was directed by Lejaren Hiller, a chemist who had gravitated to the music department and who had cocreated in the mid-1950s the first substantial example of music composed using a computer algorithm. Tenney's two years in Illinois afforded him a solid academic training in acoustics, analog electronics, and the techniques of early electronic music, but they also yielded three other outcomes that would prove even more significant.

The first of these was that, in the university's Electronic Music Studio, Tenney produced a now-classic work of tape music entitled *Collage #1 ("Blue Suede")* (1961). In it he took the unprecedented step of manipulating materials recognizably derived from a preexisting pop song: Elvis Presley's version of "Blue Suede Shoes" (section 3.3). Conceived as an exploration and celebration of the Presley source, Tenney's *"Blue Suede"* marked a technical and aesthetic convergence between the cultural insurgence of early rock and roll, the frequent use of quotation in Charles Ives's music (which Tenney was then practicing at the piano), and the concurrent development of collage technique in Schneemann's works on canvas. More generally, it furnished a harbinger of sampling culture and the "postmodern" erosion of stylistic boundaries around high art in the coming decades.

Second, Tenney obtained an assistantship with composer, instrument builder, and music theorist Harry Partch, who was resident at the university on a non-teaching fellowship. Partch was the principal progenitor of just intonation in both theory and practice in the twentieth century, and he designed and constructed a substantial number of unique instruments in order to accurately realize the nonstandard tuning of his music. Tenney's responsibilities included helping to maintain these instruments and performing upon them in Partch's ensemble. Most consequentially, he digested Partch's theoretical writings on just intonation. The influence of these would remain dormant in Tenney's music for more than a decade before significantly informing his own musical and theoretical investigations of harmony.

Finally, near the end of his time in Illinois, Tenney completed his master's thesis, entitled "Meta/Hodos," which advanced a groundbreaking theory of musical form and texture ([1961] 2015; section 3.4). Earlier music theories had generally been concerned with the description of received practice or—especially with respect to new music—the formulation of style-specific guidelines. In contrast, Tenney sought general *perceptual* principles that would be applicable across diverse styles, including the contemporary ones with which he was engaged. His approach adapted visual principles from Gestalt psychology to describe factors governing the perceptual grouping of musical elements both in time and polyphonically. He then went further to consider the characteristics of and relationships between such perceived groupings. Despite its very limited availability, over the coming decades "Meta/Hodos" would develop a widespread underground readership among composers and scholars interested in new music. For Tenney himself, it would provide a technical foundation for many compositions scattered throughout his subsequent career.

Following graduation, Tenney accepted a position at Bell Telephone Laboratories (Bell Labs) in New Jersey (chapter 4). Officially, he was employed to conduct psychoacoustic research. According with his keen interest in timbre, Tenney's scientific research involved the synthesis of musical tone colors, in connection with which he developed a theory of timbre that emphasized the importance of transient and modulatory features in sound. Unofficially, however, Tenney was retained to serve as a musical consultant to engineer Max Mathews, who was developing a pioneering computer music system called MUSIC. MUSIC would become the first widely used program for sound synthesis, and Mathews would go on to make groundbreaking contributions to musician-computer interaction, leading later writers to dub him "the father of computer music." While at Bell Labs with Mathews, Tenney created some of the very earliest pieces of music synthesized or algorithmically composed with the aid of a computer, including what is, as far as I have ascertained, the first digitally synthesized work produced by a professional composer: *Analog #1 (Noise Study)* (1961; section 4.6). A number of features added to the system at Tenney's request became standard in later computer music systems, including audio noise generators, filters, and the capacity to determine musical parameters via compositional algorithms. As both the available technologies and his timbral theories developed, Tenney incorporated them into his computer compositions, which attained a peak of technical and musical sophistication in *Phases* (1963;

section 4.7) and *Ergodos II* (1964). These works combined control over many sound parameters with complex polyphony and multileveled formal hierarchies, which were algorithmically produced by inverting the analytic procedures of "Meta/Hodos" into generative ones.

These final pieces completed at Bell Labs also represent the endpoint of Tenney's gradual digestion of the radically nondramatic, sound-focused aesthetic advanced by composer John Cage. Around 1950, in works such as *Music of Changes* (1951), Cage had begun overtly using chance procedures to determine certain musical features that traditionally would have been subject to a composer's discretion, thereby disrupting the customary interpretation of such features as expressing composerly intent. In particular, Cage's approach shed dramatic large-scale formal shaping in favor of unpredictable and varied local detail. As Tenney, over the course of his time at Bell Labs, deliberately confronted Cage's aesthetic, the dramatically conceived arch form of *Noise Study* ceded to the nonnarrative post-Cagean equanimity of *Ergodos II*, each minute of whose rich sonic tapestry statistically resembles its every other minute. One possibility promoted by Cage's partial undercutting of authorial intent as a source of musical meaning was a compensatory shift in listeners' attentions toward their own perceptions and perceptual processes. If Tenney's output seldom again approached the statistical invariance of *Ergodos II*, his turn from an expressive conception of music toward a post-Cagean, listener-focused orientation would prove to be lasting.

In the latter half of the 1960s, Tenney held research positions in acoustics, first at Yale University and then at the Polytechnic Institute of Brooklyn. Composition was not an aspect of his duties, and his creative output temporarily abated. On the other hand, his activities as performer were vigorous during this period (chapter 5). In 1963 he founded the Tone Roads Chamber Ensemble with performer-composers Malcolm Goldstein and Philip Corner, codirecting it with them until 1969. By programming the music of American experimental composers from preceding generations alongside more recent music, Tone Roads concerts—and Tenney's activities as performer, composer, writer, and teacher more generally—helped consolidate the critical conception of an American experimental-music tradition extending from Charles Ives through Henry Cowell and Varèse to Cage and later experimentalists (section 5.2).

Tenney's involvements with avant-garde art movements then burgeoning in New York also deepened in the mid-1960s (section 5.1). In the creative hothouse of downtown Manhattan, a vigorous cross-pollination between artistic disciplines was under way, bringing together emerging artists, musicians, dancers, poets, and filmmakers in a profusion of small venues. Prominent elements included the confluence of artists now known as Fluxus; the Annual Avant Garde Festivals, curated by cellist and performance artist Charlotte Moorman; and the Judson Dance Theater. Tenney was involved with each of these.

Fluxus was a fluid international group of interdisciplinary artists that emerged in the early 1960s. Broadly influenced by Dada and Cage, their performances typically featured indeterminacy, humor, attention to the commonplace, and an economy of means and notation (section 5.3). Although not himself a member, Tenney performed the works of Fluxus artists and alongside them, and his own music sometimes appeared on Fluxus programs. He also produced collaborative works with two prominent members: *Entrance/Exit Music* (1962) with George Brecht (volume 2, section 3.2) and the computer-generated poem *A House of Dust* (1967) with Alison Knowles (volume 2, section 4.7). Commencing in 1963, Moorman's Annual Avant Garde Festivals drew in part from the same community of artists as Fluxus but presented a broader range of programming, with the early festivals emphasizing music. Tenney's computer music appeared regularly on these early programs, to which he also contributed as an organizer, performer, and/or conductor.

Meanwhile, an emphasis on painterly gesture in Schneemann's work was gradually propelling it off the canvas and into three dimensions, literal movement, and finally what today might be called performance art (but which she referred to as *kinetic theater*) (section 5.4). Tenney supplied music for or performed in several of Schneemann's now-classic actions addressing gender and the body. In her *Meat Joy* (1964), for instance, he took the central masculine role, improvising with wet paint, raw meats, paper, transparent plastic, brushes, ropes, and other nearly naked performers. The handful of relatively little-known works that Tenney himself produced in the mid-1960s reflect his involvement with Schneemann and/or downtown artists, especially in their incorporation of interdisciplinary performance and the body. In *Choreogram* (1964), for instance, musicians develop approaches to reading the movements of dancers as a score (section 5.5), while Tenney's two *Thermocouples* (1965) are theatrical duos conceived around Schneemann and himself (volume 2, section 4.5). Beginning in 1965, both Schneemann and Tenney began to directly confront the ongoing Vietnam War in their art, resulting in a rare outcropping of overtly political works from Tenney. This included the *Thermocouples*, his soundtrack for Schneemann's antiwar film, *Viet-Flakes* (1966; volume 2, section 4.6), and the harrowing electronic *Fabric for Che* (1967) (section 5.6), whose maelstrom of noise and glissandi seems to anticipate the underground noise music of the 1980s.

For Tenney, the end in 1968 of his long-standing relationship with Schneemann and the beginning of a new marriage was a personal watershed accompanied by artistic and professional ones (chapter 6). A musical renovation was marked by the production of one of his best-known and most singular compositions: *For Ann (rising)* (1969; section 6.2). It was, on the one hand, the last piece of electronic music that he would compose and, on the other hand, a refined manifestation of features that would characterize his instrumental music of the coming years. These features include rigorously simplified formal design, sonic continuity, and gradual change (or stasis), all of which serve to abet radically active and self-aware listening. For most of its duration, this still-shocking work presents a strictly nonevolving periodic texture of concurrent sine waves rising in parallel. The voluntary or involuntary movement of the listener's attention about the texture consequently becomes a crucial determinant of their musical experience.

In 1970 Tenney abandoned the cultural ferment of New York City for the relative calm of a teaching position at the newly opened California Institute of the Arts near Los Angeles. Over the ensuing decade his involvements with collaboration and performance gradually ceded to compositional and theoretical pursuits. As a composer, his productivity quickly resurged as he continued to develop the new direction signaled by *For Ann (rising)* within an instrumental medium. Extending his interests in gradual predictable processes and sonic continuity, he produced another of his best-known and most distinctive works: *Postal Pieces* (1965–71), a set of concise scores printed on postcards (section 6.3). These included *Koan* (1971; section 6.3.1) for solo violin and *Having Never Written a Note for Percussion* (1971; section 6.3.2), which comprises only an enormously dilated dynamic swell for rolled percussion. The austere and predictable forms of these pieces permit active aural exploration of fine local detail while achieving an almost sculptural monumentality over time.

Around 1972, a new interest in harmony emerged in Tenney's work that would become his principal compositional preoccupation in the coming decades. Having manifested first in his music, this interest would induce a corresponding program of intense theoretical research following his move to Toronto in 1976 (chapter 7). (Although Tenney's theoretical investigations of harmony began only *after* his interest in the topic had already manifested compositionally, I discuss his harmonic theories in chapter 7 *before* addressing the music in order to introduce analytically useful concepts and terminology.) As in his previous approach to theorizing form in "Meta/Hodos," instead of responding to received harmonic theories or practices, Tenney would seek a more broadly applicable framework comprising general perceptual principles. He asserted that such a theory "should be *descriptive*—not pre- (or pro-)scriptive—and thus, *aesthetically neutral*" (Tenney [1983] 2015, 281). In this case, the principles sought were to be ones governing the perception of tones in combination. His wide-ranging research program would encompass a semantic history of the terms *consonance* and *dissonance* (section 7.4) and a decomposition of harmonic perception into multiple distinct facets or *harmonic relations*, along with proposed quantitative measures of those relations (sections 7.5–7.8).

Compositionally, Tenney's new interest in harmony was at first primarily reflected in music referencing the *harmonic series* (chapter 8). This series is a naturally occurring nontempered intervallic structure exhibited by the components of periodic acoustical signals such as spoken vowels and most definitely pitched musical tones. Tenney was fascinated by a special perceptual property of the harmonic series: the propensity under suitable conditions of its multiple components (its *harmonics*) to undergo *harmonic fusion* into a unitary percept with a unique pitch, a tendency upon which speech recognition and most music rely. He subsequently devised various ways of exploiting the structure of the series and its psychoacoustical properties compositionally. *Clang* (1972) for orchestra (section 8.2) employs gradual processes, as in Tenney's immediately preceding music, but these now included a process designed to progressively approach the conditions for harmonic fusion. *Spectral CANON for CONLON Nancarrow* (1974; section 8.3) explores not only harmonic fusion and the intervallic structure of the harmonic series but also rhythmic analogs to that structure. *Harmonium #1* (1976; section 8.4) features step-by-step "modulations" between subsets of different harmonic series, while *Three Indigenous Songs* (1979; section 8.5) represents a meticulous transcription of the acoustical components of speech for performance by an instrumental ensemble.

Among Tenney's measures of harmonic relatedness, one emerged that would underpin major new developments in his music of the early 1980s (chapter 9): this was a concept of *proximity* in a multidimensional *harmonic space*. Emerging inconspicuously in the intonational details of *Harmonium #3* (1980; section 9.2), this new conception would eventually lead Tenney to compose works of vast scale in nonstandard tuning systems, such as *Bridge* (1984; section 9.3) and *Changes: 64 Studies for 6 Harps* (1985; volume 2, section 7.11). In their increased textural complexity and formal articulation, these compositions contrasted sharply with his relatively continuous and overtly processual music based on the harmonic series. They also marked Tenney's first return to computerized algorithmic composition since his departure from Bell Labs in 1964, albeit now within a purely instrumental medium. Alongside them, works further exploring the harmonic series and harmonic fusion would continue to appear, such as *Koan for String Quartet* (1984; section 9.4), a remarkable harmonization of the earlier *Postal Piece* for solo violin.

In 1985–86 personal crises intervened in Tenney's life and work (chapter 10). In one brief terrible span he lost both a lung and a spouse to cancer. These calamities derailed the intense theoretical program that he had been pursuing, and he would not attempt to pick up its threads for more than a decade. His compositional production recuperated gradually after he remarried in 1987, now following a more eclectic course that would include percussion pieces, harmonically oriented compositions such as *Critical Band* (1988; section 10.1), retrospective works, homages, his first overtly political music since the late 1960s, and distillations from his own theories of formal Gestalt perception, such as 1993's *Flocking* (section 10.2). During this period, awareness of Tenney's work began to broaden, especially in Europe after a residency there in the early 1990s. For the first time, he began to receive a steady stream of commissions.

Tenney's compositional interests returned to the harmonic series with *In a Large, Open Space* (1994; section 11.2). In this singular work, audience members are free to wander about the performance space, throughout which stationary performers are distributed. Dissonant microtonal harmonies drawn from the upper reaches of the series are often prevalent, and for the next few years Tenney would further explore these particular intervallic resources. In algorithmically composed works such as *Diaphonic Study* (1997; section 11.3), for instance, he would revisit his early attraction to consistent dissonance by combining upper reaches of the series with stochastic models of the American dissonant-counterpoint style associated with Crawford and Ruggles.

In 2000 Tenney returned to teach at the California Institute of the Arts after an absence of twenty-four years. His late compositions include elaborations of such long-standing interests as harmonic perception, dissonance, and homage, and in his final work Tenney returned to harmonic space as a compositional model for the first time since 1990. Completed only weeks before his death, *Arbor Vitae* (2006; section 11.4) for string quartet brings together in a strikingly novel way many of Tenney's characteristic concerns, including gradual process, computerized stochastic composition, dissonant textures, nonstandard intonation, and harmonic perception.

1.2 Aesthetic and Methodological Bases: Music in Sound

1.2.1 Auditory Experience and John Cage's "Total Sound-Space"

Any contextual understanding of Tenney's music and thought must proceed from a recognition that after 1962 his very conception of music itself derived in large part from a post-Cagean experimentalist perspective. His outlook thus departed fundamentally from the received Western aesthetic mainstay of subjective expression.

In 1957 John Cage wrote, "One may give up the desire to control sound, clear his mind of music, and set about discovering means to let sounds be themselves rather than vehicles for man-made theories or expressions of human sentiments" ([1957] 1961, 10). Tenney would come to recognize in Cage's concern for sounds in "themselves" a radical reconceptualization of music *itself*. In his earlier received view, music was an expressive medium, and the understanding of music was thus tied to understanding the intentions of the composer. A more efficient means of upsetting that communicative model can scarcely be imagined than Cage's overt adoption of chance operations as partial compositional determinants, first in his Concerto for Prepared Piano and Chamber Orchestra (1950) and then in the epochal *Music of Changes* (1951) (Pritchett 1996, 70–71, 78–88). To whatever extent features of Cage's music were randomly determined and understood as such, composerly intention and the understanding of music as being expressive thereof were thwarted. Tenney consequently took Cage's emphasis on sounds "themselves" to represent, as he would put it late in life, a "decisive shift of focus from *the thoughts and feelings of the composer*—and their 'communication' to a relatively passive audience—to *the immediate auditory experience of the listener*—which may be said to be 'occasioned' by the work of the composer but assumes an active, participatory audience" (Tenney 1996a, 395–96; see section 1.2.1). Expanding on the historic significance for Western art music of this shift as he understood it, Tenney remarked:

> [Cage] wrote "Sounds we hear are music."[2] If we take that as a definition and take it seriously, it implies a very radical redefinition of music. . . . It begins in 1951 with the *Music of Changes* and marks a change in aesthetic viewpoint such that 1951 can be said to be the beginning of the end of a period of about 350 years, a period that began with the beginnings of opera, with Monteverdi and the Camerata. I think a case could be made . . . that this whole 350-year period, from 1600 to 1950 roughly, is really the operatic era, that the conception of the function of music (and here was a wonderful new discovery on the part of the composers of opera in the early seventeenth century) was a new conception of what music could do: it can express human emotion. . . . It wasn't long before it came to be taken for granted that this was what music was about and that it was all that music should be—that this was somehow natural. Well, that's OK, but it's not the only thing that it can be. Cage shifted our attention from the composer to the listening experience by repeatedly talking about sound, the nature of sound, and a music based on the nature of sound and by not focusing on the ideas or the emotions of the composer. I think it's going to turn out that, although the history books now tend to assume that a new era somehow began around the early part of this century, we'll see the work of Schoenberg and the second Viennese school, Stravinsky, and so forth, as really an end: the end of the long period, closing with what Charles Hamm called "terminal modernism." . . . I think that Cage's importance is to be understood as implying the end of a 350-year period. (Mumma et al. [1995] 2001, 173–74)

Regarding his impetus to compose, Tenney accordingly invoked his own intellectual and experiential curiosity as listener rather than any desire to express or communicate:

> I'm interested in music as an objective thing out there . . . [that] we want to go and hear because it provides some kind of special experience that can't be gained any other way. But it's not a self-expressive process. I don't have something to "say," unless I happen to be working with a text. . . . Composition for me is mostly motivated by curiosity. First of all, an interest in answering the question what will it sound like if I do such and such? But then, also, a desire to hear it. It's a desire for . . . a certain kind of sensory experience, which does not involve communication. (Tenney 2000a, 25)

Tenney's mature music consequently eschews musical devices that he viewed as suggesting narrative drama or rhetoric. These included thematic development: "I've never been very much interested in thematic work. The idea of a theme which maintains itself right through today in serial music, has never interested me at all because what it seems to introduce is rhetoric, as though this is the meaningful statement and now I'm going to show you how I can play with that and do other things with it. That's the drama of the music. It just doesn't interest me. I'm interested in sound and textures and forms" (Tenney 2005b). Tenney's unique and characteristic conception of "forms" further extended this antirhetorical stance:

> I think that it probably has been a thread going through my music from almost the very beginning. It's a conception of *form as an object of perception*, which is actually very different [from] other people's definitions of form. Most earlier definitions of form have been as a means to some end. Sonata form [is] based on a discipline of rhetoric. That's a strategy of persuasion. It's to try to make sure that the listener understands the relationships of themes and modulations and so forth. So it's a means to . . . another end. Schoenberg defined form as a means to ensure comprehensibility. Again, a means to an end, not a thing in itself. But I like to think of it literally as just something at a large hierarchical level that's equivalent to things that at a lower level constitute what we think of as content or timbre or just the nature of the sound. (Tenney 2005b, emphasis added)

Instead of focusing on thematic development, narrative drama, and traditional formal functions, Tenney turned his attention to the experience of sound. Indeed, one of his central concerns (and, I think, achievements) was to establish self-reflective exploration of the perceiving self as a topic proper to music. Whereas some artists have been drawn to complex symbolic systems, Tenney often seems to have been looking in the opposite direction: down a long evolutionary lineage toward the most basic perceptual processes of the organism. Asked whether he was interested in "sound for the sake of sound," he replied, "It's sound for the sake of perceptual insight—some kind of perceptual revelation. . . . In a way, science is about the same thing, but its enterprise seems to be to understand the nature of reality through thought and intellection. It seems to me art is about understanding reality to the same extent, and as singularly, but through a different modality—through perception" (Tenney 1978a, 16). In Cage's redirection of attention toward the experience of the listener, Tenney thus identified an open-ended avenue for artistic research into the nature and possibilities of sonic experience. "I guess all of my music can really be called experimental but in a sense different from how John Cage uses the word," Tenney wrote. "It's more literally an experiment like a scientific experiment, and in . . . scientific work, one experiment always does lead to another one. New questions are raised, which a given experiment does not answer, but it does raise the questions" (1984a, 10).

This semantic distinction notwithstanding, the listener-oriented aspect of Cage's thinking provided an important framework for Tenney's particular experimentalism not only with respect to its broad aesthetic orientation but also its programmatic details. In the statement "Experimental Music," Cage had set forth a description of a multidimensional "total sound-space" that Tenney would later quote:

> The situation made available by [tape-music techniques] is essentially a total sound-space, the limits of which are ear-determined only, the position of a particular sound in this space being the result of five determinants: frequency or pitch, amplitude or loudness, overtone structure or timbre, duration, and morphology (how the sound begins, goes on, and dies away). By the alteration of any one of these determinants, the position of the sound in sound-space changes. (Cage [1957] 1961, 9, quoted in Tenney [1983] 2015, 288)

In fact, a good deal of Tenney's work after 1961 can be understood as *extending* Cage's conception and exploration of sound-space, especially with respect to dimensions that Cage's description in "Experimental Music" had either omitted or collapsed. In particular:

- While Cage's pivotal *Music of Changes* (1951) admits a great variety of sounds, it exhibits only a few types of sound *groupings*—single sounds, "aggregates," and "constellations" ([1952] 1961, 58)—all of which are relatively localized in time. In practice, however, temporal groupings are perceptible hierarchically on many timescales and concurrently. In his computer music of 1963–64, Tenney would combine chance operations with grouping principles from "Meta⁄Hodos," thus framing formal grouping as entailing dimensions that are proper to sound but that were overlooked in Cage's enumeration (section 4.5). It is in this light that one can understand Tenney's repeatedly declared "concern with *form* not as a rhetorical device (as in the sonata) or as a means to ensure 'comprehensibility' (Schoenberg's motivation) but simply as another *object of perception*—like the sounds themselves but at a larger holarchical level" ([1996a] 2015, 396).[3]
- Cage's invocations of "overtone structure" and "morphology" elide or gloss over important acoustical determinants of perceived timbre such as modulations and envelope structure, which would become topics of both scientific and musical investigation for Tenney while at Bell Labs (section 4.4).
- In the 1950s and 1960s, not only was Cage uninterested in harmony as he then construed it (that is, as historical convention), but he forcefully repudiated it: "Harmony, so-called, is a forced abstract vertical relation which blots out the spontaneous transmitting nature of each of the sounds forced into it. It is artificial and unrealistic" ([1954] 1961, 152). Beginning in the 1970s, however, Tenney would become specifically interested in *harmony*, albeit in the nontraditional sense of perceptible relationships immanent in pitch combina-

tions—in other words, as involving inherent dimensions of sound perception (chapter 7). Speaking in 1984, Tenney remarked: "In general, I think that all my life as a composer, it's been concerned with sound. Now, what does that mean? When you begin to work that out that can mean a concern with a lot of different aspects of sound and for many years, the aspects of sound that interested me most involved timbre, tone quality, texture, and form. But in the last ten years or so, that interest has shifted. It involves pitch now, and what I call harmony. . . . But I would like it to be understood that this is an aspect of *sound*" (1984c, 8, emphasis added). Cage himself would in turn ultimately develop an interest in harmony in the late 1980s, in which instance the direction of influence between Cage and Tenney reversed (section 10.1).

1.2.2 Composition as Design

Tenney's reckoning with Cagean aesthetics coincided with his sojourn at Bell Labs in New Jersey during the early 1960s, officially as a member of the research staff studying psychoacoustics but unofficially as a musical consultant and composer of computer music (section 4.2). The unlikely convergence of his antidramatic turn with practical experience in software design bore fruit in a working methodology that would prove to be one of the most durable and consequential aspects of his practice: top-down overall design.

In a 2001 interview, Tenney was asked whether, when he was composing a piece, the process of scoring only began after he already knew how the work would manifest itself: "In the last 40 years, yes. Originally, I was working . . . just intuitively and the way so many of my students do now from the first note to the second to the next. I try to get them to work out some other way to plan a piece—to think about the whole thing before they start doing notes. And that has been the way I have worked ever since I was at Bell Labs, where working with a computer you have to plan everything out" (2005a). On another occasion, he elaborated: "I can hardly conceive of a piece without knowing its overall shape. It's the way I start composing. After I've made the precompositional decisions about instrumentation, notation, and tuning, the next job is working on graph paper laying out these large formal shapes" (Gann 1991, 78). He sometimes compared the advantages of this methodology to aerial viewing: "I remember flying over Arizona and seeing all the land forms and realizing that, if I were down there on the ground, I wouldn't be able to see these incredible land forms. And I thought, 'That's what working with a computer is like!' It gives you the possibility of distance. You can all at once take in this large thing that you couldn't take in without the technology. Instead, you'd be involved in details" (Pritchett et al. [1995] 2001, 205–6).[4]

In most of Tenney's music after 1960—whether electronic or instrumental—local features were accordingly determined not by individual compositional decisions but by the enactment of more global plans, principles, and procedures. He typically avoided extensive intervention in local musical details—when they proved unsatisfactory to him, this usually occasioned refinements at a more global level. For instance, in distinguishing his use of constrained random processes from compositional indifference, Tenney remarked: "It was not from indifference but from a gradual realization that I could really enjoy a result that I hadn't shaped in a precise way, a direct way, . . . that *if the compositional procedure was properly designed*, I could let it go and be pleased with every result that it could have" ([1990] 2015, 359, emphasis added).

Tenney's renunciation of compositional discretion at the local level serves in part to strategically deter receptive modes that appeal to composerly intent or narrative drama, whose absence facilitates the listener's redirection of their attention toward their own perceptions and perceptual processes. However, the orientation of Tenney's compositional methodology toward global planning and principles also supported another pervasive and oft-remarked quality in his work. This is a rigorous economy of means whereby some of his best-known scores occupy only a page or two of manuscript paper or a few lines of text. Other outwardly complex and multifaceted works were generated by algorithms that molded random processes according to a few elemental principles applied systematically. The resulting economy and logical elegance of Tenney's compositional designs are often striking aesthetic features in themselves.

1.2.3 Hearing with the Body

Tenney avoided pronouncements that inclined toward the transcendental. Such reticence, along with the often-technical character of his writing, might leave the misimpression that his sensibility was a decidedly Apollonian one. Circa 2003, in one of my last exchanges with him, I asserted that there was a potent unspoken dimension to his music that might be called "spiritual," for lack of a better word. He emphatically agreed but went no further. His characteristic reticence to explicate this aspect of his art was rooted in a conviction that it was essentially ineffable. When pressed by an interviewer regarding his tendency to redirect discussion toward technical or theoretical issues rather than slipperier "spiritual" matters, he replied: "I find it dangerous to talk about. As soon as you step into those fields and try to talk about them, then, you see, everybody goes off in different directions. And then you say, 'What is it? Is it this or is it that or is it the other thing?' And I say, 'Well, I don't know. What I know, it's these relationships.' [*laughter*] I like them. I think they're beautiful. I think there's a powerful thing that they can bring out of us, but it's mysterious. It's ineffable" (Tenney 1996c, 9). This response simultaneously evades the discussion of intangibles while affirming their importance. Similarly, when his student Peter Garland asked how to compose music that is deep and authentic, Tenney's reply—"It is a question of feeling things *more deeply*"—decisively prioritized a passionate, if not necessarily unintellectual, relationship to music (Garland 1990, 485). Indeed, the experience of Tenney's music can often be elemental and visceral at the very same time that it inseparably provokes intellectual fascination. Composer Tim Perkis has described this duality as "a characteristic blend of opposites in Tenney: a sense of all hell breaking loose in some strangely and beautifully ordered way" (n.d.).

Crucial to any understanding of Tenney's work is the recognition that his exploratory curiosity embraced intellection and sensuous experience together. This integrative aspect is succinctly captured in composer Gayle Young's description of Tenney's direction of a rehearsal for his *Harmonium #1* (1976): "He was eager to share with us not only the numerical basis of the tunings used, but also the *physical experience of hearing* the new harmonies and recognizing the higher overtones. In performing the piece, we learned to engage with sound at all levels: physically, perceptually, and intellectually" (2006, emphasis added). In practice, Tenney regarded intellect, perception, and the body as essentially continuous with one another. This synthetic perspective helped to reconcile the wildly diverse activities of an artist who in the 1960s was involved with computer music research and writing, new music concertizing, and carnal theatrical performances—all more or less concurrently.

> I like to think that there is no significant separation between the physical and the mental, that both intellectual and physical involvement in musical activity are part and parcel of the same thing. We can't help thinking so we might as well . . . do some good thinking. We can't help responding to music physically, kinetically, choreographically even, and that's fine. I love the title [dancer-choreographer] Yvonne Rainer gave to one of her dances back in the Judson Dance Theater in the '60s: *The Mind is a Muscle*. I like to turn that around by saying that the body has its own form of intelligence as well. So I can see them always as part of the same process. (Tenney 2004b)

Accordingly, the phenomenological aspect of Tenney's work must be understood against his personal experience of listening as a bodily process with a potential to be at the same time intellectually engaging and viscerally affecting.

His rare pronouncements regarding the wellsprings of aesthetic experience as he knew it correspondingly suggested that he saw it as related to the history of human evolution within the physical world.

> We have evolved to have very strong emotional and "spiritual" responses to nature and natural processes. . . . I feel that way, anyway. Now . . . we've been through a few thousand years of a kind of antagonistic relationship to nature on the part of . . . Western society as a whole. But . . . I believe even that the religious impulse, at least the part of it that I can relate to, is a response of awe in the face of nature. (Tenney 1996c, 9)

I think the real world's textures—or textures that have this character—are beautiful: the stars in the sky, the leaves on the trees, the noise of the traffic on the street corner, the birds in the forest, etc. These are beautiful textures to me. I think of Jackson Pollock for example. It's not just interesting and radical and non-figurative, and all the rest. It's gorgeous. It's beautiful stuff. . . . What's important here is the immediate sensual response to textures of that kind. (Tenney 2000a, 77)

Such comments might suggest that Tenney's attitude toward sound and nature was one of receptive contemplation. In actuality, he came to believe that our perceptual capacities are not essentially fixed and given but that their development is ongoing and that—within limits—we can participate in it.

I have the notion that we're all involved in our current evolutionary process, through cultural evolution, and things really do change quite radically. It is purely mental and sensory. Our brains are changing and to the extent that each of our sensory systems includes parts of the brain, and those parts are changing. It's mainly the artists who are causing that change, defining those changes. (Tenney 2000f)

It's important to realize that the auditory system is not just the ear, not even just the inner ear, but it involves part of the brain, necessarily and whenever you have circuits in the brain involved, they are changeable, they are malleable, so we are literally changing the way we hear by the experience of, the effort to make these new kinds of music. (Tenney 2000c)[5]

Regarding this evolutionary process, he elaborated further to percussionist Amy Knoles in a 2004 interview:

I'd like to think [that this process] is exemplified by the fact that the first performance of Schoenberg's *Pierrot Lunaire* [1912] only occurred after Schoenberg had directed 120 hours of rehearsal. With the best musicians in Vienna! . . . And now, a student ensemble . . . can put it together in six hours and play as well as they did. So what's going on there? . . . I think it's a cultural evolutionary process. . . . And we all are involved in that. . . . I feel like I'm involved as a composer when I ask players to do new things like some unusual tuning or whatever, and you players are deeply involved in this because you are making it happen as you are performing these things! (Mosko and Tenney 2004)

CHAPTER 2

Early Works and Influences (1934–59)

James Carl Tenney was born on August 10, 1934, in Silver City, New Mexico. He would retain only vague memories of the following decade, during which his family migrated westward in stages through small-town Arizona to the environs of Phoenix (Tenney 2004a). Tenney recalled that he began piano lessons at age eight, although his interest in music was initially muted: "I would much rather have been outside playing baseball than inside practicing" (1988b, 1). In fact, his first strong intellectual enthusiasms were elicited by science rather than music: "The curious thing about it all is that I can date the beginning of my conscious life to a very precise point in time—it was the summer of 1945. Somehow my memory before that is very vague and amorphous but I have a feeling that something turned on when I was eleven and the direction that it took was an interest in science, a kind of very hungry curiosity about the world" (Tenney 1984c, 2). In parallel with his musical career, Tenney would always thereafter maintain a passionate interest in the sciences, and this would inform both his creative and his theoretical work.

When he was about fourteen years old, Tenney's parents separated, and his mother moved with him and his two younger sisters to Denver, Colorado.[1] It was around that time that Tenney's interest in music began to develop rapidly. Initially, his energies were directed principally toward piano performance, and like many young pianists he worked his way through examples of Baroque, Classical, and Romantic repertoire. Soon he began secondarily to try his hand at composition. His earliest attempts have not survived, but he later recalled a particular enthusiasm for the music of George Gershwin: *Rhapsody in Blue* knocked me over when I first heard it and I really loved it. . . . And so the first music I wrote was kind of Gershwinesque" (Tenney 1988b, 1). His attraction to twentieth-century styles intensified as he subsequently absorbed the music of Satie, Debussy, Ravel, Bartók, Prokofiev, Hindemith, Barber, and—later—Schoenberg and Webern.[2]

2.1 Stan Brakhage and *Interim* (1952)

For his final year before college, Tenney attended South High School in Denver, Colorado, being attracted by the strong reputation of its programs in the arts (Tenney 2004a). There he fell in with a group of peers from the Drama Club who dubbed themselves the Gadflies after the metaphor adopted, according to Plato's *Apology*, by Socrates in order to describe his provocative sociopolitical function. Remarkably, several members of this group would later have notable artistic careers. They included filmmaker Larry Jordan, animator-producer Stan Phillips, composer Ramiro Cortéz, and—most significantly for Tenney—Stan Brakhage, who would become the most celebrated experimental filmmaker of the second half of the twentieth century. Over the course of a fifty-year career, Brakhage's work would progress from a nonnarrative poetic lyricism to a purely abstract "moving visual thinking" achieved by means of painting, dyeing, scratching, and/or collaging materials directly upon film stock, with or without exposure as well (James 2005).

Brakhage had graduated the year before Tenney arrived at South High and had left Denver to attend Dartmouth College in New Hampshire on scholarship. After a couple of months, however, he suffered what he would later describe as a "nervous breakdown" and returned to Denver. There he promptly rejoined his old circle, which now included Tenney (S. MacDonald 2005, 44). The close friendship that the two quickly formed would endure until Brakhage's death in 2003.

Among the group's diverse activities, its members sustained an informal film club, viewing works by D. W. Griffith, Sergei Eisenstein, Vsevolod Pudovkin, René Clair, Jean Cocteau, and others. When one friend lamented that filmmaking was prohibitively expensive, Brakhage retorted that they would themselves make a film. At his insistence, all then began collecting unused amateur film equipment. The result was Brakhage's first film, *Interim* (1952), a silent neorealist psychodrama in the mode of Roberto Rossellini and Vittorio De Sica that was shot in the railyards under Denver's viaducts. Tenney was not involved in the filming or editing but was recruited by Brakhage in the summer of 1952 to score the finished film, being given free rein to do so. The resulting soundtrack would become his first acknowledged composition: "I was just a piano student with hardly any experience yet in composition, but for some reason Stan believed that I was destined to become a composer and asked me to compose music for *Interim*. I wrote it for piano and for several months after the film was made, I had to play it 'live' whenever it was shown because none of us could afford the cost of recording it on a soundtrack. Incidentally, that belief of his was probably one of the main reasons I did become a composer" (Tenney [2003a] 2005, 58).

At a duration of 25 minutes, Tenney's *Interim* (1952) is remarkably substantial and assured for a first serious foray into composing. Reflecting on the project many years later, the composer recalled: "I think what I did was study the film, watch it a number of times with timings, working out sections with the film that had certain characteristics where the music would change. Then I simply worked out the timings for these sections. I worked at the keyboard quite intuitively after that point. . . . I didn't have any procedures or particular ways of composing in mind. I mean, I was eighteen years old" (Tenney 2005a). Accordingly, the ten sections of *Interim* exhibit a succession of styles reflecting the various musical influences that Tenney had been digesting. He later recalled these as "Satie. Gershwin. [*laughs*] Bartók. . . . Already Schoenberg was in there in some ways, but not yet as strong as some of the other influences" (Tenney 2004a). In the fourth section, a delicate Satie-esque perambulation titled "walking together" accompanies the first meeting of the film's young lovers (figure 2.1[b]). This leads to the warmly romantic music of "at the stream," with its intimations of Debussy and Gershwin. In "approaching storm," rumbling bass clusters evoke distant thunder. As rain erupts on-screen, Brakhage's lovers sprint for cover against the fleet Bartókian scherzo of "running," the right hand's punctuating melody in octaves creating sharp dissonances against a continuous $\frac{5}{8}$ ostinato in the left hand (figure 2.1[c]). Other harmonic techniques in evidence include quartal harmonies, planing, and the combining of varied transpositions, the last two appearing together in the opening measure (figure 2.1[a]).[3]

Following the completion of *Interim* in the summer of 1952, Tenney enrolled at the University of Denver on an engineering scholarship with the intention to eventually pursue architecture. This choice reflected a combination of lingering doubts about his own musical talents along with his (and his mother's) concern for his employability in light of the financial strain experienced by the family following his parents' divorce (Smigel 2012, 65). Tenney continued to take private piano lessons, however, and now added private lessons in harmony. Meanwhile, he digested whatever scant information he could find regarding modern music.[4] He later recalled listening avidly to the earliest commercial recordings of works by Arnold Schoenberg, Anton Webern, Alban Berg (*Wozzeck*), Charles Ives, and Edgard Varèse and to John Cage's *Sonatas and Interludes* (1948) for prepared piano (Tenney 1996c, 19–20). In 1951 he had attended a concert in Denver of *Sonatas and Interludes* performed by Cage himself, an experience that he recalled "blew me away" (Swed 2002) and that would contribute to his later interest in timbre. He obtained scores for Schoenberg's piano pieces op. 11 and op. 19, as well as Webern's Variations, op. 27, discovering a lasting attraction

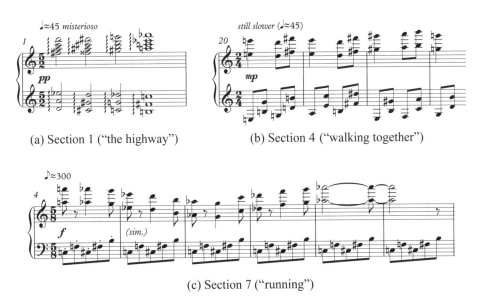

(a) Section 1 ("the highway")

(b) Section 4 ("walking together")

(c) Section 7 ("running")

FIGURE 2.1. Excerpts from three sections of Tenney's score to Stan Brakhage's film *Interim* (1952).

to Schoenberg's preserial atonal music (but not his twelve-tone music) and to Webern's music both preserial and serial.

After two years in engineering school, Tenney found himself missing direct and intensive engagement with performance and composition. Brakhage, who was continuing to make films while shuttling between Denver and San Francisco, admonished his friend to engage with both music and the wider world: "Your letter, along with things I have heard, indicates to me that you are standing still, Jim, in the worst possible position and at the worst possible time in your life. . . . Get out of that town at once before it is too late and get somewhere (anywhere) where you can begin accomplishing something. Don't be a damn fool."[5] Finally reaching a personal and professional watershed, Tenney applied to the piano performance program at the Juilliard School in Manhattan. He was accepted on scholarship for the fall of 1954.

2.2 Manhattan and Meeting Carolee Schneemann

Brakhage soon followed Tenney to New York with the purpose of meeting such pioneering experimental filmmakers as Joseph Cornell, Maya Deren, Willard Maas, and Marie Mencken. The two impecunious friends shared accommodation, including what Tenney recalled as a "horrible cold-water flat down in Little Italy," possessing only an electric heater (Tenney 2004a).

Brakhage hoped to use Varèse's *Ionisation* (1931) and certain of Cage's *Sonatas and Interludes* as soundtracks for two of his recent films (Tenney [2003a] 2005,

59). To obtain permission, the irrepressible Brakhage arranged meetings directly with the two composers, inviting Tenney along. Varèse subsequently invited the two young artists to a party that he was organizing at his home in Greenwich Village. Tenney had been thinking of asking Varèse for lessons, but at the party— feeling shy and insufficiently tutored—he instead approached composer Chou Wen-chung, a former student of Varèse (Tenney 1988b, 4–5). Thereafter until 1956 he attended weekly composition lessons with Chou, focusing on notation, instrumentation, orchestration, and form. Over the course of the next ten years, however, he would also occasionally meet informally with Varèse in order to solicit the elder composer's feedback on his recent work (section 4.1).

In May 1955 Tenney fatefully attended a concert of music by Bach and Ives at Town Hall in Manhattan. During the intermission, he struck up a conversation with a young woman whom he had noticed once or twice before in local cafés. This was artist Carolee Schneemann, who was on leave from Bard College and studying painting at Columbia University. Of that fateful concert intermission, she later recalled, "I said, 'I'm a painter and I treat space as if it's time.' And he said, 'I'm a musician and I treat time as if it was space.' And off we went for thirteen years" (Schneemann 2002, 113). The ensuing partnership of Schnee- mann and Tenney would fuse a remarkable set of mutually reinforcing elements: intense attraction, voracious curiosity, intellectual rigor, creative synergy, and a reciprocal supportiveness that was both emotional and practical (sections 3.3, 5.4). In the coming decade, some of their most celebrated and influential artistic breakthroughs would be made in adjoining rooms.

Sometime in the winter of 1955–56, Brakhage, Schneemann, and Tenney convened at a restaurant on 42nd Street in Manhattan. Schneemann was meet- ing Brakhage for the first time as the impecunious trio split a single bowl of spaghetti and rhapsodized about art and their ambitions (Schneemann 2005, 79–80). Although Brakhage would soon return to Colorado, the three quickly forged a powerful bond that would be nourished in the coming years through fervent correspondence and frequent cross-country trips. Schneemann recalled, "We were obnoxious, visionary kids. I was going to transform the visual world. Jim was going to radicalize sound, and Stan was going to open thresholds of poetry and film" (2002, 113). Their enduring friendship was founded upon—and in turn powerfully fortified—this shared Romantic ideal of the artist as culturally transformative visionary. The tempering of this intellectual commitment in the crucible of their early friendship must be counted as one of the most important formative factors in Tenney's artistic development.[6]

Meanwhile, Tenney's piano studies were proving less auspicious. The principal attraction of the Juilliard School for him had been the presence on faculty of pianist Eduard Steuermann, who had worked closely with Schoenberg and had premiered many of his keyboard works. To Tenney's disappointment, however, Steuermann's approach as a teacher seemed strictly conservative: "He just wanted me to take standard repertoire, which meant Bach, Beethoven, and Brahms. Then, maybe, once every three years you could have something else" (2006, 23).

Concurrently, Tenney's growing passion for composition was consuming steadily more of his attention at the expense of his piano studies. Within a year of starting at Juilliard, Tenney had left the program and was earning a living as a typist while composing and taking lessons with Chou.[7] During this period of time he completed four movements of a suite for six instruments entitled *Seeds* (1956/1961), adding two more movements a few years later. He would subsequently come to describe *Seeds* as his effective "opus 1"—the first of his compositions that he felt transcended the rank of mere student work (section 2.4).

2.3 Lionel Nowak, Carl Ruggles, and Charles Ives's *Concord* Sonata

In the summer of 1956, at Chou's suggestion, Tenney successfully applied to work as a music copyist at the Bennington Composers' Conference, which was hosted on the grounds of Bennington College in Vermont (Tenney 1988b, 5). By such means, he was able to support himself while attending the conference during the three summers of 1956–58. In the first year of his attendance, he had a lesson with composer Lionel Nowak, who was on the staff of the summer conference but who was also a member of the regular music faculty at the college. Nowak so impressed Tenney with both his teaching methods and his support for new musical directions that the young composer inquired whether it would be possible for him to complete his undergraduate education at Bennington, despite it nominally being a women's college at the time.

With Nowak's support, Tenney was admitted to Bennington on scholarship that fall, he and Schneemann marrying as a condition of eligibility for the award. There he studied composition with Nowak, conducting with Henry Brant, and conducting, acoustics, and the history of tuning systems with Paul Boepple (Tenney 1978b). For the first time, Tenney found himself in a position to consistently hear his music performed soon following its composition, and he accordingly produced an outpouring of student works during his two years in the program. Their succession overall evinces a rapid development in Tenney's command of form and orchestration. Compelling examples include the meticulous Webernesque *Improvisation* (1956) for solo cello and the economical song-cycle *Thirteen Ways of Looking at a Blackbird* (1958) for bass voice and chamber ensemble on a text by Wallace Stevens.

At least as influential for Tenney as his formal studies at Bennington was the close and lasting friendship that he and Schneemann developed during those years with composer Carl Ruggles. In the 1920s, Ruggles had been associated with the so-called American ultramodernist group of composers that also included Henry Cowell, Ruth Crawford, Dane Rudhyar, and Edgard Varèse:

"Ruggles lived in the little town of Arlington, which was about fifteen miles north, and he wasn't really teaching, formally. But I spent so much time with him, going over his music with him and showing him mine and getting his opinions about it, that I have no qualms about saying I studied with him, even though they were not what you would call composition lessons" (Tenney 1993a, 402). Moreover, near the end of his undergraduate studies Tenney made a deliberate point of trying to find a personal musical response to the rhapsodically expressive and dissonant contrapuntal style of Ruggles: "And when I tried to do that, what came out was something totally different, but it had the property that it involved melodies in dissonant counterpoint in relation to each other. And that is best exemplified in . . . *Sonata for Ten Wind Instruments* [1958/1971]" (Tenney 2000a, 28).

Tenney would remain friends with Ruggles until the latter's death in 1971, composing *Quintext*, V: "A Choir of Angels for Carl Ruggles" in 1972. He would maintain a theoretical interest in Ruggles's music as well. In 1974 correspondence, he penned detailed analytical remarks regarding each composition by Ruggles, among which was included the following noteworthy characterization of his melodic style: "Ruggles's melodic lines shape themselves as wave upon wave—or more precisely, smaller waves upon larger waves . . .—the larger waves usually arching in a gradual build-up/then/let-down of tension. This wave-upon-wave model is manifested by dynamics and even rhythm."[8] Although lyricism is a relatively rare feature of Tenney's music, such a melodic model might be discerned not only in early pieces such as *Monody* (1961) but also in the compounded swells of *Beast* (1971) and *Cellogram* (1971), in the winding melody of the *Chorales* series (1973–74), and even as late as *To Weave (a meditation)* (2003). Tenney would publish a further study of Ruggles's melodic style using statistical techniques in "The Chronological Development of Carl Ruggles' Melodic Style" (Tenney [1977a] 2015). This statistical perspective would, moreover, presage Tenney's intensifying engagement in the late 1990s with the dissonant melodic and contrapuntal styles that were practiced by Ruggles and Ruth Crawford and dubbed *dissonant counterpoint* by Henry Cowell and Charles Seeger (Seeger [1931] 1994; Spilker 2011). During that period he would explore algorithmic approaches to incorporating aspects of dissonant counterpoint in his own music (section 11.1).

While at Bennington, Tenney initiated a personal performance project that would require several years to achieve complete fruition: learning to play the monumental Piano Sonata no. 2 (*Concord, Mass., 1840–60*) (1915) of Charles Ives, commonly known as the *Concord* Sonata. Regarding his impetus to do so, Tenney later recalled: "My performance of other people's music has always been motivated by my desire to understand that music better. I know when I first started to learn the Ives Concord Sonata many years ago that was the reason—I wanted to hear into it. It seemed to me that learning to play it was a way of doing that" (Tenney 2005a). He learned the movements in numerical order, eventually performing the complete sonata from memory beginning in 1966 (section 5.2). Although Tenney subsequently downplayed the impact of Ives's style on his own music, he acknowledged its effect on his classic tape collage, *Collage #1 ("Blue Suede")* (1961) (section 3.3). Moreover, Ives's characteristic superposition of musical layers seems to inform the concept of *complex polyphony* that Tenney would soon formulate in his influential treatise on musical form, "Meta↓Hodos" (Tenney [1961] 2015) (section 3.4). These forthcoming musical and theoretical works would mark the maturation of a radical musical intelligence in the period following his graduation from Bennington in June 1958.

2.4 *Seeds* (1956/1961)

FLUTE, CLARINET, BASSOON, HORN, VIOLIN, CELLO
7 mins. approx.

In the winter of 1955–56, following several months of composition lessons with Chou Wen-chung in New York City, Tenney completed a set of four short pieces entitled *Seeds*. These were subject to minor revisions in 1961, at which time two movements were added, bringing the total to six.[9] Reflecting late in his career, Tenney remarked: "[*Seeds*] is, in some ways, what might be called my opus 1. It was written in 1956 when I was twenty-two. I was still a student. It's the earliest piece in the body of my work that I don't have to apologize for or qualify that it was just a student work. It seemed to me, right away then, that I had found my stride as a composer" (Tenney 2000d).

Still clearly evident in *Seeds* are Tenney's primary formative influences, which he himself identified as "Webern's *Bagatelles*, Varèse's *Octandre*, and Cage's *Sonatas and Interludes* for prepared piano—especially in the way they have focused my attention on timbre" (Tenney 1968a). Its movements already display, however, the formal rigor and material economy of Tenney's characteristic style. Moreover, his preoccupation in *Seeds* with timbre would resurface in his computer music of the early 1960s and periodically again thereafter. The title thus reflected not only the extreme brevity of the movements (with durations ranging from 30 to 90 seconds) but also Tenney's intuition at the time that "they contained within themselves in at least embryonic form most of what might later become manifest in my work as a composer" (Tenney 1978b).[10]

The influence of Varèse's *Octandre* (1923) and *Intégrales* (1925) on *Seeds* is variously detectable in its annunciatory woodwind figures, dissonant chordal punctuations, penetrating high-register woodwind ascents, and counterpoint of dynamic swells. On the other hand, the recollection of Anton Webern's Six Bagatelles for String Quartet, op. 9 (1910/1913) extends beyond concision to textural transparency and a meticulous deployment of timbre, which serves as both a formal delineator and a variegated and alluringly sensuous aspect of

sound. These timbral functions are visible in figure 2.2, which provides a reduction of the initial seven measures of the first movement of *Seeds*. A striking
timbral technique that recurs in other movements is the dovetailed transfer of
a pitch from one instrument to another, indicated in the figure using arrows.
In movement I, an opening flute motive abruptly concludes on an E_5 that has
already been slyly insinuated as a cello harmonic, thus creating a timbral and
spatial shift. The motive and effect are immediately repeated, but this time the E
moves to the clarinet before shifting back to the cello. The cello harmonic then
sustains through a third appearance of the flute motive before—in a reversal of
precedent that precipitates the climax of this opening subsection—both it and
the flute's final E are clipped (rather than extended) by a pizzicato violin. The
flute leaps upward from a D-sharp (prepared a measure earlier in the clarinet)
to a climactic A-sharp, which is then passed to the violin and back with cre-
scendos. In measure 7, a dissonant low-register aside provides a sharp timbral
contrast, the new colors in the cello and bassoon vying with each other through
a succession of dynamic variations and reattacks.

The principal motive of movement I is succinct, dissonant, and variously
instantiated, recalling early Second Viennese School practice. As a pitch-class
collection in its closest voicing, it would comprise a pair of semitones flanking
a minor third. (In other words, it is a member of set class 0145, as marked above
the staff in figure 2.2. It first appears in measures 1–2 at transposition T_4—four
semitones above pitch class C = 0—as pitch classes E, F, G-sharp, and A, that
is, as pcs 4, 5, 8, and 9.) In the figure, forms of the motive (variously transposed
and voiced) are indicated using gray filled polygons. It appears both melodically
as the flute motive and harmonically (verticalized, transposed, and revoiced)
as punctuating chords. When the beginning of the second section of the movement (not shown) intrudes on the bassoon and cello exchange of measure 7, this
same motive recurs in a new melodic incarnation: as an ascending arpeggiation
through a more open voicing.

Formal articulation in *Seeds* recalls an aspect of Webern's early atonal music in
the correlation between formal sections and completions of an *aggregate* (which
is an exposition of all twelve pitch classes of the chromatic scale). In Webern's
own account of his practice in the Bagatelles, op. 9: "Here I had the feeling,
'When all twelve notes have gone by, the piece is over.' . . . In my sketch-book I
wrote out the chromatic scale and crossed off the individual notes. . . . The most
important thing is that each 'run' of twelve notes marked a division within the
piece, idea, or theme" (Webern and Reich 1963, 51). In practice, Webern regularly
permitted close pitch-class repetitions in the form of repeated or alternating
notes. Tenney's practice was yet more liberal with respect to the exact repetition of motivic materials, but—in accordance with Webern's account—formal
sections delineated by parametric changes (of timbre, density, tempo, rhythm,
dynamic, motive, and/or register) tend to comprise the presentation of a single

FIGURE 2.2. *Seeds*, I, opening section (mm. 1–7, concert score).

aggregate. Thus the opening section shown in figure 2.2 comprises all twelve pitch classes: eight appear in the opening melodic tetrachord and its ensuing chordal transposition, pitch class 10 (A-sharp/B-flat) is reserved for the melodic climax, and the remaining three appear as the contrasting pitch-class cluster of measure 7. This pattern of developing one portion of the aggregate at relative length in the first part of a formal unit is a pattern common enough in Tenney's early music that the appearance of the aggregate's residual pitch classes often provides an audible cue to an approaching formal division. The two remaining sections of *Seed*'s first movement also encompass single aggregates. The second section (not shown) is a compressed variation of the first with new voicings and timbres, development of the basic motive again preceding that of the trichordal cluster. The final section begins with the reappearance of the motive in its original form, before its harmony is directly superimposed on that of the cluster, the climactic A-sharp/B-flat getting the last word.

The registral fixing of pitch classes is a feature less reminiscent of early Webern than of his later serial works, such as the Symphony op. 21 (1928). Within any single aggregate presentation, Tenney generally assigns each pitch class to a particular octave. Occasional deviations facilitate playability or create special effects, as in a voice exchange between bassoon and clarinet in measure 6 of *Seeds*' first movement.

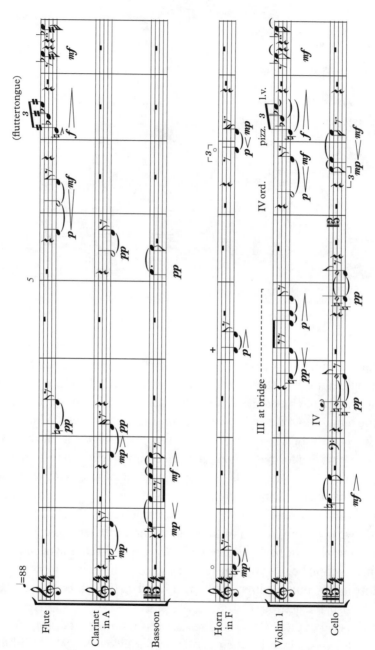

FIGURE 2.3. *Seeds*, II, opening section (mm. 1–8, concert score).

The second movement is a particularly striking exploration of timbral shifts. It adheres to a single pitch for much of its duration before finally completing its single aggregate. The primary conceptual precedent is Schoenberg's concept of *Klangfarbenmelodie,* or "tone-color melody" (Schoenberg 1978, 421), with Tenney later writing, "I have been concerned with timbre in various ways ever since *Seeds,* with its movement that is all a timbre-melody (in Schoenberg's sense of it)" (Brakhage, Tenney, and Markopoulos 1963, 81).[11] As shown in figure 2.3, at the opening a continuous D_4 is passed between instruments with careful instrumental dovetailing. The interattack duration sequence in measures 1–2 (which is 2–4–2–3–3–2 eighth notes) is repeated in measures 3–4 using a different sequence of instruments. The same rhythmic pattern commences yet again in measure 5 before a delayed attack in measure 6 occasions an accelerated rhythmic catch-up in the second part of the measure. This leads to a dramatic upward arpeggiation through new pitch classes in measure 7, concluding the first section. The second section immediately returns to passing of the D at more regular but also shorter time intervals. The arpeggiation recurs in inverted and prime forms, while Cs and C-sharps passed back and forth between the cello and bassoon expand the pitch-class palette into a trichordal cluster dispersed across the low registers. The conclusion churns through the remainder of the aggregate in a mere two measures, the D_4 momentarily disappearing. It finally returns alone once more, haltingly passed between instruments before the rhythm of the penultimate measure subsidingly recalls that of the first.

Of the set, the third movement most closely evokes the concision of Webern's Bagatelles, consuming only a single page of score. Uniquely among the movements of *Seeds*, its two complete aggregates are exposed in the same pitch-class sequence (in other words, using an untransposed twelve-tone row). The first occupies a spare 4.5 measures, while the second is exhausted in a dense 1.5-measure knot of doubled attacks and pitch-passing between instruments. Two rudimentary motives appear. The first is a minor- or major-second neighbor note figure that opens the movement as a hand-glissando in the horn and concludes it as a high trill in the flute. The second is a measured trifold repetition of a single pitch, a gesture that ultimately migrates from the high flute through cello harmonics to the low bassoon, peeking out slightly stuttered in E_4s and F-sharp$_6$s amid the dense tangle of the second aggregate.

Each remaining movement exhibits a unique musical character realized using the general compositional methodology observed in the first three. The movements written in 1961 exhibit a greater textural complexity, the last also being the longest in the set.[12]

While the overtly dramatic formal designs and motivic working of *Seeds* would largely disappear from Tenney's mature style, its deep engagement with timbral and textural variation would portend his lasting concern with them. In a late program note for *Seeds*, he remarked, "It is this original concern with timbre which ultimately—inevitably—[became] the desire for and insistence upon maximum richness and variety in the computer music" (Tenney 1968a). Moreover, it seems but a small step from *Seeds*, movement II, to the indeterminately shifting timbres of the single-pitched *Swell Piece No. 2* (1971). In a 1973 letter to Schneemann, Tenney would go so far as to write, "I've been writing quite a lot of really fine music, and my work has changed in many ways—some radically (in other ways, of course, nothing has changed, it was all there in *Seeds*)" (Schneemann 2010, 196).

CHAPTER 3

Tape Music and "Meta/Hodos"
(1959–61)

3.1 Lejaren Hiller and Harry Partch

Having received his undergraduate degree from Bennington in June 1958, Tenney returned with Schneemann to New York, where he spent the remainder of the year casting about for prospective graduate programs. A brief stint at New York University proved unsatisfying (Tenney 1988b, 7), but a new master's program in electronic music drew him in January 1959 to the University of Illinois: "I attended the University of Illinois because I had read a tiny little notice in the New York Times saying that for the first time anyplace, certainly for the first time in North America, a course in electronic music was going to be given at that university toward the end of 1958" (Pritchett et al. [1995] 2001, 199).[1] This new program was directed by Lejaren Hiller, a former chemist who had switched to the music department. Together with colleague Leonard Isaacson, Hiller had produced *Illiac Suite* (1957) for string quartet, generally regarded as the first substantial example of algorithmic composition made using a computer (Roads 1996, 830). From Hiller, Tenney would take courses on acoustics, electronic music, and information theory that would have a lasting influence on his thinking, and he would work in the electronic music studio that Hiller had been assembling since 1958.

Concurrently, Tenney studied composition with Kenneth Gaburo and conducting with Bernard Goodman but, more consequentially, he obtained an assistantship supervised by Harry Partch, a composer, theorist, and instrument builder who was at the university on a nonteaching fellowship.[2] Tenney assisted in maintaining Partch's collection of invented just-intoned instruments, and he performed in the elder composer's Gate 5 Ensemble on a large lyre-type instrument dubbed Kithara II (Tenney 1988b, 27–28): "I got a pretty good immediate feeling of that whole instrument building project, and the tuning, and teaching people to play the instruments and all of that, because I was involved in the second performance of [Partch's] *The Bewitched* [1955]" (Tenney 1996d, 119). Most importantly, Tenney would also digest Partch's seminal writings on just intonation in *Genesis of a Music* (Partch [1949] 1974), the crucial influence of which would remain dormant for some twelve years before emerging in Tenney's own explorations of harmony and intonation. Tenney's personal relationship with Partch proved more tenuous than his intellectual one, however: Partch fired him, purportedly because Tenney insisted on arguing the merits of composers such as Webern and Cage whom Partch did not like (Tenney 2006, 30).

3.2 The University of Illinois Electronic Music Studio

In a 1939 lecture, Edgard Varèse had foretold many of the musical possibilities to be afforded by future technology. Almost presciently, he predicted these to include

> liberation from the arbitrary, paralyzing tempered system; the possibility of obtaining any number of cycles or if still desired, subdivisions of the octave, consequently the formation of any desired scale; unsuspected range in low and high registers; new harmonic splendors obtainable from the use of sub-harmonic combinations now impossible; the possibility of obtaining any differentiation of timbre, of sound-combinations; new dynamics far beyond the present human-powered orchestra; a sense of sound-projection in space by means of the emission of sound in any part or in many parts of the hall as may be required by the score; cross rhythms unrelated to each other, treated simultaneously, or to use the old word, "contrapuntally" (since the machine would be able to beat any number of desired notes, any subdivision of them, omission or fraction of them)—all these in a given unit of measure or time which is humanly impossible to attain. (Varèse and Chou 1966, 12–14)

Varèse's bold vision of technology's promise would prove deeply inspiring for Tenney, as it would for many young composers of the midcentury: "Varèse had a vision of the possibilities of electronic music as the realization of the vision of music as sound. And that was important to me. That's what got me into electronic music, in 1959, and into computer music in 1961" (Tenney 2000e, 28).

Unfortunately, the actual state of the art in 1959 would turn out to be acutely disappointing to Tenney. On the cobbled-together equipment in the Illinois studio he labored in vain to produce sounds whose richness and subtlety approached those that he had achieved in the instrumental medium (Tenney 1993a, 401–2). The primitive nature of the facility is attested by Hiller's own description of it, published in September 1961, a few months after Tenney's graduation

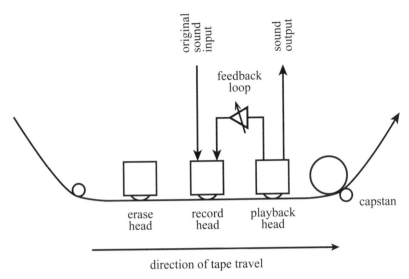

original sound input

sound output

feedback loop

erase head

record head

playback head

capstan

direction of tape travel

FIGURE 3.1. Schematic of the tape-head echo system available in the University of Illinois Electronic Music Studio circa 1960.

(Hiller 1961, 39–41). Due to budgetary constraints, most of the available equipment was either hand-built in the studio or salvaged from laboratories or radio stations that were discarding outmoded components. Available sound sources comprised sine-, sawtooth-, pulse-, and square-wave generators, as well as a ten-partial additive synthesizer, white noise generator, theremin, microphone, portable tape recorder, and—crucially, as it would turn out for Tenney—phonograph.[3] A control console salvaged from a radio station performed all signal routing and mixing, affording eight inputs and four outputs. Outputs could be routed to loudspeaker, frequency counter/timer, oscilloscope, or reel-to-reel tape decks for recording and playback. A bandpass (or *formant*) filter was available to boost one band of frequencies and to suppress others, although the creation of multiple such *formant peaks* in a frequency spectrum required the overdubbing of multiple filtered recordings of the same sound. Reverberation was achieved by feeding back the signal from a tape deck's playback head through a gain adjustment to the deck's own record head, as illustrated in figure 3.1. A net negative gain would induce a decaying echo of whatever signal was passing the playback head, and the time delay between echoes could be varied by adjusting the speed of the tape. On the other hand, a positive gain would accumulate echoes to yield howling feedback at a frequency determined by the tape speed (Hiller 1963, 113–14).

Perhaps more impressive than the list of possibilities that the studio afforded was the list of those that it did not. There were no provisions for vibrato or for amplitude envelope control, and adjustments to parameters were made by hand with dials in real time as needed (Hiller 1961, 40, figure 6).[4] As Tenney later described: "It was very difficult to make a piece using synthetic sounds because essentially what we had were a few Lafayette sine- and square-wave generators. You turned the dial to set the frequency and then you turned it on. We didn't have gates, we didn't have voltage control—we had nothing that everyone takes for granted in analog synthesis ever since Buchla and Moog created their synthesizers" (1993a, 401). In reality, a composer would typically spend less time creating and recording sounds than in subsequently manipulating recordings of them via classic tape-music techniques. The studio included three tape decks, permitting the mixing of two recordings to produce a third, although synchronization was manual and had to be achieved through trial and error. Via the physical cutting and splicing of tape, recordings could be edited for purposes of montage or to create effects, such as the obscuring of a sound's source by the removal of its attack. Tape speed could be increased/decreased in order to raise/lower the pitch of a recording with a commensurate decrease/increase in its duration. Recordings could be played backward to create novel timbres and envelopes.

Confronted with the studio's primitive facilities, Tenney soon became disillusioned: "I had been turned on by Varèse's vision of electronic music in the future. When I saw this studio, I said, this is not the future, this is terrible!" (Pritchett et al. [1995] 2001, 199). By Hiller's account, Tenney temporarily drifted away from the studio toward involvement with Partch and his ensemble (Hiller 1987, 514). However, as the date of his intended graduation approached Tenney again struggled in mounting frustration to produce original electronic music to show for his time spent in the studio. A creative breakthrough arrived only after he abandoned purely synthetic sound for prerecorded sources, resulting in the classic *Collage #1 ("Blue Suede")* (1961).

> I worked on [a] piece, where I was attempting to work with synthesized tones and play with timbre, but I didn't like it. I didn't like those sounds, finally—there wasn't enough of a way to loosen them up, they just sounded mechanical to me. So it was rather a frustrating time, that first year or two at Illinois, because I kept trying to do something with very little success, until I moved in the direction of concrete sounds. It wasn't until the computer-synthesis program became available [to me later at Bell Labs] that I felt I could really work with purely synthetic sound. (Tenney 1993a, 402)

3.3 *Collage #1 ("Blue Suede")* (1961)
for Carolee Schneemann
ELECTRONIC MUSIC (ONE-CHANNEL FIXED MEDIA)
3 mins., 20 secs.

> I had been deeply moved by Varèse's *Déserts* and *Poème Électronique*, and by his vision of the new musical possibilities realizable through electronic technologies. In 1959 I began graduate work at the University of Illinois, attracted there

by the fact that courses were about to be offered in electronic music (perhaps for the first time anywhere). Under the generous tutelage of Lejaren Hiller, and in a studio that was extremely primitive by today's standards, I began to work in the new medium, but with absolutely no success at first. In spite of all my earlier expectations, the synthetic character of the electronically generated sounds seemed to resist my every effort to use them in a way that was musically satisfying to me. *Collage #1 ("Blue Suede")* arose, initially, as an act of desperation in the face of these difficulties, but once begun, it was completed in one feverish week in the studio. (Tenney 1978b)

A few months earlier, in the simpler and relatively obscure *Improvisations for Medea* (1960), Tenney had already produced music for a theatrical production via studio manipulation of his own prerecorded piano improvisations. In *Collage #1 ("Blue Suede")*, he again resorted to the manipulation of prerecorded rather than synthetic materials, but this time from an unprecedented source: Elvis Presley's 1956 recording of Carl Perkins's song "Blue Suede Shoes."

In 1961 rock and roll was still a novel and renovating force in popular music. Both Tenney and his then partner, artist Carolee Schneemann, were enthusiasts who often danced to it at home (Corrin 2016, 115–16). The importation of rock and roll into an academic electronic music studio, however, brazenly transgressed the boundary between high and low art that midcentury modernism had fastidiously observed, thus foreshadowing its erosion by the advent of pop art and postmodernism generally.[5] Moreover, Tenney would later remark that the use of a popular source represented "a great answer to academia" (2005b). It was a choice that repudiated any potential association of electronic music with academic cerebralism in favor of rock and roll's earthiness.

> I had been very excited when I first became aware of Elvis Presley. I loved it. I'd never enjoyed popular music before that. What "popular music" meant at the time was Perry Como and Frank Sinatra, which I hate to this day. When Elvis Presley came in, I was really bowled over. I loved the sexual energy of it and his voice was tremendous. I needed no more rationale for using it than that I loved it. I knew I was going to cut it up and collage it, but I wanted it to carry the resonance of the original. (Tenney 2000f)

A variety of factors incited Tenney's adoption of collage technique specifically. By his own account, the brevity of concatenated source snippets and the rapidity of the resulting montage in *"Blue Suede"* were suggested by John Cage's dense tape collage *Williams Mix* (1952), which Tenney had heard at Cage's 25-Year Retrospective Concert in 1958 and on the subsequently released recording thereof (Tenney 2000f). Additionally, in 1958 he had begun learning the monumental Piano Sonata no. 2 (*Concord, Mass., 1840–60*) by Charles Ives, and by the spring of 1961 he had conquered the first movement and was preparing the second for performance. Despite his devotion to Ives's music as a performer,

Tenney denied the overt influence of its style on his own music, including its collage-like incorporations of recognizable tunes. *"Blue Suede,"* however, he singled out as a notable exception: "There because I'm quoting, because I'm fragmenting, because I'm superimposing, juxtaposing these things. And the quotation aspect of it, the fact that at a certain point the voice becomes recognizable, has a psychological effect that is like that of recognizing a tune in Ives" (Tenney 1996d, 133).

The works of Ives, Varèse, Cage, and Presley, however, were but a few elements among others within a complex dynamic of influences that Tenney and Schneemann together were actively digesting around the turn of the decade. The most significant of these were surely the influences that they exerted on each other. As Schneemann put it, "We were like elements of shredded paper, flowing and fluid. In the discrepancies, extra energies would come, as with collage, when you tear a piece of paper apart and an unexpected dynamic emerges between the two sections" (2016). Schneemann's work as a painter was already embracing collage, influenced in part by the experience of hearing Tenney obsessively practicing fragments of Ives in the next room. In turn, her new collages would affect Tenney's work as composer and performer. According to Schneemann:

> Once we were together, we melded our processes. . . . Fragmentation and harmonization—the fracture through which there is an incremental aspect of image or sound—we had really parallel aesthetic dilemmas. How to perfect a form and how to release it. How to keep it from being predictable while establishing a rigorous structure. . . .
>
> I was engrossed, devoured by collage process, and part of that has to do with the richness of juxtaposition that I'm hearing in the music. When Jim looks at the collage, he begins to fragment his compositions, or reinterpret phrasing in the piano works that he's mastering. (Corrin 2016, 115, 119)

The aesthetic, technical, and emotional economy between Tenney and Schneemann is reflected in the titles and dedications of their works during these years. In the 1950s Tenney served as subject for portraits by Schneemann (Breitwieser 2015), while she made a number of remarkable drawings and collages to serve as his score covers.[6] Schneemann's *Quarry Transposed (Central Park in the Dark)* (1960)—a construction on board comprising Masonite panels, wood strips, photographs, a red glass pitcher, nails, wire, paper, and oil paint—borrows its subtitle from a work by Ives for chamber orchestra. Her *Tenebration* (1960) is, as its title suggests, dedicated to Tenney and features oil paint on canvas, paper, wood strips, cloth, and photographs of Wanda Landowska, Johannes Brahms, and Ludwig van Beethoven. Her *Sir Henry Francis Taylor* (1961) comprises Masonite panels, plaster structure, Tenney's underpants, a swing, glass, photographs, and oil paint. Reciprocally, the primacy of Schneemann's influence on *"Blue Suede"* is reflected not only in its dedication to her but also in the choice of title: *collage,* after all, is a word more routinely used by artists than by musicians. Indeed, Eric Smigel quotes an April 1961 passage from Schneemann's personal diary in which she describes *"Blue Suede"* as "the new piece *Collage I*, grown out of my work and ideas on materials" (2017b, 9).

"Blue Suede" was realized using just a handful of basic studio and tape-music techniques, including "cutting, splicing, reversing tape direction, changing speeds, and very primitive reverberation" (Tenney 2001). Processed or unprocessed snippets of the source recording were sequenced into tracks using—for the first time in Tenney's music—post-Cagean chance procedures.

> When I made the piece, it involved cutting up tape into little pieces, throwing them into a basket, shaking it up, pulling them out and splicing them back together not knowing which direction they were going or what. And then when I got enough to run on a tape-recorder I would listen to it and edit it. And as I remember, the only thing I ever had to change was when the fragments were too long. I didn't want it to be like quotations. I wanted it to be sort of an exciting celebratory texture that would have some of the timbral characteristics of the original. (Tenney 2005b)

Figure 3.2 provides a timeline of the music showing how *"Blue Suede"* was assembled from four separate audio tracks. As is shown, no more than two of those tracks sound at any given time. Spectrograms of 10-second excerpts from individual tracks appear as call-outs above and below the timeline.[7] These depict the distribution of sound energy across pitch registers as a function of time. (Appendix B provides a brief general introduction to the spectrographic analysis of sound.)

In the order in which they are first heard, the four component audio tracks are as follows. The reader is urged to closely compare these descriptions with the spectrograms in figure 3.2, which illustrate many of the features mentioned, and with the audio.

I. *Low-Register Track.* Tape snippets—mostly vocal—of the source recording (at one-quarter speed but otherwise unprocessed) are concatenated with noisy reverberated higher-speed snippets. The specific source is aurally unrecognizable, but occasional pitch glides derived from vowel sounds (visible in the top left spectrogram) evoke an exaggeratedly low-register (hypermasculine) vocal quality. Snippet direction may be forward or reversed, so some reverberations increase rather than decrease in amplitude. Multiple reverberation periods appear, but one strongly predominates: a period of roughly 0.15 second that will later assume an important unifying rhythmic function. Once track II has entered, silences appear irregularly interspersed between the snippets of sound, this occurring during the region filled with vertical dashes in the timeline of figure 3.2. As the figure indicates, these silences disappear near the end of the track as the dynamic level increases in preparation for the entrance of track III.

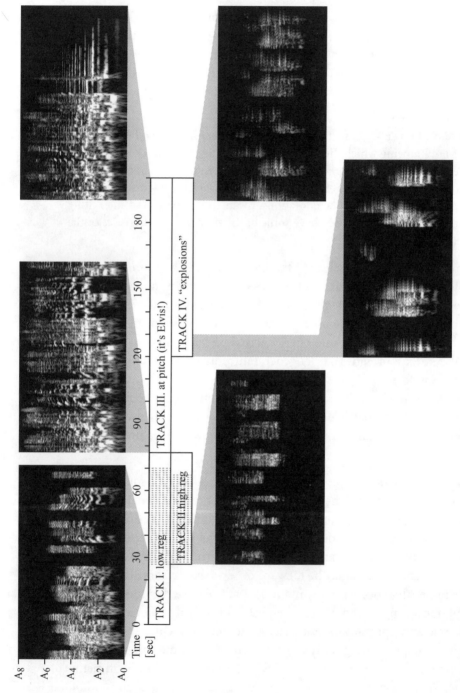

FIGURE 3.2. The four audio tracks comprising *Collage #1* ("*Blue Suede*"), with representative spectrograms of 10-second excerpts using a log-frequency (i.e., pitch) ordinate ranging from A_0 to A_8.

II. *High-Register Track.* Superimposed on track I, reverberated snippets appear at three different tape speeds (1', 2', 4') so that the audio skips by octaves between registers. The primary impression is one of modulated electronic noise bursts, but the tonal qualities of distorted music and voice are occasionally discernable. The reverberation period for the lowest tape speed is roughly 0.15 second (as in track I), and this is respectively halved and quartered at the higher tape speeds. Silences are irregularly interspersed among the snippets of sound, as again indicated by vertical-dashed fill in figure 3.2. These rests are not coordinated with those in track I, so silences in these two tracks sometimes align to introduce a new element of silence into the total mix. A rhythmically frustrated "start-stop" quality results, accumulating a tension that is discharged when the silences in both track I and track II abruptly disappear and the dynamic level increases, propelling the music toward the pivotal entrance of track III.

III. *At-Pitch Track.* Concatenated snippets of the source at its original speed suddenly commandeer the texture, appearing unprocessed but in either forward or backward direction. For most listeners, recognition of Presley as the source artist is virtually immediate at this point, abetted by several substantial (albeit backward) vocal samples near the beginning of the track. The durations of snippets range roughly from 0.1 to 0.5 second (with an average of about 0.25 second), although the perceived attack density is somewhat higher due to the internal articulation of source snippets by instrumental attacks. Most snippets originate from the opening 30 seconds of the Presley source recording, with snippets of the same content often recurring. The A-major tonality of the source's twelve-bar blues form is detectable throughout, although the random splicing process yields a highly irregular set of blues changes, to say the least. The dynamic level of the track gradually declines from its beginning so as to foreground the entrance of track IV and then very gradually increases so that the dynamics of the two tracks converge. Via tape-speed manipulation of the source's final ringing chord, Tenney engineered the tongue-in-cheek conclusion of a rockish plagal cadence to the wrong tonic (E).[8]

IV. *Reverberant "Explosions."*[9] Sudden onsets are followed by decaying reverberations. The provenance of the material is difficult to identify; a low-speed recording of the Presley source variously filtered is a possibility. The registers and bandwidths of the "explosions" are diverse. Their pitch salience also varies; when it is clear, pitch most often refutes the A-major tonality of track III, reinforcing the perceptual autonomy of the two tracks. A 0.15-second delay period is used throughout. This reverberation rate clearly recalls that of the reverberated sounds on track I in the early part of the piece. However, it also approximates the eight-note rhythmic value of the original source appearing concurrently in track III, a correspondence that promotes a rhythmic meshing of the two tracks. Initially, the explosions in track IV are foregrounded relative to track III, being relatively loud and clustered in overlapping groups. Although the average attack density in track IV remains fairly constant, this clustering of attacks gradually abates so that by the end of the track the explosions overlap less and are distributed more uniformly in time, as shown in figure 3.2. Concurrently, the dynamic level of track IV progressively decreases to approach that of track III, which has been increasing. As a result of these several factors, the two tracks rhythmically and dynamically mesh as the conclusion approaches. Their elements gradually achieve a flowing rhythmic dialogue that might conjure the improbable image of Elvis jamming with Varèse.

For the first 77 seconds of Tenney's tape collage, studio manipulations render the Presley source unrecognizable. Only the occasional suggestion of a distorted vocality remains amid a welter of bass rumbles and treble flutters. When the famous source finally becomes identifiable it does so unexpectedly but unmistakably, the listener tripping across the threshold of sudden recognition. This reveal affects perception not only of the ensuing but also of the preceding music, which is retrospectively inferred to be derived from the Presley source as well—a conclusion that has been primed by the vague earlier suggestions of vocal quality. As Smigel (2012, 77) suggests, *"Blue Suede"* might be construed as an orchestration and performance of the mental process of recognition itself, in which sundry percepts suddenly fit with a common preexisting concept. From that locus of conjunction it is not just perceptions that ramify but connotations. It is as though a door in the hermetic space of the tape studio has been flung open to reveal society at large and the participation of music therein.

Whereas many rockabilly aficionados might prefer Carl Perkins's earlier recording of "Blue Suede Shoes," Tenney seized upon the Presley version, which had proven vastly more popular and whose social resonances were correspondingly greater. The use of such a highly identifiable source recording of another artist and the engagement with its particular connotations make Tenney's collage perhaps the earliest example of a transgressive musical practice later dubbed *plunderphonics*. The term was coined by Canadian composer John Oswald (1986), who defined a *plunderphone* as "a recognizable sonic quote, using the actual sound of something familiar which has already been recorded," adding that "the plundering has to be blatant" (1989[?]).[10] In the words of writer and musician Chris Cutler, "It wasn't until 1961 that an unequivocal exposition of plunderphonic techniques arrived in James Tenney's celebrated *Collage No. 1* ('Blue Suede'), a manipulation of Elvis Presley's hit record 'Blue Suede Shoes'. The gauntlet was down; Tenney had picked up a 'non art', lowbrow work and turned it into 'art'; not as with scored music by writing variations on a popular air, but simply by subjecting a gramophone record to various physical and electrical procedures" ([1994] 2004, 11). In Oswald's assessment, relative to earlier works that involved in some way the transformation of preexisting sources, "the difference with 'Blue Suede' is how it audaciously used a very recognizable existing recording of another musical work. This blatant appropriation pioneered the discovery, for myself and many others, of an ocean of sampling and plunderphonics in following decades."[11]

As Schneemann observed regarding collage in general, from Tenney's fragmentation of the Presley source "an unexpected dynamic emerges" between parts. In particular, disruption of the source's superficial linguistic meanings foregrounds the connotations of its timbres and rhythms. Filmmaker Stan Brakhage remarked that "its editing is for the purpose of creating metaphor, so that whatever the words are of 'Blue Suede Shoes,' recutting allows submerged grunts and vulgarities to emerge from the track" (1993, 119).[12] In rock and roll, sexual energies whose expression had been socially suppressed came bubbling to the surface in mid-1950s youth culture, manifested in the bodily engagement of driving rhythm, emphatic earthy vocals, and overwhelming volume. Tenney and Schneemann recognized these barely concealed subtexts of embodiment and pleasure in early rock and roll, and *"Blue Suede"* represents in part an acknowledgment and celebration of them. Speaking of Tenney's collage and the concerns that they shared at the time of its making, Schneemann remarked: "It's about pleasure. So that's kind of a forbidden threshold conceptually around us. Pleasure is too personal or expressionistic or too precise. . . . And momentum. . . . So this is just to emphasize that the body comes in. The pleasured body is part of what we're thinking about against the traditional cultures around us."[13] Accordingly, Schneemann reported that they danced not only to Presley's recording but also to Tenney's collage. Revealing a sly private meaning to the title, she added that she did so in blue suede shoes purchased from Capezio Dance Shop.

3.4 "Meta/Hodos" (1961)

> You know, it's not the problem that everybody's stuck in the old theory. Lots
> of people have admitted that we need a new theory. But what they're after
> is a new theory that will function like the old one did. And this is a mistake.
> (Tenney 1996d, 92)

One of Tenney's most significant creative accomplishments during his graduate studies at the University of Illinois was theoretical rather than musical. This was a thesis entitled "Meta/Hodos: A Phenomenology of Twentieth-Century Music and an Approach to the Study of Form," which he completed in June 1961, discovering only afterward that his degree program did not require a thesis (Tenney 1988b, 12). Although it received a very limited publication in 1964, the text remained effectively unavailable commercially until the mid-1980s. Privately circulated and photocopied versions of it developed a remarkably widespread readership, however, especially among composers seeking a theoretical framework that could accommodate contemporary musical forms (Polansky 1983, 259; Tenney 2015, 437).

"Meta/Hodos" applied principles from the psychology of perception to the analysis of musical form and texture. It thus made consideration of the listener's experience its starting point, in radical contrast with the concern to codify received practice that was characteristic of traditional music theory. Although Tenney's own music would not begin to reflect the ideas developed in "Meta/Hodos" until after he had left Illinois, they would appear in diverse manifestations throughout the remainder of his career. In particular, he would invert the analytical procedures developed in his thesis into generative compositional techniques in his algorithmic music of the 1960s and again after 1980. Thus, while an exhaustive treatment of the contents of "Meta/Hodos" is neither required nor practical here, an overview of its main ideas as manifested in Tenney's compositional practice is necessary to any detailed understanding of his mature music.

During his undergraduate studies Tenney had already begun casting about for a theoretical framework sufficiently broad to accommodate the music in which he was then most interested, as well as his own developing compositional practice. He later recalled this pursuit as follows:

> 1956–57: . . . begin to search for some theoretical base relevant to my own sensibility. Feeling, somehow, that Schoenberg (and even Webern) went wrong at this point (in the theory, not in the music). Read Stockhausen with interest and some reservations; read Xenakis with somewhat more interest and still greater reservations; (will later read Partch with combined fascination and despair). (Tenney 1968a)

> I read Messiaen's book in French and . . . Pierre Schaeffer's *À la Recherche d'une Musique Concrète* and, what else, Cowell, *New Musical Resources*, Schoenberg's writings, and finally, Partch's book. . . . Oh, Schillinger was another. (Tenney 1988b, 11)

None of these sources ultimately proved satisfying for Tenney, largely because they were too closely wedded to particular styles and structures, while he was seeking a conception sufficiently general to accommodate a more expansive field of musical experiences: "I think I wanted something that would give me a way of understanding the music that was important to me—which is to say Varèse, Webern, Cage, Schoenberg—of understanding that music and at the same time giving me some kind of a technical basis to move forward on my own work without it sounding like any of theirs, necessarily, . . . so that needed to be more general and less stylistically specific than any of those sources were" (Tenney 1988b, 11).

The greater generality that Tenney was seeking he ultimately found through an analysis of the tendency of musical events to form perceptible groupings and morphologies. His approach was inspired by the writings of the early twentieth-century German psychologists Max Wertheimer, Wolfgang Köhler, and Kurt Koffka.

(a)   (b)

FIGURE 3.3. (a) Visual grouping by spatial proximity.
(b) Visual grouping by parametric similarity.

Just kind of by accident, I was reading in all sorts of things including work in perceptual psychology, and I came across this wonderful paper by a German psychologist called "The Laws of Organization of Perceptual Forms" [1923], or something like that. Max Wertheimer. And I right away saw that some of the things he was doing, that he was applying to visual perception, could fairly easily be transferred to auditory perception, musical perception. But as I studied the literature and searched it down, I saw that nobody had done that. They were all very visual-oriented. (Tenney 1988b, 13)

Around 1912, Wertheimer—along with Köhler and Koffka—had founded the theory of Gestalt psychology, which sought to determine the principles according to which perception rendered the complexity of the world manageable to the mind. In the words of Koffka, as quoted by Tenney in "Meta/Hodos" ([1961] 2015, 32), "the laws of organization which we have found operative explain why our behavioral environment is orderly in spite of the bewildering spatial and temporal complexity of stimulation. Units are being formed and maintained in segregation and relative insulation from other units. . . . Without our principles of organization . . . the phenomenal changes produced by these changes of stimulation would be as disorderly as the changes of stimulation themselves. . . . Order is a consequence of organization, and organization the result of natural forces" (Koffka [1935] 1962, 175). Thus "Meta/Hodos" is, first, an analysis of the acoustical factors that promote the formation of perceptually coherent musical groupings—*temporal gestalt units*—and, conversely, the segregation of such groupings from one another.

In particular, Tenney seized upon classical Gestalt psychology's principles of grouping by *proximity* and *similarity*, which are illustrated in the visual modality in figure 3.3. In part (a) of the figure, elementary gestalt units (unfilled circles) visibly group in threes. Each three-element group coheres as a spatial gestalt on account of the proximity in space of its adjacent constituent elements and—conversely—is segregated from the other groups by virtue of the relative remoteness of its constituents from theirs. Figure 3.3(b) illustrates visual grouping by similarity, wherein three groups each internally comprising three similar elements (unfilled or filled circles) cohere by virtue of the similarity of their constituent elements and—conversely—segregate from one another on account of differences between the elements in adjacent groups. Moreover, visual gestalt grouping operates hierarchically: within each part of figure 3.3, elementary units (circles) cohere in three three-unit groups, while the two parts of the figure, (a) and (b), in turn constitute two larger groupings that cohere by virtue of the proximity of the adjacent three-unit groups that comprise them and that conversely are segregated on account of the larger separation between the two parts of the figure.

Tenney adapted these concepts to the auditory realm, in which he translated spatial proximity as temporal proximity and visible similarity as audible similarity.[14] He referred to temporal gestalts that—in their musical context—possess no significant internal temporal divisions as *elements*. In much of music, an element corresponds to a single attack (a note or chord), although trills, tremolos, and rolled chords may sometimes function as elements. The next smallest temporal gestalt unit Tenney dubbed the *clang*. In traditional Western contexts, clangs often have the cardinality—if not necessarily the thematic function—of motives. The level above the clang in the hierarchy of groupings is the *sequence*. Tenney would not introduce names for higher levels until the late 1970s, at which time he would add *segments* and *sections*, respectively (Tenney with Polansky [1978] 2015, 203).

Figure 3.4(a_1) and (b_1) graphically illustrate auditory grouping induced by factors, respectively, of (a) proximity in time and (b) similarity in the value of some sonic parameter. Tenney discussed various other factors effective in the evocation of temporal groups (repetition, accent, and expectations or recollections aroused by the piece or past musical experiences), but he took the factors of temporal proximity and parametric similarity to be primary (Tenney [1961] 2015, 41, 48). In the figure, the ordinate might be any musical parameter (any distinctive attribute of sound in which two elements might be distinguished from each other), pitch being just one possibility.[15] The durations and parametric values of individual elements are represented using solid black horizontal lines. The sequence illustrated in part (a_1) of the figure comprises three clangs of four, five, and four elements, respectively, assuming for illustrative purposes that any variation in other parameters is negligible. Each of these three clangs coheres as a temporal gestalt unit primarily by virtue of the relative temporal proximity between its successive elements. Conversely, each clang is segregated from neighboring clangs primarily by its relatively greater temporal separation from their nearest elements. In part (b_1) of the figure, on the other hand, three clangs that are contiguous in time nonetheless segregate into distinct gestalts by virtue of difference in their parametric "registers." A more complete characterization of either sequence would usually necessitate the depiction of additional musical parameters, whose variations might or might not cooperate with one another in the determination of temporal grouping.

The same principles that induce intragroup cohesion and intergroup segregation at the clang level can operate at other hierarchical formal levels (i.e., on various timescales). Thus, while parametric changes and/or temporal separation between successive clangs can perceptually delineate them, those same factors can also serve to delineate sequences, segments, and so forth. Segregation of

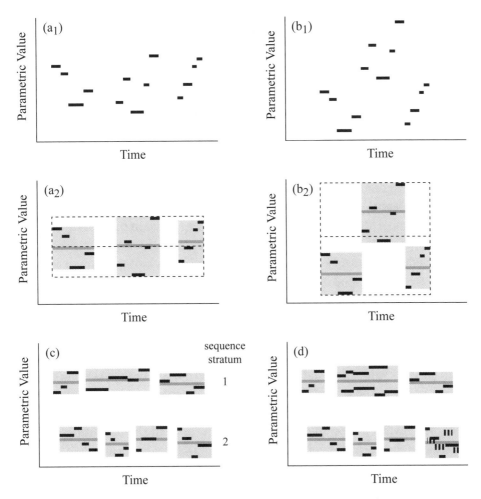

FIGURE 3.4. Auditory grouping of elements into clangs by (a) temporal proximity and (b) parametric similarity. (c) A polyphonic sequence comprising two strata of monophonic clangs. (d) A polyphonic sequence comprising two strata, which include some polyphonic clangs.

higher-level temporal gestalt units may be the product of relatively greater disjunctions in time or parametric range. Commonly, segregation of higher-level groupings may occur when a parameter that has been relatively static finally changes. For instance, if dynamic has been fairly uniform and hence has not participated in the delineation of recent clangs, a significant change in dynamic may initiate a new sequence. In such a case, dynamic can be said to have served as a *factor of cohesion* within the preceding sequence and a *factor of segregation* between it and the new sequence.

As thus far described, "Meta⁄Hodos" offers a perceptually based theory of musical *segmentation*. In other words, where musical examples exhibit hierarchies of temporal groupings, the analytical approach described in "Meta⁄Hodos" attempts to account for the sonic factors that delineate groupings and induce their hierarchies. It proceeds further, however, to develop for such temporal gestalt units a theory of *form* that Tenney took to have three aspects: *state*, *shape*, and *structure*.[16]

By the *state* of a gestalt Tenney meant the ensemble of what he called its overall or *statistical* features. These are the gestalt's *mean* (or *average*) parametric values, the *ranges* of those values, and total *duration* of the gestalt. For the two sequences of figure 3.4(a_1) and (b_1), these statistical features are depicted at the clang level in figure 3.4(a_2) and (b_2) by the addition of gray rectangles. The width of each rectangle corresponds to the duration of the associated clang, its height corresponds to the clang range in the ordinate parameter (whatever it is), and a solid horizontal gray line indicates the clang mean in that parameter. It is similarly possible to define at the hierarchical level of the sequence a sequence mean, sequence range, and sequence duration for each of the two sequences, and these are indicated in the figure using dashed frames. At the element level in this particular example—as in much monophonic traditional music—each element has a unique parametric value so that each element mean simply equals that value, while each element range is nil.

By *shape* or *morphology* Tenney meant the profile of a parameter induced by changes in its value, although gestalts at various hierarchical levels may display shapes native to those levels.[17] The individual elements of figure 3.4 are all parametrically static and thus possess no shape, but the first clang of figure 3.4(b_2) has roughly a reversed checkmark shape, while the last clang has an almost linearly increasing shape. Tenney observed that at hierarchical levels above that of the element, the perceived shape in a particular parameter is largely determined by differences between the states of gestalt units *at the next lower hierarchical level*. Thus, the most salient aspect of parametric shape in the sequence of figure 3.4(b_2) is the rising-then-falling figure outlined by the gray clang-mean lines of its three constituent clangs. By contrast, the sequence-level shaping of parametric value in figure 3.4(a_2) is so slight as to perhaps be audibly nil because all clang means are very similar. This might, however, help to foreground a subtler shaping that appears in another statistical feature: clang range. In both sequences, shaping in a third statistical feature is also visible: clang duration decreases at the end of the sequence.

By *structure*—Tenney's third and final aspect of form—he meant perceived relationships between parts. For example, if the two sequences of figure 3.4(a_2) and (b_2) appear in the same piece of music, then a thorough account of its structure would include the observation that each clang of the second sequence is related to a corresponding clang in the first sequence by some vertical translation (which would correspond to pitch transposition if the parameter involved were pitch). Moreover, structural relationships can potentially appear between different parameters and/or between gestalts appearing at different hierarchical levels.

In conjunction with its theory of form, "Meta‡Hodos" includes an analysis of musical texture. Tenney defined a temporal gestalt (at any hierarchical level and in any polyphonic stratum) to be *monophonic* if all of its next-lower-level temporal gestalts are heard one at a time; otherwise, it is *polyphonic*. Figure 3.4(c), for instance, shows a polyphonic sequence comprising two distinct strata of clangs. The two strata are differentiated by a parametric separation that is large compared to the parametric variation within each individual stratum. The distinguishing parameter may be any parameter, but pitch affords particularly extensive possibilities for complex polyphonic layering, since it exhibits a uniquely large number of discriminable values. Polyphony may appear at multiple hierarchical levels, as shown in figure 3.4(d), which retains two strata of clangs, as in figure 3.4(c), but introduces two polyphonic clangs within those strata. In particular, the second clang of the upper sequence stratum exhibits two strata of elements distinguishable by difference in the ordinate parameter, while the last clang of the lower sequence stratum exhibits two strata of elements roughly coextensive in the ordinate parameter but with dashes meant to suggest that they are distinguishable in some other musical parameter. Such *compound polyphony* recalls the frequent concurrence of semiautonomous musical layers in the music of Charles Ives, whose music was an early touchstone for Tenney and whose enormously complex *Concord* Sonata he was practicing while in Illinois. In the 1990s Tenney remarked, "My own music has not reflected very much of a direct influence from Ives, but my ideas about music have been deeply affected. . . . [F]or example, my ideas about what a music theory would have to be able to do is very much determined by keeping in mind that it has to be able to deal with the music of Ives" (Tenney 1996d, 133).

Tenney had an enduring affinity for etymologies. He derived the title of "Meta‡ Hodos" from the root of the modern English word *method* as "along the way."[18]

meth′ od, n. [F. *méthode*, fr. L. *methodus*, fr. Gr. *methodos*, method, investigation following after, fr. *meta* after ‡ *hodos* way]. (Tenney [1961] 2015, 13).

"Meta‡Hodos" accordingly represented to Tenney certain steps toward a theory of formal perception, with an expectation of further developments by himself and others (2004b). In the 1970s he would axiomatize and extend the analytical principles of "Meta‡Hodos" in "META Meta‡Hodos" (Tenney [1975a] 2015) before recasting them to permit algorithmic analysis of musical examples using a computer (Tenney with Polansky [1978] 2015).[19] Nonetheless, his thesis of 1961 had already captured the essential features of a conception of form that would undergird much compositional work throughout his subsequent career and his forthcoming computer music in particular. Regarding the pragmatic supporting role of theoretical research with respect to his compositional production, he remarked, "The theory has always done that for me. Never was undertaken for any other reason" (Tenney 1988b, 46).

CHAPTER 4

Computer Music and Ergodicity (1961–64)

In my view, James Tenney is the first composer who made a
significant musical use of computer synthesis of sound.
—Jean-Claude Risset (1987, 549)

The primitive technical means available in the medium of tape-music composition had proven frustrating for Tenney, the musical success of *Collage #1 ("Blue Suede")* (1961) notwithstanding. Near the conclusion of his master's program at the University of Illinois, however, his supervisor, Lejaren Hiller, pointed out to him a recent journal article, "An Acoustic Compiler for Music and Psychological Stimuli" (Mathews 1961), that renewed his excitement about the potential of electronic music. The article described a new software system for the computerized generation of sound that engineer and amateur musician Max Mathews had been developing at Bell Telephone Laboratories (Bell Labs) in Murray Hill, New Jersey. Tenney remembered later: "I was very excited about it, as soon as I read it—remember this is in a context in which I'd had a great deal of difficulty with electronic music—after all of the excitement and the dream of being able to do everything, or anything, in fact it turned out I couldn't do anything that satisfied me. But when I read that article, my response to it was 'This is a medium that I can work with'" (1988b, 16). The detailed and definite control over the acoustic signal promised by Mathews's digital system must have struck Tenney as an enormous advance over the crude analog equipment with which he had been wrestling in Illinois.

Near the beginning of 1961 Tenney visited Bell Labs, where he met Mathews and engineer John R. Pierce, who subsequently invited him in writing to return and use their facilities.[1] Tenney gratefully replied that he would surely do so if he managed to find a job nearby after graduation. He was much surprised to subsequently receive in the mail a job offer to conduct research at Bell Labs itself. This research was to be undertaken in psychoacoustics, although this description in part served as a cover under which Tenney would advise and help to further develop the computer music system (Tenney 1988b, 18; Wood and Pierce 1991, 22).

Tenney himself provided a detailed analytical and technical account of his work at Bell Labs in a classic report entitled "Computer Music Experiences, 1961–1964" (1964). That essay remains an indispensable resource not only for readers interested in Tenney's computer music but also for anyone interested in the early development of computer music generally. His account begins with the following elegant condensation.

> I arrived at the Bell Telephone Laboratories in September 1961 with the follow-ing musical and intellectual baggage:
>
> 1. numerous instrumental compositions reflecting the influence of Webern and Varèse;
> 2. two tape-pieces produced in the Electronic Music Laboratory at the Uni-versity of Illinois—both employing familiar, "concrete" sounds, modified in various ways;
> 3. a long paper ("Meta/Hodos: A Phenomenology of Twentieth-Century Music and an Approach to the Study of Form," June 1961), in which a descriptive terminology and certain structural principles were devel-oped, borrowing heavily from gestalt psychology. The central point of the paper involves the clang, or primary aural gestalt, and basic laws of perceptual organization of clangs, clang-elements, and sequences (a higher-order gestalt unit consisting of several clangs);
> 4. a dissatisfaction with all purely synthetic electronic music that I had heard up to that time, particularly with respect to timbre;
> 5. ideas stemming from my studies of acoustics, electronics, and—espe-cially—information theory, begun in Lejaren Hiller's classes at the Uni-versity of Illinois; and finally
> 6. a growing interest in the work and ideas of John Cage.
>
> I leave in March 1964 with:
>
> 1. six tape compositions of computer-generated sounds, of which all but the first were also composed by means of the computer, and several in-strumental pieces whose composition involved the computer in one way or another;
> 2. a far better understanding of the physical basis of timbre and a sense of having achieved a significant extension of the range of timbres possible by synthetic means;
> 3. a curious history of renunciations of one after another of the traditional attitudes about music due primarily to a gradually more thorough as-similation of the insights of John Cage. (Tenney [1964] 2015, 97–98)

TABLE 4.1. Compositions completed by Tenney at Bell Labs, including works that were computer synthesized (CS) and/or algorithmically composed with the aid of a computer (AC)

Title	Month	Year	CS	AC	Medium	Duration
Analog #1 (Noise Study)	12	1961	✓		one-channel tape	4'23"
Entrance/Exit Music*	08	1962	✓		one-channel tape	6'30"
Five Stochastic Studies	11	1962	✓	✓	one-channel tape	11'
Stochastic (String) Quartet	01	1963		✓	instruments or tape	2'40"
Dialogue	04	1963	✓	✓	one-channel tape	4'00"
Radio Piece	07	1963	✓	✓	one-channel tape	2'04"
Ergodos I	08	1963	✓	✓	two one-channel tapes	10'22"
Phases	12	1963	✓	✓	one-channel tape	12'20"
Music for Player Piano	01	1964		✓	player piano	5'45"
String Complement	02	1964			string(s)	variable
Ergodos II	03	1964	✓	✓	two-channel tape	18'25"
Instrumental Responses	04	1964			instrumental	variable

* Composed in collaboration with George Brecht.

Tenney would later describe his sojourn at Bell Labs as one of the most productive periods in his artistic career. In less than three years, and in addition to conducting acoustical and psychoacoustical research, he would produce the spate of groundbreaking compositions listed in table 4.1. They would include, as far as I have been able to ascertain, the earliest example of computer-synthesized music made by a professional composer (*Noise Study*), the first music to be both algorithmically composed and synthesized using a computer (*Five Stochastic Studies*), and some of the earliest examples of instrumental music algorithmically composed with the aid of a computer that are not imitative of a traditional style (*Stochastic String Quartet*). With respect to computerized digital synthesis in particular, certain technical facilities were only then available at Bell Labs. Mathews recalled that "we were the only ones in the world at the time who had the right kind of digital-to-analog converter hooked up to a digital tape transport that would play a computer tape. So we had a monopoly, if you will, on this process" (Roads and Mathews 1980, 16).[2]

Tenney's groundbreaking contributions to the early history of computer music composition have long gone underacknowledged, although that has begun to change (Kahn 2012). Multiple factors may have contributed to this relative neglect. First, after departing Bell Labs in 1964 Tenney made no new computer music, and he gradually fell out of touch with its community and consequently it with him. Moreover, like much of Tenney's other music, recordings of his computer music remained commercially unavailable for decades after its creation. *Analog #1 (Noise Study)* and *Stochastic String Quartet* appeared on early compilation LPs, but not until 1992 would most of his electronic music see commercial audio release. Finally, it is impossible to overlook the drastic divergence in style of such radically nondramatic works as Tenney's *Phases* and *Ergodos* pieces from that of most computer music produced in the 1960s and 1970s. It may be that misunderstanding or antagonism regarding the specifically post-Cagean aesthetic embodied by most of Tenney's computer music has collaterally impeded recognition of its technical and historical significance.

In terms of technique, the succession of Tenney's computer music exhibits a steady increase in complexity and algorithmic control with respect to both texture and synthetic timbre. However, it also records his progressive intellectual and compositional absorption of the aesthetic concepts that would most influence the subsequent course of his life's work. First among these was a process-oriented conception of form generation arising from the ideas of Edgard Varèse, John Cage, and biologist D'Arcy Thompson.

4.1 Edgard Varèse, D'Arcy Thompson, and "Growth to Form"

Given the profound changes in aesthetic that Tenney underwent while at Bell Labs, it is remarkable that, in contrast, his technical approach was relatively consistent throughout most of this period, although subject to progressive refinement. Beginning with the *Five Stochastic Studies* (1962), this approach involved the creation of multileveled hierarchical formal structures by inverting the analytic procedures of "Meta*f*Hodos" into synthetic ones. The perceptual principles formulated in "Meta*f*Hodos," however, were sufficiently general that they could easily have been applied deterministically to produce generic forms. Tenney instead combined those principles with the use of random procedures to generate diverse forms that were, to varying degrees, unpredictable. This process-oriented approach to composition seems to have arisen in response to a confluence of musical and scientific currents in Tenney's thought of the late 1950s and early 1960s. Premier among these was Varèse's conception of form as a product of process.

Tenney first encountered Varèse's music via the earliest commercial recordings thereof, which were released in 1951.[3] Tenney and filmmaker Stan Brakhage subsequently met Varèse in person soon after arriving in New York in 1954 (section 2.2). Although Tenney never undertook formal composition lessons with him, until Varèse's death in 1965 Tenney often met informally with the elder composer: "I played for him tapes of most of the music I had done up to that time, and showed him scores of instrumental pieces and he gave me criticisms and we had many, really important, to me, very important talks. That's why I like to say, informal studies in composition with Varèse, because I learned a great deal of what I know about composition from him" (1976). Reciprocating, the Tone Roads Chamber Ensemble that Tenney cofounded in 1963 (section 5.2) would perform music by Varèse, and in 1964 Tenney would conduct a then-rare all-Varèse program as part of the Second Annual Avant Garde Festival of New York (all with Varèse in attendance). Notably, in response to Varèse's keen interest, Tenney provided Varèse with a tour of Bell Labs and its computer music facilities in the 1960s (Tenney 2005c).

Varèse's process-oriented notion of form would, in turn, buttress the algorithmic turn in Tenney's computer music. Varèse explained this formal conception through an analogy to crystal growth: "Conceiving musical form as a resultant—the result of a process, I was struck by what seemed to me an analogy between the formation of my compositions and the phenomenon of crystallization. . . . There is an idea, the basis of an internal structure, expanded and split into different shapes or groups of sound constantly changing in shape, direction, and speed, attracted and repulsed by various forces. The form of the work is the consequence of this interaction. Possible musical forms are as limitless as the exterior forms of crystals" (Varèse and Chou 1966, 16). If metaphorical as far as Varèse's compositional practice was concerned, his description of form as a *consequence* of objective processes playing out nonetheless represented a conception in arresting contrast to received architectural, rhetorical, and dramatic models of form. A more literal example of form as the outcome of process would be afforded by the compositional techniques of John Cage in the 1950s. These would include the flipping of coins in the *Music of Changes* (1951) and the marking of preexisting imperfections on paper in *Music for Piano 1–84* (1952–56), among other systematically applied procedures (Cage [1958] 1961; Pritchett 1996). By the time of his arrival at Bell Labs, Tenney had already employed post-Cagean chance procedures in assembling his own *Collage #1 ("Blue Suede")* (1961), and the use of randomly generated values in his computer music owes a debt to Cage's example.

In a 1959 letter to Varèse, Tenney revealed a less obvious influence on his interest in form-generating processes, connecting it explicitly to Varèse's analogy with crystal growth: "I have thought a lot about . . . the analogy between music and crystal structure. Somewhat along this same line, perhaps, is the relation of music to organic structure, and I would like to recommend a book that I believe will interest you very much. It is *[On] Growth and Form* by D'Arcy Wentworth Thompson."[4]

Thompson (1860–1948) was a celebrated Scottish biologist and mathematician who made a case that biological forms reflect physical and mathematical principles because organic growth takes place under the influence of physical forces. Tenney was introduced to Thompson's classic treatise *On Growth and Form* (1917) by Schneemann, who had discovered it at Bard College before the two met. She recalled their mutual interest in Thompson's ideas as reflecting an interest in natural forms and physiological processes: "We're looking at seashells and stones and rocks and ferns and the patterns of growth that produce distinctive form, . . . the astonishing variability and complexity of forms. How are they produced, why is it like that? And how does this inflect on what I'm making and building and for Jim on what he's hearing and thinking about for hearing as a physiological domain."[5]

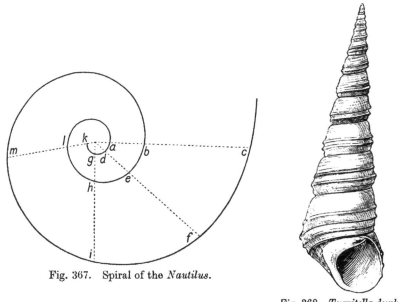

Fig. 367. Spiral of the *Nautilus*.

Fig. 368. *Turritella dupli-cata* (L.), Moseley's *Turbo duplicatus*. From Chenu. × ½.

FIGURE 4.1. Two figures from *On Growth and Form* (Thompson [1917] 1992, 813).

Among Thompson's famous illustrations are ones concerning the morphology of shells, understood as a nonliving physical record of the constrained growth of the living mantle of the shellfish (figure 4.1). These illustrate his general conception of form as a record of the forces that have acted upon a growing system, as articulated in an excerpt from *On Growth and Form* that Tenney recruited for the epigraph to section II of "Meta/Hodos": "The form, then, of any portion of matter . . . and the changes of form which are apparent in its movements and in its growth, may in all cases alike be described as due to the action of force. In short, the form of an object is a 'diagram of forces,' in this sense, at least, that from it we can judge of or deduce the forces that are acting or have acted upon it" ([1961] 2015, 36–37, quoting Thompson [1917] 1992, 16).

Thompson's attention to the influence of chemicophysical forces on the development of organic forms appears to have triggered for Tenney an association with a specifically psychological sense of the word *force* as deployed by the Gestalt psychologists, whose theories of visual perception supplied the principal foundation for Tenney's own theories of formal perception in music. For instance, in "Meta/Hodos" Tenney also quoted Gestalt theorist Kurt Koffka's assertion that "[perceived] order is a consequence of organization, and organization the result of natural *forces*" ([1935] 1962, 175, emphasis added). The Gestalt psychologists described the factors of similarity and proximity as exerting psychological *forces* that promote the cohesion or segregation of visual gestalts.

An audit of Tenney's use of the word *force* in "Meta/Hodos" reveals that he employed it often and consistently in this narrow psychological sense. To choose one among many possible examples, concerning a passage from the *Concord Sonata* by Charles Ives, Tenney wrote: "The same general relationships can be seen to apply to the remainder of the example, where parametric similarities always constitute the primary cohesive force within each of the monophonic sequences, parametric dissimilarities being the primary segregative force exerted between them" ([1961] 2015, 58).

What is unclear from "Meta/Hodos" alone is the manner in which Thompson's concept of form as the product of processes subjected to constraining forces would later inform Tenney's music. Evidence that it did so is provided by Tenney's rather enigmatic 1968 recollection that "the particular form of *Phases* [1963] was probably inspired by my readings of D'Arcy Thompson and Wilhelm Reich" (1968a). More revealing with respect to specifics is the following excerpt of a 1963 letter from Tenney to filmmaker Stan Brakhage in reference to their mutual reading of Thompson: "My thinking—since ["Meta/Hodos"]—has gradually centered more and more on this question of the total form, considered as a process (because unfolding in time), and finding numerous analogies with other processes, of which organic growth (to form) is only one example, though surely the most engrossing" (Brakhage, Tenney, and Markopoulos 1963, 83). This passage makes clear that Tenney's formal thinking during the height of his period at Bell Labs involved not only the Gestalt theories of "Meta/Hodos" but also a conception of overall forms as products of processes unfolding in time, especially growth processes. Since the forms of Tenney's music in this period are literally the products of variously constrained generative processes—particularly in the sense that the inchoate fecundity of the computer's random number generator was algorithmically subjected to form-imparting constraints ("forces")—a work like *Phases* might be regarded as the musical analogue of a Thompsonian nautilus shell or Varèsian crystal.

Explicit reference to Thompson and formative "forces" would disappear from Tenney's writings after 1964, but a model of form as the product of a generative process variously constrained would persist. It would resurface not only when Tenney returned to algorithmic composition in the 1980s but also in an array of works after 1970 involving constrained choices to be made by performers (section 6.1.1).

4.2 John Cage, Variety, and Ergodicity

Tenney's earliest exposure to the music of John Cage came via the *Sonatas and Interludes* (1946–48) for prepared piano, which he first heard on record and subsequently in a 1951 concert performance by Cage in Denver, where the young Tenney was still residing. Tenney recounted that he was "blown away" by the performance, which helped to sharpen his interest in timbre (Swed 2002). His personal acquaintance with Cage began in 1954, soon after he and a friend—filmmaker Stan Brakhage—had moved to New York City. Brakhage sought out Cage because he wanted to use the latter's music in a film soundtrack and brought Tenney along to their meeting (section 2.2). Tenney subsequently attended a number of performances of Cage's music in the 1950s, including the 25-Year Retrospective Concert of Cage's Music at New York's Town Hall in 1958, for which he and Schneemann traveled from Vermont (Tenney 1995a). In the printed program he encountered Cage's seminal essay "Experimental Music," including the famous pronouncement that "one may give up the desire to control sound, clear his mind of music, and set about discovering means to let sounds be themselves rather than vehicles for man-made theories or expressions of human sentiments" ([1957] 1961, 10).

After returning to the New York area from Illinois in 1961, Tenney was often in contact with Cage and involved in performances of his music. The Tone Roads Chamber Ensemble that Tenney cofounded in 1963 with performer-composers Philip Corner and Malcolm Goldstein included works by Cage on many of their programs (Arms 2013, 92–97; section 5.2). When in September 1963 Cage organized the first verifiably complete performance of Erik Satie's marathon *Vexations* (ca. 1894), Tenney participated as member of a relay team of pianists.[6] Tenney and Cage would subsequently serve together as assistant conductors in a famously contentious February 1964 performance of Cage's *Atlas Eclipticalis* with *Winter Music* by the New York Philharmonic under Leonard Bernstein, in which orchestra members mounted a minor rebellion (Miller 2001, 547–51; Piekut 2011, 28–61). In July 1965 Cage would again call on Tenney to perform in his *Variations V* at Lincoln Center (Miller 2001). In the summer of 1967 Tenney participated in a reading group convened by Cage to discuss recent writings by Buckminster Fuller, among other texts (Tenney 2000f; Kahn 2012, 142; D. Patterson 2012, 53), and in June 1968 at Something Else Gallery, Tenney organized what may have been the first continuous public reading of James Joyce's *Finnegans Wake*, an event in which Cage participated as member of a relay team of readers, as did Cage's friend, the mythologist and Joyce scholar Joseph Campbell (Higgins, Clay, and Friedman 2018, 155; Tenney 1996d, 145–46).[7] In a 1988 interview, Cage remarked that Corner, Goldstein, and Tenney might well have been incorporated into the regular meetings of the "New York School" of Cage, Earle Brown, Morton Feldman, David Tudor, and Christian Wolff in the 1960s if it were not for Feldman's blanket opposition to expanding the group (Duckworth 1999, 16).[8]

Against the backdrop of his heightened involvements with Cage, around 1963 Tenney consciously resolved to attempt to assimilate in his own work the radically listener-centered aspects of Cage's music and thought since 1950 (section 1.2.1). He later recalled: "In retrospect, one of the important things about my 'encounters' with Cage is that I was not an immediate or easy convert. I had strong reservations about some aspects of his aesthetic philosophy, and it took some considerable time for me to arrive at a sympathetic understanding of his position" (Tenney 1995a).

This progressive intellectual and artistic reckoning is clearly reflected in Tenney's computer music output, which proceeded from a Varèsian abstraction of city sounds and a dramatic arch form in *Analog #1 (Noise Study)* (1961) to a nonmimetic and antidramatic post-Cagean equanimity in *Ergodos II* (1964). That Tenney's groundbreaking work in computer music at Bell Labs and his intellectual reckoning with Cage's aesthetic took place concurrently might well be a coincidence, but it entails that the resulting music cannot be understood without a complementary reckoning on the parts of the reader and analyst.

Listeners familiar with such rigorously "minimal" works as Tenney's *For Ann (rising)* (1969) or his *Postal Pieces* (1965–71) will appreciate the sharp contrast between the aesthetic they manifest and one that he had articulated just a few years earlier:

> If I had to name a single attribute of music that has been more essential to my esthetic than any other, it would be variety. It was to achieve greater variety that I began to use random selection procedures in the *Noise Study* (more than from any philosophical interest in indeterminacy for its own sake), and the very frequent use of random number generation in all my composing programs has been to this same end. I have tried to increase this variety at every gestalt "level"—from that of small-scale fluctuations of amplitude and frequency in each sound (affecting timbre), to that of extended sequences of sounds—and in as many different parameters of sound as possible (and/or practicable). (Tenney [1964] 2015, 111)

If some of Tenney's later works appear outwardly simple in prescription and focused in material (if complex in perception nonetheless), this statement apropos his computer music embraces an overtly maximalist variety in every perceptible dimension. In part this reflects a post-Cagean embrace of all sonic possibilities, one to which Cage had described chance operations and indeterminacy as suited: "In view, then, of a totality of possibilities, no knowing action is commensurate, since the character of the knowledge acted upon prohibits all but some eventualities. . . . An *experimental* action, generated by a mind as empty as it was before it became one, thus in accord with the possibility of no matter what, is, on the other hand, practical" (Cage [1955] 1961, 15).

A pertinent concept from probability theory that appears repeatedly in Tenney's writings is that of *ergodicity*. It is likely that he first encountered it during his master's program at the University of Illinois in a course on information theory taught by Lejaren Hiller (Tenney [1964] 2015, 97; Hiller 1963, 123). The concept has important roles in both information theory and chemistry (which was Hiller's academic discipline before he began his research in music; Hiller 1987, 514). In Tenney's usage it denotes a property of a musical sequence—specifically, that all excerpts of that sequence exhibit statistical similarity to one another.[9] He associated these characteristics with the music of Cage in particular:

> Most of Cage's works since 1951 exemplify an important new formal type that I have elsewhere called "ergodic." I use this term (borrowed from thermodynamics) to mean *statistically homogeneous* at some hierarchical level of formal perception. For example, it can be said about many of Cage's post-1951 pieces (and something like this often *is* said, though usually with negative implications not intended here) that any two- or three-minute segment of the piece is essentially the same as any other segment of corresponding duration, even though the details are quite different in the two cases. I interpret this to mean that certain *statistical properties* are in fact "the same"—or so nearly identical that no distinction can be made in perception. (Tenney [1983] 2015, 289)

Accordingly, the two pieces in which Tenney—by his own account—most closely approached the aesthetic of Cage were entitled *Ergodos I* (1963) and *Ergodos II* (1964) (Tenney 2000f). Both are dedicated to Cage.

In his early computer music works, Tenney had imposed time-varying probabilistic constraints as inputs to the composing program in order to induce large-scale parametric shaping. His progressive assimilation of Cage's influence, however, would be reflected in a gradual progression from the dramatically conceived forms of pieces such as *Analog #1 (Noise Study)* (1961; section 4.6) and *Dialogue* (1963) to the consistency-in-variety of the two *Ergodos* pieces.

> Both the *Stochastic String Quartet* and *Dialogue* made use of programming facilities that enabled me to shape the large-scale form of a piece in terms of changing means and ranges in the various parameters in time. Now my thoughts took a different turn—an apparent reversal—as I began to consider what this process of "shaping" a piece really involved. Both the intention and the effect here were involved in one way or another with "drama" (as in Beethoven, say)—a kind of dramatic "development" that inevitably reflected ("expressed") a guiding hand (mine) directing the course of things now here, now there, and so on. What seemed of more interest than this was to give free rein to the sounds themselves, allowing anything to happen within as broad a field of possibilities as could be set up. (Tenney [1964] 2015, 121)

Accordingly, in *Ergodos I*, *Music for Player Piano*, and *Ergodos II*, Tenney progressively removed such predetermined, time-dependent formal constraints, ultimately allowing the algorithm to stochastically determine all formal features on multiple timescales throughout the piece, with no preestablished restrictions on parametric values other than the fixed limits of the synthesis system. Regarding such ergodic forms, Tenney later remarked: "Such a form is quite unlike the dramatic and/or rhetorical forms we are accustomed to in earlier music and has been the cause of much of the negative response to Cage's music of the last thirty years. A different attitude is obviously required of the listener to be able to enjoy an ergodic piece—and it is perhaps ironic that it is an attitude that most people are able to adopt quite easily in situations outside the usual realm of 'art' (e.g., the sounds of a forest)" ([1983] 2015, 289). Correspondingly, Tenney's computer music of 1963–64 bears less formal or aesthetic kinship with most other electronic music of the decade than with the (primarily instrumental) music of Cage in the 1950s, of which *Music of Changes* is the archetype. Accordingly, Tenney's music of 1963–64 must be understood in the context of Cage's musical precedent.

In this respect, Tenney's work seems to have created a degree of aesthetic confusion quite early: "What Bell didn't realize but gradually became aware of was how subversive my activities there were bound to be, due to the fact that my aesthetic philosophy was very close to Cage's thinking, whereas that was not the case with the people at Bell Labs. They didn't have the faintest notion of what he was up to" (Pritchett et al. [1995] 2001, 191). Ironically, the engagement by Tenney with Cagean ideas and methods has the surprising implication that Cage exerted a covert influence on the early *technical* development of computer music.

> Because of my interest in Cage's work, his ideas had a significant influence on the early development of computer music—without his ever realizing it. It was at my suggestion, for example, that the random noise generator was added to the set of "unit generators" available in the design of "instruments," and that it was made possible to have the input specifications of a computer instrument be determined by the output of an algorithmic composition program (which in my usage was always "stochastic"). In addition, much of my work on timbre was influenced by Cage's thought, especially in its concern with environmental sounds, and "sound in general." (Tenney 1995a)[10]

Although Tenney's adoption of a post-Cagean listener-centered aesthetic would prove permanent, after 1964 he only rarely revisited the strict statistical homogeneity of his *Ergodos* pieces—doing so, for instance, in *Ergodos III* (1994), a memorial tribute to Cage. At a remove of three decades, he remarked: "[*Ergodos II* represents] my closest point in my own kind of aesthetic trajectory to Cage's trajectory. And it was very conscious. . . . I like the result quite a bit . . . [but] you have to give up certain kinds of expectations that you might have with respect to form. So I was able to get that close, and then gradually, I guess, over the years, beginning around then, clarify for myself what I wanted to be doing with it, and how it was different from Cage's aesthetic." Clarifying this difference, Tenney added, "I like to shape things, even if I use a random process. What fascinates me is the varieties of forms that are possible. Cage, I think, was not so interested in this. . . . For me [Cagean ergodicity is] one possible kind of form among an infinite number" (1996d, 144, 150).[11]

4.3 Max Mathews and MUSIC

The sequence of software systems for computer music that Mathews had been developing came to be known as MUSIC-N, beginning in 1957 with a version later dubbed MUSIC I (Roads 1996, 87–90, 787–91). A number of the fundamental structural features that he introduced in those systems persist in various computer-music systems to the present day. A characteristic of MUSIC-N programs was the division of their inputs into a *score file* and an *orchestra file*. The score file comprised a sequence of *notes* (stipulations of note onset times, durations, frequencies, amplitudes, etc.). The orchestra file, on the other hand, comprised the specifications for one or more software *instruments* that would "play" (in other words, generate digital audio associated with) notes assigned to them in the score file.

The version described in the early article encountered by Tenney was MUSIC III, which Mathews had developed with mathematical acoustician Joan Miller in 1960. This groundbreaking version was the first to permit the construction of instruments from basic interconnectable modules that Mathews called *unit generators*, sometimes referred to as UGENs by later authors. UGENs were software modules with predefined data inputs, data outputs, and functionality. UGEN inputs could derive from a note in the score file or from the output of another UGEN, such that their interconnection abstractly resembled the patching together of hardware units in a music studio. By interconnecting these relatively simple software modules (UGENs), instrument designs of unlimited complexity could in principle be implemented. Available UGENs included a periodic function generator (or *oscillator* UGEN) that accepted amplitude and frequency inputs. With a frequency input in the audible range, it would output a specified periodic digital audio waveform, while at low frequencies it could be used to produce a specified envelope function applicable to various note parameters such as amplitude (as described below). Other UGENs available in MUSIC III included random number generators outputting pseudorandom values with inputs for gain and rate, adders that would sum multiple inputs to a single output, and—always as the final stage in any instrument design—an output module that would write audio samples to magnetic tape for later digital-to-analog conversion and playback over loudspeakers. In 1963 the MUSIC III system was superseded by MUSIC IV, which included at Tenney's request the implementation of a bandpass (or *formant*) filter UGEN with controllable parameters of center frequency and bandwidth (basically representing a movable and sizable registral window outside of which sound components would be substantially suppressed). This filter was used in *Phases* (1963) and *Ergodos II* (1964) in addition to the previously available functionality. MUSIC IV also introduced a capacity for stereophonic output, which Tenney exploited in *Ergodos II*.[12]

By today's standards, computation was extremely slow and expensive on the early IBM computers in use at Bell Labs in 1961. Digital synthesis of audio with passable fidelity required the computation of thousands of output samples per second of music, so that—even though real-time audio generation was not intended—the amount of computation feasible for individual samples was still limited.[13] In order to make digital audio synthesis more practical, instead of always computing the values of audio waveforms and parametric envelopes from scratch, these were typically derived from reusable tables of values computed just once near the beginning of each software run and stored in computer memory for later access (Tenney 1963, 35–36, 48–49). An oscillator UGEN could subsequently generate a tone of desired frequency with a waveform corresponding to the contents of such a prefilled *wavetable* by indexing through the table at an appropriate rate, skipping and/or interpolating between entries as needed, and wrapping back to the beginning of the table each time its end was reached. At longer timescales, such tables could also be used to create parametric envelopes (which were curves specifying parametric changes over the course of a single note, such as variation in the note's amplitude corresponding to attack, sustain, and release portions). Such envelopes could be generated by reading a table containing the envelope's values at a rate such that it would be scanned just once from beginning to end over the course of the note's duration. Software routines were available to prefill the tables with stock functions, such as piecewise linear functions specified by their breakpoints, an exponential function usable for amplitude envelopes, or sums of amplitude-weighted sinusoids (upon which an oscillator UGEN could subsequently draw in order to generate audible tones with corresponding harmonic partials). Custom table-filling routines could also be written.

In order to illustrate the potential of the system's interconnectable modularity for purposes of software instrument design, figure 4.2 represents graphically the design for a rudimentary instrument capable of producing notes with frequency modulation (FM, or *vibrato*) and a particular amplitude envelope. Oscillator UGENs are represented as U-shaped modules and labeled according to the prefilled wavetable (F1, F2, or F3) from which they read values, while a two-input adder is represented by a triangle and the final output stage by a square. Each oscillator UGEN has an amplitude input at top left and a frequency input at top right, the latter determining the rate at which the oscillator repeatedly scans its associated wavetable. (Wavetable contents are illustrated as continuous functions, although in actuality they are tables containing digital samples of those functions, with interpolation between samples sometimes required.) For the instrument in this illustration, the required input values for tone durations, peak tone amplitudes, nominal tone frequencies, FM amplitude, and FM rate would be listed as note data in the score file, which might be entered manually or generated with the aid of a dedicated composing subroutine (section 4.5). By

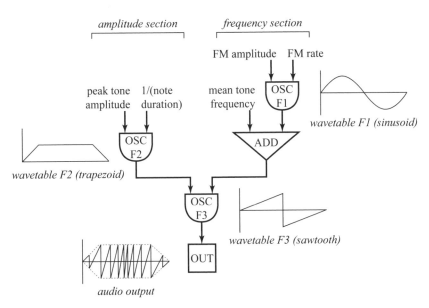

FIGURE 4.2. A simple MUSIC-N instrument capable of producing tones exhibiting sawtooth waveforms, frequency modulation (FM, or *vibrato*), and trapezoidal amplitude envelopes.

reading iteratively through wavetable F1, the oscillator at upper right produces a sinusoidal modulating signal for the production of vibrato, typically with a small amplitude and a frequency of a few cycles per second. As shown, values of this sinusoid are summed with a constant nominal audio frequency for the tone and fed to the frequency input of the bottom oscillator. That oscillator reads iteratively through wavetable F3 at the corresponding rate, outputting a sawtooth waveform whose frequency accordingly varies sinusoidally about the nominal frequency for the tone, thus exhibiting a vibrato effect. On the left of the figure, an oscillator reads a trapezoidal amplitude envelope function from wavetable F2 at a low frequency that equals the reciprocal of the currently speci-fied note duration, so that the entire table is scanned just once over the course of the current note. The output from this oscillator feeds the amplitude input of the bottom oscillator to impose the corresponding amplitude variation on the audio waveform, which is routed to the output UGEN.[14]

Possible variations and elaborations of this instrument include ones in which the output of a modulating oscillator is fed to the amplitude input of the envelope generator to produce amplitude modulation (AM, or *tremolo*). AM and FM could be combined, and either type of modulation could include both periodic and random components. Instead of producing modulated tones, sufficiently high rates of purely random AM and/or FM can be used to produce noise signals with controllable bandwidths and registers, a fact that Tenney exploited in most of his computer music. Following the advent of MUSIC IV, audio signals could be routed to the audio input of a bandpass filter. The center-frequency input of that filter could be controlled by the output of yet another oscillator that was slowly scanning a wavetable containing a simple linear ramp function, thus producing a gradual *formant transition* or "wah" in the audio output from the filter, and so forth. Software instrument design could thus become an integral part of the composer's creative process, there being in principle no limit to the instrumental variety and complexity attainable by combining UGENs.

Tenney published a detailed description of the MUSIC IV system in an article entitled "Sound-Generation by Means of a Digital Computer" (1963) and of his own evolving instrument designs in "Computer Music Experiences, 1961–1964" ([1964] 2015), to which the interested reader is directed for more extensive and specific technical documentation. However, the principal *motivation* for his progressive technical refinements is easily summed: it was to approach the levels of timbral richness and diversity that had eluded him in the Illinois studio and that he associated with acoustic instruments and environmental sounds.

4.4 The Acoustic Correlates of Timbre

In hiring Tenney, Mathews and Pierce had been seeking the advice of a professional musician to help guide the development of their computer system's musical potential. Given his affinity with Varèse and Cage, however, Tenney's perspective on what constituted musical material was broader than the conventional instrumental resources of which they had likely been thinking: "From the very beginning of my work at Bell, I said I want to start with the whole world of sound, so what kind of programming structure would I have to design here that would have all the variables needed to get that noise that I just heard down the street? I would walk around New York City listening to sounds and ask myself, how would I generate that?" (Tenney 2000f). Indeed, his first composition at Bell Labs was *Analog #1 (Noise Study)* (1961), a tapestry of evolving noise bands inspired by traffic sounds (section 4.6).[15]

For a year thereafter, Tenney focused not on composition but on scientific research concerning the acoustical correlates of perceived timbre ([1964] 2015, 104–11; [1965] 2015). One topic of these investigations concerned the perceived effects of slight *amplitude modulation* (AM, or *tremolo*) and *frequency modulation* (FM, or *vibrato*) on tones, which interested him in part as a prospective remedy to his dissatisfaction with the timbres of prior electronic music. He concluded that the introduction of random amplitude modulation plus a combination of random and periodic frequency modulation—within stipulated amplitude and frequency ranges—engendered the naturalistic tone quality that he was seeking. Notably, he was not interested in the emulation of particular acoustic instruments but in achieving a timbral richness comparable to that which he associated with acoustic instruments generally: "When random amplitude modulation is applied to the synthesized tone along with the combination of periodic and random frequency modulations . . . the result is a quality of tone that compares very favorably with that of a tone produced by a conventional musical instrument; it no longer seems 'mechanical,' 'lifeless,' 'electronic,' and so on, adding that element of richness to the computer sounds that I had so long felt necessary. Since these experiments, every instrument I have designed—with the intention of producing interesting tones—employed these modulations" (Tenney [1964] 2015, 107).[16]

Tenney's basic repertoire of synthetic sounds thus ranged between two poles:

- noise bands with the controllable parameters of amplitude, center frequency, and bandwidth, and
- tones, each with a fixed harmonic spectrum (associated with a particular wavetable) and the controllable parameters of amplitude, frequency, AM rate, AM depth (amplitude), FM rate, and FM depth.[17]

However, the same sorts of modulations that—at low rates—would add random vibrato or tremolo to a tone would—at faster rates—transform that tone into a noise band. In practice, Tenney's musical materials often fell somewhere between the archetypes of *noise* and *tone* in the form of *noisy tones* or *pitchy noise bands*. Over the course of any given note, furthermore, all of the controllable sound parameters could be independently varied, typically using the outputs from sundry envelope generators so that, for instance, continuous transformations from one sound type to another were possible.

4.5 Algorithmic Composition

For his first piece of computer music—*Analog #1 (Noise Study)*—Tenney produced the score file manually, laboriously determining note parameters by random means such as coin-tossing (section 4.6). Given this post-Cagean processual approach to composition and the capacity of the computer for rapid random number generation, he subsequently became interested in using the machine not only to synthesize sound but also to compute musical parameters. At Tenney's request, in October 1962 Mathews added to MUSIC III a facility for the score file to be generated by a software subroutine written by the composer (Tenney [1964] 2015, 111–13).[18] "When I began to use this, I was immediately working with random number generation in a kind of process that I ended up calling a stochastic process, adapting the term from [Iannis] Xenakis's writings, but redefining it in a way that seemed more suitable to my own musical ideas and that is also applicable to a good deal of Cage's work" (Pritchett et al. [1995] 2001, 192).[19] By this means Tenney produced his *Five Stochastic Studies* (1962) and ensuing computer music works. As computerized algorithmic compositions, their few precursors include Lejaren Hiller and Leonard Isaacson's

Illiac Suite (1957) for string quartet, some of Pierre Barbaud's music circa 1960, and the *ST* series by Iannis Xenakis, which was also completed in 1962 (Ames 1987a; Harley 2004, 25–28). Tenney, however, enjoyed one technical advantage over these preceding artists insofar as the facilities at Bell Labs allowed him to generate sound as part of the computational process, eliminating the need to manually transcribe computer outputs into conventionally notated scores for instrumental performance.

An understanding of Tenney's compositional methodology in his computer music requires the introduction of certain basic concepts from statistics and probability theory. First, it must be admitted that, in the words of computing pioneer John von Neumann, "anyone who considers arithmetical methods of producing random digits is, of course, in a state of sin" (1951, 36). In actuality, the "random" sequences produced by computers are *pseudorandom*—in other words, they are the outcomes of deterministic processes but exhibit certain desired statistical properties associated with randomness. In fact, any pseudo-random sequence begins from a *seed* value that must be chosen in advance and from which the sequence may be exactly regenerated on subsequent occasions. Furthermore, such sequences are periodic, although the period of any pseudo-random number generator (PRNG) suitable for digital audio applications will be quite long in order to avoid audible repetition.

Statistical properties typically required in pseudorandom sequences include a lack of correlation between values separated in the sequence (by lags up to its period length) and the production of some target distribution of values. The distribution most commonly produced by PRNGs—and the one that was most often used by Tenney in the determination of musical parameters—is a *uniform* or *rectangular distribution* wherein all values occur (in the long run) equally often within a given numeric range but never outside that range. Such a uniform distribution is exemplified by the sequence of outcomes from rolling a fair die, wherein (again, in the long run) all values from one through six appear with equal relative frequentness and no other values appear. Such a distribution is illustrated in figure 4.3(a). Another distribution that Tenney occasionally used is the *triangular distribution,* illustrated in figure 4.3(b). Such a distribution can be produced by summing pairs of independent uniformly distributed random numbers. Triangular distributions feature in the game of craps, wherein the values appearing on each of two thrown dice may individually be uniformly distributed, but their sums do *not* all appear with equal frequentness. In particular, $1 + 1 = 2$ (*snake eyes*) and $6 + 6 = 12$ (*boxcars*) are rare compared to 7 (a *natural*), because the latter can result from multiple different combinations of die values (viz., $1 + 6$, $2 + 5$, $3 + 4$, $4 + 3$, $5 + 2$, or $6 + 1$). Whatever the distri-bution, its mean and range are often important characteristics: the mean and range of the particular uniform distribution of die values in figure 4.3(a) are 3.5 and [1,6], while those for the triangular distribution of figure 4.3(b) are 7.0

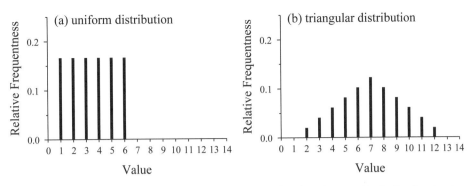

FIGURE 4.3. (a) A uniform distribution. (b) A triangular distribution. Each distribution is normalized such that its values sum to unity.

and [2,12]. Both of these distributions are symmetrical about their mean values, although asymmetrical distributions are also possible. A typical software PRNG will produce a huge number of different numeric outcomes (not just the six of a standard die). These can subsequently be scaled and/or offset to yield desired ranges and means as the application warrants. In practice, it is often the case that the resulting distributions represent values so closely spaced that musical parameters derived therefrom will be perceived as continuously rather than discretely distributed (in other words, the quantization of parametric values will be too fine to detect by ear). If coarser granulation is desired among the random values (e.g., to model the outcomes from rolling a six-sided die), these finely granulated outputs can be arithmetically quantized as needed.

In Tenney's computer music, time-varying constraints were applied to the distributions of various pseudorandomly determined musical parameters. Depending on the piece, the parameters stochastically controlled in this fashion might include pitch, dynamic, note duration, attack density, vertical density (notes per chord), amplitude envelope, steady-state timbre (choice of wavetable), modulation parameters, the number of polyphonic voices, and others. The constraints on their distributions were determined from a combination of input data supplied by the composer and autonomously unfolding stochastic computations performed by the composing algorithm. For each parameter, these constraints typically comprised a time-dependent scaling and offset applied to the output from a PRNG, causing the statistical mean and range of the resulting parametric values to change over time, sometimes continuously and sometimes discontinuously (as though the horizontal positions and widths of the distributions illustrated in figure 4.3 were made to vary in time).

These statistical parametric variations were designed to engender musical forms—specifically, perceived gestalt segmentation and parametric shaping on multiple hierarchical timescales. In "Meta†Hodos" Tenney had already formulated a theory relating statistical changes in musical parameters to perceived musical segmentation and shaping (cf. section 3.4). Accordingly, the algorithm for determining parametric constraints in his computer music inverted that *analytic* methodology into a *generative* one: "When I got to Bell Labs, I soon realized that ["Meta/Hodos"] was going to provide a compositional basis for me, and I couldn't have quite anticipated it when I wrote it. . . . [B]ut using a computer I was able to really put in algorithmic form many of the things that I had expressed in a kind of analytical and descriptive way. They turned out to be immediately applicable in computer compositional algorithmic work" (Tenney 1988b, 31). Where "Meta/Hodos" had explained perceived temporal grouping as a consequence of changes in parametric states—in other words, of changes in the means and/or ranges of one or more sound parameters—Tenney's composing subroutines manipulated parametric states in order to *induce* the perception of temporal gestalts. In accordance with "Meta/Hodos," this was typically done so as to promote temporal gestalt formation on multiple hierarchical levels (time-scales), from elements to clangs, sequences, and—when he returned to algorithmic composition in the 1980s—even higher levels, depending on the piece.

The essential features of Tenney's algorithmic approach to determining musical parameters are illustrated by an invented example in figure 4.4, which focuses (arbitrarily) upon the parameter of pitch. Element pitches are depicted using solid black horizontal lines, clang ranges using foreground dark gray polygons, and a sequence range using a background light gray polygon. Other musical parameters—including the durations of the gestalts depicted—would be determined independently but in an analogous fashion. Typically, element attack times and durations would be determined independently of each other so that elements within a clang would sometimes overlap in time, and the last element of a clang might sustain into the following clang, as shown in the figure. In other words, the temporal extent of a clang corresponded to the time interval during which its elements might attack, not necessarily to their full temporal extent.

Figure 4.4(a) shows an isolated clang comprising six elements. In this example, the mean of the clang's pitch distribution was assigned a rising linear trajectory, which is depicted using a finely dashed line. In other words, the distribution from which element pitches were randomly selected possessed a time-varying mean that linearly increased over the course of the clang, in tandem with which its range varied according to the height of the gray filled region. In practice, this variation would be effected by assigning to each element a pitch value generated by a PRNG whose output had been scaled and offset to have the mean and range depicted in figure 4.4(a) *at the attack time for that element*. The usual result would be a clang that exhibited an overall rising trend in pitch. This provision for linear trajectories in the parametric means of low-level gestalts is common in Tenney's algorithmic music. It supplements the purely descriptive formalism of "Meta/Hodos" with an element of composerly discretion, promoting musical gestalts that, while diverse, often exhibit a particular gestural quality: statistical direction.[20]

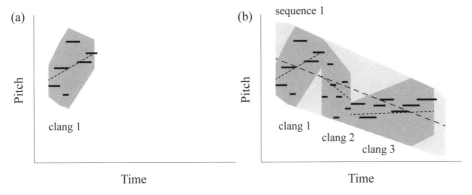

FIGURE 4.4. An example illustrating the algorithmic determination of pitches for (a) the elements comprising a clang and (b) three clangs comprising a sequence.

If there were to be sequence-level organization in the piece, then—as depicted in figure 4.4(b)—the means and ranges of clangs would be randomly determined within a range associated with their parent sequence. As with clangs, the sequence could be given a statistical parametric shape by varying the mean value about which its clang means were randomly selected. In the figure, clang means were selected from within a sequence distribution whose mean (depicted using a coarsely dashed line) decreased linearly with time, resulting in a net downward trend in pitch among the three successive clangs in the sequence.[21]

In practice, the composing algorithm made determinations in a top-down rather than a bottom-up fashion, so that—for the example of figure 4.4(b)—the duration, mean, and range for the illustrated sequence would be determined first, then those for the first clang therein, and then the first element in that clang. Successive elements would then be specified until the first clang was filled, with the algorithm then proceeding to similarly specify the second (and subsequent) clangs, ascending the formal hierarchy to determine the attributes of the second sequence when the first had been filled with completed clangs, and so forth. If there were to be higher levels of temporal gestalt organization (involving segments etc.), then the computations would proceed analogously at those levels, determining yet longer-range segmentation and parametric shaping.

The elements depicted in figure 4.4 all have unique pitches, but in practice they could be colored noise bands or chords comprising multiple tones, and vertical density (the number of simultaneous tones) could be a stochastically controlled parameter. Furthermore, multiple independent strata of such gestalts (such as polyphonic *voices*) could unfold concurrently. The number of such voices could itself vary under stochastic control, and polyphony could persist over the course of different timescales, sometimes appearing for the duration of a clang and at other times for the duration of a sequence or larger unit. Thus, for instance, a particular segment might comprise multiple concurrent sequences throughout, and some of those constituent sequences might themselves comprise a polyphony of concurrent clangs, while others would be "monophonic at the clang-level" (in other words, they would comprise only one clang at a time; cf. figure 3.4[c] and [d]). Such a *compound polyphony*—comprising multiple musics of distinct character proceeding concurrently and independently—recalls passages in the work of Charles Ives, of whose music Tenney had been a devoted student and performer since the 1950s.

A figure analogous to figure 4.4 could be drawn for all other stochastically controlled musical parameters (durations, dynamics, etc.). In instances where change in the distribution of one parameter (such as pitch) was insufficient to induce a perceived temporal gestalt boundary (e.g., between clangs), it would often be reinforced by concurrent changes in the distributions of other parameters. In the unusual event that such collusion between parameters was still inadequate to delineate the gestalt boundary, a single aggregate gestalt would instead be perceived, and, conversely, the random nature of value generation could occasionally induce a perceived gestalt boundary by happenstance where none was entailed by the nominal parametric distributions. Furthermore, just as flipping a coin will sometimes produce a short succession of outcomes (such as four heads in a row) that is uncharacteristic of what their distribution would have been in the long run, short successions of gestalts would not always be representative of the nominal distributions from which their parameters were drawn. This is exemplified in the final clang of figure 4.4(b), whose elements do not reveal the extent of the low register into which they might have ranged if there had been more of them or if the PRNG had been differently seeded. In any event, Tenney appears to have happily accepted such occasional consequences inherent in probabilistic procedures in exchange for the great variety of discriminable gestalts that they produced. Although the product of a stochastic algorithm, these gestalts constitute a fully determinate music, but one that exhibits a great variety of parametric shapes. As Tenney later remarked, even in a texture derived from an ergodic process, "you don't have statistical constancy, you have a shape that you didn't determine, which is nice. . . . We'll hear all kinds of shapes. But it's something that is not imposed by the composer" (1996d, 64).

4.6 *Analog #1 (Noise Study)* (1961)
ELECTRONIC MUSIC (ONE-CHANNEL FIXED MEDIA)
4 mins., 23 secs.

Noise Study represents a pioneering contribution to the history of *computer-synthesized* music. Its conception did not, however, germinate from the rarefied scientific discourses of Bell Labs, where it was produced. Instead, it arose as a remarkably direct importation of everyday modern life into that high-tech environment. In "Computer Music Experiences, 1961–1964," Tenney described how the idea for *Noise Study* arose during his commutes between New Jersey and Manhattan:

For several months I had been driving to New York City in the evening, returning to the Labs the next morning by way of the heavily traveled Route 22 and the Holland Tunnel. This circuit was made as often as three times every week, and the drive was always an exhausting, nerve-wracking experience, fast, furious, and "noisy." The sounds of the traffic—especially in the tunnel—were usually so loud and continuous that, for example, it was impossible to maintain a conversation with a companion. It is an experience that is familiar to many people, of course. But then something else happened, which is perhaps not so familiar to others. One day I found myself listening to these sounds, instead of trying to ignore them as usual. The activity of listening, attentively, to "non-musical," environmental sounds was not new to me—my esthetic attitude for several years had been that these were potential musical material—but in this particular context I had not yet done this. When I did, finally, begin to listen, the sounds of the traffic became so interesting that the trip was no longer a thing to be dreaded and gotten through as quickly as possible. From then on, I actually looked forward to it as a source of new perceptual insights. Gradually, I learned to hear these sounds more acutely, to follow the evolution of single elements within the total sonorous "mass," to feel, kinesthetically, the characteristic rhythmic articulations of the various elements in combination, etc. Then I began to try to analyze the sounds, aurally, to estimate what their physical properties might be—drawing upon what I already knew of acoustics and the correlation of the physical and the subjective attributes of sound.

From this image, then, of traffic noises—and especially those heard in the tunnel, where the overall sonority is richer, denser, and the changes are mostly very gradual—I began to conceive a musical composition that not only used sound elements similar to these, but manifested similarly gradual changes in sonority. ([1964] 2015, 98–99)[22]

Analog #1 is a curious title for a piece facilitated by groundbreaking *digital* technology.[23] Presumably it refers to an association between the sounds of the piece and the *analogous* sounds of traffic in the tunnel, although Tenney's comments make clear that he was less interested in re-creating that environment than in abstracting its sonic character. In any event, both Tenney and subsequent commentators usually refer to the piece simply as *Noise Study*.

The word *noise*, however, carries multiple implications of its own. These include ones derived from aesthetics ("unmusical" sounds) and engineering (unwanted signal components).[24] However, it is a third relatively narrow technical sense of *noise* that is most obviously evoked by *Noise Study*, that being *broadband noise*: an acoustical signal in which energy is distributed across some continuous range of frequencies rather than concentrated at discrete frequencies (see appendix B). Examples of broadband noise include the sounds of traffic, ocean surf, sibilants, ventilation, and gas combustion.

Approximations to sustained broadband noise are relatively uncommon in Western art music before 1960, barring special programmatic effects inadmissible in general musical contexts (such as militaristic snare drum rolls, real or imitation cannonades, and piano clusters imitating surf noise). Early modern examples include the colored friction noises producible by some of Luigi Russolo's *intonarumori* instruments (ca. 1913), the airplane propellers of George Antheil's *Ballet mécanique* (1924), and the sustained unprogrammatic clusters that appear near the conclusion of Edgard Varèse's *Ionisation* (1931). In the postwar electronic medium, the outstanding example is Henri Pousseur's *Scambi* (1957), which comprises only filtered analog noise sounds. Since the 1960s, however, sustained broadband noise has become a musical commonplace not only in electronic music but also in instrumental music. The reasons for this advent are presumably diverse, but its contrast with the traditional privileging of tone in Western art music is conspicuous, so cultural critique or reaction may contribute.[25] Tenney's own comments on the subject of tone and noise, however, critique as a whole the artificial imposition of such categorical partitioning on the continuum of sound.

> [*Noise Study*] goes from wide-band noise to very narrow-band noise, and these are almost like sirens, the sound going up and down. They are very narrow bands, so you hear them as tones. So already that dichotomy between noise and tone was implicitly wiped out, replaced by the idea of a continuum.
>
> The terms noise and tone imply a categorical distinction that I don't believe exists. Every sound we hear has some noise element in it, every sound we actually hear in our environment, including those of the orchestra, and most noises have some tonal aspect to them. We keep reverting to the distinction because it is in our language. But our language is not really very well equipped to deal with what I'm proposing except by using a more general term like sound, and speaking of any sound or all possible sounds describing a continuum of sounds. There is no dividing line. (Tenney 2000f)

The acoustical waveforms associated with broadband noises are random or quasi-random, and it was through the use of pseudorandom number generation that Tenney created the sounds used in *Noise Study*: "Very early after arriving at Bell Labs I asked for a noise generator for *Noise Study*. It immediately opened up wonderful possibilities because the characteristics of each noise (what would have been called a "note" in [Max] Mathew's terminology) could be interpolated from one condition to another in a single sound. It could start narrow-band and go to wide-band or start soft and go loud or low and go high, etc. *Noise Study* was dependent on that kind of possibility" (2000f). Using Mathews's MUSIC III program, Tenney was able to produce noise bands of varying amplitude, bandwidth, and center frequency via random amplitude modulation of sinusoidal signals ([1964] 2015, 99–101). This procedure involved modulating (i.e., multiplying) a sine wave by a sequence of algorithmically generated pseudorandom values. The center frequency of the resulting noise band was determined by the frequency of the sine wave, while the noise bandwidth was determined by the rate of the random number generator's output. This approach was used to generate five polyphonic voices of sound, each comprising a concatenation of noise sounds (or "notes," in Mathews's expanded sense of the term). *Noise Study* consists of this original computer-generated *layer* of five voices on tape along with overdubbed half-speed and double-speed versions thereof (strategically aligned) for a total of three such layers. In the final version, as many as fifteen voices thus sometimes sound concurrently, although at any one time many of them are not individually discriminable.

Figure 4.5(a) provides a complete spectrogram for the original single-speed layer alone, with its five registrally segregated voices visible near the outset.[26] Aligned with this in parts (b)–(f) of the figure are Tenney's compositional sketches indicating probability distribution profiles for various musical parameters ([1964] 2015, 102).[27] These parameters are:

(b) note duration (whose reciprocal is temporal density) within each voice,
(c) sound intensity,
(d) noise bandwidth,
(e) the mean pitch level (or center frequency) of each voice, and
(f) the possible range about this mean within which the pitch level of each voice may vary.

Thus, for example, note duration at the opening was selected at random within the gray filled region in figure 4.5(b) at 0 seconds, the dashed line representing the mean value of possible durations. Within each voice, the duration of each concatenated note would be determined at the conclusion of the previous one and thus within different numeric ranges as indicated in the figure. In subsequent pieces, Tenney would program the computer to make such random selections automatically, but in *Noise Study* they were still made laboriously by hand. The composer indicated that various methods of random value generation (including coin tossing) were used for this purpose, the results being scaled and offset as necessary ([1964] 2015, 101–2).

As indicated in figure 4.5, the layer comprises five sections, each shorter than the last, although the boundaries of the first three sections cannot be precisely identified by ear due to the continuity of changes across them. Although the five voices in this layer are *visually* discriminable in figure 4.5(a) at the opening, due to their registral contiguity they are not *aurally* discriminable at first but instead create the impression of a single band of white noise spanning all registers. Only as the bands begin to change is their independence revealed. The subsequent articulation of each voice into discrete "notes" by sudden parametric changes is audible and visible in the spectrogram. Moreover, the center frequency, intensity, and bandwidth of each note may gradually change over its course. In sections I–III and V, this internal variation represents a linear interpolation between initial and final values chosen for each note. These values are randomly selected from the permissible range with the exception that, according to Tenney, "for

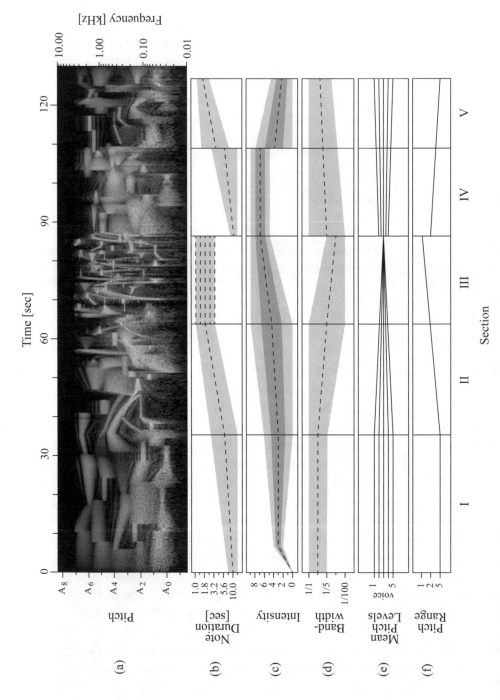

FIGURE 4.5. The structure of *Noise Study*'s single-speed layer alone. (a) Complete spectrogram of the layer. (b)–(f) Tenney's compositional sketches (redrawn) indicating parametric probability distribution profiles for *Noise Study*.

center frequency, the toss of a coin was used to determine whether the initial and final values for a given note were to be the same or different (i.e., whether the pitch of the note was constant or varying)" ([1964] 2015, 101–2). Accordingly, although their bandwidths and intensities may still vary, the center frequencies of about half of the notes shown in figure 4.5(a) are constant. The result is a striking interplay between stability and instability in pitch that intensifies as the movements of the gliding bands gradually increase.

Initially, the mean pitch registers of the voices are well-separated and the excursions of their center frequencies are restricted so that voices do not cross or substantially overlap in register, as figure 4.5(e)–(f) indicate. Over the course of sections II and III, however, these constraints are progressively relaxed so that voices no longer "stay in their lanes" but increasingly cross in register, as is visible in part (a) of the figure. Mean temporal density and sound intensity concurrently increase. Narrower noise bandwidth values gradually become available over the course of section II, resulting in notes with clearer pitch definition. Indeed, by the climactic conclusion of section III, narrow bandwidths prevail so that relatively clear pitches are heard, often gliding wildly across registers and one another.

The most striking transition of the piece occurs at the boundary of sections III and IV as the mean note duration abruptly increases. Concurrently, the range of available bandwidth values greatly expands so that broad bandwidths not heard since the opening suddenly reappear. Furthermore, in section IV (only) two new dynamic envelopes temporarily supplant the linear interpolations of the preceding sections. As illustrated in figure 4.6, these are a *swell* and a *notch*, both exhibiting extrema at two-thirds of their durations. Applied to a noise band, the abrupt onset of the latter yields a sound akin to a cymbal strike or the crash of an ocean breaker. Both of these envelopes are visible in section IV of figure 4.5(a) near 105 seconds, at which time a swell envelope dynamically shapes a roughly constant-width noise band centered near 2 kHz, while a notch envelope is applied to a narrowing noise band centered near 1 kHz.

The parameters described in figure 4.5(c)–(f) all return at the conclusion to roughly the same statistical distributions they displayed at the opening. The result is a skewed arch form with its crux at the boundary between sections III and IV, about two-thirds of the way through the layer's duration. Regarding this skewed symmetry, Tenney later related it to the time-honored formal benchmark of the golden section: "Both *Noise Study* and what you hear when you drive through the tunnel have a similar shape—the deeper you get into it the more you are submerged and then as you come out it comes on again—yet it was still fairly symmetrical. But there was a deliberate asymmetry [in *Noise Study*] that may relate back to Bartók's use of Fibonacci ratios and similar things which I still use" (2000f).[28] On the other hand, figure 4.5(b) shows that in temporal density sections IV and V offer a varied repetition of sections I and II rather than an

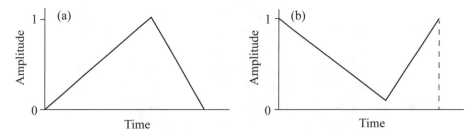

FIGURE 4.6. Dynamic envelopes employed in section IV of *Noise Study*.

arch. A sudden slackening in mean temporal density (and mean intensity) at the beginning of section V evokes a sense of release and hastens the conclusion by abridging the dissipation of musical energy already begun in section IV. The form of the layer thus combines contrasting types of quasi-symmetries in its different musical parameters. This counterpoint of symmetries is preserved when the layers at different speeds are superimposed.

Tenney's initial plan was that the single-speed layer alone would constitute *Noise Study*. However, he experienced a growing dissatisfaction with the musical result:

> First, I would have liked it to be denser (vertically) or cover a wider range of vertical densities; and second, the range of temporal densities (speeds, note-durations) seemed too narrow—the slow sections did not seem slow enough nor the fast sections fast enough. . . . After some consideration of these problems, a very simple solution occurred to me that corrected both conditions in one stroke. . . . The original analog tape was rerecorded at half speed and at double speed, and these were mixed with the original. . . . This device, while sure to antagonize certain purists and undertaken with some hesitation on my part, seemed to give me more nearly what I was after—to correspond more closely to the original image—than the first analog tape by itself, and this is its final form. (Tenney [1964] 2015, 103–4)

The layers at different speeds were synchronized such that the boundaries between their respective sections III and IV all aligned, thus preserving and emphasizing the arch form of the original layer. Figure 4.7 supplies a spectrogram of the complete result. Brackets above the image indicate the durations of the individual layers, and a vertical line marks the point of their alignment. Relative to the corresponding musical features in the original single-speed layer, features in the faster layer elapse twice as quickly and sound one octave higher, while features in the slower layer elapse half as quickly and sound one octave lower. The result is thus a mensuration canon between the three layers.

Tenney remarked in 1964 that "so far, no one listening to the piece has even noticed the repetitions (at different speeds and in different octaves) that resulted from the overlay—though they are plain to my ear and will surely be heard by

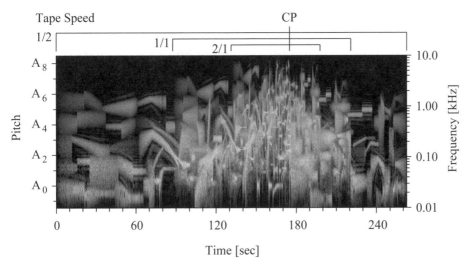

FIGURE 4.7. Complete spectrogram of *Noise Study* (all layers combined).

anyone told about them in advance" ([1964] 2015, 104). Among the more easily discernible correspondences are the entrances of successive layers at roughly 0, 90, and 130 seconds; the high-frequency, elbow-shaped features near 70, 120, and 150 seconds; and the pairs of horizontal high-frequency noise bands at 190, 200, and 230 seconds. Furthermore, the point of alignment between the three layers of the canon represents what Kyle Gann (1995) has dubbed—with respect to the many mensuration canons found in the music of Conlon Nancarrow—a *convergence point* (*CP*).[29] In the vicinity of such a point, imitation between canonic layers becomes more conspicuous due to the close temporal proximity of corresponding figures. For example, just before the convergence point of *Noise Study*, quickly sweeping glissandi (among other features) can be heard rapidly echoing across the layers, emphasizing this pivotal moment as climactic even if it is not recognized as a canonic convergence point per se.[30] The peeling away of successive canonic layers as they reach their conclusions (at roughly 195, 220, and 260 secs.) is also audible due to the thinning of the texture and the quieting of the highest register at those moments. However, the fact that Tenney resorted to the canonic structure post hoc in order to ameliorate perceived textural deficiencies in the single-layer version—along with his apparent unconcern that the canon went undetected by naive listeners—suggests that such imitative structures were peripheral to his compositional interests in *Noise Study*. Judging by the composer's remarks quoted at the outset of this section, more central compositional concerns included musical recruitment of the sound types he encountered in the tunnel (in particular, noise bands of diverse and varying widths) and the sorts of gradual sonic changes that they displayed.

Tenney acknowledged that *Noise Study* bore the musical influence of his mentor Varèse (more so than of Cage, whose music and thought he was still absorbing). For instance, although Varèse insisted that *literal* sonic depiction of the city played no part in his work, according to his widow, the abstracted environmental sounds of foghorns on the Hudson River and the sirens of fire engines both found their way into his music (Ouellette 1968, 57; L. Varèse 1972, 150). More overtly, Tenney's description of his climactic narrow band noises as rising and falling "almost like sirens" evokes the literal sirens featured by Varèse in *Amériques* (1921) and *Ionisation* (1931). This siren-like quality in turn foreshadows the prominent reappearances of glissandi in a number of Tenney's own later compositions.

Also resurfacing in later pieces would be an interest in musical continuity, portended by Tenney's interest in the "gradual changes in sonority" characteristic of sound in the tunnel. Although the texture of *Noise Study* is still articulated into discrete temporal gestalts ("notes") by parametric contrasts, the gradual modulation of parameters and the frequent perceptual fusion of registrally adjacent noise bands occasionally suggest music comprised of a single continuous but complexly modulated sound. Finally, the skewed arch or swell, which would become a common formal device in Tenney's music after 1970, makes an early appearance in *Noise Study* both at the level of global parametric shaping and in the local dynamic envelope of figure 4.6(a). Thus a number of style features appear in *Noise Study* that would lie dormant for the next few years before reemerging in Tenney's music.

4.7 *Phases* (1963)
for Edgard Varèse
ELECTRONIC MUSIC (ONE-CHANNEL FIXED MEDIA)
12 mins., 20 secs.

Late in his career, when asked to name personal favorites among his works, from his computer music of the 1960s Tenney would invariably cite *Phases*. It combines a distinctive large-scale form with a major advance in the ability to generate sophisticated textures and rich acoustic detail using a computer. Its breath-like cycles and varied sonic efflorescences lend the impression of a strange and autonomous ecosystem of sounds.[31] Most palpably among Tenney's early music, *Phases* evokes D'Arcy Thompson's process-oriented conception of "growth (to form)" under the tangible influence of forces, the prolific but inchoate production of the pseudorandom number generator having been molded in time by the forces of stochastic control into a musical formation that recorded their effect (section 4.1).

Relative to Tenney's preceding computer music, in *Phases* the listener is most immediately struck by a greatly enhanced nuance and detail—even quirkiness—among local sound events. The composer recounted that before making it, "I spent a great deal of time listening to all kinds of natural and mechanical sounds as these occur in the environment, trying to determine their acoustical properties and, especially, the kinds of fluctuations in various parameters that were most often taking place within each sound. The whole 'world' of environmental sounds (including sounds of musical instruments but no longer limited to these) became a kind of 'model' for the range of sounds I wanted to be able to generate with the computer" (Tenney [1964] 2015, 123). Accordingly, Tenney developed a new software instrument and concomitant compositional algorithm (PLF5) in part as an attempt to capture the natural complexity of environmental sounds.[32] The algorithm (PLF3) used for the preceding pieces *Dialogue* and *Ergodos I* had incorporated stochastic control over six parameters: frequency, amplitude, note duration, amplitude modulation (AM, or tremolo) rate, waveform number (timbre), and amplitude envelope number. PLF5, however, dramatically increased the number of controlled parameters to twenty. For instance, in addition to control of frequency and frequency modulation (FM, or vibrato), Tenney introduced a table of selectable frequency envelope functions—*ornaments* applicable to a nominal pitch—with an additional parameter controlling the size of their excursions. The diversity of these curving and gliding ornaments is visible in figure 4.8, which provides spectrograms of selected excerpts from *Phases*. Another important addition was that of a bandpass (or *formant*) filter permitting variation ("wah") in a tone's spectrum that was independent of its fundamental frequency. This filter afforded control over its center frequency (CF) and bandwidth (BW), and *Phases* accordingly incorporated stochastic control of mean CF, CF envelope (changes in CF), mean BW, and BW envelope (changes in BW). (Appendix B provides a brief general introduction to the spectrographic analysis of audio signals along with a survey of basic acoustic genera and their specifications.) Finally, whereas *Dialogue* had treated tone and noise as disparate categories of signal, in *Phases* they become merely the endpoints of a continuum. This was achieved by allowing the possible rates of random amplitude modulation to range from zero (a steady tone) through intermediate values (an unstable tremolo) to maximum (a noise of large bandwidth). In general, a noise signal appeared in combination with a tone residing at its center frequency, the proportion of noise to tone being controllable. The complete list of twenty controllable parameters from Tenney's archival notes is reproduced in table 4.2. To it have been added explanatory remarks and references to examples visible in the spectrograms in figure 4.8.[33] The reader is encouraged to spend some time comparing the contents of the table with both the spectrograms and the corresponding audio in order to appreciate the extraordinary richness of musical detail in *Phases* and its orderly statistical evolution.

No less significant than the enrichment of sonic detail were the textural enhancements achieved in *Phases*. Specifically, Tenney's new PLF5 composing subroutine could generate formal hierarchies that were more sophisticated in two respects than those of his previous computer music:

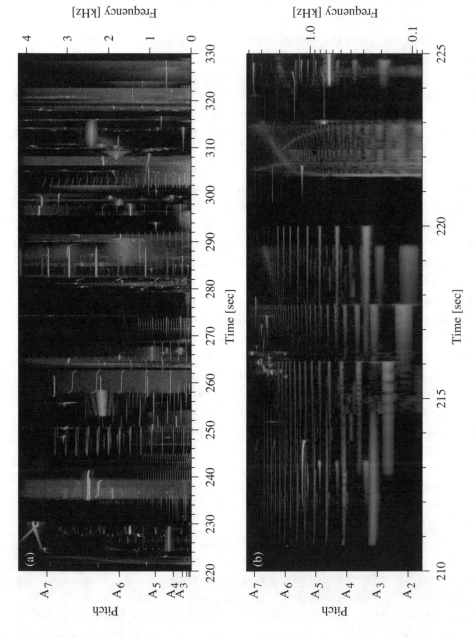

FIGURE 4.8. *Phases.* (a) Spectrogram of a lengthy excerpt using a linear frequency ordinate. (b) Spectrogram of a shorter excerpt using a linear pitch ordinate.

TABLE 4.2. Controlled parameters in *Phases*

Parameter	Remarks	Examples from figure 4.8; (a) or (b) indicates which part of the figure
1 note duration		(a) higher mean at left, lower mean at right
2 amplitude	scales envelope	(a) lower mean at far left
3 mean fundamental frequency		(b) lower and higher strata of clangs visible
4 frequency envelope range	intervallic width of pitch ornaments	(a) large for glissandi 224–30 secs. 3.8 kHz, smaller for chirp 298 secs. 3.6 kHz
5 range (width) of frequency modulation	vibrato width	(a) large for glissandi 224–30 secs. 3.8 kHz, (b) large for 0.25 kHz tone
6 range of amplitude modulation (AM)	controls ratio of noise to tone	(a) mostly noise 286–90 secs. 1.6 kHz, clear tone with noise 320–23 secs. 1.5 kHz
7 mean AM rate / noise bandwidth (BW)	noise bandwidth	(a) nil for steady tones, low for warble effects, large for noise bands 320–30 secs.
8 range of AM rate envelope	noise bandwidth flare	(a) narrower 252–58 secs. 2.2 kHz, wider 321 secs. 3.0 ± 1.2 kHz
9 mean center frequency (CF) of formant filter	formant region	(a) low 241–44 secs. 0–0.5 kHz, (b) higher 218–20 secs. 2–3 kHz
10 range of filter CF envelope	movement of CF	(b) large 221.5–223.0 secs. (four separate rapid sweeps)
11 mean BW of filter		(b) wider 218–20 secs. 2–3 kHz, narrower 222–23 secs. 1.8–0.4 kHz
12 range of filter BW envelope	amount of BW expansion/contraction	(a) 218–20 secs. 2–3 kHz, BW expands, admitting increasing number of partials
13 upper-frequency limit (no. of harmonic partials; eight possibilities)	1, 2, 3, 5, 8, 13, 21, or 34 partials (Fibonacci sequence)	(a) higher mean at left, lower mean at right
14 amplitude-envelope function number	selected from table of functions	
15 frequency-envelope function number	*ornament* selected from table of functions	many shapes visible
16 note-rest probability		(a) higher at right
17 clang-rest probability		(a) three-element clang 296–300 secs.
18 probability of clang-mean interpolation for: note duration	interpolation, if any, is applied to all voices in the clang	1.5–2.0 kHz is likely interpolated in note duration (decreasing) and frequency (increasing)
19 amplitude		
20 frequency		

- The earlier two-level hierarchy of temporal gestalt groupings—comprising elements and groups of elements (clangs)—was extended to a three-level hierarchy comprising elements, clangs, and groups of clangs (called *sequences*).
- As was the case previously, polyphony was possible at the level of elements—so that clangs could contain multiple simultaneous strata ("voices") of elements—but now multiple polyphonic strata of concurrent sequences could also be generated. Each sequence, however, contained only one clang at a time. Typically, one to three concurrent polyphonic strata are audible in *Phases*, distinguished most commonly by their separation in pitch register.[34]

As shown in figure 4.8(b), in *Phases* a brief sequence appears from 215 to 218 seconds in a high-register polyphonic stratum. This sequence comprises two successive clangs that are discriminable by difference in their mean note duration. Over the course of a sequence, its parametric means follow randomly determined linear trajectories; in this case, the mean pitch rises slightly over the course of the sequence. For individual clangs, means in the primary parameters of note duration, amplitude, and frequency may be held constant or—as indicated in lines 18–20 of table 4.2—with a certain probability they also may exhibit linear trajectories. In figure 4.8(b), for instance, from 210 to 220 seconds the mean fundamental frequency of a single clang in a low-register polyphonic stratum appears to fall.[35]

The most distinctive and intriguing aspect of formal design in *Phases*, however, appears at the largest timescale. As reflected in its title, at this scale the music features slow sinusoidal oscillations in the mean values of key musical parameters. A few of these cyclical mean-parametric trajectories are depicted using black curves in figure 4.9, which is reproduced from Tenney's published sketches ([1964] 2015, 126).[36] Gray filled regions correspond to total parametric ranges. The oscillations proceed at different rates in different parameters so that they exhibit diverse phase relationships to one another over the course of the piece. The bracket above the figure indicates the time interval corresponding to the spectrogram in figure 4.8(a), which confirms that over this time interval:

1. mean note duration decreases,
2. mean amplitude is generally high but lower toward the far left and far right of the spectrogram,
3. mean AM rate increases so that the prevalence and bandwidth of noise increase,
4. mean formant filter bandwidth increases in tandem with the mean AM rate, bandwidths becoming so broad by the end of the excerpt that the filtering is less noticeable, and
5. the mean upper limit of spectra (governing the mean number of harmonics appearing in tones) decreases.

It is possible to follow each of these statistical variations by ear.

The large-scale retrograde formal symmetry evident about the 6-minute mark in figure 4.9 is not merely statistical—the audio of the second half is the exact reverse of that in the first half. The location of this literal retrogression is unlikely to be detected by a naive listener in part because it is located amid a passage of nondescript low-frequency noise, although the relationship between the opening and concluding moments of the piece is more noticeable. On the other hand, this large-scale retrogression does have one clearly audible consequence: in the first half, amplitude envelopes featuring gradual attacks and relatively rapid releases are much more prevalent than the opposite so that, in the second half, rapid (quasi-percussive) attacks become the more common type.

In contrast with Tenney's later affection for *Phases*, his appraisal of the piece in 1964 was uncertain. Its cyclical form suggested to him a retreat from the post-Cagean renunciation of formal shaping toward which *Ergodos I* had represented a decisive step: "By comparison with the ergodic form of *Ergodos I*, this was a small step backward—an experiment, really, to determine whether this kind of variation might produce a larger form more interesting than the ergodic one without sacrificing much in the way of variety. At this moment, the experiment remains inconclusive—I have not yet lived with these pieces long enough to be sure of my own reactions to them in these large-formal terms" (Tenney [1964] 2015, 126). Significantly, however, this decidedly nonergodic form does not signal a return to dramatic or rhetorical design. Whereas environmental sounds provided the model for the local sonic detail of *Phases*, in a late interview Tenney likened its form as well to environmental processes in a passage that recalls Thompson's paradigm of form-imparting forces in nature: "In *Phases* the shaping . . . is basically not dramatic at all, but there is shaping nevertheless involving very slow, wave-motion-like tides, ocean tides, very slow increases and decreases of certain variables defining the characteristics of the sound" (2000f).[37] The undulating parametric counterpoint in *Phases* is correspondingly bold but nonrhetorical, projecting its form as a percept. Later in his career, Tenney would repeatedly embrace a conception of *form as an object of perception*, in light of which *Phases* seems to anticipate his characteristic formal concerns some years *after* his relatively brief exploration of Cage-inspired ergodicity.

Regarding the dedication of *Phases* to Edgard Varèse, looking back, Tenney remarked: "[It] referred to him because he was the primary visionary seeing ahead to electronic music, the earliest of them in my view, and that vision of his was extremely powerful for me, and it's what led me to work in the medium of electronic and computer music for a decade" (2005c). The sounds of *Phases* share with the music of its dedicatee a raw sensuous presence and individualized sculpting. Also, like Varèse's *Hyperprism* (1923) and *Intégrales* (1925) especially, it features a multilayered texture in which sounds of quiet dynamic seem not accompanimental but as worthy of close attention as louder ones. In *Phases* this

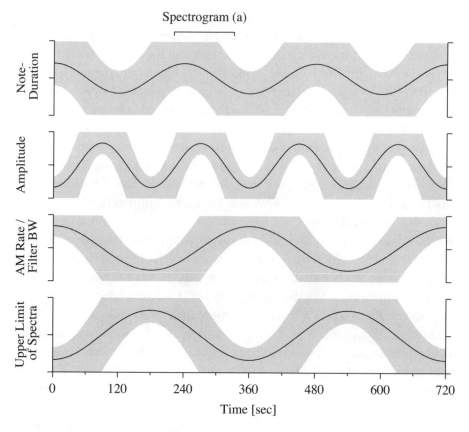

FIGURE 4.9. Counterpoint between selected parametric distributions in *Phases*. The bracket above the figure indicates the duration of the spectrogram in figure 4.8(a).

sense of increased dynamic "depth of field" is greatly facilitated by the enhanced dynamic range and control afforded by digital synthesis. Nonetheless, beyond such abstract similarities, the relationship of *Phases* to Varèse's style is oblique. Tenney recalled playing the work for Varèse: "He played it on his system in his studio, which included this old Ampex tape deck and this enormous loudspeaker [on which] you could imagine him playing his own music at top volume and filling all of Sullivan Street with the sound. So I remember it was beautiful to hear it in that kind of situation. He seemed very pleased with it even though, or maybe because, it was not at all like his music" (1976).

CHAPTER 5

Performance and the Social (1964–68)

Tenney's move to New Jersey in September 1961 to begin work at Bell Labs brought him again into proximity with New York City. With his partner, Carolee Schneemann, he divided his time between a rented house near his workplace and her loft in Manhattan, and both of them soon became vigorously involved with the burgeoning developments in avant-garde and intermedia art that were taking place downtown. During the coming years, Tenney participated in a wide array of such contexts as conductor, pianist, actor, or organizer, and most of his groundbreaking computer music was premiered not in institutional settings but in downtown lofts or performance spaces on programs shared with dance, poetry, and performance art.

5.1 Downtown in the 1960s

Amid the juxtapositions and mixtures of media in Downtown Manhattan venues, many of the important emerging artists of the 1960s generation crossed paths and influenced one another's work. The sharing of programs, venues, resources, skills, and camaraderie among musicians, dancers, poets, directors, visual artists, performance artists, filmmakers, and technicians helped to foster artistic hybridization well before artist and poet Dick Higgins coined the term *intermedia* in middecade. Recalling this extraordinary convergence, composer and pianist Philip Corner remarked: "None of these worlds was incompatible. All of these people were around, and if you were at all interested in painting, poetry, or dance, you met them. People would use each other in their works. The barriers were breaking down; everyone brought in special qualities" (Banes 1983, 84).

Shortly after their move, Schneemann and Tenney met Corner through violinist and composer Malcolm Goldstein, with whom Tenney was already acquainted from the Bennington Composers' Conferences (Tenney 1988b, 21–22; Goldstein 1984, 4). Together in 1963, Corner, Goldstein, and Tenney founded the Tone Roads Chamber Ensemble, whose concerts would do much to consolidate the concept of an American experimental music tradition (section 5.2). More immediately, though, both Tenney and Schneemann would become involved through Corner with the dancers, musicians, and visual artists who would soon found the Judson Dance Theater, whence postmodern dance principally arose.[1] This group worked mainly at Judson Memorial Church in Greenwich Village, where Schneemann would soon begin to present her kinetic theater works.

Tenney and Schneemann would concurrently become involved with the confluence of artists that came to be known as Fluxus, as well as with the annual New York Avant Garde Festivals, directed by cellist Charlotte Moorman (Moorman [1973] 2003). Like many downtown artists, they moved fluidly between sundry coalitions and venues that spanned Happenings, Fluxus, the Judson group, Moorman's Avant Garde Festivals, Pitt Street Concerts (hosted by Corner and dancer Beverley Schmidt [Blossom]), Something Else Gallery (in the home of Dick Higgins and Alison Knowles), the Living Theater, the Bridge Theater, the Pocket Theater, the New School for Social Research, and others. For instance, although not a member of Fluxus, Tenney would perform the works of Fluxus artists, and his own work would sometimes appear on Fluxus programs. His electronic music was featured during each of the first five Avant Garde Festivals (1963–67), in which he also often served as organizer, performer, or conductor. At the 1964 festival, for instance, he played the piano part in the North American premiere of Karlheinz Stockhausen's *Originale* (1961) at Judson Hall—a contentious event that purportedly fractured Fluxus (Higgins 1979, 27). Although numerous Fluxus artists performed in this legendary production, it was picketed by Fluxus founder George Maciunas and philosopher-musician Henry Flynt, while poet Allen Ginsberg managed to both picket *and* perform (Piekut 2011, 62). For his part, between stints at the keyboard Tenney could be observed clambering up scaffolding in a "feral costume" designed by Schneemann—or "fur G-string and fur ears," as Moorman put it ([1973] 2003, 173).[2]

Despite Tenney's involvement as performer with artistic developments downtown, his compositional activity was at first little affected by them. While at Bell Labs he remained focused on the computer music that he was making there and its progressive integration of Cagean aesthetics with his own theories of formal perception. This changed, however, following his departure from Bell Labs in March 1964 to take up research positions in musical acoustics first at Yale University in New Haven, Connecticut (1964–66), and then in the electrical engineering department of the Polytechnic Institute of Brooklyn (1965–69) (Mathews et al. 1965; Tenney [1966a] 2015). Despite his continuing employment in technical fields, Tenney's artistic focus in the mid-1960s turned sharply away from computer music toward concerns more aligned with the downtown interdisciplinary activity to which some of his friends were already central. Relinquishing sound synthesis, computer algorithms, and the design of formal hierarchies, *Choreogram* (1964), *Chamber Music* (1964), *Three Theater Pieces* (1965), and *Viet Flakes* (1966) instead exhibit an overt theatricality and/or politicization that are peculiar to this era of his output. In their incorporation of the body as artistic material or in their engagement with the political and social climate of the time, some of these works were informed by Tenney's partnership with Schneemann and his participation in her kinetic theater performances. Others were spurred by his close interactions with Fluxus artists such as George Brecht, Philip Corner, and Alison Knowles. As he would recall more than a decade later, "This was a time for me of considerable searching for new directions in my own work, including extensions of music toward theater, and some participation in the activities of the Fluxus group. It was also a time of intensifying concern with social and political problems—civil rights, Vietnam war protests, etc.—and my only politically inspired pieces were done during this period" (Tenney 1978b).

However, this was also a period during which Tenney's overall compositional productivity declined markedly, and it would not resurge until after his move to California in 1970. In contrast with his prodigious compositional output while at Bell Labs, from mid-1964 to mid-1965, and again following his divorce from Schneemann in 1968, there were periods of more than twelve months during which Tenney completed no new pieces of his own. In part this abatement was due to the stringent demands of his research appointments. These primarily involved hardware and software development, and he later recalled: "I was . . . spending more time at that, it always seemed to me, than actually composing. And that aspect of it got frustrating. It also meant that I had very little time to do anything else, any other kind of music" (Tenney 1993a, 406).

Moreover, although the later 1960s would beget the signature works *Fabric for Che* (1967) and *For Ann (rising)* (1969), Tenney's creative output of 1964–70 is stylistically uncharacteristic of his oeuvre taken as a whole. His works from middecade seem particularly atypical and remain relatively unknown; he seldom remarked upon them later, and most have gone unpublished until recently. Nonetheless, based on a comparison of Tenney's musical style before 1964 with that following 1966, it would appear that his aesthetic underwent significant and durable change during the intervening years. In the wake of this period, there emerged a number of style features that would persist in much of his music of the coming decades, including a rigorous notational and formal economy, manifest generative processes, a more active role for the listener, and a heightened tangibility of raw sensation. These developments are illuminated by Tenney's personal interactions and by his confrontations with notation, performance, and embodied experience in the mid-1960s, as explored in sections 5.3 and 5.4.

5.2 Tone Roads and an American Experimental Tradition

In the 1950s and early 1960s, Tenney had felt acutely the lack of a musical heritage within which he could situate his own developing experimentalism. Finding no unifying tradition yet delineated, he gamely undertook to construct one. He made no pretense of being unbiased: "There was a point in the '50s, when I was a student, when I felt the need for a tradition of our own, not just defined by its differences from the European tradition—some of the European composers of the twentieth century are very much a part of my sense of my tradition. I decided to simply define that tradition in my own way. So, I put together the list of composers whose work was important to me, and many of them happen to be American composers" (Tenney 1991, 33). Recalling the Tone Roads Chamber Ensemble and associated concert series that he inaugurated in 1963 with composer Malcolm Goldstein and pianist Philip Corner, Tenney remarked: "When my friends and I started Tone Roads, the motivation was to connect [and] to bring back together all these disparate individual achievements and show them to be connected in some way. Not directly in the way of influence on each other necessarily, but just maybe only that we, the later generation, could see them as all part of a tradition" (2005b).[3]

If Tenney's efforts at tradition-building were first undertaken for the benefit of himself and his particular community, they would come to be broadly influential. Writer Douglas Kahn asserted to Tenney that he was, "perhaps more than anyone else, associated with being responsible for championing an American rogue tradition among composers, which would include Ives, Ruggles, Nancarrow, Cage and others, and Partch is right in there too" (Tenney 2000f), while composer Warren Burt put it to Tenney that he was "one of the leading scholars for years promoting the history of American music . . . [and] that tradition is finally being acknowledged as a viable historical thing through the works of people like you" (Tenney 1987c). In writer and composer Peter Garland's assessment, "Tenney has been responsible, both as a composer and teacher, for re-identifying today's work with the historical lineage of the American experimental tradition—a connection that the serial and post-serial movements have tended to play down (witness the eclipse composers like [Carl] Ruggles, [Dane] Rudhyar, and [Conlon] Nancarrow went into in the 1950s)" (1984, 3).

Goldstein recalled that in the 1960s academic and critical establishments generally privileged twentieth-century European music over American examples: "At that time nobody ever mentioned Ives or Varèse. They mentioned Berg, Schoenberg, and Webern" (2006). Corner recalled:

> "Stoky" [conductor Leopold Stokowski] has already lost one prestigious (respectable) orchestra, the Philadelphia; a career sacrifice for new music. So in the 60s playing the "classics" of this century was as radical as creating, say, Fluxus. Earle Brown was to say to us, when we created the Tone Roads Ensemble . . .

"You guys shouldn't have to be doing this." Unbelievable to recall that at that time no-one was playing Ives or Ruggles, just a little Varèse. Some simpler pieces of Henry Cowell. John Cage was known—but notorious. (1995, 6)

On its twelve concert programs of 1963–69, Tone Roads (named after two pieces of that title by Ives) brought together music by Ives, Cowell, Ruggles, and Varèse at a time when they were seldom performed and the concept of an American experimental tradition was still nascent. Pointedly, such works were heard alongside more recent music by the "New York School" of Cage, Earl Brown, Morton Feldman, and Christian Wolff (Goldstein 1984, 4–5). Late Tone Roads programs would add music by Philip Glass, Gordon Mumma, and other younger composers, including Corner, Goldstein, and Tenney themselves, thereby threading a connection all the way from Ives to contemporary experimental music.[4] In Goldstein's telling, "The basic impulse was always rooted in Tenney's vision: 'the continuity of an American experimental tradition'" (Goldstein 1984, 6) (albeit one to which the French-born Varèse was notably conscripted).

Tenney garnered a reputation as a champion of Ives's music in particular. It was frequently included on Tone Roads programs, which included the apparent premieres of Ives's *Tone Roads No. 3* (1911–15?), *Scherzo: Over the Pavements* (ca. 1910?), *In Re CON MOTO Et Al* (ca. 1915–16), and a number of his songs (Sinclair 1999; Arms 2013, 92–97). In 1966 Folkways Records released a double album of Ives's songs performed by Tenney and tenor Merle "Ted" Puffer with liner notes by Tenney (Tenney [1966b] 2015; 1988b, 28–29). Particularly noted were Tenney's performances in the 1960s and 1970s of Ives's monumental Piano Sonata no. 2 (*Concord, Mass., 1840–60*) (1915). He learned the movements of the *Concord* in their numeric order, mastering the first ("Emerson") sufficiently to perform it before leaving Bennington in June 1958 (Tenney 1988b, 29–30; Goldstein 1984, 4; section 2.3). He worked on the difficult second movement ("Hawthorne") during his graduate studies in Illinois (1959–61) and first performed it in New Jersey and New York in 1963. Finally, he conquered the last two movements ("The Alcotts" and "Thoreau"), following which he performed the complete sonata from memory at Yale University and various venues in New York in 1966.[5] He would continue to perform it periodically in the 1970s and would return to doing so in the 2000s.

Tenney's performance and advocacy encompassed various other activities as well. In September 1964 he organized and conducted a rare all-Varèse program as part of the Second Annual Avant Garde Festival of New York (Rothfuss 2014, 366). In many other solo and ensemble performances throughout the 1960s, he presented, as pianist or conductor, both American and international music by Erik Satie, Ives, Cage, Webern, Varèse, Ruggles, Morton Feldman, Earle Brown, Karlheinz Stockhausen, George Brecht, Toshi Ichiyanagi, Alvin Lucier, and Scott Joplin (before the Joplin revival of the 1970s). After moving to California in 1970, he continued as pianist to perform Ives, Ruggles, and Joplin, and he founded and directed a shorter-lived Tone Roads West (1973–75), which programmed music by Ives, Cage, Varèse, Cowell, Joplin, and Lou Harrison alongside that of emerging composers John Luther Adams and Peter Garland. Composer Dane Rudhyar had stopped composing around 1930 and was essentially forgotten by the musical community until Tenney and Garland sought him out in the early 1970s, reviving both the performance of Rudhyar's music and his activity as composer (Oja 2001).[6] Tenney's scholarly publications would include a study of Ruggles's melodic style ([1977a] 2015), extensive essays supplying the first substantial published analyses of Conlon Nancarrow's music (1977b), and a consideration of the implications of Cage's thinking for music theory ([1983] 2015). As late as 2002 Tenney recorded Cage's complete *Sonatas and Interludes* (1948) for commercial release (2003c).

Finally, in his own compositions Tenney advanced—and situated his music with respect to—a particular historicization of experimentalism by linking selected earlier artists via homage and technical synthesis. In a 1967 letter to Cage, Tenney wrote, "What is required now, it seems to me, is a sort of radical eclecticism—like that eclecticism that Ives described as 'every composer's duty.'"[7] *Collage #1 ("Blue Suede")* (1961) accordingly fuses Varèse-inspired tape techniques, post-Cagean chance procedures, and the collage aesthetics of Ives and Schneemann with the insurgent energy of rock 'n' roll. *Spectral CANON for CONLON Nancarrow* (1974) combines Nancarrow's characteristic instrumentation of player piano and interest in tempo canons with gradual process and the harmonic series. *Chromatic Canon* (1980/1983) weds minimalist phase-shifting with Second Viennese duodecaphony, while *Bridge* (1984) manages a conceptual rapprochement among the musics of John Cage, Harry Partch, and Charles Ives. Tenney's works of the late 1990s would synthesize many of his earlier concerns within newly dissonant textures inspired by such American dissonant contrapuntalists as Ruth Crawford and Carl Ruggles (section 11.1). His oeuvre includes many other such distinctive hybrids. Even Tenney's characteristic practice of dedicating compositions to elder composers, if primarily an expression of appreciation, also contributes to historicization. Musicologist Bob Gilmore (2008) lists nearly fifty such dedications appearing in or beneath Tenney's titles. These are distributed throughout his oeuvre, from the early Sonata for Ten Wind Instruments (1959) for Carl Ruggles to *Essay (after a sonata)* (2003), whose title refers to Charles Ives's *Essays before a Sonata* (1920). It may come as no surprise that Tenney's primary mentors appear as dedicatees—Cage is the most frequent beneficiary with seven dedications, followed by Varèse with four—but he also honored many others, including artists whom he did not know personally (such as Henry Cowell, Ruth Crawford, Giacinto Scelsi, and Stefan Wolpe) and even ones with whom his personal relationship had been strained (such as Harry Partch, who was twice a dedicatee).

Like all histories, the particular formulation of an experimentalist tradition that Tenney helped to consolidate in the 1960s privileged certain content and omitted much more. In particular, it mainly projected the work of white artists rather than, for instance, the experimentalism that had been flourishing among Black musicians of the 1960s in New York (Lewis 2008, 29–43). It should be noted that despite his significant contributions to the concept of an American experimental tradition, by the 1980s Tenney himself was repeatedly expressing a need to transcend aspects of it. In particular, he emphasized that "the nationalistic focus of this kind of thing is quickly becoming less and less useful; there's got to be some sense of *world* history that we partake of, a sense of tradition that draws from many different cultures" (Tenney 1991, 34).

5.3 Fluxus and Friends

Even ostensibly canonical members of Fluxus have not always agreed on what defined it as a collective, if indeed it was one. In the appraisal of Joe Jones, it represented the sphere of influence of founder George Maciunas, through which diverse individuals drifted for various spans (Bonito Oliva 1990, 175). George Brecht, on the other hand, offered a more broadly inclusive formulation: "[Certain] misunderstandings have seemed to come from comparing Fluxus with movements or groups whose individuals have had some principle in common, or an agreed-upon program. In Fluxus there has never been any attempt to agree on aims or methods; individuals with something unnamable in common have simply naturally coalesced to publish and perform their work. Perhaps this common thing is a feeling that the bounds of art are much wider than they have conventionally seemed, or that art and certain long-established bounds are no longer very useful" ([1964] 1990, 1).

Tenney never described himself as a member of Fluxus, although in the 1990s I once heard him jokingly refer to himself as a member of an expanded collective called "Friends of Fluxus." He was involved with various performances of works by Fluxus artists, and his own music was sometimes featured on Fluxus programs, such as when his *Collage #1 ("Blue Suede")* (1961) was heard at the 1963 Yam Day festival and when his *Chamber Music* (1964) appeared on the program of the 1964 Fluxus Symphony Orchestra concert at Carnegie Hall. He appeared in Yoko Ono's notorious *Film No. 4* ("Bottoms") (1966) and produced collaborative works with two other canonical Fluxus artists: *Entrance/Exit Music* (1962; volume 2, section 3.2) with George Brecht and *A House of Dust* (1967; volume 2, section 4.7) with Alison Knowles. Although Tenney later downplayed any effect of his involvements with Fluxus on his own compositional development (Mosko and Tenney 2004), certain aesthetic commonalities with his later music are sufficiently noticeable to warrant a brief examination.

Asked whether there was "an actual sense of joining a group or movement" in his involvement with Fluxus artists, Tenney's reply inclined toward Brecht's:

Not really, no. In my sense of it, it was a bunch of individuals who liked each other and got along together and had ideas to collaborate in programs. . . . Of course, now it's crystallizing into this historical object called Fluxus, right? That's taught me to suspect that most of the movements in history have been equally fluid and elusive and just accidental—or not entirely accidental, but nice confluences of different individuals. The notion of a movement is not the way I felt about it. These were just individuals; I was interested in their work, and there was mutual interest in the work, and we could do programs together. (1993a, 406–7)[8]

If Fluxus lacked an agreed agenda, certain characteristic attitudes and techniques are nonetheless discernable in many of its members' works. Before Maciunas gave Fluxus its name, John Cage's late 1950s courses on experimental composition at the New School had convened several key members (including George Brecht, Al Hansen, Dick Higgins, and Jackson Mac Low). The lingering influence of Cage on many Flux-works is detectable in an attention to experiential time (as in music), an important role for notation (which was usually textual), and the invocation of indeterminacy in performance (Kahn 1993). Interdisciplinary and intermedia works were characteristic. A decidedly antielitist and anticommercial overtone manifested in the use of inexpensive materials, small scale, brevity, humor, and a focus on the quotidian. A desire to efface the boundary between art and life was a frequent subtext. One recurring feature was a parodying of high-art ritual that convoked influences from Dada, Marcel Duchamp, and Cage's 4'33" (1952) (in its illumination of the rituals and parerga surrounding performance). Pieces tended to invite an actively observant and analytical attitude on the part of the audience, whose direct engagement or participation was often involved.

Many of these features are exemplified among the works of Fluxus artist George Brecht. His best-known creations are probably the various *event scores* that he produced between 1959 and 1962, which quickly became emblematic Flux-works. Each event score consists of a single small card bearing a title and maximally succinct textual instructions or propositions that leave open diverse possibilities for realization. Two examples are shown in figure 5.1. Similar scores were later produced by other Fluxus and Fluxus-adjacent artists, including Dick Higgins, Alison Knowles, George Maciunas, Mieko Shiomi, Yoko Ono, Ben Patterson, Ben Vautier, and La Monte Young. Brecht would typically mail newly created scores in small sets to various friends, including Tenney, and they would become a staple of Fluxus performances.[9] Characteristically, they reveal in certain mundane actions a striking semiotic power and multireferentiality when those actions are mindfully performed, observed, or merely considered. Brecht

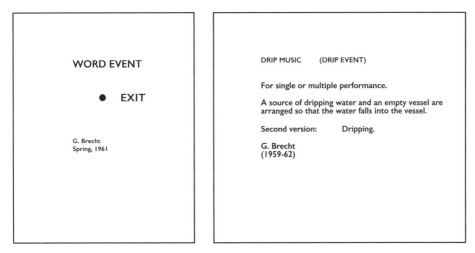

FIGURE 5.1. Two event scores by George Brecht. (a) *Word Event.* (b) *Drip Music (Drip Event).*

developed his concept of the event score in Cage's experimental composition course in 1959 (Robinson 2009), and the influence of music persisted in these scores insofar as the element of time remained essential. However, Brecht was interested in extending the scope of his work to include all aspects of experience, not just sound. In 1973 Brecht recalled: "Afterwards I tried to develop the ideas that I'd had during Cage's course and that's where my 'events' come from. I wanted to make music that wouldn't only be for the ears. Music isn't just what you hear or what you listen to, but everything that happens. . . . Events are an extension of music" ([1973] 1978, 83–84).[10]

Despite Tenney's interactions with Fluxus artists—including a collaboration with Brecht on the computer-synthesized *Entrance/Exit Music* (1962)—not until his departure from Bell Labs in the spring of 1964 would his own work begin to embrace senses in addition to hearing. If the linkage of sound and dance in *Choreogram* (1964) and the scripted theatrical actions of *Three Theater Pieces* (1965) owe more to Tenney's interactions with Schneemann and the Judson Dance Theater (section 5.4), his spotlighting of the total concert environment in *Chamber Music* (1964) was classic Fluxus, complete with event-score format and dedication to Brecht. Despite its later recontextualization as one of Tenney's sound-focused *Postal Pieces* (1965–71), his initial conception of *Maximusic* (1965) was likely in part theatrical—its manic middle section is sandwiched between periods of near immobility on the part of the solo percussionist. (Moreover, evoking Fluxus's parodistic mode, it was apparently intended to caricature aspects of the contemporary percussion repertoire [volume 2, section 5.4.1].) During this period, the Brechtian term *event* would begin to appear with regularity in Tenney's notes along with affirmations of multisensory art as an ideal.[11] These would culminate in the summer of 1965, when he would pen the following declaration in his notes: "It is not 'new sounds' we are after, but new situations. It has become necessary to discover or invent a new totality of sense-events, a new configuration of these, an environment as complete yet as unpredictable as might occur at any other moment in our lives."[12] Ironically, a few months thereafter Tenney would abandon multimodal work to again concentrate on music in particular. His composition of the soundtrack for Schneemann's film *Viet-Flakes* (1966) would provide a conduit back to work in sound specifically.

More durable for Tenney than his passing interest in intermedia was his attraction to a conceptual focus and an economy of means that are also exhibited by many Flux-works and of which the event scores of Brecht and La Monte Young supply prime exemplars.[13] The earliest example of such an aesthetic in Tenney's work would be the austere process form of *Entrance/Exit Music* (1962), a collaboration with Brecht comprising a gradual sonic transformation between sine tone and broadband noise. While a strain of reduction is detectable in the statistical and processual uniformity that underlies the variegated surfaces of Tenney's *Ergodos I* (1963) and *Ergodos II* (1964), rigorous conceptual focus and economy of means would overtly assert themselves in *Swell Piece* (1967) and (decisively) in *For Ann (rising)* (1969). They would remain features of his characteristic style thereafter. While such economy would most obviously manifest itself in Tenney's *Postal Pieces* (1965–71), many of his subsequent scores likewise fit on one or two pages, and even his most apparently complex compositions usually reveal upon close examination a core of focused exploratory intent from which digression has been ruthlessly pruned.

Speaking of his works following his move to California in 1970, Tenney would recall in 1988:

> Something was happening in those, that hadn't been happening before, or it hadn't been happening before *For Ann (rising)* in 1969. In some of the pieces from then on you see an effort at a kind of distillation, to a simpler form, a simpler manifestation. In fact something that I think would more justifiably be called minimalism than what [is] currently called minimalism, which is not minimal at all, it's just simple. I mean it's just repetition of an idea. But real minimalism, which can be traced back to, you know, Cage *4'33"* in 1952, or La Monte Young's *Composition 1960*, where it's just a statement about letting butterflies loose in the auditorium or something like that, that's minimalism and I think *For Ann (rising)* is truly minimal in that good sense, in that sense of being a kind of distillation down to the simplest possible thing. (1988b, 40–41)

Although Tenney here identifies *For Ann (rising)* (1969) as the watershed in his trend toward formal distillation, he also mentions the particular precedents of La Monte Young's classic event score and the single piece that arguably most influenced Fluxus: Cage's *4'33"*. Indeed, *Entrance/Exit Music* (1962) and the succinct quasi-Fluxian text scores of Tenney's *Maximusic* (1965) and *Swell Piece* (1967) (dedicated to Alison Knowles) exhibit a rigorous simplification that predates *For Ann (rising)* and the other *Postal Pieces*. Thus the intellectual and aesthetic roots of Tenney's own brand of conceptual and material streamlining—of which *For Ann (rising)* represents the signal instance—appear to stretch back at least as far as the first half of the 1960s.

5.4 Carolee Schneemann, Antonin Artaud, Wilhelm Reich

The artist and thinker with whom Tenney interacted most significantly during the mid-1960s remained Schneemann, of course. Until their separation in early 1968, they lived and worked extraordinarily closely together (Schneemann 1979, 2014). Tenney took prominent performing roles in some of Schneemann's best-known kinetic theater works, beginning with *Meat Joy* (1964, NYC performance) and continuing through *Water Light / Water Needle* (1966, Mahwah version), *Noise Bodies* (1966), *Snows* (1967), and *Night Crawlers* (1967). Her kinetic theater works *Chromelodeon* (1963), *Looseleaf* (1964), and *Snows* featured live or prerecorded sound collages cocreated with Tenney, and the soundtrack for her antiwar film *Viet-Flakes* (1966) comprised Tenney's *Collage #2 (Viet Flakes)*, made from commercial recordings cooperatively selected by the two of them. Concurrently, he would undertake with her a sustained multiyear collaboration on the making of her experimental film *Fuses* (1964–67). In turn, Schneemann's increasing engagements with the body as artistic material, with performed actions, and (after 1965) with the impact of the Vietnam War all seem to echo in Tenney's creative output of the period (sections 5.5–5.6; volume 2, sections 4.5–4.6).

As an emerging painter working in the wake of Jackson Pollock's gestural abstraction, Schneemann was already exploring in the 1950s an activation of the viewer's kinesthetic sense through the material traces of the artist's gestures in paint and collage (see section 3.3). Her practice of collage had been absorbing a growing diversity of materials while moving progressively into three dimensions and—in *Fur Wheel* (1962) and *Four Fur Cutting Boards* (1963)—literal movement through mechanization. She extended this preoccupation with physical gesture into live performance—what she would call *kinetic theater*. This process began as early as *Labyrinths* (1960), an event staged while she and Tenney were still residing in Illinois that took good advantage of friends and a downed tree at her residence. Upon arrival in New York, she quickly became active in the Happenings movement, performing in artist Claes Oldenburg's *Store Days* (1961), and soon she was mounting her own kinetic theater works, principally with the members of the Judson Dance Theater. Speaking of the nascent field of what is now called *performance art*, Schneemann wrote: "Our work seized dynamic implications of Abstract Expressionism to extend the active visual surface of painting into actual physical space and time, and to de-materialize the frame, the object, the aesthetic commodity" (1991, 31). In the photographic series *Eye Body: 36 Transformative Actions* (1963), she would take the radical step of placing her own body as an element within a collage before inserting it into her kinetic theater by performing in what remains one of her best-known works: *Meat Joy* (1964). Schneemann described this famous action as an extension of her increasingly three-dimensional and kinesthetically evocative work in painting and collage, writing that it was "an erotic vision that came through a series of very visceral dreams of expanding physical energy—off the canvas, out of the frame" (Reilly 2010, 29). *Meat Joy* accordingly culminated with its eight male and female performers improvising on the floor amid wet paint and raw meats, the instructions reading: "Wet fish, heavy chickens, bouncing hot dogs—bodies respond sporadically; twitching, pulling back, hands reaching, touching, groans, giggles . . . slips, flops, flips, jumps, throwing and catching, drawing, falling, running, slapping, exchanging, stroking. Tenderly, then wildly" (Schneemann 1979, 80). Schneemann dedicated *Meat Joy* to Tenney, who played opposite her in the central male role for its North American premiere (Schneemann 2018, 53).

Alongside the gestural implications of abstract expressionism, *Meat Joy* absorbed such influences as dramatist-essayist Antonin Artaud's visceral and non-narrative "theater of cruelty," the gender politics of writer Simone de Beauvoir, and psychoanalyst Wilhelm Reich's analysis of sexual energies and their political ramifications. According to Schneemann, "In 1959, I found Simone de Beauvoir. I felt all alone while my sense of gender politics was revealed by *The Second Sex.* . . . From de Beauvoir, I can go to Artaud for other suppressed meanings of the body and its larger extensivity. At the same time, my lover, the composer James Tenney, and I were reading Freud and Wilhelm Reich. Reich, with de Beauvoir and Artaud, gives me permission to begin to introduce the body into a literal space" (Juhasz 2001, 67).

Reading Artaud and Reich together with Schneemann, Tenney likewise developed an intense engagement with their ideas. In the late 1960s, he would personally undergo post-Reichian bioenergetic therapy in New York with Alexander Lowen (a student of Reich), continuing even after his move to California in 1970 (Tenney 2000f). Teaching at the California Institute of the Arts in the early 1970s, Tenney offered a reading course at the request of students in which he prominently included texts by both Artaud and Reich alongside ones by Ezra Pound and Charles Olson (Garland 2007, 54). As late as 1981 he would compose the song "Listen . . . !" in a popular style, "in memoriam John Lennon (and Wilhelm Reich)," the title borrowing from that of Reich's book *Listen, Little Man* (Reich and Steig 1948). On the other hand, although Artaud's and Reich's names appear occasionally amid Tenney's notes, evidence linking their ideas to specific aspects of his music are not to be found. The historian sometimes risks mistaking influence for resonance, and it may be that the writings of Artaud and Reich served less to influence Schneemann and Tenney than to reinforce or articulate particular aesthetic dispositions or potentialities that they already harbored. Whatever the case, in light of their attraction to these thinkers, I am prepared to indulge in some limited speculation regarding their significance to Tenney's art.

Artaud imagined a revitalized "concrete" theater addressing the audience primarily through the senses rather than through narrative: "Words say little to the mind; extent and objects speak; new images speak, even new images made with words. But space thundering with images and crammed with sounds speaks too, if one knows how to intersperse from time to time a sufficient extent of space stocked with silence and immobility. On this principle we envisage producing a spectacle where these means of direct action are used in their totality" (1958, 87). This description of a multisensory spectacle deemphasizing narrative seems apposite to Schneemann's kinetic theater works, and she wrote that Artaud was indeed influential in her conception of *Meat Joy* (Schneemann 1979, 62). For his part, in "Meta/Hodos" Tenney had quoted Artaud's description—inspired by Balinese theater—of a prelinguistic and gestural "pure theater" giving rise to a new and nongeneric conception of form, as well as to new types of content ([1961] 2015, 61, quoting Artaud 1958, 62). Especially resonant with Tenney's subsequent work, however, was Artaud's proposed alternative to narrative: a theater acting directly and powerfully through the sense organs (i.e., through the body). Among Artaud's comments on sound specifically, the following would surely have caught Tenney's notice: "The need to act directly and profoundly upon the sensibility through the sense organs invites research, from the point of view of sound, into qualities and vibrations of sounds to which we are absolutely unaccustomed, qualities which contemporary musical instruments do not possess and which compel us to revive ancient and forgotten instruments or to create new ones" (Artaud 1958, 95). Perhaps the most noteworthy part of this passage is less Artaud's call for unaccustomed sounds than his insistence on acting "directly and profoundly upon the sensibility through the sense organs," as opposed to through conventional, representational, or quasi-rhetorical devices. The aim of achieving an impact primarily through somatic rather than symbolic means might be discerned in certain of Tenney's obscure theatrical pieces of the midsixties, such as the two harrowing *Thermocouple*s of 1966. Perhaps more importantly, however, it persisted as a crucial undercurrent throughout much of his subsequent music despite its exclusion of overt theatricality. Among many examples that might be adduced, *Having Never Written a Note for Percussion* (1971) is perhaps the paradigmatic instance. Despite the pervasive impact of Cage's thought upon Tenney's work since 1963, the sensuous but cool aesthetic of Cage can scarcely accommodate the overwhelming visceral impact of *Having Never*. Its effect seems closer to Artaud's ideal of powerful organic engagement. The closest musical precursor may be the looming dissonances of *Déserts* (1954) by Varèse, who in 1932 had himself attempted an operatic collaboration with Artaud (M. MacDonald 2003, 235–41). It seems likely that Tenney's attention to somatic impact—perhaps traceable to his experience of Varèse's music—was buttressed not only by his reading of Artaud but also through his close ongoing dialogue with Schneemann and committed participation in her sensual and Artaud-informed kinetic theater performances.

The significance for Tenney of Wilhelm Reich's thinking is even more challenging to assess with any certainty. His interest in it at least reflects again a concern with the body, as well as his growing attention to politics and society in the 1960s. In 1961, a colleague at Bell Labs introduced Tenney to the *Selected Writings* (1960) of Reich and both he and Schneemann read them closely (Tenney 2000f; Kahn 2013b, 247–48). Schneemann commented: "The late 1950s and early '60s was a time of profound erotic suppression—I've written about that ad nauseam—and here was this brave, challenging, and remarkable psychoanalytic delving into the forms of suppression that related to governance, to militarism, to patriarchy" (2016). Reich argued that neuroses resulted from the accumulation of bodily stresses, which prevented "complete discharge of all dammed-up sexual excitation through involuntary pleasurable contractions of the body" during orgasm (1971, 79). The resulting residual undischarged sexual energy would induce frustration, inclination to cruelty, and—in extreme cases—fascistic personality traits. Reich's connection of complete sexual fulfillment with a progressive sociopolitical agenda was attractive to many artists of the 1950s and 1960s, including Stan Brakhage, William S. Burroughs, and Allen Ginsberg, and Reich's writings became an important intellectual tributary to the sexual revolution of the 1960s (Elder 1997, 149). Schneemann's engagement with Reich's liberatory program is reflected in her description of *Meat Joy* "as an erotic rite to enliven my guilty culture" (1991, 31).[14] On the other hand, Reich's connection of cruelty and authoritarianism with sexual repression informed her works of the second half of the decade, including the experimental film *Viet-Flakes* (1966) and her major kinetic theater work *Snows* (1967). She has commented that for both Tenney and herself, "Reich did make an impression particularly because of the militaristic government that we had. His analysis of sexual oppression and fascism was especially helpful to us" (2014, 41).

As with Artaud, however, specific verifiable examples of Reich's influence on Tenney's creative work are difficult to pinpoint. That it was nontrivial, however, is attested by a remarkable program note dating from 1968 regarding his computer composition *Phases* (1963): "The particular form of *Phases* was probably inspired by my readings of D'Arcy Thompson and Wilhelm Reich, but the sensuous core of it still has to do with Edgard Varèse, and the piece is dedicated to him" (Tenney 1968a). Tenney does not elaborate, and so any identification of specific features in *Phases* that reflect the influence of Thompson and Reich must remain conjectural. Perhaps the undulating mean parametric curves of figure 4.10—which Tenney (2000f) later likened to tidal motion—might recall Reich's proposition that any form of vital energy "would have to explain simply the basic pulsatory function (contraction and expansion) of life, as it manifests itself in respiration and the orgasm" (1973, 192). Comparison of the cyclical parametric unfoldings in *Phases* to changes over time in a living system—an ecosystem or metabolism—is undeniably vivid, but whether this was in fact an explicit part of Tenney's conception of the work remains uncertain.

The Reichian dichotomy between liberation and fulfillment versus repression and violence remained a concern for Schneemann and Tenney in 1966–67 as their works began to more explicitly address the ongoing Vietnam War. A relatively overt Reichian aspect seems to emerge in Tenney's *Three Theater Pieces* (1966). This is particularly evident in *Thermocouple #1*, the second of the set, in which two performers first engage in gently affectionate contact with electrostatically charged glass rods before the performance changes course with an abrupt eruption of howling high-volume acoustic feedback. This contrast of the intimate and erotic with the aggressive and disturbing suggests the two sides of a Reichian coin: the concomitants of sexual liberation and repression.

Tenney's engagement with Reich was not uncritical, however, so any fastidiously literal Reichian reading of his work—even that of the mid-1960s—would likely be inappropriate. In an unsent letter dated 1964–66, for instance, he proposed a fundamental overhaul of Reichian theory that would entirely eliminate reference to Reich's trademark (but scientifically untenable) concept of a vital energy called "orgone." Tenney's hope was that the theory could thereby ultimately be placed on a more orthodox scientific footing.[15] Reflecting two decades later, he would remark: "I think Reich was on to something that I'd never seen in any other place about whole-organism integration that relates to the sexual function. I still think it is interesting, but you have to wade through so much. In the later writings there is so much that is questionable and indefensible, but the first few books are still very important" (Tenney 2000a).

5.5 *Choreogram* (1964)

ANY NUMBER OF PLAYERS, USING ANY INSTRUMENTS
OR SOUND SOURCES (WITH DANCERS)
variable duration

"Choreo-" derives from the Greek *choros*, denoting the art of the dance, while the combining form "-gram" derives from *-gramma*, indicating something written or drawn. Thus, Tenney's idiosyncratic title translates roughly as "dance text." Accordingly, the notation read by the musicians is supplied by the visible positions and actions of dancers. Dating from near the end of his tenure at Bell Labs, *Choreogram* thus represents the beginning of Tenney's brief period of intermedia works in which sonic elements would constitute just one facet of a multisensory experience. They would continue with *Chamber Music* (1964), for any number of performers anywhere; *Maximusic* (1965), for percussion; and *Three Theater Pieces* (1965).

Tenney's interest in notational experiments had been provoked by his examination of the radically unconventional piano part to John Cage's *Concert for Piano and Orchestra* (1958).[16] The production of his first unconventional scores—*Choreogram* and *String Complement*, both dating from February 1964—was undoubtedly buttressed by this study. However, unlike Cage's example, both of these works require musicians to assume a responsive relationship to their environment, reacting to it in real time. In *String Complement*, performers monitor the prerecorded electronic sounds of Tenney's *Ergodos I* (1963) or *Ergodos II* (1964), which prompt their individual readings of the graphical instrumental parts. In *Choreogram*, Tenney's instructions to the performers assert that "the score is the dance itself, each player's part the positions and movements of one or more dancers."

Apparent influences on the interactive aspect of *Choreogram* included the work of Tenney's partner, artist Carolee Schneemann, and that of the Judson Dance Theater. Beginning with *Glass Environment for Sound and Motion* (May 1962) and continuing through a series of classic kinetic theater works presented at Judson Hall in 1963–64, Schneemann began to integrate the body and live action within her prior practice of collage (Schneemann 1979). *Choreogram* integrates these same new elements with Tenney's own primary medium (music). More broadly, Tenney was a frequent presence at Judson Hall, where his electronic music appeared on programs alongside dance and where he helped to supply musical complements not only for Schneemann's work but also for that of other members of the Judson group (Banes 1983). The relation between experimental music and experimental dance was thus already a concern for him, as well as for two other musicians who were even more closely involved with Judson: Tenney's friends Philip Corner and Malcolm Goldstein. A year earlier, for instance, Corner had presented there his *Certain Distilling Processes* (1962), a work in which improvising dancers effectively conduct musicians' navigation of a partially graphical score (B. Patterson et al. 1965, 182–88; Piekut 2018, 72). Corner's subsequent *Flares* (1963) involved projected graphics that were interpreted simultaneously by dancers and musicians (including Tenney).[17]

Choreogram extends this direction of interdisciplinary research by eliminating the fixed score object altogether in favor of the bodies of the dancers themselves. The nature of the dance is not itself prescribed, so that the traditional expectation that dancers must follow the music is inverted. The musicians respond to the dancer(s) using an interpretive scheme that they themselves develop in accordance with broad guidelines stipulated in Tenney's performance instructions. In particular, "each player determines—ahead of time, and independently of other players—a specific, one-to-one correlation between 'dancer-variables' and

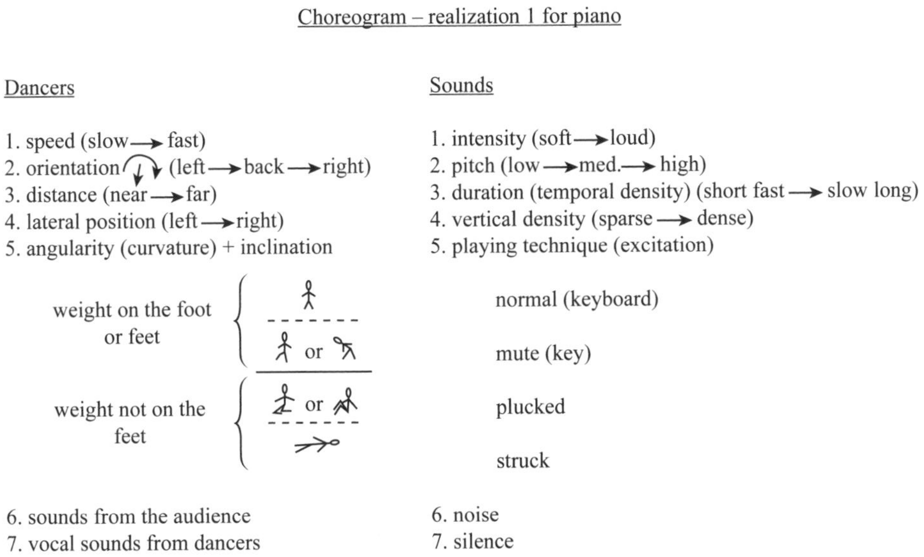

Choreogram – realization 1 for piano

Dancers

1. speed (slow → fast)
2. orientation ↻↓ (left → back → right)
3. distance (near → far)
4. lateral position (left → right)
5. angularity (curvature) + inclination

weight on the foot or feet { ————— }
weight not on the feet { }

6. sounds from the audience
7. vocal sounds from dancers

Sounds

1. intensity (soft → loud)
2. pitch (low → med. → high)
3. duration (temporal density) (short fast → slow long)
4. vertical density (sparse → dense)
5. playing technique (excitation)

normal (keyboard)

mute (key)

plucked

struck

6. noise
7. silence

FIGURE 5.2. An example of possible correlations between "dancer-variables" (*left*) and "independently variable parameters of the sounds" (*right*), redrawn from the performance instructions for *Choreogram*.

independently variable parameters of the sounds he can produce. The number of such correlations is up to the player, but should number at least three, if possible." Tenney supplies nonexhaustive lists of possible "dancer-variables" and sonic parameters. The latter included pitch, intensity, tempo, articulation, and tone color, as well as modulations in pitch (vibrato) and amplitude (tremolo)—a listing that recalls the composer's prior research on timbral perception and the acoustical parameters of the computer-synthesized music that he was still composing at Bell Labs (section 4.4). The instructions also include two concrete examples (for piano) of possible mappings between dance and musical variables, the first of which is reproduced in figure 5.2. In this illustration, speed of bodily motion is translated as musical dynamic, orientation of the body is interpreted as pitch (presumably with a skip from one registral extreme to the other at frontal orientation), distance of the dancer (presumably from the musician) is translated as temporal density, lateral position of the dancer as vertical density (the number of simultaneous sounds), and so forth.

The instructions stipulate that special allowances be made for the musical states of noise and silence: "The player should establish a condition or set of conditions in which he will remain *silent*, and a condition or set of conditions in which he will produce *noises* or other sounds not 'normal' to his instrument or sound-source, or by means of auxiliary sound-sources."[18] In each case, these conditions are to be such that they are likely to occur at least once in performance. Unlike the other parametric mappings, the conditions for noise and silence are permitted to involve any characteristics of the performance environment, which may include the dance but also sounds or activities among the audience or other musicians, lighting conditions, and so forth. Additionally, "each player is free to establish these silence- and noise-correlations in any way he chooses, with one exception: this is that complete inactivity within the space of the dance—such as before the dance begins and after it ends, must mean inactivity ('silence') on the part of the players (thus, no preludes, interludes or postludes!)." Finally, each musician is free to decide whether the values of the "dancer-variables" correspond to the state of an individual dancer, to the states of two dancers ("in which case a degree of ambiguity will be introduced, to be resolved by the player in any way he chooses"), or to the average conditions of the entire ensemble of dancers. This interpretive choice—and even the details of the mapping between dance and sound—can be changed in the course of a performance if there seems to be a good reason to do so, although "this should not be done arbitrarily or . . . very often."

The example mapping supplied in figure 5.2 might be viewed as relatively natural insofar as low energy states tend to correspond across media (e.g., slow dancing corresponds to soft dynamics and fast dancing to loud dynamics). A different mapping might anticorrelate these parameters to produce a sort of inverse relationship between them (such that slow dancing might correspond to loud dynamics). The instructions require that values of the sonic parameters have a maximal range and that they be distributed as nearly uniformly as possible over that range. Interpreted strictly, this goal of uniform distribution would entail that—as in the example of figure 5.2—continuously variable sound parameters (such as intensity) should be mapped from continuously valued dance parameters (such as speed) rather discretely valued ones (such as "weight-on-feet"). This condition may help to make the association between continuously variable sound parameters and their corresponding dance parameters more easily perceptible; for instance, a strictly monotonic change in the dance parameter will thus be reflected by a strictly monotonic change in the sonic one. On the other hand, silence and/or noise may be triggered by conditions having nothing to do with the ongoing dance, temporarily disrupting the dance-sound correspondence. Moreover, the word "noise" affords a potentially wide range of sonic interpretations, which (depending on the performer's approach) may introduce indeterminate or improvisatory elements.

Tenney's final note to the performers makes clear that the music should not be conceived as an expressive response to the dance: "It is not the composer's intention that the sounds that occur should have any dramatic or psychological relation to the dance, nor is it intended that such relations should never occur. The sounds' relation to the dance will be appropriate to the extent that they do not reflect any intention on the part of the performer(s) to make them so." To borrow terminology from communications engineering, the musical performance represents a transduction of the dance signal into a musical one, with noise and silence representing extraneous intruding elements akin to static in a telephone signal. Recent usage might dub this process a *sonification* of the dance. At Bell Labs, Tenney worked routinely with transductions of voltage into sound, and in his journals of the era he draws a parallel between that process and a performing musician's interpretation of a musical part, so *Choreogram* might be viewed as involving a transduction process extended to still other types of input signal (in this case, observed bodily movement).[19] Indeed, from later in 1964 and 1965, Tenney's archives preserve sustained ruminations concerning signals and their transformations or transductions across media, and such transformations would figure again in his conception for *Metabolic Music* (1965), for performers with bioelectric equipment.[20] However, *Choreogram* goes beyond mere transduction insofar as both signals (dance and music) are presented together, so that their perceived relations become a component of the aesthetic experience. The correlated moment-by-moment response of the musician(s) to the dancer(s) thus extends, across media, Tenney's long-standing interest in texture by supplying a musical counterpoint to a terpsichorean theme.[21]

5.6 *Fabric for Che* (1967)

ELECTRONIC MUSIC (TWO-CHANNEL FIXED MEDIA)
9 mins., 50 secs.

There are few musical precedents for *Fabric for Che*'s combination of furiously dynamic detail with relentless statistical constancy. According to composer Peter Garland, Tenney once remarked, "I kind of wanted to start where Varèse left off in *Poème électronique*," which is presumably a reference to the wailing distorted glissandi that crisscross siren-like during the final seconds of Varèse's classic 1958 tape composition.[22] My own first association upon hearing *Fabric* was with much later music: the dense, harsh, and unrelenting Japanoise of the 1980s and 1990s (Novak 2013). Although I have now heard the piece many times over the course of decades, its precipitous beginning still disorients my senses and emotions, furnishing the musical equivalent of a trap door suddenly opening beneath my feet.

In Tenney's archives, the following rather uncharacteristic note from the composer is scrawled among the work tapes for *Fabric*: "Music is a physical process (acoustics). And it involves psychological processes (imagination, perception). But it is also, and most importantly, a *social* process."[23] This declaration is perhaps unexpected in connection with a wordless piece comprising computer-generated sounds on tape. In 1969, however, when asked "Have you, or has anyone, ever used your music for political or social ends?" Tenney went further: "Yes, I have. I can think of two compositions where there were political connotations. In both cases it was integral enough to my idea of the music for me to say that it was part of the whole thing. This is the way it should be used. One called *Viet Flakes* to go with a film, the other *Fabric for Che*" (Austin, Kahn, and Gurusinghe 2011, 217).

The title refers to the Argentinian Cuban guerrilla leader Ernesto "Che" Guevara. Guevara had been assassinated after his capture by the Bolivian army in October 1967, shortly before the completion of *Fabric for Che*. In an archival document from 1968 entitled "Background—fragments of an unkept diary," Tenney expanded on this association.

> I would be, when I may be, a pacifist. But I see no alternative—in this world of tyrannies—to armed struggle, on the part of the tyrannized, against the (so well armed) forces of repression at the service of tyrants (or abstracted, oppressive systems). Thus I was sympathetic with Guevara's "adventure," and deeply moved when it became clear that he really had been killed. Especially so because he seemed to have a sensibility quite beyond that of brute force—even of that on the side of a "just cause"—a sensibility that could say, and help me to believe, "It takes love to make a revolution." (1968a)

Tenney also connected the piece to his ongoing opposition to American military involvement in Vietnam. This association occasioned a minor scandal when *Fabric* was premiered at the Polytechnic Institute of Brooklyn, where Tenney was employed as a research acoustician.

> They asked me to do a little talk about computer music. But I was sure that they were doing all kinds of defense research at the engineering school, and that at my talk there was going to be representatives of the military or Defense Department, or corporations under defense contracts in attendance. I thought to myself, why do I need to talk about computer music to these guys? I said I'd rather not. I just didn't want to have anything to do with them. And they said, "Oh, come on, please." So finally I said okay. (Tenney 2000f)

Technical details regarding computer music composition and synthesis occupied Tenney's short presentation until its closing moments, when he introduced the recently completed *Fabric* as an example demonstration: "I made a kind of brief statement before I turned it on, that it had something to do with my disgust with the Vietnam War, and then I pushed the button and blasted it at them at 110 decibels [*laughs*]. So that was my little demonstration" (2003b).

On other occasions, however, Tenney was more equivocal about the meaning and motivations for the piece: "The original motivation for it was, I'm sure, not political, but acoustic; it was music. But it had a character that was a bit like an angry statement, and somehow—I don't even remember the sequence of things—but I ended up calling it that" (2003b).[24] Regarding his "acoustic" concerns in particular, continued reflection upon the new technical possibilities afforded by the electronic medium were leading Tenney to question whether the temporally discrete nature of sounds produced by acoustic instruments was

TABLE 5.1. Audio source tracks for *Fabric for Che*

Track name	Subtrack	Duration (mins.)	Content	Creation date
1	A1	1	1 computer-synthesized voice	Mar. 1964
	B1a	1	bandpass-filtered broadband noise	Nov. 1967
2		1	4 computer-synthesized voices	Dec. 1964
3		1.25	4 computer-synthesized voices	Mar. 1964
4		1.25	4 computer-synthesized voices	Mar. 1964

a musical necessity. Commenting upon *For Ann (rising)* (1969), he remarked, "I began thinking instead about a notion of continuity, which I first used in the piece called *Fabric for Che* (1967), where by not hearing the beginnings or the ends of sounds I wanted it to be a kind of a terrible, incredible turmoil" (2000f).

Fabric for Che was constructed using traditional tape-music techniques applied (primarily) to computer-generated sounds on reel-to-reel tapes that Tenney had recorded years earlier near the end of his time at Bell Labs.[25] As indicated in table 5.1, most of the tape tracks dated from 1964 and bore polyphonic combinations of computer-synthesized voices. The sole exception was a component of filtered noise whose bandwidths and center frequencies were swept at various rates (producing sounds ranging in character from jet take-offs to thunderclaps). This noise track was generated around the time that *Fabric* was completed, possibly without recourse to a computer.

Figure 5.3 provides a spectrogram of an excerpt from track A1 (one of two subtracks constituting track 1), showing the registral distribution of sound energy as it varies over time. (Appendix B provides a brief general introduction to the spectrographic analysis of audio signals.) The subtrack comprises a single computer-generated voice and exemplifies the typical characteristics of all such voices in *Fabric*. As shown in part (a) of the figure, frequency trajectories are linear in time. Fundamental frequency contours exhibit occasional discontinuous or extremely rapid transitions (leaps), but continuous transitions are more common. There are no intervening silences. In addition to changes in their frequency and amplitude, tones are subjected to varying rates and amplitudes of random frequency modulation. Effects characteristic of this technique are pervasively audible, ranging from the insectile buzzing of irregular vibrato to babbling, boiling, or effervescing noise sounds.[26] From 10 to 14 seconds into the track, as shown in the figure, a nearly pure tone glides downward, while from 16 to 20 seconds, a noise band descends in register with an audible pitch corresponding to its center frequency. From 25 to 26.5 seconds, the amplitude of random modulation diminishes quickly so that an ambiguously pitched noise band becomes a relatively pure tone. At 30 seconds, a complex tone with seven harmonics appears, gliding upward. At 37 seconds, a lower-register complex is

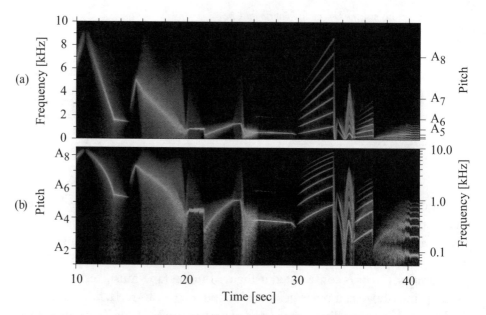

FIGURE 5.3. Spectrogram of an excerpt from track A1 using (a) an ordinate that is linear in frequency versus (b) an ordinate that is linear in pitch. (Stereo channels are summed.)

subjected to diminishing modulation so that its sound changes progressively from broadband noise to a tone with erratic vibrato.

Figure 5.3(b) displays the same spectrogram using an ordinate that is linear in pitch rather than frequency. Comparison between the two parts of the figure reveals a characteristic of the glissandi that contributes crucially both to the formal unity of the music and to its affective impact: all of the computer-generated trajectories are linear in frequency and thus concave downward in pitch (i.e., in log frequency), which is the directly perceived parameter. In other words, in pitch the slopes of ascending glissandi gradually decrease, like the paths of projectiles influenced by gravity or increasing resistance. On the other hand, the slopes of descending glissandi increase in magnitude, as though plunging ever more precipitously. In both cases, the degree of nonlinearity increases with the registral span of the glissando.

The stereo tracks listed in table 5.1 were repeatedly overdubbed at different tape speeds in order to produce an extremely dense texture.[27] The mixing process is illustrated in figure 5.4(a). Black arrowheads indicate tape direction. Different content is indicated using solid versus dashed lines, while greater line thickness indicates a lowered tape speed. As shown in the top line of the figure, tracks 1 and 2 (each 1 minute in duration) were mixed, and the result was repeated, alternate repetitions of the tape being reversed in direction, as indicated by the arrowheads. Tracks 3 and 4 (each 1.25 minutes in duration) were treated similarly, yielding a large-scale 4:5 polyrhythm of tape durations against the previous

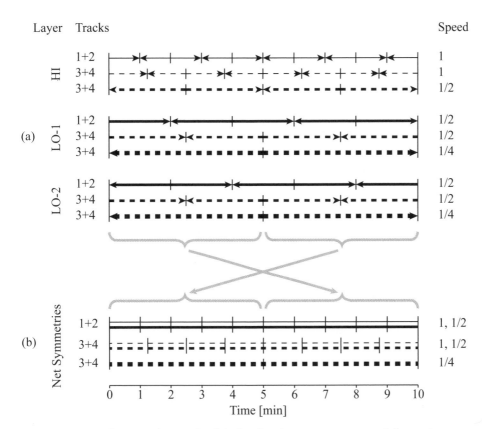

FIGURE 5.4. (a) The mix scheme of *Fabric for Che*. (b) Decomposition of the total mix into components with differing axes of retrograde symmetry.

mix. In addition, half-speed versions of tracks 3 and 4 (sounding one octave lower) were mixed and repeated, with their first iteration reversed in direction relative to the full-speed version. All of these tracks were then mixed together into a layer that Tenney marked "HI." A half-speed version of HI was then split into two halves ("LO-1" and "LO-2"), which were mixed with HI to produce the final audio. Finally, the first and second halves of the final result were swapped (without audio reversal), as indicated by the crossed gray arrows in the figure.

Close inspection of figure 5.4(a) reveals that some voices are duplicated in the final mix; in particular, the "3 + 4" components of LO-1 and LO-2 comprise identical audio. With reference to table 5.1 but excluding such duplications, there are forty-seven independent computer-synthesized voices present (plus three versions of the broadband-noise subtrack). However, this tally is an oversimplification because the copies of duplicated voices are not perfectly synchronized with each other in the mix! These slight asynchronies are visible in figure 5.5, which provides a spectrogram of the entire first half of the piece. For instance, the very low frequency glissandi that appear in the first half-minute of the music appear in ganged pairs at a lag of about 1 second. Because their trajectories are

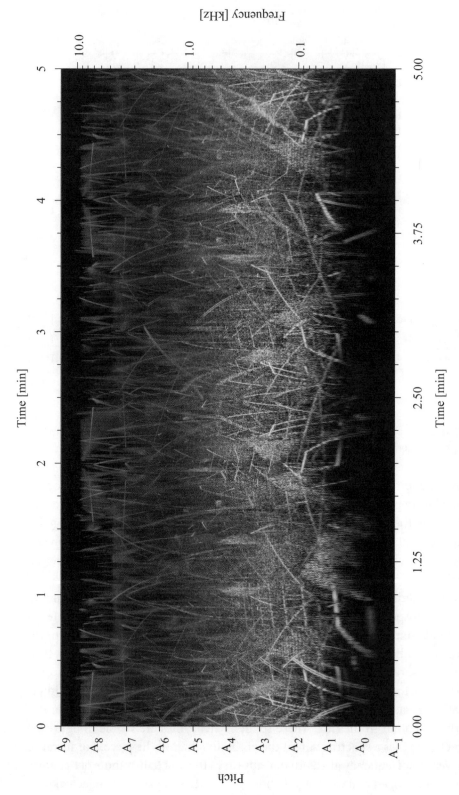

FIGURE 5.5. Spectrogram of the entire first half of *Fabric for Che* (with stereo channels summed).

linear in frequency, these pairs are separated by a constant frequency difference; thus, the pitch interval between them contracts as they ascend in register. At low frequencies these intervals can be as wide as a fifth, while in high registers they can produce beating microintervals. A treble example is visible approaching the 3-minute mark, ascending between A_4 and A_7. Such dyadic glissandi are recurrent and audibly striking features.

As a result of the alternation between forward and reversed tape directions and of the mixing of forward with reversed versions of the half-speed tracks, the final mix can be decomposed into three layers exhibiting different retrograde symmetries, whose numerous axes are represented by verticals in figure 5.4(b). These symmetries are also visible in figure 5.5, wherein the numbered ticks above and below the spectrogram correspond to instants at which certain sets of audio components retrogress. As indicated in figure 5.4(b), as a whole the piece is a palindrome: all components are retrograde symmetric about its midpoint at 5 minutes, including the quarter-speed components that are symmetrical *only* about that point. This central reversal is aurally conspicuous and is often recognized by listeners who have no foreknowledge of it. The other axes of symmetry are less recognizable as such because at each one only a subset of the many sounding features retrogrades. The partial retrogrades around 2.5 and 7.5 minutes are audible—especially if the listener is expecting them—but the other axes typically go undetected. Thus it would be inaccurate to describe the *perceived* large-scale formal organization of *Fabric* as one involving retrograde symmetries or the polyrhythmic superimposition of different periodicities. Even when heard, due to the limitations of memory, the reversals of musical features about axes of temporal symmetry are perceived as *local* features no more than a few seconds in duration, not as aspects of large-scale organization.

All of these retrograde symmetries have audible consequences, however, even when the locations of their axes go unnoticed. This is the case because retrograde relationships are recognizable (or at least suggested) between isolated sonic features that are not necessarily close to the axis of symmetry or to one another. To choose just one example, in figure 5.5 to the left of the 2.5-minute mark (roughly between 2 minutes and 2 minutes, 10 seconds) a light gray leftward-pointing triangular region is visible in the neighborhood of E_3. This region corresponds to a tone undergoing increasingly wider and more rapid random frequency modulation, whose audible character thus progresses from a tone with erratic pitch vibrato to noise. The reverse of this ear-catching process appears symmetrically to the right of the 2.5-minute mark. Other instances of this feature are faintly visible in the figure around 20 seconds and 4 minutes, 40 seconds. Moreover, these features derive from track 3 at half speed, so full-speed versions of them are also visible; these appear transposed up one octave and in rhythmic diminution flanking the 1.25-minute and 3.75-minute marks. The relationships between all of these features are audible, although the impression created is less one of large-scale symmetries or periodicities than of transformational relationships between particular isolated elements. Such relationships almost have the character of motivic variation, but in the absence of any developmental linearity, the effect is more akin to sporadic and surprising recurrences of various sonic "species" within a teeming electroacoustic ecosystem.

A number of factors contribute to the musical impression of "terrible, incredible turmoil" at which the composer indicated he was aiming.

- New and distinctive sound events arise in rapid succession, often luring the ear away from a previous sound before its cessation. Alternatively, sounds frequently end or subside to reveal others previously unnoticed, an effect that is particularly striking when rapid pitch variation momentarily abates to reveal a more slowly moving background in some register. In both cases, as Tenney indicates, the beginnings or ends (or both) of sounds go unheard as the ear is deflected from one object to another, each of which is only partially apprehended. In a passive hearing, attention is thus pinballed about the texture. Alternatively, attention can be deliberately directed to particular registers or sounds, although these forays tend to be brief because other sonic activity soon draws the ear away again.
- The impression of playing perceptual catch-as-catch-can is greatly compounded by the sheer density of discriminable sonic information simultaneously presented. As attention voluntarily or involuntarily ranges between sounds and across registers, the listener remains acutely aware that much sonic activity is escaping notice.
- The pervasive instability of sonic parameters also contributes to the impression of musical tumult. Pitches are never constant but glide independently at rates ranging from precipitate to glacial. Similarly, noise characteristics such as bandwidths and registers are in constant flux. The independent variation among sounds makes more of them readily discriminable than if they were static or covarying. The corresponding impression is one of swarming motion within a musical space whose dimensions correspond first to pitch and time but also to an apparent proximity (suggesting foreground, middleground, and background features) correlated with dynamic and rate of change.
- The title alone is sufficient to open a semiotic dimension that is impossible to ignore, although listeners will surely apprehend its specifics in divergent ways. The prevalence of unstable broadband noise may evoke the release of energy in friction or turbulence (engine noise, combustion, ordnance, cries). The concave-downward glissandi may seem to struggle upward against resistance or to plunge dizzyingly in sudden debacle. Various personal or sociopolitical correspondences would not be difficult to invent, but for most listeners the evocation of crisis is likely to be general rather than particular.

The intense flux and variety of local detail are balanced by powerful unifying factors operative at larger timescales. Most striking is the rigorous statistical constancy in certain musical parameters: each 30-second segment largely resembles every other one in its density of sounding tones, registral compass, average dynamic, timbral palette, balance between noise and tone, and distribution of glissando lengths and speeds. Presumably, the title *Fabric* alludes to this statistical homogeneity, as well as to the interweaving of sound components. Figure 5.5 shows that the downward concavity of pitch trajectories is similarly consistent. Finally, the recurrence of transformationally related figures promotes perceived unity among the musical materials.

The shockingly abrupt commencement and termination of the piece—as though its "fabric" has been cut from a roll—are aptly characterized by Tenney in the following 1970 passage concerning *extrinsically limited* forms in general: "'Reaching an *extrinsic* limit.' . . . The effect here is as though looking at a landscape through an open window—the perceptual boundaries are defined 'arbitrarily' (by the window frame) rather than being inherent or 'intrinsic' to the process ('landscape') itself; music that ends this way often begins this way also, and we might call it a 'windowed' form of closure" ([1970] 2015, 157). By implication, the music of *Fabric for Che*—like the history of social and political struggles—continues indefinitely beyond the temporal frame within which it appears.

Despite its unprecedented texture, *Fabric for Che*'s constructive logic has precursors in Tenney's earlier electronic music. The attainment of great textural density by superimposing the same computer-generated tracks at different speeds recalls *Analog #1 (Noise Study)* (1961), whose climax briefly approaches the churning complexity of *Fabric*. The superimposition of different periodicities brings to mind the cyclical structure underlying *Phases* (1963). On the other hand, the profusion of glissandi, the distribution of activity across nearly the entire musical frequency range, the continual shunting of attention between musical features, and the potential to tailor one's musical experience by deliberately directing the ear to different registers all anticipate Tenney's watershed *For Ann (rising)* (1969), in which the Varèsian siren found an apotheosis.

CHAPTER 6

Process and Continuity
(1969–71)

The late 1960s brought major changes to Tenney's personal circumstances. Most significantly, early 1968 brought divorce from his first wife, artist Carolee Schneemann. Although the end of this thirteen-year personal and creative partnership was painful for both parties, they would resume mutually supportive communication in the following decades. At the time, however, Tenney entered a creative hiatus lasting more than a year. As previously, much of his time and energy was consumed by his employment in acoustical research, now in the electrical engineering department at the Polytechnic Institute of Brooklyn. He remained active as a performer, however, even resuming formal piano studies with noted teacher Dorothy Taubman (Tenney 1988b, 30). During this period he continued to codirect and perform in Tone Roads concerts and served as an original member in the ensembles of both Steve Reich (1967–70) and Philip Glass (1969–70).[1]

The lapse in his compositional output was finally broken with *For Ann (rising)* (1969), a work dedicated to the woman who would become his second wife, Anne Christine Tenney.[2] December 1969 brought the birth of a daughter, Mielle, whose imminent arrival motivated Tenney to reassess his lifestyle in New York City. In March 1970 he consequently moved with his family to California in order to assume a position teaching composition and piano at the newly opened California Institute of the Arts (CalArts) in Valencia that fall.

> At the time I was living in a loft down on Bleecker Street near the Bowery, and it was bums outside and cockroaches all over the walls and it was pretty awful. And I thought, "This is no place to bring up a kid." . . . So, shortly after she was born, we moved to California, and that was the end of my New York career. . . .

For quite a little I really was quite happy with the change, with the difference. I guess I really wanted nothing more than to get out into another environment and be distant from the kinds of intense stimulation that is one's life in New York. I felt like I didn't need it so much. What I needed was another kind of environment for doing my own work. And that's what it gave me. For a while. (Tenney 1988b, 27, 33)[3]

Tenney was hired in part as an expert on electronic and computer music. Ironically, his move to California would mark an end to his production of purely electronic music, *For Ann (rising)* (1969) being the final instance. Neither would he employ the computer as a compositional tool again until the 1980s, well after departing CalArts. Tenney later explained that "what they had [at CalArts] was analog-synthesis equipment which I had never really worked with. I'm not a knob-turner, and if you're not a knob-turner, analog synthesis is not very comfortable. After my frustrations at Illinois, and the fact that I got into the computer work so early, the analog systems just weren't for me. But I found at CalArts that I was surrounded by fantastic performers—really good players—so I started writing music for acoustical instruments again" (1993a, 405).

In fact, Tenney would find disengagement from technology creatively liberating. In a 1971 letter to Schneemann, he wrote, "The job is a very good thing—I feel lucky in having it, and to be free of the old technology/research thing I was bound to for so long."[4] The consumption of time and energy by the technical duties associated with his prior positions at Yale and the Polytechnic Institute had contributed to his diminished productivity in the second half of the 1960s. Shedding them for the very different responsibilities of teaching at a West Coast art school would trigger for Tenney a period of intense compositional productivity that would yield some of his best-known music. Concomitantly, it would usher in major developments in both his style and technique: "My involvement with technology during the 1960s had been very demanding of both time and energy, and other aspects of my compositional personality had had to be postponed. The log-jam thus created was finally released in California, with *Quiet Fan for Erik Satie* (for chamber orchestra, 1970), several 'Koans' (for violin, cello, bass, harp, and percussion, 1971), *Clang for Orchestra* (1972), *Quintext* (1972), *In the Aeolian Mode* (1973), *Chorales for Orchestra* (1974), *Spectral CANON for CONLON Nancarrow* (for 'harmonic player-piano,' 1974), and *Three Pieces for Drum Quartet* (1974–75)" (Tenney 1978b).

In *Quiet Fan for Erik Satie,* there first emerged a new interest in harmony that would endure throughout Tenney's remaining career. This soon led him to compositional explorations of the harmonic series, which would appear in *Clang* and *Quintext.* Another major development, however, had already decisively manifested in *For Ann (rising)* (1969), and it would crucially underpin the ensuing ones: this was an attraction to simple generative processes combined with gradual musical pacing.

6.1 Gradual Processes

6.1.1 Process

As composing has been traditionally practiced, significant decisions by the composer regarding the nature of musical events manifest at points in time that are widely distributed over the course of a composition. In contrast, strict examples of so-called *process music* define a set of *initial data* (the *initial state*) and a set of *generative rules* for deriving musical events from those data. The sequence of musical events then unfolds in time according to those predeterminations and without further decision-making by the composer (Nyman 1999, 4–9). The events determined by the process may be actions to be executed by performers, or, if the process is automated, they may instead or additionally include acoustic events, as in Tenney's computer music. Invoking the designation *process music* or *process piece*, however, often implies that the music-generative process possesses a particular property: that it provides a relatively economical prescription for a realization of the piece compared to an explicit sequential listing of the musical events in a typical realization. Indeed, the scores to many process pieces fit economically on a single page or less (Lely and Saunders 2012). Such "data compression" may be permitted by inclusion in the process of indeterminate elements to be resolved only in execution and/or an efficient formulation of the generative rules (e.g., by the use of iterative procedures).

A seminal example of a generative musical process is the one used by John Cage in the making of his score to *Music of Changes* (1951). Cage's initial data comprised a set of charts containing various invented musical features. By his account, the generative rules involved an iterative process of selecting entries from the charts using chance procedures and then combining those selections to yield musical figures. These figures were then inscribed in a fully prescriptive and largely conventional score for subsequent performance by a pianist (Cage [1952] 1961). In process pieces of the 1960s and 1970s, a composer might instead describe in a relatively succinct *process score* some music-generative procedure to be enacted by performers in real time rather than enacting it themselves in advance. A classic example is Steve Reich's *Piano Phase* (1967), wherein two pianists—beginning in unison—each repeat the same brief melody in steady eighth notes, one pianist periodically accelerating slightly so as to slowly pull ahead of the other. A new and surprising aggregate musical pattern subsequently appears each time that the lag between performers is an integral number of eighth notes. Typical performances of *Piano Phase* last 15 to 20 minutes, but its published score comprises only thirty-two measures (and, in principle, three measures with instructions would suffice).

Generative processes feature in most of Tenney's music since 1960. His early attraction to them was nourished by Edgard Varèse's analogy between musical forms and the products of crystal growth and by D'Arcy Thompson's theories of organic growth under the influence of physical forces (section 4.1). His random sequencing of tape snippets in *Collage #1 ("Blue Suede")* (1961) inherited chance procedures from Cage's music of the 1950s, such as *Music of Changes*. Tenney's computer music of 1963–64 automated chance procedures using stochastic algorithms, which—given an economical set of initial input data—generated all aspects of the music down to individual digital samples without further intervention by the composer.

With his return to instrumental composition in the 1970s, Tenney's compositions continued to feature generative processes. In many of these pieces, the indeterminate factor of stochastic computation was supplanted by one of constrained choice in performance. This post-Cagean element of indeterminacy sometimes took the form of what Tenney termed an *available-pitch procedure*, with *Clang* (1972) providing the earliest instance (section 8.2). In such a procedure, each performer independently selects and plays pitches from a limited collection, which typically undergoes a composed evolution that is itself rule-governed. On the other hand, some of his pieces of this era involve processes that are thoroughly deterministic. These include a number of texturally complex canons in which the internal structure and/or entrance schedules of the canonic voices are rule-governed, *Spectral CANON for CONLON Nancarrow* (1974) providing an example (section 8.3). Other pieces such as *Saxony* (1978) represent hybrids in which a canonic aspect is induced by a fixed tape-delay system while the players pursue a partially indeterminate available-pitch procedure.

A distinction must be respected between a generative process itself and the listener's apprehension of it as such. A musical example may not be recognized as the outcome of a generative process if that process is sufficiently complex or involves indeterminacy. For instance, Tenney's electroacoustic algorithmic composition *Ergodos II* (1964) is a process piece in the sense that the computer's inputs and fixed generative rules were stipulated in advance, after which the generation of musical particulars proceeded autonomously of the composer. No listener, however, is likely to intuit the details of the underlying generative process (or perhaps even its existence) from the highly unpredictable sequence of audible features in *Ergodos II*. In contrast, a characteristic of many paradigmatic process pieces is a lucid algorithmic simplicity by virtue of which the generative process (in whole or in outline) is readily inferable by ear. Examples include many of Reich's early compositions, including *Piano Phase*, and many of Tenney's pieces of the 1970s. Inference of the processual algorithm from its audible upshot is often abetted by some combination therein of gradual pacing, predictability, and didactic exposition (as in a succession of canonic entrances).

Apprehensibility of the process can in itself serve a number of significant musical functions.[5] The first of these renovates Arnold Schoenberg's conception of form as primarily serving "to express ideas in a comprehensible manner" by making them memorable (1975, 381, 399). Tenney was interested neither in expression nor in musical "ideas" in Schoenberg's thematic sense. Moreover, his own principal conception of form was as an object of perception, and he typically disavowed with respect to his own work Schoenberg's conception of form as a means for ensuring comprehensibility (Tenney [1996a] 2015, 396). Nonetheless, I would argue that in many of his pieces, lucid process in fact supports global structural comprehensibility in the sense that it situates musical events or conditions within a manifest logical framework—in other words, that it overtly rationalizes their advent at particular times and/or in particular contexts rather than others. Indeed, in a late unpublished interview, Tenney appeared to reconsider his earlier narrower pronouncements, admitting that "maybe in some cases I have been influenced by Schoenberg's idea about form, which was that form is a means of ensuring comprehensibility, that it can be used to clarify content" (2000c).

Moreover, such manifest processual logic sometimes has potent affective consequences. For instance, a gradual monotonic process may evoke a sense of inexorable direction and attendant expectation. Such expectancy sometimes furnishes the setup for musical surprises, as when a predictable executional trajectory begets an unpredicted perceptual outcome. Precisely because the performance involves an apparently prosaic and predictable process, such revelatory events may evoke responses of wonder with powerful connotations of transcendence. Examples include the surprising resultant patterns that periodically emerge in Reich's *Piano Phase* as the lag between instruments smoothly increases, as well as the flood of noise that overwhelms the ear in Tenney's *Having Never Written a Note for Percussion* (1971) as the results of the player's continuously intensifying excitation of the tam-tam cross discrete acoustical and psychoacoustical thresholds. Similarly, Tenney's accumulative canons—such as *Spectral CANON for CONLON Nancarrow* (1974) and *Wake for Charles Ives* (1974–75)—eventually produce complexly structured resultants that are not easily foreseen from the apparently simple materials and inexorable processes set forth at their openings.

On the other hand, considered at the largest formal scale, Tenney's efficient processes often yield austere and monolithic global forms that suggest a musical counterpart to minimalist sculpture. The iconic shapes of pieces such as *Koan* (1971) and *Having Never Written a Note for Percussion* (1971) linger in memory, providing vivid illustrations of Tenney's concept of form "as an object of perception"—as a "thing in itself" rather than a means to an end (section 1.2.1). The singular boldness of these large-scale morphologies is often accentuated by a suppression of medium-scale formal features, typically via very gradual change.

6.1.2 Gradualness

To say that the change in some measure of a quantity is *gradual* assumes a particular temporal span within which that quantity is observed and over the course of which change in the given measure is deemed modest. That measure might simply be related to the instantaneous value of the quantity. Alternatively, it might be some statistical attribute of the quantity's values—such as their mean, range, morphology, or interrelations—observed over the course of a movable temporal frame or *analysis window* that is shorter than the full temporal record. For instance, the local sound configurations of John Cage's *Music of Changes*—which Cage calls "aggregates" and "constellations"—last just a few seconds each, and they are audibly diverse. On the other hand, the statistical attributes of the music when observed over any given minute are roughly similar to those obtaining in any other minute, demonstrating a statistical parametric constancy that Tenney termed *ergodicity* (section 4.2). Thus *Music of Changes* is locally unpredictable but globally predictable. Its form evinces no medium- or large-scale parametric shapes or structures that might delineate sections, trajectories, transitions, climaxes, or releases. Instead, at large scales it exhibits apparent stasis—the limiting case of gradualness. In other words, a large-scale "bird's-eye" view of the music is information poor, while a smaller-scale "ant's-eye" view (on the scale of a few aggregates or smaller) is relatively information rich. If a concerted listening gravitates to musical information where it can be found, after an initial period of adjustment the listener is apt to preferentially focus on the details of aggregates/constellations and perhaps the comparison of temporally proximate configurations. Indeed, in comparison to traditional piano music, listeners to *Music of Changes* often report a heightened awareness of local articulations, durations, releases, dynamics, timbres, partials, noises, and the morphologies and proportions of all of these separately and together. The suppression of distinctive medium- and large-scale formal features thus promotes attention to local details that might otherwise be overlooked or disregarded.

Tenney's process pieces of the early 1970s often restrict even further the timeframes on which musical information is primarily available, promoting attention to features at very large and very small timescales. They might thus be regarded as extrapolations of Tenney's interests of the early 1960s in—at the large scale— temporal gestalt formation and—at the small—the analysis of timbre. As noted above, the characteristic proportions of salient perceptual objects in such pieces extend, on the one hand, to their monumental overall morphologies. On the other hand, articulation at the local level is sometimes suppressed to the limiting condition of sonic *continuity*. In a November 1971 letter to Carolee Schneemann, Tenney described his recent music: "The key word is Continuity—as though the whole piece were one single sound, and it often is just that. Much less interested now in a 'sequence of events'. They tend to be more static—or approximate a kind of static equilibrium. Stemming, perhaps, from aspects of the *Noise Study* and *Fabric for Che*" (Schneemann 2010, 183).

Approaching this limit of nearly static continuity, the music invites a radical auditory reorientation: a shift in the balance of attention away from the tracking of information presented sequentially and toward the scanning of information presented synchronously. Concurrently audible sound components obligingly proliferate in the awareness of an attentive listener. Absent conventional cues regarding the musical importance of particular percepts, all audible features become potential objects of interest. Not even the criterion of salience escapes this anarchic leveling of value hierarchies: the fact that a sound component is barely audible by no means entails that it is less worthy of close attention—the opposite might as easily be true. Indeed, features so delicate that careful concentration is required in order to discern them at all—such as harmonic partials in *Swell Piece No. 2* (1971) or *Koan* (1971)—may participate in remarkable structures. Progressive concentration of attentional focus in order to discern ever finer sonic features and relationships produces an experience of form that goes *into* as much as *along*.

In these works, the listening experience is typically animated in part by subtle acoustical variations and in part by the voluntary or involuntary travel of the listener's attention among registers, aspects of sound, apparent foreground/background, and perceptual gestalts versus components thereof. This indeterminate subjective factor makes an important contribution to form as experienced in much of Tenney's work since the late 1960s, in which each listener is invited to trace their own unique aural pathway through the music. In such cases, the musical texture often comprises a profusion of concurrent features so that listening attention cannot apprehend all of them together but instead roves among them like the beam of a searchlight traversing a landscape or an eye scanning a painting. The paradigmatic example is surely *For Ann (rising)* (1969), the body of which is acoustically periodic but perceptually highly variable. As Tenney put it:

> In music . . . it is possible to create a situation in which the indeterminate character of the future is suspended for a while, thereby suspending also anticipation, surprise, and thus, drama—leaving nothing to be concerned with but the *present*. In *For Ann (rising)*, as in the later "Koans" and a few other pieces, this "present" involves micro-variations in the sounds themselves, made more perceptible by the pieces' determinate forms, but it also involves the listener's internal, subjective processes in a way that is less obscured by drama—here, the music is *in you*. (1978b)[6]

6.1.3 Ramps and Swells

Tenney's penchant for continuous parametric transformations over time often manifested in particular archetypal morphologies: the *ramp* and the *swell*. These shapes are found throughout his oeuvre but emerge with particular clarity and abundance in his music after 1970. They may appear on any temporal scale and in any musical parameter as its determinate value, as its mean statistical value, or as a bound on its range. They may occur subject to various transformations such as offsets, scalings, deformations, and reflections, as illustrated in figure

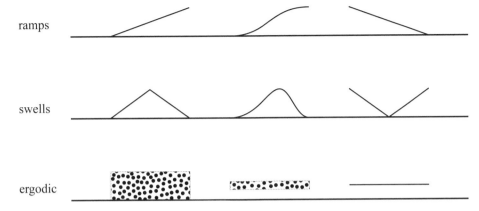

FIGURE 6.1. Some elementary formal morphologies common in Tenney's music.

6.1. A ramp, for instance, may be distorted so that it departs and approaches its extremal values more gradually, and for this purpose Tenney sometimes expressed it mathematically as a segment of a raised cosine curve. A constant value might be construed as either a ramp or swell in the limiting case where the parametric range is reduced to zero.

The swell or arch shape takes its name from the dynamic envelope applied to individual tones in *Swell Piece* (1967). Although it can be decomposed into the succession of an ascending ramp and a descending ramp, the swell appears so often in Tenney's music that it warrants a separate designation. Especially when appearing at large formal scales, the swell may be smoothed and asymmetrical, with its peak shifted to near its golden section (approximately 0.618 of its total duration; section 4.6, note 31).

More complex formal morphologies can be constructed by concatenation or superimposition of these elementary ones. In the successive sections of Tenney's computer-generated *Dialogue* (1963), for instance, each parametric mean describes an offset linear ramp. In the determinate pitch trajectories of *Koan* (1971) for solo violin, opening and closing intervallic swells are superimposed on a gradually ascending ramp. Such a concatenation of opening-and-closing intervallic swells is itself a notably common form in Tenney's music, appearing variously elaborated in *A Rose Is a Rose Is a Round* (1970), *Quiet Fan for Erik Satie* (1970/1971), *Beast* (1971), *Koan* (1971), *Cellogram* (1971), *Koan for String Quartet* (1984), and *To Weave (a meditation)* (2003).

Tenney discusses ramps and swells as part of his typology of large-scale formal morphologies in a 1970 essay entitled "Form in Twentieth-Century Music" ([1970] 2015, 157). To these he adds a third formal archetype: the statistically static or *ergodic* form, which is also depicted in figure 6.1.[7] Tenney associated ergodic forms with the music of John Cage in the 1950s and used them in a number of his own compositions as well. They are discussed more extensively in section 4.2.

6.2 *For Ann (rising)* (1969)

ELECTRONIC MUSIC (ONE-CHANNEL FIXED MEDIA)
11 mins., 45 secs.

Although *For Ann (rising)* is one of Tenney's best-known works, decades after composition its profound reconception of music listening remains a radical aesthetic challenge and provocation. It presents at once an extreme of rigidly determined minimalist audio design and a perceptual experience of great potential variability, ranging from the austere to the rococo. To an unprecedented degree the music invites the active participation of the listener in the constitution of their subjective experience, pursuing a post-Cagean listener-centered aesthetic to an extraordinary culmination.

For Ann (rising) was composed in New York City not long before Tenney's departure for California to take up a teaching position at the recently opened California Institute of the Arts. It presages the dramatic changes in his musical concerns that would accompany this move.

> In March 1969, I made what turned out to be my last piece of electronic (or computer generated) music—*For Ann (rising)*. I suppose this piece represents some sort of reaction away from the complexities of most of my earlier work—as it was perhaps a reaction to the complexities of life in New York in the 1960s. I like to think that it was not a negation, however, but a kind of turning inward, through which I first began to feel the possibility of old dichotomies dissolving—continuity vs. discontinuity, determinacy vs. indeterminacy, etc.—becoming indistinguishable at a point reached when either is carried to an extreme.[8]

For Ann (rising) presents a static texture of overlapping sine-wave glissandi that rise in parallel from the extreme bass to the extreme treble. The piece went through a succession of early incarnations, each using a different technical approach to try to more accurately realize a smooth and prolonged glissando. The first used a tape recording of a descending chromatic scale played on the piano with the sustaining pedal depressed, which was then reversed to ascend and to deemphasize attacks. Delayed versions of this recording were then superimposed (Tenney 2008, 84–85). Tenney found the result noisy and insufficiently smooth, so he made a second version by manually sweeping the frequency of a hardware oscillator. In order to achieve the full frequency sweep, the range setting of the oscillator had to be switched, necessitating the splicing together of separate tape recordings in order to assemble a complete glissando. Still dissatisfied with imperfections remaining at the splice, Tenney telephoned a friend, composer Jean-Claude Risset, who had taken up a position at Bell Labs following Tenney's departure. He asked Risset to send him a single computer-generated glissando, from which he then created the complete piece using tape-mixing techniques (Tenney 2000f).[9] Plans to commercially release this recording on 45 rpm vinyl, however, came to naught after Tenney refused to allow the record company to issue a retrograded version of the recording as the B-side: "I had actually listened to a section of a very early version of it and I found it depressing. It was like always coming down. [*laughter*] It was a real downer! [*laughter*] So I refused to let it be done" (Tenney 1996d, 27).[10] As a result, *For Ann (rising)* was not commercially released until 1984, at which time it appeared on an audio cassette accompanying a magazine issue dedicated to Tenney's work.[11] However, not even this version was entirely free from technical issues, betraying the difficulty of achieving accurate timing with tape techniques: the glissandi become quite unevenly spaced by the end of the recording.

Finally, in 1991 sound engineer Tom Erbe generated an accurate high-fidelity version of *For Ann (rising)* to Tenney's specifications via computer synthesis. The results are represented in figure 6.2, which provides a spectrogram of the opening to *For Ann (rising)* showing the registral distribution of sound energy as a function of time.[12] The final version comprises 240 identical sine wave sweeps. Each of these lasts 37.8 seconds and rises linearly in pitch at a rate of 4.2 seconds per octave for a total of nine octaves from A_0 to A_9. Each sweep has a trapezoidal amplitude envelope that rises from zero to full gain in the first two octaves, stays at full gain for the five middle octaves, and drops from full to zero gain over the course of the top two octaves of each sweep. A new sweep starts every 2.8 seconds. The resulting pitch interval between registrally adjacent sweeps is a minor sixth in 12TET.[13] Once a full complement of glissandi has entered, the aggregate texture persists without any further objective evolution whatsoever, repeating periodically every 2.8 seconds for more than 10 minutes. At any one moment during this span, thirteen or fourteen glissandi are simultaneously present, and seven or eight of them are at full gain. At the conclusion of the piece the last sine tones implacably rise into the treble, vanishing as they finish their glissandi so as to retrograde-invert the opening.[14]

The aggregate signal heard in *For Ann (rising)* is related to that of the *Shepard tone*, named after cognitive scientist Roger N. Shepard, alongside whom Tenney worked at Bell Labs in the early 1960s (Shepard 1964). Shepard tones have both discrete (scalewise) and continuous (gliding) incarnations. A continuous version corresponds closely to the signal found in *For Ann (rising)*, but with an octave rather than a minor sixth between adjacent sine tones. In a classic Shepard tone, the strong perceptual fusion of the octave-separated tones, coupled with the smooth fade-in of sine waves in the bass and their similar fade-out in the treble, produces the paradoxical sensation of a single tone that continually rises without getting any higher. An analogue in the visual modality is a Penrose staircase, which appears to rise (or fall) continuously without changing net elevation (Penrose and Penrose 1958), a famous example of which appears in artist M. C. Escher's lithograph *Ascending and Descending* (1960). Tenney, however, contrasted Shepard's motivations as a cognitive scientist to his own as a composer.

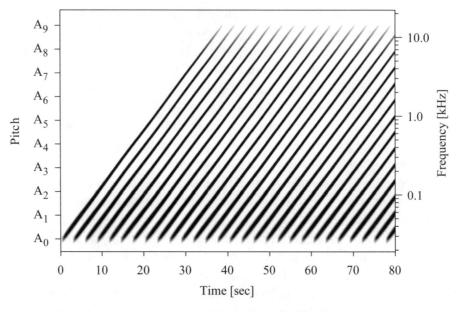

FIGURE 6.2. A spectrogram of the first 80 seconds of *For Ann (rising)*.

I didn't want to create an illusion, I was just trying to carry forward a notion developed toward the end of my Bell Labs period into a piece some five years later. I was working with the idea that it was not necessary anymore to think in terms of discrete sounds that began and ended in relatively short times. It occurred to me that this was a hangover from a time when the only way we could produce sounds was by an action that caused an object to vibrate, which would then stop vibrating after a little while. So I began thinking instead about a notion of continuity, which I first used in the piece called *Fabric for Che* (1967). (Tenney 2000f)[15]

Whereas Tenney's *Ergodos II* (1964) had embraced *statistical* homogeneity, *For Ann (rising)* extended such formal consistency to an absolutely deterministic periodicity. Despite its *acoustical* uniformity, however, the music is by no means *perceptually* static but instead evokes a varied profusion of audible impressions as the ear moves between sonic features. The perceptual articulation of such a continuous sound signal cannot be accounted for by a conventional theory of musical segmentation that attributes the delineation of temporal units to sonic contrasts. In fact, around the year 2000, Tenney made to me the astonishing remark that he had composed *For Ann (rising)* in part to subvert the precepts of "Meta∤Hodos" ([1961] 2015), his own influential treatise on musical segmentation. "Meta∤Hodos" posited that in music the perceived segregation of temporal gestalts (at various hierarchical levels) was induced by changes appearing in one or more musical parameters (such as pitch, dynamic, timbre, etc.; section 3.4), and Tenney applied this principle pervasively in his computer music of the early 1960s. The uninterrupted acoustical continuity of *For Ann (rising)*, on the other hand, affords no such perceptual contrasts in order to cue temporal segmentation.[16]

Such segmentation of auditory stimuli at various temporal scales into discrete events and event groupings is customarily an indispensable component of the perception of speech and music. The perceived parametric characteristics of such groupings (such as their register, duration, tempo, dynamic, timbre, and the profiles thereof), as well as relationships between those characteristics, provide a basis for the cognition of most music; consequently, criteria for segmentation also constitute a basis for explicit analysis of most music as heard. In the absence of the cues to temporal segmentation that music customarily affords, the analyst must confront the extraordinary prerequisite question of what it means to "listen to *For Ann (rising)*" at all.

The work seems to demand an analytical approach as unorthodox as its musical content. The reader is encouraged to have a recording of *For Ann (rising)* at hand in order to gauge their own experience of it, a measure without which the following descriptions are unlikely to be very meaningful. I will consider three plausible listening modes that I will call *observant*, *exploratory*, and *ludic*, each of which in turn implies a more active role for the listener than the last.

An *observant* listening to *For Ann (rising)* comes closest to the receptive mode customarily engaged in passively listening to music in a familiar style, in which the perception and cognition of musical features largely proceed automatically without significant moment-to-moment exercise of the listener's discretion. An important distinction is that the apprehension of the music's static character soon suspends anticipatory listening and instead invites attention on the part of the listener to local phenomenal detail and a self-reflexive observation of their own perceptual apparatus's response to the unusual stimulus.

Tenney's choice of a tempered minor sixth between sine tones—rather than the octave interval characteristic of classic Shepard tones—proves significant because it deters their ready fusion into a single pitched percept, the individual tones instead being relatively easy to discriminate in pitch. In an observant listening mode, hearing tends to follow some such individual glissando for a brief duration before involuntarily switching to another one, this process repeating again and again as the ear wanders to various registers. The lowest register seems relatively quiet on account of both the ear's reduced sensitivity at low frequencies and the amplitude envelope applied to the sine tones, but it also seems darker, and tones therein exhibit a slight warble as they enter. Tones in the frequency range from 2 to 5 kHz, where the ear's sensitivity is greatest, seem not only loudest but also most *present* or near. The register above 5 kHz is generally quieter in accordance with the ear's reduced sensitivity therein, but tones develop a bright sizzle at its high end. Sometimes odd impressions of amplitude modulation or frequency quantization (the sense that pitches are ascending in steps rather than continuously) appear as if in the periphery of attention, but careful fixation on any single tone reveals no such variations.

Curiously, the ear does not automatically tend to follow the seemingly obvious course of tracking a single tone to its high-register terminus. In fact, following a single tone from its low-register entrance to its conclusion proves extraordinarily difficult—I have never succeeded, although I more than once observed a grinning Tenney challenge groups of listeners to try to do so. Nevertheless, adopting such a deliberate listening strategy shifts the perceptual mode from *observant* to *exploratory* as the intentions of the listener begin to govern significant aspects of their local musical experience. Tenney alluded to such a distinction between listening modes in a late interview: "So little seems to be happening, yet there is continual change, partly because it appears to be in some way completely predictable, right? The mind starts moving around in the sound in an extremely interesting way, and everyone is taking a different path through it. You can just sit there and follow unintentionally and find yourself going here and there or you can actually focus your hearing and cause yourself to change your focus within the texture" (2000f).

Attempting to follow without distraction a single glissando throughout its entire ascent amounts to adopting an *attentional trajectory* such as depicted in figure 6.3(a), wherein a thick gray line representing the focus of listening attention coincides with a thinner black line representing a single complete glissando. For me, as indicated above, this particular trajectory proves infeasible in practice. Despite careful concentration, like an unskilled surfer, my ear at some point invariably "falls off" whichever glissando it is attempting to follow in favor of some lower one. On the other hand, many other attentional trajectories prove quite feasible, and some of these are depicted in the remaining parts of figure 6.3. For instance, it is possible for a listener to follow a single glissando upward from an arbitrarily chosen initial pitch just long enough for the next lower glissando to reach that pitch, at which time the listener can then switch their attention to the lower glissando. Repeating this process creates a loop whose period equals the 2.8-second lag between successive glissandi, as shown in figure 6.3(b), thus providing a regular rhythmic articulation. In other words, *For Ann (rising)* has a slow but perfectly clear *beat*, but only if the listener forms an intention to listen in a manner that reveals it. This is characteristic of what I am calling an *exploratory* listening mode, wherein the explicit intentions of the listener determine important aspects of their musical experience.

The formulation of other exploratory listening programs occasions curiosity and inventiveness. For instance, the attentional trajectory of figure 6.3(b) can be transposed to higher and lower registers, while figure 6.3(c) shows two variations of that trajectory that traverse registers. The latter may be easiest to hear by directing attention along the *average attentional trajectories* represented by dashed black lines, a procedure that again summons surfing or skiing metaphors as the ear touches briefly on each glissando in succession. The discontinuities where the ear skips from one glissando to another again articulate regular rhythms, although their tempos differ from that associated with figure 6.3(b). An attentional trajectory coinciding with a glissando will be unarticulated (for however long the ear can follow it!), while other attentional trajectories will be articulated at tempos that increase with the divergence of their average slope from that of the glissandi. More complex paths can be formulated, such as the periodic trajectory depicted in figure 6.3(d), which leaps back and forth between registers. The many other possible listening schemes include trajectories that follow more complex contours, ones that undergo directed processes such as accelerando and ritardando, and even multiple trajectories in counterpoint with one another.

At some point, the listener may well opt to discontinue the formulation of explicit listening tasks in favor of improvisatory play, creating their own unique aural experiences as they direct their attention across the matrix of glissandi like a skier bouncing among moguls. In such a *ludic* listening mode, *For Ann (rising)* resembles less a *composition* than an *instrument* that the listener plays with their attention.

The unusually active role offered to the listener by *For Ann (rising)* accords with Tenney's belief that an epochal aesthetic shift had been induced by the work of John Cage. In a late unpublished essay, Tenney described this change as reorientation toward a more listener-centered musical culture.

> One of Cage's answers to the question "what is your definition of music?" [was] to the effect that "it is work." Another time, in response to the same question, he answered "sounds heard." I especially like this definition, and I find it really interesting that *there is no composer* in this definition. What this means to me is that there has been (or is, or will be) a shift of focus in the musical enterprise from the thoughts and feelings of the composer (and often of the performer, as well) to the experience of the listener. It is thus that listening experience which is central to what music is (or was, or will be), and this should be seen as an invitation to a more active participation in the shaping of that experience by the listener, compared to the relatively passive role assumed during the "operatic era." (2000b)[17]

For Ann (rising) represents a watershed in Tenney's compositional style, as he readily acknowledged in a late interview:

> *In a way, many of your early tape pieces are positively Baroque in comparison with some of the things you've been doing over the last ten or fifteen years.*

> Yeah. And all of that changed with *For Ann (rising)*. In fact, that's the watershed. Everything before that I think of as a kind of different world. Everything after that is where I still am now. (2008, 84)

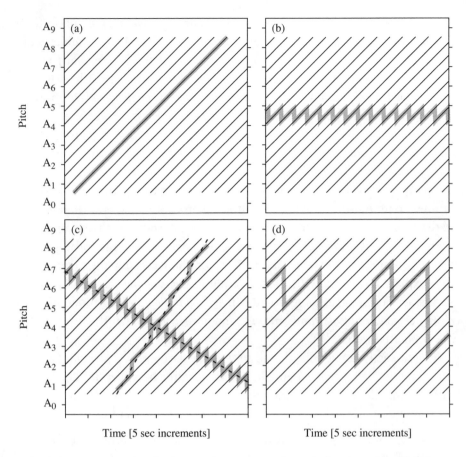

FIGURE 6.3. Some proposed attentional trajectories through the glissandi of *For Ann (rising)*.

In particular, many of his ensuing compositions would adopt economical formal designs for the close examination of perceptual processes. Moreover, many would feature complex but static (or slowly evolving) textures through which a listener could choose their own aural path with a degree of autonomy. *For Ann (rising)*, however, remains extraordinary for the directness with which it confronts that possibility. During its static middle expanse, it offers all of its musical potentialities together and continually.

6.3 *Postal Pieces* (1965–71)

durations are variable unless otherwise noted

Scorecard No. 1: *Beast*	(July 30, 1971)
Scorecard No. 2: *A Rose Is a Rose Is a Round*	(March 1970)
Scorecard No. 3: *(night)*	(August 6, 1971)
Scorecard No. 4: *Koan*	(August 16, 1971)

Scorecard No. 5: *Maximusic* (June 16, 1965)
Scorecard No. 6: *Swell Piece* (December 1967)
Scorecard No. 7: *Swell Pieces Nos. 2 & 3* (March 1971)
Scorecard No. 8: *August Harp* (August 17, 1971)
Scorecard No. 9: *Cellogram* (August 17, 1971)
Scorecard No. 10: *Having Never Written a Note for Percussion* (August 6, 1971)

Along with *For Ann (rising)*, the *Postal Pieces* are, to many listeners, the best-known and most emblematic of Tenney's compositions. They comprise eleven works succinctly notated on ten postcards ("scorecards"), which were mailed to friends and colleagues.[18] Each piece has a dedicatee, many of whom were Tenney's colleagues at the California Institute of the Arts, while others were friends from his years in New York. Most were completed in 1971—five of them in a period of just three weeks during the summer. Three, however, were completed earlier and recruited for the set well after the fact, as indicated in the above listing.

The *Postal Pieces* captured a sudden burst of exploratory energy following the aesthetic watershed of *For Ann (rising)* and seemingly nourished by the composer's fresh start in California. Tenney commented on his changing musical concerns in a text that he considered for distribution on a final eleventh nonmusical scorecard entitled *Valentine Manifesto* but that has only recently been published. The following is an extended quotation from that statement.

I have always been concerned with the tangible experiencing of sound, and I have failed more often than I have succeeded in realizing this or manifesting it in my music. The problem here has usually seemed to be a kind of disparity between technique or texture or even tempo and this "tangibility" that I was after—this sense of *sounding* sound. In the last four or five years, though, my work has changed in a direction that perhaps comes closer to this ideal than it ever had before. The objective characteristics that seem to have brought this about are CONTINUITY and SIMPLICITY, and these have thus almost become esthetic goals in themselves. By continuity I mean primarily temporal continuity—less a marking of time or even an organizing of discrete events in time and more a continuous flow *in* time, evoking a more internal, subjective experiencing of both sound *and* time. As for simplicity, it is as in my own life now, finding richness and nourishment in the common-place, the undramatic, as though reaching for a kind of peace, and a joy in that peace. But the "simple" is never simply that—there are complexities and resonances as deep as we are willing or able to perceive them. Finally, the format of these scores (as post cards) relates to (and is an attempt to solve) an old problem of mine, namely, getting the music out—into the world. It has always been difficult for me to complete the act of composition to the point of launching a new piece on some life of its own apart from me—and thus to take full responsibility for its potential existence as a sound- (as well as a social) phenomenon. I have had plenty of cooperation from the publishing fraternity in perpetuating this problem of mine, but perhaps it's not entirely the fault of my numerous (non-) publishers. Some of the pieces in this series are old, some are new. Some of them are obviously trifles, some are not. In any case, events have conspired to bring them into their present form.[19]

Tenney's new interest since *For Ann (rising)* in the perceptual affordances of continuity largely replaced the concern with parametric and formal variety that characterized his computer music of the early 1960s (cf. section 4.2). He elaborated on the intended musical effects of this new continuity in a 1978 interview with composer Gayle Young.

> *Your postcard pieces, for example, are essentially a single musical gesture that continues until it's over.*
>
> They involve a very high degree of predictability. If the audience can just *believe* it, after they've heard the first twenty seconds of the piece, they can almost determine what's going to happen the whole rest of the time. When they know that's the case, they don't have to *worry* about it anymore. . . . What they can do is begin to really *listen* to the sounds, get inside them, notice the details, and consider or meditate on the overall shape of the piece, simple as it may be. It's often interesting how within a simple shape there can be relationships that are surprising. It's curious—in a way, the result in this highly determinate situation is the same as in an indeterminate one, where things are changing so rapidly and unpredictably that you lose any sense of drama there, too. Now people react to that in two different ways: some are angry about it, because they expect, and demand, meaningful drama. But if you can relax that demand and say, "no, this is *not* drama, this is just 'change'" [*laughs*]—then you can listen to the sounds for themselves rather than in relation to what preceded or what will follow. (Tenney 1978a, 16)[20]

For the listener, a necessary first step may be a recalibration of their assumptions regarding what counts as noteworthy musical material from relatively gross features such as tones, chords, motives, and meters to ones that are subtler and often less readily audible. These may include high partials, quiet beating patterns, subtle timbral contrasts, and other aspects that, in their delicacy, recede toward the horizons of virtuoso listening. As Tenney indicated in *Valentine Manifesto*, "the 'simple' is never simply that—there are complexities and resonances as deep as we are willing or able to perceive them." The experience of the observer is partly constituted by their own choices of when, where, and how to direct their attention. As in much of Tenney's music since *For Ann (rising)*, this entails an active listening posture in which the listener assumes some autonomous responsibility and initiative for navigating the sound world that the composer and performers have made available.

The following sections explore two of the best-known and most emblematic of these remarkable pieces: *Koan* for solo violin and *Having Never Written a Note for Percussion*. The remaining *Postal Pieces* are all addressed in volume 2, section 5.4.

6.3.1 *Koan* (1971)

for Malcolm Goldstein
VIOLIN
variable duration

As Tenney described it, "*Koan* for solo violin is one of ten 'Postal Pieces': scores which fit on a postcard, and have the character of a sonic 'koan'—a difficult, often paradoxical question given to the Zen student as a means of achieving 'enlightenment.' An unpredictable experience, for both the performer and the listener, arises out of an apparently predictable, mechanical, yet finally 'impossible' musical task."[21] The most outwardly austere of the set, *Koan* epitomizes Tenney's project in the *Postal Pieces* of eliminating musical drama so that the listener can "begin to really *listen* to the sounds, get inside them, notice the details, and consider or meditate on the overall shape of the piece, simple as it may be" (Tenney 1978a, 16).

The score calls for a slow cross-string bowed tremolo that gradually ascends in register, ultimately traversing all the strings of the violin. As shown in figure 6.4, this begins with a rocking fifth on the open G and D strings, which in measure 1 very slowly closes to a unison and then opens again in measure 2 as the pitch on the stopped (G) string microtonally ascends. When the moving pitch reaches A_4 at the end of measure 2, it is transferred to the open A string and becomes the stationary pitch, below which the pitch on the (now stopped) D string gradually ascends. Thus measures 3 and 4 repeat the pattern of measures 1 and 2 transposed up a fifth and now on the instrument's inner strings. The pattern is repeated yet again on the A and E strings, before the A string's pitch in the final measure breaks free of the cycle, rising high into the treble but also fading in dynamic as the performer slowly moves the bow toward the bridge. The process thus highlights and contrasts the timbres of the various strings, progressing from the dark reedy resonance of the G string through the more subdued colors of the inner strings, to the searing luminance of the E string before concluding with the gauzy shimmer of *molto sul ponticello*.

The score is notationally unambiguous about the downbeat location, which begins on the lower pitch but switches to the higher in measure 2, alternating every two measures thereafter. In performance, however, the perceived metrical emphasis is anything but determinate, switching between the pitches in response to subtle variations in the performer's articulation or as listening attention moves from one pitch to the other. On other occasions the higher and lower pitches may segregate into separate auditory streams (i.e., *polyphonic voices*), the ear oblivious to their alternation as each pulses independently. This tends to happen most readily when the two pitches are separated by a relatively large interval, while at small intervals they tend to coalesce into a single auditory stream comprising a slow trill or tremolo.[22]

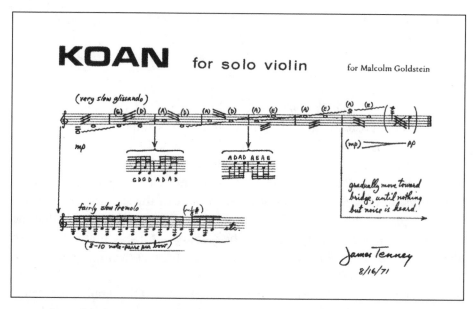

FIGURE 6.4. The score to *Koan*.

Behind the foreground sonic grill of the unbroken tremolo, subtle timbres, resonances, decays, and beatings may be descried, all of which vary over the course of the movement as the music traverses the instrument's registers. These appear because although the two pitches are temporally disjunct in the notation, in practice the strings of the instrument ring following excitation, especially the lower strings and the open string in each tremolo. Close listening thus reveals that the interval between the strings quietly sounds not only melodically but also harmonically. This becomes particularly noticeable for small intervals, where the ringing tone beats against the bowed one. In the high register, especially in the final measure, rising and/or falling combination tones sometimes become faintly audible below the two acoustical tones if the sound from the instrument is loud enough (in other words, if the listener is close enough to the performer).[23]

Figure 6.5 provides a spectrogram of an entire recording of *Koan*, showing the registral distribution of sound energy as a function of time.[24] The lowest-frequency curves represent the fundamentals of the two tones and thus provide a graphic score, while their harmonics higher in the figure display a variety of intersections and patterns. As the two tones approach unison at the end of measure 1, for instance, in addition to the beating of ringing tones mentioned above, a number of other sonic effects emerge. As the figure shows, not only the fundamentals of the two tones but also all of their higher harmonics converge. As they do so, they become particularly audible so that the ear is easily lured upward among them, in which case it discovers that these higher harmonics, like the fundamentals, are slowly trilling in pairs and beating against one another.

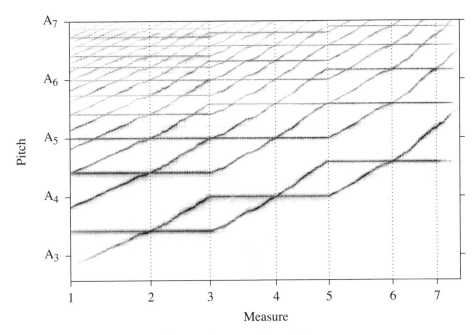

FIGURE 6.5. A spectrogram of a complete recording of *Koan*.

At the moment of unison, many ringing harmonics become clearly audible, the ear leaping upward in the series. Once thus spotlighted, high harmonic pitches remain audible as the tones quit their unison, multiple harmonic trills again opening as the ear skips among them.[25]

Harmonic alignments are audible at various points between the unisons as well. As the interval between the tones approaches a fifth their frequency ratio approaches 3/2. Every third harmonic of the lower tone accordingly converges with an even-numbered harmonic of the higher tone, since these frequencies of convergence represent the common multiples of the two fundamental frequencies. The beating of these higher harmonics aurally highlights their convergence and divergence. In a very quiet room, similar harmonic convergences may be faintly audible at other intervals corresponding to relatively simple rational frequency ratios.

Although Tenney had not yet developed an explicit interest in harmonic perception per se, the varying degrees of consonance associated with the just intervals traversed by the violin tremolos are an intrinsic dimension of the listening experience in *Koan*. The most perceptually salient of these intervals are associated with low-order *superparticular ratios*, which are ratios whose numerator exceeds their denominator by one: the 4/3 just perfect fourth, 5/4 just major third, and 6/5 just minor third. The passage of the tremolo's moving tone through these and other harmonically simple dyads is audible and sometimes marked by noticeable convergences between harmonics.[26] Tenney would later explore these harmonic implications directly in *Koan for String Quartet* (1984), a harmonization of this solo version using extended just intonation (section 9.4).

Some commentators have remarked that *Koan* gives the impression of a continual rise in pitch (Belet 2008, 32–33; Féron 2014, 106). The spectrogram of figure 6.5 shows that this is true in the particular sense that the mean of the fundamental pitches continuously and linearly rises throughout the performance. While this average ascent surely contributes to the impression of continual rise, other factors may also participate. In point of fact, neither of the two fundamentals ascends continuously; instead, they take turns rising and holding constant. However, if aural attention jumps down in register at the beginning of an even-numbered measure in order to continue tracking pitch *movement*, the experience is reminiscent of a common one in *For Ann (rising)* in which attention switches (voluntarily or involuntarily) from a glissando to the next lower one. The uninterrupted awareness of rise in pitch—even if it is not always of the same tone—may contribute to a general impression of continual rise.

Further inspection of figure 6.5 reveals subtler intimations of both continual rise and constancy. The rightward-rising diagonals surprisingly recall the spectrogram of *For Ann (rising)* in figure 6.2. Although the relative quietness of the upper partials and their perceptual fusion make it relatively difficult to aurally discriminate and move among them compared to that earlier electronic work, it is possible to a limited extent in a sufficiently quiet room. For instance, the second harmonic of the moving tone rises from G_4 through the first two measures before holding steady at A_5, at which time the third harmonic of the other tone begins to rise from that same A_5, extending the pitch glide up to B_6. With very careful attention it is sometimes possible to follow this harmonic pitch relay by ear. On the other hand, partials in common between the unmoving tones on open strings also result in certain harmonic pitches being retained for more than two measures, as when the third harmonic of the open A string (again A_5) becomes the second harmonic of the open D string at the end of measure 2. Indeed, an inaudibly high E_7 is a natural harmonic on all three of the A, D, and E strings and appears as a spectral line spanning the entire width of figure 6.5. While these connections among partials may be difficult or impossible to discriminate aurally, perhaps they nonetheless contribute to an impression of sonic continuity.

The focal depth of listening attention may at times retreat from the music's details to the unfurling of its bold large-scale morphology. Abstracted in memory, the rigorously simple form of *Koan* achieves an uncannily vivid affinity to minimalist sculpture. By implication, its gradual rise extends infinitely—a musical counterpart to Constantin Brancusi's *Infinite Column* (1918/1938). In experiential time, on the other hand, *Koan* unfolds with the inexorability of celestial motion. Its glacial progress in pitch, coupled with the metronomic pulsation of the tremolo, promotes an acute awareness of being carried slowly and steadily forward in the flow of time, past occasional formal landmarks. As the music ascends in register, its sonic complexity attenuates, refocusing attention onto basics: the pitch process and its quality of resolute advance. A committed performance amplifies this measured character. Sustaining the tremolo, preserving a steady rhythm and articulation, and achieving a uniform pacing are all challenges for the performer, whose visible concentration and resolve promote close shared attention to both sound and musical time. Like a Zen student repeating the elliptical text of a koan, by committing themselves to the discipline of *Koan*'s repetitive and humble process, performer and listener are obliquely led toward thresholds of perception.

6.3.2 *Having Never Written a Note for Percussion* (1971)

for John Bergamo
PERCUSSION
variable duration

Having Never Written a Note for Percussion is perhaps Tenney's best-known composition. Written for percussionist John Bergamo—then the director of the percussion program at CalArts—it has become something of a staple for new music percussionists but has also been recorded by rock bands and techno artists.[27]
Regarding his whimsical title, Tenney remarked:

> *Having Never Written a Note for Percussion* is one of my very most favorite pieces (though I often wonder who really wrote it). The title refers to the facts that (a) the only piece I had written for percussion before 1971 was *Maximusic*—a simply verbal score, and that (b) only one "note" is necessary to "notate" this piece. It was originally intended for any percussion instrument on which a sustained roll with the indicated dynamic variation is possible, and was intended to be played for an indeterminate length of time ("very long"), but I have since come to feel that the piece works best using tam-tam, and that it should last something between ten and twenty minutes. (1975b, 103)[28]

The following remarks address the customary tam-tam version of the piece. While it is not the only possible choice of instrumentation, this version admirably illustrates an important theme: that as the excitation of an instrument grows more energetic, the resulting sonic changes extend to much more than just loudness. If the score's single iconic swell distills the compositional impetus to a stark essence, the resulting music is surprisingly complex and ultimately disorienting.

Unlike oscillators that are effectively one-dimensional—such as the strings and air columns of most pitched instruments—a tam-tam, being effectively two-dimensional, produces pure-tone partials that do not reside in a harmonic series. In other words, its frequency spectrum is inharmonic rather than harmonic: the frequencies of its partials are not all multiples of some fundamental frequency but may instead be quite irregularly spaced.[29] An important perceptual consequence of this inharmonicity is that the gong's partials do not readily fuse into a gestalt tone with a unique pitch in the way that the partials of a harmonic

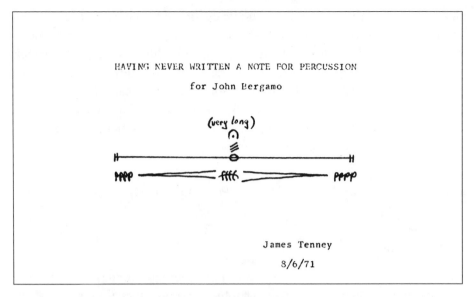

FIGURE 6.6. The score to *Having Never Written a Note for Percussion*.

series tend to do. For this reason and because of their sustained duration, individual lower partials emitted by a ringing tam-tam tend to be particularly easily discriminable by ear, provided that they are sufficiently differentiated in frequency that they do not present as a single beating tone.

Another important distinction between the inharmonic spectra of multidimensional oscillators like the tam-tam and the harmonic spectra of most pitched musical instruments is that the density of their various partial frequencies increases much more rapidly with increasing frequency (Heller 2013, 186–87, 535). This increase is visible at the right side of figure 6.7, which shows the spectrogram of a recording of the first half of *Having Never*, indicating the registral distribution of sound energy as it evolves in time. The frequency components present depend on the particular gong used, but their average spacing invariably widens toward the bass, while toward the treble it becomes extremely dense. Also visible at the right side of the figure (where the excitation is greatest) are certain darker frequency bands of greater energy and lighter bands of less. For instance, the midrange interval from about A_4 to E_6 is noticeably quieter than the ranges above and below it. Such banding is characteristic of tam-tam spectra.

In performance, the first gentle strokes of the beaters may elicit no audible sound at the audience's location. Gradually, as repeated strokes feed energy into the instrument, droning low-register tones become detectable, slowly and irregularly modulated in amplitude. At 1 minute into the performance illustrated in figure 6.7, frequency components near A_1, F-sharp$_2$, and D-sharp$_3$ are prominent, and a low hum has developed near A_0. As the force of the performer's strokes gradually increases, quieter and more closely spaced partials appear in progressively higher registers. While the amplitude of these tones is often audibly

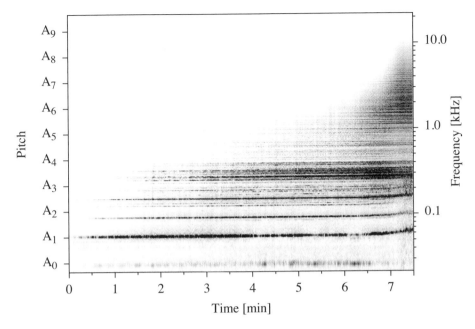

FIGURE 6.7. Spectrogram of the first half of a recording of *Having Never Written a Note for Percussion* performed on a tam-tam.

modulated as they beat against one another, they also more slowly but continually vary in amplitude in response to the precise timing and location of beater strokes. These gradual changes in prominence between closely spaced tones manifest as meandering legato melody and/or chords in the middle register (from about E_3 to A_4 in figure 6.7), unfolding above the ongoing drone of the lowest partials.

As the performer continues to increase the force of their strokes, some energy slowly moves into the tam-tam's relatively subdued midrange frequency band (which spans roughly A_4 to E_6 for the instrument of figure 6.7). Individual partials in this register sometimes swell to fleeting prominence, but the principal impression created by these many aurally unresolvable frequency components is usually one not of discrete pitch or harmony but of reverberation. Rooms, like gongs, are inharmonic oscillators, and their many aurally unresolvable high-frequency resonances are not heard individually; instead, they communicate the aural impression of listening in a reverberant space. The decay time of a room's reverberations is a perceptual cue to its characteristics, longer times evoking the impression of a larger room with hard reflecting surfaces. Louder sound events in rooms typically not only produce louder reverberation but also extend the spectrum of the reverberation upward by exciting higher-frequency resonances to audibility. Similarly, variations in the excitation of the tam-tam cause gradual variations in the intensity, shape, and high-frequency extent of its emitted inharmonic spectrum and may evoke a cavernous space filled with continually shifting reverberation that is eerily divorced from discrete excitations. In addition, the actual resonances of the performance space—large or small—are excited by the sounds proceeding from the tam-tam, reshaping the sound spectrum at the listener and enveloping them from all directions. For this reason, although the piece remains impressive on recording, live performance brings a unique immersivity to the experience of *Having Never*.

As the performer's excitation of the gong approaches its maximum intensity, the energy in the emitted sound spectrum increasingly extends upward in frequency, reaching toward the upper limit of human hearing. Due to their extreme density, these high-frequency components are perceived collectively as high-end broadband noise. At its peak, the energy in the very high register exceeds that in the midrange, with the still-active lower bands surprisingly exhibit only a modest increase in energy. In fact, it is believed that some of the energy from low-frequency resonances in a forcefully excited tam-tam is transferred after a delay into the band above 1 kHz by physical mechanisms that are still poorly understood. This feature of the instrument accounts for the characteristic delayed brightening of its sound after an isolated stroke (Fletcher and Rossing 2010, 656–60). Especially if the performer has been conserving their energy for the climax of *Having Never*, the extension of sound into the high register may happen relatively quickly as energy breaches the levee of the less receptive midrange band. The particular physics of the tam-tam thus promote a relatively precipitous change in sonic character approaching the work's climax. The listener's psychological response may likewise be quite discontinuous despite the continuity of the performer's process. As energy floods the high register, any impression of expansive space and remote reverberation collapses to one of engulfing proximity. Intense and sustained high-frequency broadband noise is rare in nature, and the sonic climax brooks few comparisons.

An interesting feature observable near the culmination of many but not all performances (depending on the particular tam-tam and the peak excitation) is a rise in pitch among the lower partials by a semitone or more, as is visible at the right of figure 6.7. Such pitch glides are usually avoided in Western instrument designs but are cultivated in Chinese opera gongs, for instance (661–63). In *Having Never*, the rise in pitch, if present, may well go unnoticed, despite which it may subtly reinforce the climactic dynamic and timbral changes.

While solo tam-tam is the most commonly used instrumentation, it is not the only effective choice possible. Other percussion instruments such as snare drum can be employed with remarkable results, and so can ensembles of like percussion instruments. The details of the music are specific to the particular instrumental choice, but the aural project of following the sonic changes as an instrument is excited with gradually increasing or decreasing energy proves robustly interesting. The measured unfolding of the performance process encourages close observation of local phenomena, revealing a wealth of sonic features and transformations that are often surprising.

CHAPTER 7

Interlude: Harmonic Theory

In 1979, in the introduction for a planned treatise on harmonic theory, Tenney penned the following recollections:

> Until a few years ago, my own work in composition was such that questions of harmony seemed completely irrelevant to it. Timbre, texture, and formal processes determined by the many musical parameters other than harmonic ones still seemed like unexplored territory, and there was a great deal of excitement generated by this shift of focus away from harmony. Harmonic theory seemed to have reached an impasse sometime in the late nineteenth century, and the innovations of Schoenberg, Ives, Stravinsky, and others in the first two decades of the twentieth century were suddenly "beyond the pale" of *any* theory of harmony—or so it seemed. I was never really comfortable with this situation, but there was so much to be done—so many other musical possibilities to be explored—that it was easy to postpone questions of harmony in my own music. This situation began to change, however, in about 1970, when I wrote the first of a series of instrumental pieces that were to become more and more involved with specifically harmonic relationships. Then it was no longer the questions that seemed irrelevant but the "answers" offered by the available theories of harmony—both "traditional" and otherwise. ([1979a] 2015, 235)[1]

A preoccupation—both creative and theoretical—with "specifically harmonic relationships" would occupy much of Tenney's attention from 1970 onward. The origins of his newfound interest in harmony are partially obscure, and he experimented with a number of initial approaches to it. In 1969 he took a brief vacation from experimental music—as he would do periodically throughout the remainder of his career—to compose a collection of three piano pieces in classic ragtime style: *Three Rags for Pianoforte* (1969). Although these charming tonal works lie outside the mainstream of his technical development, they represent his first reengagement with harmony in more than a decade. The "first of a series of instrumental pieces" to which Tenney refers above was *Quiet Fan for Erik Satie* (1970/1971), in which the guiding principles of tonality are supplanted by a deterministic pitch process that occasions an unconventional sequence of tertian harmonies. The tonal round *A Rose Is a Rose Is a Round* (1970) oscillates ceaselessly between dominant and tonic harmony. The brief chant *Hey When I Sing These 4 Songs Hey Look What Happens* (1971) uses a pentatonic pitch-class set.[2] Tenney's emerging harmonic practice thus stemmed from a short sequence of singular pieces displaying diverse brands of harmonic organization.[3]

The emergence in Tenney's music of the harmonic series as a structural resource represented the beginning of a more focused exploratory program, beginning with *Clang* (1972) for orchestra and *Quintext*, V: "Spectra for Harry Partch" (1972) for string quintet. The acoustical series and its particular perceptual correlates would reappear in various guises throughout Tenney's music of the 1970s and again in the 1990s. In the late 1970s, however, alongside formulations directly related to the harmonic series, a second model of harmonic structure began to appear in Tenney's music and writings. This involved the depiction of pitches as points within a lattice structure that he dubbed *harmonic space*. In this model, he associated close harmonic relationship between two or more pitches with their proximity to each other in the lattice. The conceptual underpinnings of Tenney's harmonic space first appeared modestly and inconspicuously among his *Harmonium* sequence of pieces, but in the ensuing decade they would provide the foundation for his most complex large-scale works.

Drawing a distinction between his constructions conceived around the harmonic series and those invoking the concept of harmonic space, Tenney remarked that "obviously there's a relationship between them, but . . . the two notions lend themselves in different ways to different kinds of musical ideas" (1996d, 203). Indeed, these distinct paradigms of harmonic structure manifested in musics of notably different character. Tenney's *harmonic-series pieces* often feature gradual formal processes and a relatively high degree of continuity. These characteristics permit and promote close attention, on the one hand, to timbre and its gradual variation and, on the other hand, to constituent tones or partials and their intervallic relationships, with fluid shifts possible between these synthetic and analytic modes.[4] In contrast, Tenney's music conceived around his idea of harmonic space often involves forms that are relatively segmented and changeable, whereas timbre assumes a role that is secondary to the perception of relationships between pitches, and an interplay between textural fusion and fission plays little part. Significantly, Tenney did not simply supplant one harmonic model with the other but continued to invoke each at different times, the overt stylistic distinctions apparently reflecting appeals to subtly different facets of harmonic perception itself.

In the 1980s Tenney came to believe that a detailed computational model of auditory pitch processing would be required in order to answer certain questions about harmonic perception and that such a model would need to involve neural timing information rather than the spectral features on which his previous formulations (described in this chapter) had focused. He left voluminous archived notes toward such a model, most of which remain unexcavated. In 1985 he suspended his theoretical investigations following upheavals in his personal life, and he would not attempt to renew them until a brief period in the late 1990s. His notes from that later era confess that he had to a significant degree forgotten about his multifaceted theories of the 1970s and 1980s regarding aggregates of harmonic series (as discussed in section 7.6). The concept of harmonic space seems to have been the one that he had kept most in mind during the interim, applying it theoretically (Tenney [1993b] 2015) if not compositionally. Tenney's theory of harmony remained incomplete at the time of his death in 2006.

In the scientific community, recent decades have witnessed extensive research regarding the characterization of pitch perception and neurophysiological mechanisms of pitch processing (Langner and Benson 2015; Micheyl and Oxenham 2010). It is to be hoped that a better eventual understanding of these topics may help to elucidate not only received harmonic practices but also a broader domain of perceptual and cognitive harmonic possibilities. On the other hand—as Tenney's theoretical and compositional work suggests—the diverse, intimate, and exploratory involvement of musicians with tone combinations as phenomena may have a significant contribution to make to such research by illuminating the sundry aspects of harmonic experience for which it must account. In any event, this chapter surveys aspects of Tenney's harmonic theories that illuminate the particular concerns, structures, and experience of his own music composed after 1971.

7.1 The Meaning of *Harmony*

Tenney traced his first intellectual encounter with the harmonic series and issues concerning intonation to a course in musical acoustics that he completed in 1956 while still an undergraduate student at Bennington College (Tenney 1993a, 393). This initial exposure to scientific perspectives on sound and perception was much extended by graduate coursework with Lejaren Hiller at the University of Illinois. Of great importance for his later harmonic theories, while in Illinois he also worked with and performed in the ensemble of composer Harry Partch, who may fairly be described as the primary progenitor of modern extended just intonation in both theory and practice. Tenney subsequently conducted acoustical research at Bell Labs in the early 1960s, and this involved the harmonic series as a matter of course due to the relationship between spectrum and timbre. Despite such early and close engagement with aspects of the series and of intonation, however, in the 1960s Tenney had been compositionally preoccupied with other matters. These included a gradual absorption of the music and ideas of John Cage, which in those years had led him to avoid constraints on pitch relations (Tenney 1988b, 15). An interest in harmonic relationships would not manifest in Tenney's music until the early 1970s, and his attention would not turn to attendant theoretical questions until middecade.

When, around 1976, Tenney began to formulate his own theory of harmony, it was conceived as conceptual scaffolding for his own compositional work and as an alternative to received theories that he found to be unsuited to nontonal music. He would come to assert, for instance, that the concept of harmonic function and the imperative resolution of dissonance were culturally and historically specific conventions, not general features of harmonic perception: "There is no harmonic function other than what we choose. That's a choice, a matter of style, culture, and compositional intention. . . . The acoustical properties of sound and the physiological, neurological properties of the ear. These are real things that are given, as well as what the brain can do with this" (Tenney [1990] 2015, 362). By focusing his attention specifically on sound perception and the functioning of the human auditory system, Tenney hoped to instead arrive at a theory that would conform with music-making more generally. Delineating this objective, he wrote: "It seems to me that what a true theory of harmony would have to be now is a theory of *harmonic perception* (one component in a more general theory of musical perception) consistent with the most recent data available from the fields of acoustics and psychoacoustics but also taking into account the greatly extended range of musical experiences available to us today" ([1983] 2015, 281).

As a composer, Tenney focused on harmonic qualities as percepts, which in part reflected his specifically post-Cagean interest in sound as perceived rather than in expressive intent or conventionalized musical practice ([1983] 2015, 280–93; cf. section 1.2). As a theorist, however, he was also critical of received harmonic theory for its narrow cultural and historical applicability. Although he recognized that a perceptually based theory would never alone provide a complete account of harmonic practice in any culture, he believed that it could serve as a reliable foundation and guide for the development of diverse stylistically specific theories.

> In choosing this acoustical approach, I was under no illusion that *all* of the problems of harmony could be solved in this way. Obviously, many other factors—emotional, intellectual, and sociological—have influenced the historical evolution of harmonic practice in music and will continue to influence our harmonic perception. But although these may well have determined the *choices* that composers have made—and the responses to these choices by their audi-

ences—the acoustical nature of the tonal materials must always have played a very large part in determining what options were available to them *from which to choose.* (Tenney [1979a] 2015, 236–37)

For many musicians and scholars of the time, however, Tenney knew that the very meaning of the word *harmony* would be associated with the Western tonal tradition specifically, and he concluded that any renovation of harmonic theory (and practice) would first require clear redefinition of *harmony* itself. In a landmark essay entitled "John Cage and the Theory of Harmony," he advanced a generalized definition of harmony "as *that aspect of musical perception that depends on harmonic relations between pitches, i.e., relations other than 'higher' or 'lower,'*" and he accordingly asserted that "*there is some (set of) specifically harmonic relation(s) between any two salient and relatively stable pitches*" ([1983] 2015, 303). He went on to set forth a list of principles to which he believed a new theory of harmony ought to adhere.

> First, it should be *descriptive*—not pre- (or pro-)scriptive—and thus, *aesthetically neutral.* That is, it would not presume to tell a composer what should or should not be done but rather what the results might be if a given thing *is* done.
>
> Second, it should be culturally/stylistically *general*—as relevant to music of the twentieth (or twenty-first!) century as it is to that of the eighteenth (or thirteenth) century and as pertinent to the music of India or Africa or the Brazilian rainforest as it is to that of Western Europe or North America.
>
> Finally, in order that such a theory might qualify as a "theory" at all in the most pervasive sense in which that word is currently used (outside of music, at least), it should be (whenever and to the maximum extent possible) *quantitative.* Unless the propositions, deductions, and predictions of the theory are formulated quantitatively, there is no way to verify the theory and thus no basis for comparison with other theoretical systems. (Tenney [1983] 2015, 281–82)

Among Tenney's archival notes there appear numerous and varied lists of "specifically harmonic relations" for which he thought that any new theory of harmony ought to be able to account. The candidates appearing most regularly in such lists are:

- octave-*equivalence*,[5]
- categorical harmonic identity between pitch intervals whose sizes fall within some *tolerance* range of one another,
- a quality of relative perceptual *fusion* for combinations of tones, associated with measures that Tenney called *intersection ratios,*
- a *proximity* relation between tones associated with a measure that Tenney called *harmonic distance,* and
- a *polarity* relation associated with the perception of roots and tonics.

A significant part of Tenney's research involved seeking potential acoustical correlates for perceptible harmonic relations and—where possible—quantitative measures of such relations based upon those acoustic correlates. Even more than the list of harmonic relations themselves, the list of their proposed measures underwent phases of expansion and pruning, from which only intersection ratios and harmonic distance would ultimately find their way to published description.[6]

Most of the above relations and measures will provide topics for more extensive discussion below. However, the recurring appearance of the *harmonic series* in Tenney's music—as well as its outsized role in discussions of harmony generally—occasions a prefatory consideration of the structure of the series and its appropriate place within an account of harmonic perception.

7.2 The Harmonic Series

A *harmonic series* is a sequence of frequency values comprising some lowest value and all whole-number multiples thereof. The lowest value is called the *fundamental frequency* of the set or, informally, the *fundamental*. A collection of sinusoidal acoustical components whose frequencies reside in a harmonic series is called a *harmonic complex*, and the individual components are called *(harmonic) partials* or, informally, *harmonics*. The spectrogram in figure 7.1(a) shows the frequencies at which energy resides in two different harmonic complexes using a linear scale on the frequency ordinate (vertical axis). (Appendix B provides a brief general introduction to the spectrographic analysis of audio signals.) The fundamental frequencies of the two complexes are 0.75 and 1.0 kHz, and each comprises ten harmonic partials, as shown. Because harmonic frequencies are multiples of their associated fundamental, they appear evenly vertically spaced, and the spacing between them is proportionately wider in the 1 kHz complex. Part (b) of the figure displays the same information using a logarithmic rather than a linear frequency ordinate, so that this ordinate is linear in the more perceptually meaningful parameter of pitch. (The logarithmic relationship of perceived pitch to acoustical frequency is discussed in Appendix A.) In pitch, the spacing between harmonics is *not* uniform but instead narrows with ascending register, although the sequence of intervals between successive harmonics is independent of the fundamental frequency, as shown in the figure (and discussed below).

Under acoustical conditions that encompass those typical of speech and pitched music, the components of a harmonic complex strongly tend to perceptually *group* so that they are heard as a unitary *auditory image* or *gestalt*. In this case, those components are said to have undergone *harmonic fusion*. Usually the resulting gestalt will possess a pitch called the *residue pitch* associated with the fundamental frequency. An auditory gestalt with a pitch is called a *tone*, so such a fused gestalt is usually called a *(harmonic) complex tone*. A residue pitch may still be evoked when certain partials are missing from the complex, and this is the case even when one of those partials is the fundamental.

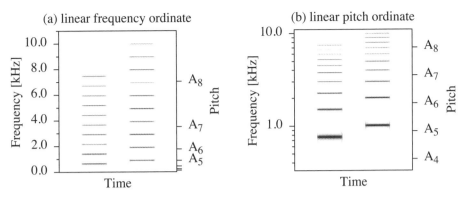

FIGURE 7.1. Spectrograms of harmonic complexes with fundamental frequencies of 0.75 and 1.0 kHz, displayed using (a) a linear frequency ordinate and (b) a linear pitch ordinate.

Partials whose frequencies are arrayed in a harmonic series are produced by physical oscillators that are uniform, flexible, and effectively one-dimensional (in other words, by ones whose other dimensions are negligible compared to their lengths). Most definitely pitched musical instruments involve oscillators that closely approximate these conditions in the forms of vibrating strings, vocal cords, or air columns. The psychoacoustical effect of harmonic fusion thus promotes the perception of musical tones and spoken vowels as unified gestalts despite the fact that acoustically they comprise multiple partials, an outcome that is basic to the apprehension of most music and speech. On the other hand, collections of partials that are *inharmonic* (in other words, ones whose partials are *not* all multiples of a single fundamental frequency) usually fuse much less readily. Church bells and gongs, for instance, are effectively two-dimensional oscillators and therefore produce inharmonic partials that often fail to perceptually group—thus the frequent impression that bell and gong strokes elicit multiple simultaneous pitches rather than only one.[7]

In the normative mode of musical hearing, a harmonic complex is accordingly perceived as a tone whose pitch corresponds to its fundamental frequency, while the (possibly evolving) relative amplitudes of its constituent partials contribute to the perceived timbre of that tone. This mode is called *synthetic listening* (Huron 2016, 132–33, 167–68). However, with close attention and sufficient tone duration, listeners can instead *hear out* (i.e., discern individually) various partials within the complex, a mode known as *analytic listening*. In this analytic listening mode, the pitches of various individual harmonics and the intervals between them become discrete objects of perception. Thus, in the synthetic listening mode, the ensemble of harmonic partials contributes to a perception of timbre, while in the analytic mode, they contribute to perceptions of pitch and/or harmony. Analytic listening becomes easier with practice and is facilitated if individual partials undergo independent variations in amplitude. Partials up to the tenth are usually the most easily discriminable, but considerably higher ones can sometimes be heard.

The first thirty-one pitches in the harmonic series above a fundamental corresponding to pitch C_2 are illustrated in figure 7.2. Harmonics are numbered consecutively from the fundamental, which is harmonic number 1. As previously observed in figures 7.1(a) and (b), harmonics are evenly spaced in frequency—all being multiples of the fundamental frequency—but pitch intervals between successively higher harmonics steadily narrow due to the logarithmic relationship of pitch to frequency. As a consequence of this logarithmic relationship, a particular pitch difference (i.e., a pitch interval) corresponds not to a particular frequency *difference* but to a particular frequency *ratio*. Perhaps the most widely known such correspondence is that between the octave interval and a frequency ratio of 2/1. Any other interval occurring within the harmonic series can be similarly denoted by the reduced ratio of its two constituent frequencies, which equals the reduced ratio of the two harmonic numbers involved.[8]

Pitch intervals within the harmonic series are said to be *just* intervals, and all of them differ to greater or lesser degree from the *tempered* intervals found on a conventionally tuned piano keyboard, with the important exceptions of the octave and its compounds. Above the staves in figure 7.2, the deviations of the harmonic-series pitches from their closest tempered counterparts are indicated as rounded to the closest integral number of *cents*, where a cent is a pitch interval equal to one one-hundredth of a tempered semitone. Any just interval can thus be expressed numerically either as an approximate pitch difference or as an exact frequency ratio. For instance, the *just fifth* between the second and third harmonics may be described either as a tempered perfect fifth (a span of seven tempered semitones) plus approximately 2 cents or as a frequency ratio of exactly 3/2, and this interval recurs between any two harmonics whose harmonic numbers stand in a ratio of 3/2. Just intervals are typically expressed as frequency ratios rather than pitch intervals due in part to this numerical simplicity and exactitude, but also because the structure of such a rational representation may help to elucidate certain perceived qualities of the acoustical stimulus, as discussed in the following sections.

Tenney's interest in the harmonic series had less to do with its *acoustical* structure per se than with the unique *perceptual* response that it evokes in listeners. His understanding of the distinction is elucidated by his late description of the auditory system's special response to the acoustical harmonic series as an evolutionary adaptation useful for source localization and recognition:

> Human beings did not create [the harmonic series]. It's not a cultural artifact. ... It is something that our auditory systems have evolved in such a way that if a tone and its harmonics sound in the environment, we will tend, unless there are cues to suggest otherwise, we will tend to hear it as a single thing, not a

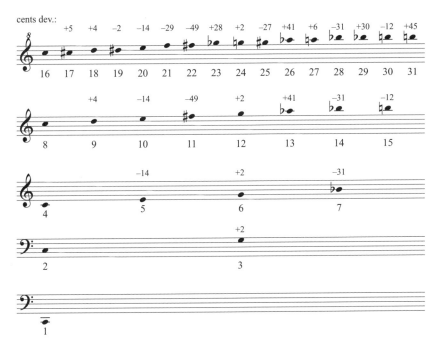

FIGURE 7.2. The first thirty-one members of a harmonic series above C₂. Pitch deviations from equal temperament (if any) are indicated above the staves in cents. Successive staves correspond to successive octaves above the fundamental, and members of the same pitch class are vertically aligned.

chord—a single sound with a pitch, an intensity, and a timbre. Which means that our auditory system has evolved to integrate that set of frequencies in a very remarkable way. (Tenney 1996c, 7–8)[9]

Tenney's emphasis on the perceptual correlates of the series over its acoustical properties is paramount to any understanding of its place in his thought and music. The response of the auditory system to the series, being distinct from the acoustical entity itself, is neither fully determined by the structure of the acoustical series nor reflective of all its properties. As a musician concerned with the experience of the listener, Tenney took the nature of perception to be the proper object of his research rather than acoustics per se.

To understand the real relation between the harmonic series and musical perception we must ask the following question: why is it that a compound tone consisting of many harmonic partials is normally and immediately perceived as a *single tone*, rather than as a "chord"? The science of psychoacoustics does not yet provide a satisfactory answer to this question, but I predict that—when it does—it will be seen that *it is the nature of harmonic perception in the auditory system that "explains" the unique perceptual character of the harmonic series, not . . . the other way around.* ([1983] 2015, 302, emphasis added)

Consequently, Tenney's conception of harmony did not reduce solely to relationships or percepts derivable from the harmonic series. On the contrary, he observed that "whoever has taken the position that somehow, because it's there in the harmonic series, we're imitating nature when we play with it—well, just immediately, the minor triad throws that theoretical position into disarray" (Tenney 1993a, 394).[10] Accordingly, while in the early 1970s (and again in the 1990s) Tenney would explore musical possibilities afforded by the harmonic series specifically, in the late 1970s his theoretical and compositional attention would turn to more general kinds of harmonic interrelations, of which the minor triad affords an emblematic instance.

7.3 Interval Tolerance and "The Language of Ratios"

Inspection of figure 7.2 reveals that many intervals commonly described as "consonant" by listeners appear between harmonics of low number. On the other hand, less familiar and more "dissonant" intervals involve higher harmonic numbers, although it is possible to find some consonant intervals between higher harmonics as well. More generally, many intervals considered relatively consonant correspond to *reduced* frequency ratios of relatively low *height* (meaning ratios in lowest terms whose numerator and denominator are relatively small numbers). On the other hand, intervals considered relatively dissonant correspond to reduced frequency ratios of greater height (meaning ones whose numerator, denominator, or both are relatively larger). I will follow Tenney in sometimes referring to such ratios and their associated harmonic percepts as relatively *simple* or *complex*, respectively. For Tenney, any theory of harmonic perception needed to acknowledge the correspondence between the adjudged relative consonance of an interval and the relative numerical simplicity of its associated frequency ratio.

Although whole-numbered frequency ratios of diverse complexity appear naturally between partials in a harmonic series, Tenney observed that such ratios may also participate in a wealth of other intervallic structures: "The harmonic series is only one limited manifestation of the kinds of possible pitch relationships that I'm interested in that relate to this thing that I'm calling harmony. They're involved because, when they're played accurately, they relate to each other as simple integer frequency relations. But they're not the only kind of set of possible integer frequency relations" (Tenney 1984c, 9). In particular, just intervals provide the harmonic substance of the music of composer Harry Partch, with whom Tenney had worked circa 1960 while a graduate student at the University of Illinois, more than a decade before his own interest in harmony and tuning emerged (section 3.1). Regarding the significance of Partch's thinking, Tenney remarked: "[Partch] wrote a book about his whole musical world called *Genesis of a Music*, which I think is one of the most important documents of twentieth-century music. And it was from that book, quite specifically, that I learned what Partch called 'the language of ratios,' which is essentially a tool for dealing with other kinds of tunings" (Tenney 1975c).[11] In the 1970s, Tenney thus found himself returning to the ideas of Partch regarding just intonation and rational frequency relationships, and these would come to provide a crucial part of the foundation of his own creative and theoretical work (Partch [1949] 1974; Tenney [1984b] 2015, 305; section 9.3).

Tenney described just intervals as *referential*—a term he chose for its neutrality. Referentiality in this sense entails that intervals whose magnitude resides within some sufficiently small *tolerance* range about a just interval will be interpreted categorically by the auditory system as referring to that just interval.

> An interval is represented by the simplest ratio within the tolerance range around its actual relative frequencies, and any measure on the interval is the measure on that simplest ratio. (Tenney [1983] 2015, 296)

> Within the tolerance range, a mistuned interval will still carry the same harmonic sense as the accurately tuned interval does, although its timbral quality will be different. . . . Thus, when we play a major triad on a tempered piano, where the major third is 14 cents larger than the just third, we are "understanding" that third as a 5/4 relationship; i.e., it has the same harmonic sense as a 5/4. It may sound unclear or even out of tune, but it's that particular (5/4) relationship "out of tune." (Tenney [1993c/2003] 2015, 379)

An implication of Tenney's postulated interval tolerance is that all intervals are harmonically categorized by the auditory system as instances of just intervals (albeit possibly "out of tune") and are thus representable as whole-number frequency ratios.[12] Moreover, the number of discriminable intervals is finite, since a relatively complex interval sufficiently close to a relatively simple just interval would not have an autonomous intervallic identity but would be heard as a version of the simpler interval. Tenney left the size of such tolerance ranges—and hence the number of discriminable intervals—as a topic for experimental investigation, although he hypothesized that the size of a just interval's tolerance range would vary inversely with its rational complexity ([1983] 2015, 294–95). Thus the tolerance range about a 2/1 octave or a 3/2 fifth would be larger than that about an 11/8 tritone.[13]

Tenney's concept of interval tolerance implies that a particular frequency ratio need not be realized exactly in order for its harmonic sense to be definitely perceived. This insistence on the categorical character of intervals distinguishes Tenney from theorists of just intonation for whom frequency ratios represent autonomous ideals and for whom the nature of human intervallic perception is extraneous. In his harmonic (and other) theories, he attributed his distinctive focus on perception to the influence of John Cage's listener-oriented aesthetic (Tenney 2005b). One consequence of this position was that Tenney took a relatively pragmatic approach to the stipulation and realization of intonations. This included, for instance, the use of finely graduated equal temperaments if these permitted sufficiently close approximation to just intervals of interest. Distinguishing his attitude from that of some other composers working with just intonation, Tenney commented: "The issue is not fundamentally 'just' versus 'tempered' in my mind. I believe it is for Ben [Johnston], as it was for [Harry] Partch. Fundamentally, for me, the issue is harmony. And, to go anywhere with harmony leads towards new tuning systems. Not just because a new tuning system will give us new harmonies, but rather because we need new tuning systems to give us some other just relationships" (1987b, 461).

On the other hand, in order to satisfactorily approximate just intervals of relative complexity, Tenney's concept of adequate intonational approximation became progressively more stringent over time. In *Clang* (1972) he accepted quarter-tone approximations to harmonic-series intervals, while in movements I and III of *Quintext* (1972) he stipulated deviations from 12TET in cents but indicated that "only a conscientious effort towards approximation is expected here." In *Three Harmonic Studies* (1974) 12TET was used to approximate the harmonic series, while in *Symphony* (1975) downward-pointing arrows above noteheads were used to identify pitches whose intonation should be "slightly flatter than the tempered pitch." By 1981, however, Tenney was employing special notations to stipulate pitches in 84TET (gradations of sevenths of a semitone, or 14.3 cents), subsequently switching to 72TET (gradations of sixths of a semitone, or 16.7 cents).[14] These temperaments permitted approximations of the just intervals used in those pieces to within ±5 cents (one-twentieth of a tempered semitone), a degree of intonational accuracy for which Tenney would regularly call beginning in the late 1980s.[15]

Tenney appreciated the potential performance difficulties engendered by his intonational demands and sought means of making them feasible that were tailored to particular pieces. These included the provision of audible intonational references (e.g., in the form of tunable electronic keyboards or scordatura strings playing natural harmonics), textures that permit tuning via monitoring the tempo of beating, the use of multiple instruments tuned sixths of a semitone apart in order to realize 72TET, the monitoring by instrumentalists of electronic tuners in live performance, and the retuning of tunable instruments such as pianos. He always believed, however, that performance practice and aural acuity would evolve such that, one day, nonspecialist players would commonly be able to accurately tune the intervals of such music by ear alone. Regarding such evolution in musicianship, he remarked:

> I definitely see it among performers that I've worked with. The interesting thing is, they can all do what I ask them to do, but they've never been asked to do it before. In music school, all you're asked to do is distinguish twelve different pitches in an octave. I ask them to distinguish many more, but in a context in

which those distinctions make harmonic sense. And the first thing they discover is they can do it! . . . The same is true with rhythmic perception and rhythmic performance. This is involved in an evolutionary process as well. (Tenney 2000c; see section 1.2.3)

7.4 A History of *Consonance* and *Dissonance*

No conception is more fundamental to traditional Western harmonic theory and practice than the economy of consonance and dissonance. The relationship of these terms to specific percepts is complicated, however, because—despite their widespread usage—they possess a complex history from which they have inherited considerable ambiguity.

Tenney himself attempted to resolve the terminological equivocacies in a detailed semiotic history entitled *A History of 'Consonance' and 'Dissonance'* (1988; manuscript dates from June 1980). In that book, he surveyed the changing implications of these terms in Western music theory since the Middle Ages, identifying five successive semantic paradigms or *consonance/dissonance concepts* (CDCs). To these Tenney applied the neutral designations CDC-1 through CDC-5 in the chronological order of their appearance in history. In his account, CDC-1 evolved from a classical Pythagorean conception of consonance as "directly tunable" (e.g., using certain accepted rational divisions of a monochord) to a prepolyphonic medieval conception of "relations between pitches" (that applied essentially to *melodic* dyads rather than simultaneous ones). CDC-2 dates from the High Middle Ages, and Tenney concluded that it ascribed consonance to the quality of sounding like a single tone, which he sometimes termed *fusion* in his notes and which psychoacousticians today sometimes call *toneness* (Huron 2016, 33–38).[16] CDC-3, dating from the Renaissance, involved the maintenance of textural clarity in a lower polyphonic voice. CDC-4 represented the functional consonance and dissonance of Western tonal common practice, wherein the consonance or dissonance of an interval is determined in part contextually as its obligation to resolve and so cannot always be determined from the inherent qualities of that interval in isolation. CDC-5 corresponded to a sensation of what psychoacousticians today refer to as *smoothness/roughness* and is related to the perception of acoustical beating.

Tenney's harmonic thinking as it developed in the period of 1976–85 came to associate CDC-1, CDC-2, and CDC-5 with subtly different aspects of harmonic perception that occasioned different harmonic measures. Moreover, CDC-2 can be regarded as a theoretical counterpart to Tenney's music invoking the harmonic series, while CDC-1 is linked to his conception of relations in harmonic space and compositions based thereon. Both CDCs will be explored further below. A prefatory account of CDC-5 is also warranted, since it is probably the concept of broadest currency among musicians today.

7.5 Roughness and Beating (CDC-5)

Between sine tones, rates of acoustical beating in the range of about 20–200 Hz produce an auditory sensation known as *roughness*. Roughness is nil when the sine tones are in unison, reaches a peak at a small interval as their frequencies diverge, and decreases again as the frequency separation increases further (Roederer 2008, 34–42; Plomp and Levelt 1965). Peak roughness occurs at an interval of slightly less than a semitone for pitches above C_4. When intervals are formed by complex tones rather than sine waves, beating between low harmonics that are close but not coincident in frequency may also evoke roughness. The eminent nineteenth-century physicist Hermann von Helmholtz observed that in intervals corresponding to simple frequency ratios, the harmonics of two complex tones either coincided precisely or were well separated in frequency so that sensory roughness was low ([1877] 1954, 179–97). On the other hand, intervals corresponding to more complex ratios contained close but noncoincident harmonics that beat to create greater roughness. He hypothesized that *dissonance* referred to roughness and *consonance* to its absence (*smoothness*). Figure 7.3 shows illustrative harmonic alignments and interactions for a 3/2 just fifth and a tempered tritone. Gray ellipses enclose pairs of low-order harmonics in the tritone that differ slightly in frequency so as to beat and induce roughness. In the fifth, on the other hand, these same harmonic pairs are either precisely aligned so as to generate no roughness or are at least spaced so as to induce less roughness. Helmholtz's roughness theory of consonance would thus predict that the fifth was the more consonant interval, in accordance with the judgment of most listeners.

Certain implications of the roughness theory may seem at odds, however, with many musicians' intuitive sense of what the terms *consonance* and *dissonance* denote. For instance, the rate of beating between two tones is determined by their frequency difference. Due to the nonlinear relationship between frequency and pitch, however, the frequency difference associated with a particular interval grows with registral height. Thus, the degree of roughness of a given interval (and hence its "dissonance" in the Helmholtzian sense) is also dependent on register, other factors being equal. On the other hand, roughness can also vary with intervallic width: the bandwidth within which frequency components will interact in the peripheral auditory system (called the *critical bandwidth*) increases below C_4, so that in the treble the two sine tones separated by a perfect fourth do not appreciably beat against each other, while in the deep bass they do (Roederer 2008, 34–42). Finally, the amplitude of beating—and hence the salience of roughness—can vary with both overall dynamic and the relative amplitudes of interacting partials (in other words, with an aspect of timbre).

Although sensory roughness is perhaps what nonmusicians most often mean when they refer to dissonance, for musicians its variation with register, intensity, and timbre may rouse a contrary intuition that the dissonance of a particular

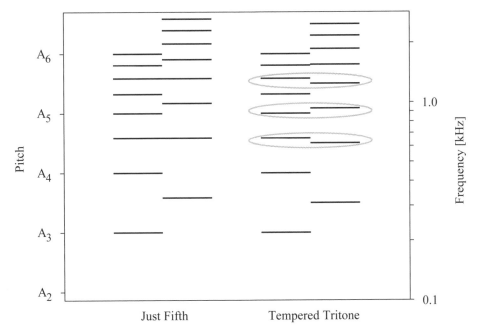

FIGURE 7.3. Comparison of coincidences between low-order harmonics for two pitch intervals between complex tones: A_3–E_4 (just) and A_3–D-sharp$_4$ (tempered). Selected pairs of beating harmonics are enclosed by ellipses.

interval type should be independent of such factors—an unease that betrays the ambiguity latent in the term *dissonance*. Tenney took the identification of roughness with dissonance in the post-Helmholtzian CDC-5 to concern timbre more than the sort of harmonic relationships with which he was primarily concerned, going so far as to suggest that it be dubbed "*timbral* consonance and dissonance" (1988a, 100). He accordingly concluded that its compositional significance pertained to orchestration rather than harmony, although "for the composer, certain aspects of Helmholtz's theory (or its more recent extensions) are quite valuable as tools in the process of orchestration ... or, more generally (as in the field of electronic music), in the manipulation and control of timbre, texture, and 'sonority'" (94).

Roughness/smoothness and beating are frequent features of Tenney's music, but often as alluring phenomena attendant to a more structurally significant manifestation of consonance/dissonance in some other sense. A notable exception is *Beast* (1971) for solo contrabass, in which the rhythmic aspect of beating is formally and phenomenally central.

7.6 Toneness and Harmonicity (CDC-2)

One alternative contemporary theory of consonance and dissonance posits that consonance corresponds to the perceptual similarity of a collection of sounds to a single tone, a quality sometimes called *toneness*. A high degree of toneness is associated with clear auditory images (gestalts) that evoke clear pitches. The origin of the toneness theory of consonance is usually credited to the nineteenth-century psychologist Carl Stumpf, who in 1898 wrote:

> The combined sound of two tones approximates—now more, now less—the impression of a single tone, and it appears that the more this condition holds, the more consonant is the interval. Even when we perceive and distinguish the tones as two, they nevertheless form a whole in perception, and this whole strikes us as more or less unitary. We find this property with simple tones, just as with those with overtones. That the octave sounds effectively like a unison, even when we can clearly distinguish two tones in it, is always admitted, although it is nothing less than self-evident, but it is a most remarkable fact. This same property becomes weaker, however, even with fifths and fourths, and still weaker with thirds and sixths. (Stumpf 1898, 35; quoted in Tenney 1988a, 30)

The perceived quality of toneness is promoted by a high degree of acoustical *harmonicity*, which is the similarity between the frequency structure of the sound stimulus and a harmonic series (Huron 2016, 27–40). Thus—broadly generalizing—the acoustical signals in the following list trend from greater to lesser toneness:

- complete harmonic complexes
- harmonic complexes with missing or mistuned partials
- inharmonic complexes (including bell, gong, and cymbal sounds)
- random or quasi-random signals (such as broadband noises and clicks)

The degree of toneness exhibited even by complete harmonic complexes is subject to registral restrictions, however. In particular, pitch strength weakens significantly for complexes whose fundamental frequencies reside below about 50 Hz (roughly G_1) (McDermott 2014b, 528). Of course, for fundamentals below the frequency range of human hearing, pitch and fundamental frequency lose their correspondence entirely. An extreme example is represented by computer-generated broadband noise, which has a period (albeit usually very long) and whose frequency structure thus mathematically corresponds to a harmonic series despite the fact that it elicits minimal toneness. On the other hand, the toneness of harmonic complexes exhibits a maximum for fundamentals near D_4, which studies suggest is close to the average pitch of global music as a whole (Huron 2016, 35). Dyads comprising complex tones possess greater or lesser harmonicity depending on the degree to which the aggregate of their partials resembles a complete harmonic series, and this resemblance decreases for increasingly complex intervals in accordance with Stumpf's description of their decreasing toneness.

Disentangling the contributions of roughness and toneness to subjective judgments of consonance and dissonance for particular isolated intervals has been complicated by the fact that in most instances these qualities tend to covary; in other words, intervals that are "consonant" (in the experimental psychologist's sense of *subjectively preferred*) tend locally to both minimize roughness and maximize harmonicity. However, in the past decade new experimental designs have permitted the separation of the two contributions (McDermott, Lehr, and Oxenham 2010; Cousineau, McDermott, and Peretz 2012; McDermott 2014a). For instance, electronic synthesis permits the generation of acoustical stimuli that are not found in nature and that vary in roughness but not harmonicity, or vice versa. Findings have indicated that preference for consonance is consistently correlated with preference for harmonicity but not with preference for smoothness (McDermott, Lehr, and Oxenham 2010). As a result of such studies, after decades of scientific dominance by the roughness theory, the toneness theory has lately moved into ascendancy as an explanation of listener preferences.

More significant for present purposes than an explanation of listeners' statistical preferences is the establishment that harmonicity and smoothness each makes a contribution to the perception of tone combinations and that these contributions are distinct (McDermott, Lehr, and Oxenham 2010, 1037). If toneness and smoothness have different qualitative referents, then the toneness and roughness theories of consonance are not in competition, and any complete account of how tone combinations are perceived will need to address not one but both phenomena.

7.6.1 Intersection and Disjunction Ratios

A combination of multiple simultaneous complex tones (a chord) corresponds to a collection of multiple harmonic series, each of which possesses its own distinct fundamental frequency. Tenney referred to such a collection as a *harmonic-series aggregate*. Tenney developed a number of quantitative measures of harmonic relatedness, some of which he associated with different CDCs. Consonance in CDC-2 he linked with Stumpfian toneness (Tenney 1988a, 30), and one of his measures associated with CDC-2 can be viewed as a gauge of harmonicity for harmonic series aggregates—i.e., of their *similarity* to a single complete harmonic series. This is the *intersection ratio* between a harmonic-series aggregate and a complete harmonic series whose fundamental frequency is the greatest common divisor (GCD) of the frequencies represented in the aggregate (Tenney [1979b] 2015, 248, 252–55). In short, this quantity represents the fraction of a *single* complete harmonic series constituted by the components of a number of complex tones sounding together. The principal caveat is that this measure assumes that the harmonic spectra of individual tones are complete and have many harmonics.[17]

A simple example of a harmonic series aggregate is illustrated in figure 7.4, in which solid black lines represent the harmonic partials of two complex tones,

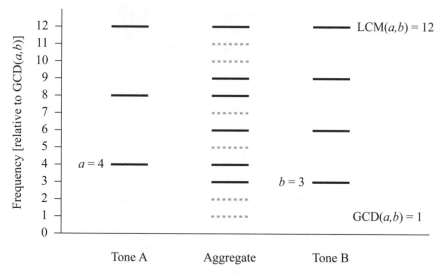

FIGURE 7.4. The partials of two harmonic complex tones (Tone A and Tone B) are shown flanking the first harmonic period of their harmonic-series aggregate.

Tone A and Tone B. Suppose that the fundamental frequencies of these two tones are in a reduced ratio a/b (in other words, that the numerator a and the denominator b have no common divisors greater than one). In figure 7.4, for purposes of this particular illustration, the fundamental frequencies of the tones are in a reduced ratio of $a/b = 4/3$, corresponding to the pitch interval of a just fourth.

Frequency values in the figure are represented in units of the GCD of the two fundamental frequencies; thus, this GCD frequency appears as the unit ordinate, and the frequencies of all partials—being multiples of this GCD—correspond to whole numbers. As figure 7.4 shows, the aggregate comprises a subset of a complete harmonic series whose fundamental is the GCD frequency, the missing harmonics thereof being depicted by dashed gray lines. In other words, the GCD frequency represents the highest frequency of which all present sound components represent harmonics. For this reason, in the sequel I will sometimes refer to the GCD frequency, or its associated *GCD pitch*, as the *conceptual fundamental* of the harmonic-series aggregate.

Tenney referred to the least common multiple (LCM) of the fundamental frequencies in an aggregate as its *harmonic period* (HP). Since the frequency ratio a/b is assumed to be reduced, the harmonic period is ab, so that the harmonic period in the example of figure 7.4 is $ab = 3 \times 4 = 12$. The figure depicts only the first such harmonic period, but the pattern of partials repeats identically in higher ones. Within one harmonic period of the aggregate, the total number of harmonics in Tone A is the LCM divided by the fundamental frequency of Tone A, which gives $(ab)/a = b$. For the specific example in figure 7.4, this is $12/4 = 3$. Similarly, within one harmonic period the total number of harmonics of Tone B is $(ab)/b = a$, or $12/3 = 4$. Now, the total number of *distinct* harmonics falling within one harmonic period of the aggregate is the number of harmonics in Tone A plus the number of harmonics in Tone B minus one, so that the LCM frequency is not counted twice. For a frequency dyad of reduced ratio a/b, this tally is

$$\frac{ab}{b} + \frac{ab}{a} - 1 = a + b - 1.$$

For the illustrated example in particular, this value is $4 + 3 - 1 = 6$, as the figure shows. For an arbitrary dyad with reduced frequency ratio a/b, the total number of harmonics in one harmonic period of the notional harmonic series on the GCD frequency is ab, so that—per the last equation above—a general expression for the *intersection ratio of a dyad with a harmonic series on its own GCD* is (Tenney [1979b] 2015, 248)

$$I = \frac{a + b - 1}{ab}.$$

This quantity represents the fraction of a single complete harmonic series (with fundamental equaling the GCD frequency) that is supplied by the harmonic-series aggregate of Tone A and Tone B. For the particular example of $a/b = 4/3$ illustrated in figure 7.4, the value of this intersection ratio is $I = 6/12 = 0.5$.

The intersection ratio I may be viewed as a measure of an aggregate's harmonicity. Its value trends to unity as the notional series on the GCD fills with sounding partials and toward zero as it thins. Figure 7.5 plots values of I for intervals between a unison and one octave. As shown, I equals 1 if the fundamental frequency of one tone corresponds to a harmonic of the other (in other words, if either a or b equals one), since in that case all harmonics in the higher tone correspond to a harmonic of the lower one. On the other hand, I trends toward zero as the harmonic period ab increases. An important caveat regarding the complex frequency ratios associated with high LCMs and low intersection ratios is that they may fail to evoke autonomous harmonic identities but may instead be heard as inflections of nearby simpler harmonies in accordance with Tenney's principle of interval tolerance (section 7.3).[18]

A complementary measure of the *inharmonicity* of an aggregate is furnished by the *disjunction ratio*,

$$D = 1 - I,$$

which is plotted in figure 7.11(b) for intervals up to a double octave.[19]

Attractions of these intersection and disjunction ratios include their interpretation as measures of harmonicity, their straightforward extension to collections of more than two tones, and the fact that they permit comparisons between tone collections of different cardinalities. Although analytic expressions for the intersection ratio become unwieldy as the number of tones increases, this ratio can be easily computed by simply counting the number of distinct partials in

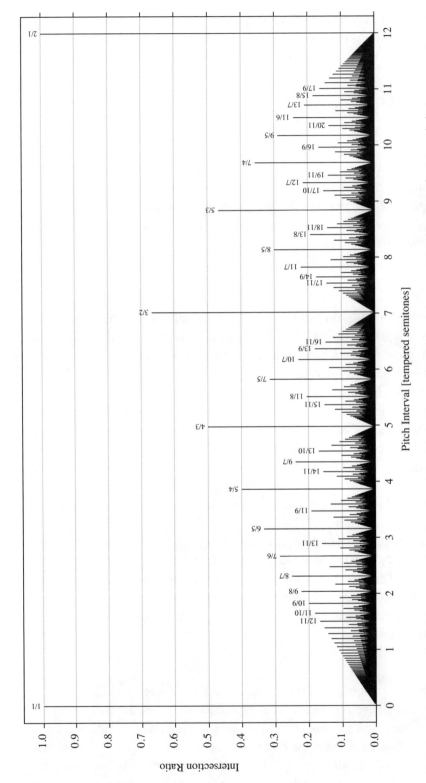

FIGURE 7.5. Values for the intersection ratio *I* of a rational dyad with a harmonic series on its own GCD frequency for intervals between a unison and an octave. Selected frequency ratios are labeled.

one harmonic period of the aggregate (in other words, up to the LCM of the fundamental frequencies involved). On the other hand, the relationship between acoustical harmonicity as gauged by these particular measures and subjectively perceived toneness has not been experimentally tested and may not always be straightforward, especially if the complexes involved fail the assumed criteria of completeness and extensiveness.

7.7 Harmonic Space (CDC-1)

In the late 1970s, Tenney began to explore a distinct set of relationships that he associated with CDC-1 (Tenney [1979b] 2015, 256). He traced that earliest of his five historical consonance/dissonance concepts from ancient Greece through the early Middle Ages, arguing that—unlike the later CDCs—it originally applied strictly to successive tones (melodic intervals). Consequently, unlike the concepts of toneness (CDC-2) and roughness (CDC-5), which seem to apply only to simultaneous complex tones, Tenney maintained that CDC-1 referred to audible harmonic relationships between both successive and simultaneous pitches and between both sine tones and complex tones. He detected traces of CDC-1's melodic aspect in Jean-Philippe Rameau's eighteenth-century rules of root progression and in the concept of *closely related keys* for purposes of modulation, as well as in the early twentieth-century writings of Paul Hindemith and Arnold Schoenberg, the latter casting it as a "relation between tones" (Tenney 1988a, 15–16).

Tenney understood this harmonic relationship as one of harmonic *proximity* between pitches.

> The earliest sense of consonance and dissonance—CDC-1—implies that at the octave and perfect fifth, for example, two tones seem much more closely related to each other than at immediately adjacent though smaller intervals (the major seventh and augmented fourth), and this has given rise to numerous attempts to order or "map" pitches in a way that somehow represents these other relations by proximities in a "space" of two or more dimensions while still preserving the relations of pitch-distance. What is implied here is a conception of *harmonic space* and a measure of the *harmonic distance* between any two points in that space that is distinct from—but not inconsistent with—the measure of pitch-distance. ([1979b] 2015, 256)

Tenney's model of harmonic space represented frequency ratios as locations within a multidimensional lattice of the sort shown in shown in figure 7.6 (Tenney [1979b] 2015, 261–71; [1983] 2015). The appearance of such lattices among Tenney's compositional plans thus betokens a significant development in his thinking beyond the harmonic-series-based structures of his music in the early 1970s.[20]

In describing the structure of harmonic space, Tenney wrote: "For a given set of pitches, the dimensions of this space would correspond to the *prime fac-*

tors required to specify their frequency ratios with respect to a reference pitch. It is a discrete space, not a continuous one, with the line segment connecting any two adjacent points in a graph of the lattice symbolizing a multiplication (or division) of the frequency ratio by the prime number associated with that dimension" ([1993c/2003] 2015, 375). Such lattices thus depict the *prime factorizations* of frequency ratios. Any whole-number ratio can be factored in one and only one way as a product of prime numbers:

$$2^{c_2}3^{c_3}5^{c_5}7^{c_7}11^{c_{11}}\ldots,$$

where the product extends to include as many prime factors as needed and where the exponents c_i are integers. For example, the frequency ratio 20/3, such as appears between the third and twentieth harmonics, can be expressed as

$$\frac{20}{3} = \frac{2 \times 2 \times 5}{3} = 2^2 3^{-1} 5^1.$$

The prime factors on the right of this expression appear with exponents that represent their multiplicities.[21] As shown in figure 7.6, based on this factorization it becomes possible to represent the ratio 20/3 as a unique point in a three-dimensional lattice whose dimensions correspond to the three prime factors involved—i.e., 2, 3, and 5 with coordinates corresponding to their exponents, (2,–1,1). The origin at coordinates (0,0,0) corresponds to $2^0 3^0 5^0 = 1/1$. Tenney referred to the three axes in this lattice as the *2-axis*, *3-axis*, and *5-axis* according to the associated prime factor and to the associated lattice as *(2,3,5) harmonic space*. This three-dimensional lattice permits representation of all ratios involving prime factors no greater than 5 or—in the parlance of Harry Partch—of ratios within the *5-limit* ([1949] 1974, 109). For example and as shown in figure 7.6, according with its coordinates, (2,–1,1) and relative to the origin at 1/1, the ratio 20/3 is located two positive (in other words, rightward) steps along the 2-axis, one negative (downward) step along the 3-axis, and one positive (outward) step along the 5-axis. On the other hand, $15/2 = 2^{-1} 3^1 5^1$ is located at coordinates (–1,1,1): one negative step along the 2-axis, one positive step along the 3-axis, and one positive step along the 5-axis.

Tenney often invoked octave equivalence to map all ratios differing only by factors of powers of two to the same lattice point, thereby reducing the dimensionality of the lattice by one. He referred to this operation as *pitch-class projection* (Tenney [1983] 2015, 296–97). It might be regarded as viewing figure 7.6 down its 2-axis from the right, so that all ratios differing only by some factor of two align visually. Each point in the resulting *pitch-class projection space* thus represents a particular *ratio class*—a collection comprising all ratios that differ only by some factor of a power of two. Following Partch's convention ([1949] 1974, 78–79), a ratio class is typically labeled with its unique member ratio that resides in the range [1, 2), as illustrated in figure 7.7.[22] As shown, the dimensional reduction permits the depiction, if needed, of an additional prime

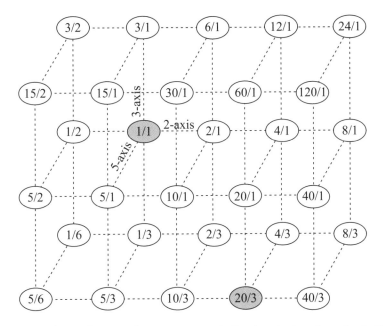

FIGURE 7.6. A subset of (2, 3, 5) harmonic space indicating the location of ratio 20/3 relative to 1/1.

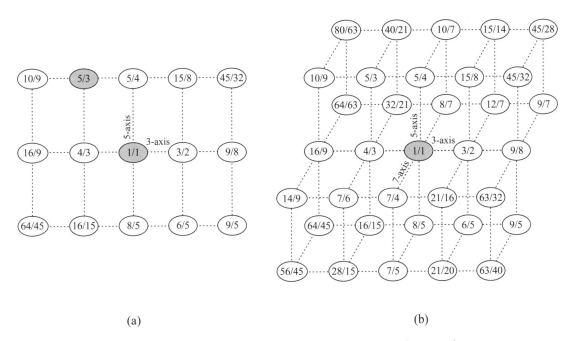

(a)   (b)

FIGURE 7.7. (a) A subset of (5, 3) pitch-class projection space showing the ratio class 5/3 that contains the ratio 20/3. (b) A subset of (7, 5, 3) pitch-class projection space.

factor such as 7 using an axis envisioned as perpendicular to the page. Abstract lattices involving additional prime factors are straightforwardly formulable but frustrate attempts at depiction because they involve more than three dimensions.

7.7.1 Harmonic Distance

Just as he posited intersection ratios as a harmonic measure linked to CDC-2, Tenney developed a measure of harmonic relatedness associated with CDC-1. This he dubbed *harmonic distance* (HD), defining it as

$$HD(a,b) = \log_2(ab),$$

where a/b is the reduced ratio between the fundamental frequencies of two tones.

By assumption, a and b have no common factors, so the argument ab is their least common multiple (LCM), and their greatest common divisor (GCD) is one.[23] By virtue of the logarithm, Tenney's harmonic distance thus corresponds to the pitch distance in octaves between the LCM and GCD frequencies associated with the tones.[24]

An alternative interpretation of the harmonic distance associated with a given interval relates it to the lowest pitch height within the harmonic series at which that interval appears. Consider two tones whose fundamental frequencies are in the reduced ratio of a/b. Now a/b is also the frequency ratio between the ath and bth partials in a harmonic series, and since it is a reduced fraction, it corresponds to the lowest instance of the corresponding interval within the series. By virtue of the general summation property of logarithms,

$$HD(a,b) = \log_2(ab) = \log_2(a) + \log_2(b) = 2\left(\frac{\log_2(a) + \log_2(b)}{2}\right).$$

$\log_2(a)$ is the pitch interval in octaves between the ath partial in a harmonic series and the fundamental of that series, and, similarly, $\log_2(b)$ is the interval of the bth partial above the fundamental. Thus the quantity in large parentheses represents the distance from the fundamental to the midpoint of the pitch interval between those two partials. The equation therefore shows that the farther that midpoint resides above the fundamental, the greater the harmonic distance between two tones whose fundamental frequencies exhibit that ratio (Tenney [1979b] 2015, 260).

Yet another important interpretation of Tenney's harmonic distance function is that it furnishes a *metric* (a measure of a distance) between points in harmonic space. Using the prime factorization of a reduced ratio a/b given at the opening of section 7.7, and exploiting certain general properties of logarithms, the harmonic distance function can be written as[25]

$$
\begin{aligned}
HD(a,b) &= \log_2(ab) \\
&= \log_2(2^{|c_2|}3^{|c_3|}5^{|c_5|}7^{|c_7|}\ldots) \\
&= |c_2| + |c_3|\log_2(3) + |c_5|\log_2(5) + |c_7|\log_2(7) + \ldots.
\end{aligned}
$$

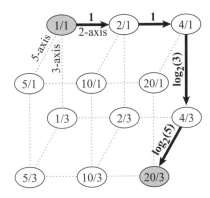

FIGURE 7.8. Harmonic distance as a rectilinear distance in harmonic space. Distances between vertices are indicated in boldface.

Suppose that the lattice axes are differently graduated according to the logarithms of their associated primes, so that points along the n-axis are separated by a distance of $\log_2(n)$. Then the above expression for HD tallies the distance in the lattice from the origin at 1/1 to the point associated with ratio a/b, assuming that measurements must be made parallel to the axes and between lattice points. Returning to the example of frequency ratio $20/3 = 2^2 3^{-1} 5^1$, corresponding to harmonic-space coordinates $(c_2, c_3, c_5,) = (2, -1, 1)$ relative to the origin at 1/1, the preceding harmonic distance formula becomes

$$\mathrm{HD}(a,b) = 2 + \log_2(3) + \log_2(5).$$

This corresponds to a sum of distances in harmonic space stepwise along a path from 1/1 to 20/3, as indicated using arrows in figure 7.8. Harmonic distance as a measure (or *norm*) of distances to the origin is extensible to distances between any two points by applying it to their reduced ratio (in other words, by treating one of the two points as though it were the origin). Such a distance measure is variously known as a "taxicab," "city block," "Manhattan," or *rectilinear* metric, as distinguished from the usual *Euclidean* ("straight-line" or "as the crow flies") metric.[26]

While harmonic distance furnishes a measure on frequency ratios (or their corresponding pitch intervals) and corresponds to a distance in harmonic space, Tenney also formulated a *generalized harmonic distance* (GD) between ratio classes in pitch-class projection space. This octave-generalized distance corresponds to the minimum value among all of the harmonic distances associated with the member ratios in a given ratio class. It equals the usual harmonic distance sum minus its integer-valued octave term. In compositional applications involving harmonic distance, Tenney typically invoked octave equivalence and worked with pitch-class collections rather than pitch collections, in which case his harmonic distance measures would take this generalized form ([1979b] 2015, 263–66; [1987a] 2015, 344).

7.7.2 Compactness and Connectedness

Tenney associated the harmonic simplicity of a pitch set with its *compactness* in harmonic space (1987b, 462). For example, if two pitches both reside on the 3-axis, then the less their separation along that axis, the greater their harmonic *proximity* (or, in other words, the less the *harmonic distance* between them).[27] Regarding the perceptual significance of such proximity in harmonic space, Tenney commented: "My hypothesis is that our ears will interpret things in the simplest way possible. Given a set of pitches, we will interpret them in the simplest way possible. This can be translated into harmonic space terms by saying that it will be the most compact arrangement in harmonic space. Well, I think that compactness, in that sense, . . . could be made very explicit by speaking of the sum of harmonic distances among these various points" (462).[28] A tempting analogy extends the civic metaphor of a "city-block metric" to imagine a compact set in harmonic space as a community of individuals (pitches or pitch classes) who, taken pairwise, are more or less distantly or indirectly related to one another but who, taken as an ensemble, reside in relative proximity and engage in various sensible interrelations.

Another property that Tenney considered significant for pitch sets was *connectedness* in harmonic space, wherein each element of a set is adjacent to at least one other element thereof ([1993c/2003] 2015, 383), presumably enabling the ear to range stepwise over the entire set via the primitive intervals. Even in the absence of such connectedness, however, traversal of primitive intervals might be implied. For instance, apparently referring to the decomposition of a 15/8 major seventh into a 3/2 fifth and a 5/4 third, Tenney remarked that "the major seventh, even when you're hearing it by itself, there are two other pitches that would give that interval itself an immediate harmonic meaning, and those two other pitches are the pitches that would correspond to the major third or the fifth" (1996d, 200).

Various familiar scales and harmonies can be associated with compact sets of lattice points in pitch-class projection space. For instance, as shown in figure 7.9 (upper left), a twelve-note just chromatic scale can be associated with a 4 × 3 configuration of points in the (3,5) plane of pitch-class projection space. (In this figure, letter names for pitch classes correspond to the closest tempered pitch class, assuming that 1/1 represents pitch class C.) As depicted, this collection contains a C major diatonic scale on and above the 3-axis (excluding the F-sharp), and a C natural-minor diatonic scale on and below it (excluding the D-flat). Major and minor triads appear respectively as upward- and downward-pointing triangular configurations in this same subspace. As illustrated, major, minor, and dominant seventh chords can be associated with other close-packed subsets, the dominant seventh chord extending into the 7 dimension. More complex harmonies can be associated with correspondingly more complex point

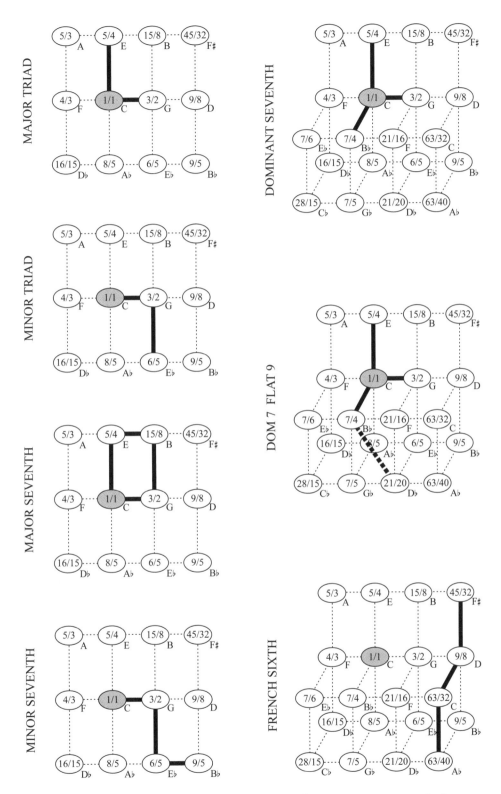

FIGURE 7.9. Selected traditional harmonies interpreted as compact sets in pitch-class projection space.

sets, including chords with altered and unaltered ninths, sharp elevenths, and so forth; the figure includes, for instance, a proposed tuning for a French sixth chord such as would traditionally resolve to a harmony on G (3/2). Tenney's notes feature a profusion of such figures corresponding to chords of diverse complexity and scales from musical cultures around the world. Only a fraction of these have been published (Tenney [1993b] 2015; [1993c/2003] 2015, 378).[29]

7.7.3 Polarity and Containment

The perception of roots, tonics, and "strong" root progressions was one of Tenney's earliest, most intense, and most sustained theoretical preoccupations. Although his unpublished writings on these topics are voluminous, very little of their substance has found its way to print. Lamenting in 1984 the difficulty of finding a suitable point of closure at which he might finally publish his accumulated theorizations, he remarked, "Recently I've come to think that maybe the most appropriate way to put it out is in the pieces" (Tenney 1984a, 13). Accordingly, his ideas regarding roots and tonics figure significantly in *Changes: 64 Studies for 6 Harps* (1985) and *Water on the Mountain . . . Fire in Heaven* (1985). Tenney's archival notes include clear indications that he did not regard his model of rootedness as settled—in which light the following partial descriptions of it should be regarded.

For convenience, the following will designate the direction along an axis in harmonic space as increasing if it corresponds to multiplication by the associated prime and decreasing if it corresponds to division thereby; for instance, in figure 7.7, rightward is the increasing direction along the 3-axis. Inspection of each pitch-class set in figure 7.9 reveals that the commonly accepted *root* of each is located at the point whose coordinate values are least, with priority given to axes corresponding to lower primes. Thus, as drawn in the figure, the tone commonly regarded as root always resides at the leftmost coordinate in the chord (i.e., at the most negative coordinate along the 3-axis), and when two or more chord members share that coordinate, then the one with the bottommost coordinate (i.e., the most negative coordinate along the 5-axis) is root, with a similar tie-breaking criterion applied to other axes as needed in order of their increasing associated primes. Regarding such apparent *polarity* within harmonic space, Tenney remarked:

> Harmonic space is not symmetrical. It clearly has an up and down. In each dimension, in fact, except between the octaves, there's an asymmetry, which is what leads to roots and tonics. And moving to the left along that three-to-two dimension is a very different manner from moving to the right. It's as if one is uphill and the other is downhill. . . . Those downhill progressions are the ones that *sound*, I guess, because they really present new information. When you move uphill you're moving into a region which you're already expressing with

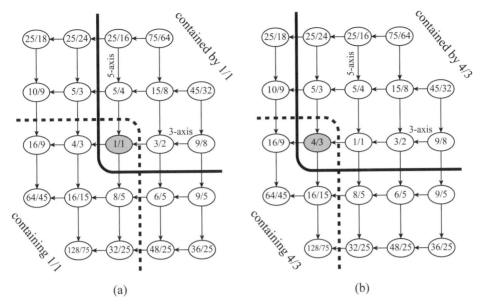

FIGURE 7.10. Containment relations in the (3,5) plane of pitch-class projection space.

the harmonic series, which is already present. But when you move downhill, you're always moving into an area that contains where you've been. The harmonic structure could move down a major third. And that, to my ear, is only a little less powerful than down a fifth. That's a strong harmonic progression. . . . It's always like from 3:2 to 1:1, and 5:4 to 1:1, or from 1:1 down to 4:3—moving in the subharmonic direction. There is a power in that direction. (1987b, 462)[30]

Suppose—as depicted in figure 7.10(a)—that the ratio class 1/1 in the (3,5) plane of pitch-class projection space represents the pitch class of the fundamental of a complex tone. Then only ratio classes residing in the first (upper right) quadrant of the plane correspond to pitch classes contained within the harmonic series of that tone. (If the 7 dimension were added to the figure to yield (3,5,7) space, then this *containment* region would correspond to the first octant and would include the ratio class 7/4.) Conversely, only ratio classes residing in the third (lower left) quadrant of the figure correspond to fundamentals whose harmonic series contain the pitch class of 1/1.[31] Progression of the fundamental through an interval corresponding to one of the ratio classes appearing in that third quadrant—as from 1/1 in part (a) of figure 7.10 to 4/3 in part (b)—thus yields a consequent tone among whose harmonics are represented the pitch classes of all harmonics in the antecedent tone but also some new pitch classes, most notably including the pitch class of the new fundamental. Thus, with respect to pitch class, this progression "downhill" (i.e., in the negative direction along the 3-axis) presents "new information" but also "contains where you've been," as Tenney indicated in the above quotation. Negatively directed motions along the 5-axis (or 7-axis) exhibit these same two characteristics, but neither obtains for positively directed ("uphill") motions along any axis. Tenney's description of "downhill" progressions as "strong" echoes Schoenberg's designation of "strong" root progressions, and he went so far as to assert that it, "to me, explains the sense of what Schoenberg calls strong root progressions" (Tenney 1987b, 464).[32]

Next, suppose that two complex tones sound concurrently or successively and that the pitch classes of their respective fundamentals correspond to 1/1 and some other ratio class in the first quadrant of figure 7.10(a). Then the former tone *contains* the latter, again in the sense that the pitch classes of all harmonics in the latter tone are represented among the harmonics of the former tone. Tenney hypothesized that such containment promoted perception of 1/1 as the root of the dyad. Similarly, a tone whose fundamental corresponds to a ratio class in the third quadrant would tend to be heard as the root if presented together with a tone of pitch class corresponding to 1/1, which it would contain in the same sense. This *polarity* that tends to assign root quality to pitch classes at more negative coordinates in harmonic space is represented in the figure using arrows. The rootedness of a dyad involving a second fundamental drawn from the second or fourth quadrant of the plane would be less clear in Tenney's model. At times he described the root in such instances as undefined, ambiguous, or possibly external to the dyad itself, although he also attempted to develop quantitative measures for root strength that could be used to decide among the candidates for the root of either dyads or larger pitch-class collections.[33] For larger pitch sets, Tenney hypothesized that the *tonal center(s)* of the collection would be the member pitch class(es) with greatest net root strength and that for each candidate all other members of the collection would make some weighted contribution to this quantity. Among the implications of employing extending just-intonation systems, Tenney hypothesized refinements and extensions of the root-tonic quality:

> In dealing with tempered pitches, I assume that approximations of the simpler intervals are involved in perception, but these yield ambiguities . . . (e.g., is a tempered maj. 2nd an approximation of 8/7, 9/8, or 10/9?)[.] Because of the ambiguities, we cannot extend the root-weighting process beyond the intervals of the "5 limit" when dealing with twelve-tone tempered pitches (in a just scale, however, the process might be extended as far as the interval-system (limit) of the scale itself, thus in Partch's system, both 7/4 and 11/8 ought to have some root-defining power).[34]

Among the projects that Tenney left unfinished at the end of his life was a model of the auditory system that he hoped would be capable, for a given pitch collection, of computing the relative strengths of various root candidates and concomitantly the degree of the collection's perceived *rootedness*. Regarding these he noted that "any theory of 'root-strength' *must* take into account the actual spacing, distribution, vertical ordering of pitches (not just as pitch-class collections), because the root-sense can clearly be altered by these factors alone. And in a melodic situation, temporal order must be considered."[35] That Tenney's thinking on the subject of roots, tonics, and harmony generally remained unfinished is attested by an archival note apparently written sometime after 1990, in which he reflected that "*re* theory of harmony: over the years I have worked out quite a large number of important basic principles which, taken together, constitute a large part of a new theory. More extensions are needed, and I must avoid being stuck in older conceptual habits, like looking for a tonic, when the more general notion of *containment*—which is *one* of several factors determining the tonic—can (and should) stand by itself, for what it's worth in non-conventional harmonic textures."[36]

7.8 Harmonic Measures and Their Applications

In this section I offer a few of my own observations regarding the properties of Tenney's harmonic measures and consider their prospective analytical applications.

Tenney's harmonic distance HD and disjunction ratio D (of a harmonic series aggregate with respect to a notional harmonic series on its GCD) are plotted in figure 7.11(a) and (b), respectively, for reduced frequency ratios corresponding to pitch intervals whose size is no greater than a double octave and whose denominators are no greater than 16. Comparison of these figures reveals that the two measures exhibit very similar but not identical structures. The most striking difference is provided by the special case of two tones separated by an interval occurring between the fundamental of a harmonic series and a partial thereof (i.e., by frequency ratios of the form 1/1, 2/1, 3/1, 4/1 . . .). The harmonic distance between two such tones increases monotonically with the interval between them, as shown near the bottom of figure 7.11(a). On the other hand, as shown at the bottom of figure 7.11(b), any two such tones will exhibit zero disjunction, since all partials of the upper tone will coincide in frequency with some partial of the lower one. More generally, absolute intervallic width tends to make a greater additive contribution to harmonic distance than to disjunction ratio. This factor also affects the ranking of intervals according to each measure, such rankings generally being similar but not identical. Figure 7.11(c) provides a ranking by harmonic distance of intervals smaller than an octave with denominators no greater than 16. Arrows indicate all changes that would occur if ratios were instead ranked by disjunction ratio. These changes affect only intermediate rankings of very similar measure, in each case decreasing the rank of certain larger intervals while increasing the rank of smaller ones. An additional noteworthy observation is that disjunction ratio is bounded above by unity, while harmonic distance has no upper bound. Thus ratios of relatively

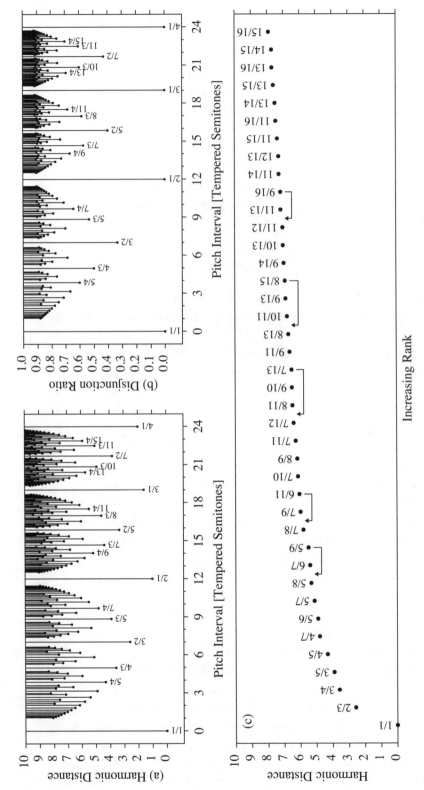

FIGURE 7.11. (a) Harmonic distance and (b) disjunction ratio for all frequency ratios corresponding to pitch intervals between a perfect unison and a double octave with denominators no greater than 16. Selected points are labeled with their associated ratio. (c) A rank ordering by harmonic distance of all frequency ratios smaller than one octave and with denominators no greater than 16. Arrows show the changes if ratios were ranked by disjunction ratio instead.

high measure are often less quantitatively differentiated by disjunction ratio than by harmonic distance.[37]

On the other hand, certain similarities between the two measures are clear. For instance, according to either disjunction ratio or harmonic distance, ratios of relatively low measure (relatively "consonant" or "simple" intervals) tend to be well separated from one another in magnitude, and the lower the measure, the greater their separation. This separation between relatively simple intervals is inherited from the structure of the rational number system itself, wherein reduced fractions of low denominator are better separated from their neighbors than reduced fractions of relatively greater denominator (Hardy and Wright [1938] 1979, 30). For example, as shown in figure 7.11(a) and (b), no comparably simple ratios are found in the immediate neighborhood of the 2/1 octave—which is instead populated by relatively complex ratios—and the same holds for the moderately less simple 4/3 just fourth, although it is not so well-buffered in this respect as the octave.[38] In Partch's rendition, "Each consonance or comparative consonance is a little sun in its universe, around which dissonant satellites cluster" ([1949] 1974, 151).

Although Tenney speculated regarding the potential analytical usefulness of his harmonic distance function (1987b, 462), he himself never applied his harmonic measures to the analysis of music—not even his own. In his work as a composer, they contributed to his conceptual framework for harmony, and harmonic distance in particular sometimes served as a compositional or pre-compositional tool. On the other hand, Tenney's formulations turn out to be ripe for retrospective application to the analysis of certain of his pieces. For instance, in his compositions that feature gradual microtonal intervallic expansions and/or contractions, harmonic measures like those of figure 7.11 can illuminate the order and timing with which particular harmonic entities appear, as well as the general character of variation between neighboring harmonic events. For instance, the aforementioned separation between relative consonances lends to their traversal an inherent musical drama, since the advent of a relatively consonant interval furnishes an abrupt contrast with the increasingly dissonant intervals through which that consonant interval is approached and the similarly dissonant ones through which it is departed.

More particularly, if they are regarded as time sequences, then figure 7.11(a) and (b) each delineates a recognizable rhythmic structure: a multilayered divisive polyrhythm. Each span between successive frequency ratios of denominator 1 is divided into two parts by the ratios of denominator 2 that it contains, into three parts by those with denominator 3, and so forth, with coincidences between rhythmic layers devolving to the layer with the lowest denominator. In particular, the octave interval between 1/1 and 2/1 is divided into n parts by the ratios with denominator n that are contained within it, projecting a divisive polyrhythm of the form 1:2:3:4:5: . . . If intervallic width varies linearly in time, then—as figure 7.11(a) and (b) show—this stratified divisive polyrhythm is subjected to a continuous accelerando or ritardando, depending on whether the interval is expanding or contracting, respectively. Each of the two illustrated harmonic measures of a frequency ratio is an increasing function of the ratio's denominator, so that—as the figures again reveal—the value of the measure reflects in part the rhythmic location at which that frequency ratio appears, since this denominator corresponds to the *tuplet layer* within the polyrhythm. In particular, local minima in the harmonic measures (corresponding to marked local "consonances") appear at relatively simple *tuplet divisions*. Within the octave, certain salient local minima in these measures are associated with frequency ratios either of the form $(n + 1)/n = 1 + 1/n$ (such as 2/1, 3/2, 4/3, 5/4 . . . , which are sometimes called *superparticular* ratios) or of the form $(2n − 1)/n = 2 − 1/n$ (such as 1/1, 3/2, 5/3, 7/4 . . .). These particular frequency ratios tend to furnish the principal harmonic landmarks in a gradual intervallic expansion or contraction, although secondary landmarks may be audible between them. For instance, during the course of a smooth intervallic expansion from a unison to an octave, the advent of each successive superparticular ratio always corresponds—when discriminable—to the strongest consonance heard since the initial unison. (A dedicated exploration of the structure of multilayered divisive polyrhythms is available in Wannamaker [2012].)

There may be no general grounds to prefer one harmonic measure to the other if they furnish gauges of different qualities. The disjunction ratio of a harmonic-series aggregate with a harmonic series on its own GCD is complemented by its corresponding intersection ratio (section 7.6.1), which might be advanced as a gauge of harmonicity (and thus, under suitable conditions, fusion and toneness). Harmonic distance, on the other hand, is intended to quantify a different sense of harmonic relation—one that pertains not only to concurrent complex tones but also to successive or sine tones and that is qualitatively distinct from Stumpfian "resemblance to a single tone." As mentioned above, Tenney associated the two measures with decidedly different historical concepts of consonance and dissonance (CDC-1 and CDC-2, respectively). Eventually, science may grapple on its own grounds with empirical questions concerning the extent to which the various CDCs and measures Tenney proposed are psychologically meaningful and distinct, how closely they fit experimental data, and what neurophysiological correlates they might possess. For the particular music-analytical purposes of this book, the limited differences in intervallic ranking produced by intersection ratio and harmonic distance are unimportant. Instead, these measures prove useful primarily insofar as their correlation with pertinent aspects of intersubjective musical perception is sufficient to permit the attention of a reader to be directed to specific audible features and trends.

CHAPTER 8

Canons and the Harmonic Series (1972–79)

For a few years following his arrival in California in 1970, Tenney's teaching position at the California Institute of the Arts provided him with relative financial stability and greater freedom to compose, helping to initiate a highly productive and exploratory period in his musical output. Before too long, however, CalArts itself entered a period of financial instability. After the increasingly tenuous support for Tenney's position finally collapsed entirely, he spent the 1975–76 academic year teaching at the University of California, Santa Cruz (Tenney 1988b, 34). His personal life also underwent major transitions during this period, with separation from his second wife leading to divorce in 1974, followed by a new marriage in 1975 to violist Ann Holloway. After a year spent in Santa Cruz, Tenney accepted a relatively secure position at York University in Toronto, Canada, where he would teach for the next twenty-four years (from 1976 until 2000). During this period, his personal biography became less outwardly eventful as he focused closely upon composing, research, and family life.[1]

Surveying his output since the move to California, Tenney remarked in 1978: "Although these pieces are quite different from each other in many respects, most of them are characterized by one or more of the following: (1) simple, often highly predictable forms, (2) a frequent use of *canon* as a structural device (though the canonic relations are often rendered imperceptible by the musical textures), and (3) a renewed concern with *harmony*, sometimes involving deviations from tempered tunings, but nearly always related in some way to the *harmonic series*" (1978b). Radically simple and predictable process-generated forms had been a characteristic feature of Tenney's music since *For Ann (rising)* (1969), as discussed in section 6.1. Tenney's canons may be regarded as a subclass of such process-generated forms. Some are rigorously deterministic, with themes whose internal structures and entrance schedules are rule-governed, as in *Spectral CANON for CONLON Nancarrow* (1974; section 8.3), the *Three Pieces for Drum Quartet* (1974–75), and the *Three Pieces for Mechanical Drum* (1974–75, composed for a robotic instrument constructed by sound sculptor Stephan von Huene). Other instances involve indeterminate elements, such as the de facto canons produced in a number of pieces employing tape-delay systems, such as *Saxony* (1978) and *Glissade* (1982). Usually the composer specified the use of such systems primarily in order to thicken the musical texture—he referred to them as "the poor man's orchestra"—but he sometimes additionally exploited their reiterations to achieve contrapuntal effects or aggregate patterns.

The preeminent development in Tenney's music of the 1970s, however, was the emergence of harmonic perception as a topic, beginning with his adoption of the harmonic series as an intervallic and structural resource in *Clang* (1972) and *Quintext* (1972). Moreover, after his middecade move to Toronto brought him relative stability in both employment and personal life, Tenney embarked on a program of intense *theoretical* research regarding harmony, the results of which would crucially inform his music of the coming decades. This chapter and the next accordingly assume familiarity on the part of the reader with the discussions of Tenney's harmonic theories as presented in chapter 7. The following selected analyses illustrate particular concerns and methodologies that were characteristic of Tenney's music in the mid-1970s and that would make periodic later appearances as well.

8.1 The Harmonic-Series Music

Section 7.6 introduced the concept of *toneness* (the perceived similarity of a given acoustical stimulus to a single tone) along with that of a frequent acoustical correlate of such toneness: *harmonicity* (objective similarity to a harmonic series). As such, harmonicity often provided a crucial formal parameter in Tenney's compositional practice between 1972 and 1978, and it is relevant in varying degrees to many of his compositions thereafter as well. Asked what circumstances led to his use of the harmonic series in composition, he replied:

> That's really hard for me to reconstruct. I wrote two pieces that year, 1972, which used it: a piece for orchestra called *Clang* and a piece for string quintet called *Quintext*. In both of them I used the harmonic series in this compositional way. I can't frankly remember how that came to me—I think it had to do with looking for some new way to integrate a composition. And I've always been fascinated by the sheer acoustical and psychoacoustical fact involved there, that the auditory system integrates what, from an acoustical standpoint, is a complex set of frequencies. For one reason or another—and this is an extremely important theoretical question as far as harmony is concerned—the auditory system is

able to integrate that complex set into a singular percept. And I think it's quite possible that just something about that, I began to think of it as a possibility for compositional integration. The whole interplay between multiplicity and singularity, complexity and simplicity, began to interest me. Of course, this is not a new goal in music; it's an old notion of variety within unity. (Tenney 1993a, 393)

Accordingly, a number of Tenney's pieces can be understood as involving processes that gradually increase or decrease toneness through the manipulation of harmonicity.

The late piece *Diapason* (1996) for chamber orchestra provides a lucid example of a gradual approach to harmonicity. At its opening, pitches are restricted to very high harmonics of a low fundamental, and all of the lower harmonics of this fundamental are absent. The resulting harmonicity is therefore low because the aggregate of sounding partials is far from comprising a single complete harmonic series. Gradually, however, the pitch set of the ensemble descends through the harmonic series, achieving complete harmonicity once the fundamental is finally supplied. Various other realizations of such gradual approaches to or departures from harmonicity appear in Tenney's *Three Harmonic Studies* (1974), *Symphony* (1975), *Saxony* (1978), *Septet* (1981), *Voice(s)* (1982/1984), and *Critical Band* (1988; section 10.1).

A different musical process involving harmonicity appears in the concluding section of *Clang* (1972) for orchestra (section 8.2). Therein massed instrumental pitches initially correspond to high harmonics of an infrasonic fundamental. This unplayed and unheard fundamental resides far below the frequency range wherein acoustical harmonicity would evoke perceived toneness. However, toneness is then gradually approached as, in each ensuing section, the sounding pitch set is conformed to the harmonics of a new fundamental that is one octave higher than the last. Variations of this migration by a harmonic series into and through the register wherein harmonicity evokes toneness can also be found in *Glissade*, V: "Stochastic Canonic Variations" (1982), *Form 2* (1993), the *Diaphonic* series (1997; section 11.3), and *Panacousticon* (2005).

Yet another tactic for approaching and retreating from harmonicity figures in the first of Tenney's seven-part *Harmonium* series (1976–2000). *Harmonium #1* (1976; section 8.4) features note-by-note "modulations" between subsets of different harmonic series. These subsets constitute salient *milestone harmonies*, with harmonicity decreasing during the transitions between milestones but increasing upon arrival at each new one.

A striking outgrowth of Tenney's interest in harmonic fusion is represented by three works in which he painstakingly transcribed the acoustical components of selected spoken texts for performance by an instrumental ensemble. The archetype of these was *Three Indigenous Songs* (1979; section 8.5), which was followed by *"Ain't I a Woman?"* (1992) and the remarkable *Song 'n' Dance for Harry Partch* (1999).

Other pieces, while not necessarily making formal use of harmonicity, derive scales from subsets of the harmonic series. For instance, the *Chorales* series (1974–75) uses octatonic scales comprising tempered approximations to the pitch classes of a fundamental and its first seven prime-numbered harmonics. On the other hand, the first and third movements of *Quintext* (1972) use a thirteen-note scale comprising the pitch classes of a fundamental and its first twelve odd-numbered harmonics (corresponding to the lowest thirteen distinct pitch classes appearing in the harmonic series).

In its explorations of the harmonic series, invocation of the duality of harmony and timbre, orchestrations of spectral features, and frequent use of gradual processes, Tenney's harmonic-series music invites comparisons to the mid-1970s *spectral music* of such European composers as Gérard Grisey, Tristan Murail, and Horatiu Radulescu (Anderson 2000; Fineberg 2000a, 2000b), although Tenney reported that he did not become aware of their work until the 1990s (2008, 82). In two articles (Wannamaker 2008a, 2008b) I explore in detail the ways in which his work paralleled, anticipated, or contrasted with developments in Europe, but perhaps the paramount distinction was Tenney's relatively concentrated focus on the nature and operation of perception. The concept of spectral structure accordingly provided him with a sometimes-useful framework for associated explorations rather than a source of structural and processual templates more generally.

8.2 *Clang* (1972)

ORCHESTRA
15 mins., 20 secs.

Clang is Tenney's earliest composition to invoke the harmonic series as a structural resource, and it introduced a number of techniques that he would continue to use throughout his subsequent career. These include available-pitch procedures, the derivation of scales from pitch classes in the harmonic series, and the filtering of a texture via changes in its *conceptual fundamental* (section 7.6.1).

The title is derived from Tenney's theories of temporal gestalt perception in music (section 3.4). In that context, a *clang* is the smallest musically significant temporal grouping larger than an indivisible element. The simple monumental form of *Clang* indeed suggests—perhaps only poetically—such a fundamental unit enormously dilated in time, although the title has a more straightforward onomatopoeic sense as well. The large-scale form comprises two successive gradual processes—the first accumulative and the second dissolutive—as shown in figure 8.1. These are initiated, separated, and concluded by three *fortissississimo* percussive "clangs." The second clang marks the onset of the dissolutive process and occurs about two-thirds of the way through the work. It thus divides the work roughly at its golden section, a juncture that would often furnish a formal pivot in Tenney's subsequent music.

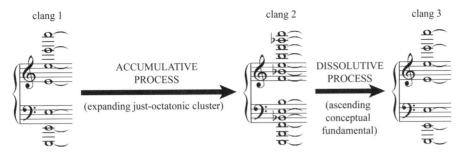

FIGURE 8.1. Formal scheme of *Clang* showing reduced "clang" chords.

The gradual progressions in *Clang* employ, for the first time in Tenney's output, a partially indeterminate process to which he would often resort thereafter and that he referred to as an *available-pitch procedure*. The instructions in the score characterize this as follows: "The notation indicates available pitches to be played by sustained-tone instruments (including rolls on the percussion instruments) in the following way: each player chooses, at random, one after another of these available pitches (when within the range of his or her instrument), and plays it beginning very softly (almost inaudibly), gradually increasing the intensity to the dynamic level indicated for that section, then gradually decreasing the intensity again to inaudibility. . . . After a pause at least as long as the previous tone, each player then repeats this process." The available-pitch set changes periodically, causing the pitch content of the music to gradually evolve.

Clang uses throughout a scale comprising the pitch class E and the pitch classes of its first seven prime-numbered harmonics. These are approximated using equal-tempered quarter tones for partials 11, 13, and 7, as shown in figure 8.2. Quarter-tone inflections are indicated both in this figure and in the score using parenthesized accidentals, which denote inflections that are half as large as for the unparenthesized accidental. Relative to 12TET, this quarter-tone notation improves the approximations to a number of harmonic-series pitch classes; the residual deviations from 24TET are indicated in cents above the staff of figure 8.2. With regard to intonation, however—and in contrast with increasingly stringent stipulations in Tenney's later music—the score indicates that "great precision is obviously not expected here—in fact, the beats resulting from slight discrepancies from the actual harmonic frequencies are welcome—but an effort should be made to improve the approximation as much as is possible or practical."[2] The resulting pitch-class collection roughly resembles the 12TET octatonic scale that alternates half steps and whole steps, but with certain quarter-tone alterations. The approximations to just intervals that it provides are heard in various combinations as the ensemble enacts the available-pitch procedure.

The opening percussive "clang" sounds a pitch-class unison comprising all Es between E_1 and E_7, inclusive. The following accumulative process presents a measured expansion of the available-pitch gamut, starting from E_4 alone and

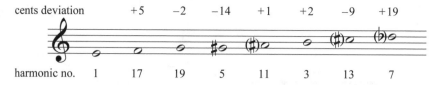

cents deviation		+5	−2	−14	+1	+2	−9	+19
harmonic no.	1	17	19	5	11	3	13	7

FIGURE 8.2. The pitch-class set used in *Clang*. Quarter-tone inflections are denoted by parenthesized accidentals. Deviations of the corresponding harmonic-series pitch classes from these approximations in 24TET are shown above the staff in cents.

gradually adding adjacent pitches from the just-octatonic set. The score indicates that "the effect intended . . . is a single, continuous pitch with gradually changing timbre, followed . . . by a gradually expanding, quasi-random texture of changing timbres and pitches." In stages, the range of available pitches is slowly expanded symmetrically above and below E_4, rather as though an imaginary registral window were being progressively widened so as to admit an increasing number of pitches. Meticulous orchestration is employed to ensure that changes in dynamic and timbre are smooth. For instance, after the initial clang the various instruments enter fractions of a choir at a time. The entrances of the various percussion instruments are likewise delayed to varying degrees, the timpani entering last. The result is by no means static—the evolving available-pitch procedure slowly amasses a dark, churning ocean of sound from which variegated tones, timbres, and microtonal harmonies hauntingly effloresce.

When all pitches in the just-octatonic set between E_1 and E_7 have become available, the accumulative process stops and the second clang sounds, all sustaining instruments falling briefly silent in response and then continuing just as before. This second clang contrasts markedly with the first and last, as shown in figure 8.1. Whereas the opening and concluding clangs are extreme consonances, the second is an extreme dissonance. However, it also contrasts sharply with the dense dissonant cluster that it locally interrupts due to its distinctive timbre, extension, and more open voicing.[3]

At the time of the second clang, all available pitches (and their harmonics) can be regarded as harmonics of a fundamental at E_{-3}. This notional infrasonic pitch thus represents the *conceptual fundamental* of the collection (as discussed in section 7.6.1). The stages of the ensuing dissolutive process represent successive upward octave transpositions of this conceptual fundamental, with those tones (and only those tones) that cannot be interpreted as harmonics of each new fundamental dropping out of the available set at each stage.[4] The process is illustrated for two successive sections (corresponding to successive available-pitch sets) in figure 8.3, wherein filled noteheads indicate pitches that will be deleted from the available-pitch set in the next section. In section 10 of figure 8.3, the conceptual fundamental of the collection is E_{-1}, whose harmonic numbers 5,

FIGURE 8.3. Two successive sections (i.e., available pitch sets) from the score to *Clang*, between which the conceptual fundamental changes from E_{-1} to E_0.

7, 11, 13, 17, and 19 are approximated by the filled noteheads in the figure. These and only these odd-numbered harmonics of E_{-1} will not be harmonics of the new conceptual fundamental E_0 in section 11 of figure 8.3 and are accordingly omitted from the available-pitch set for that ensuing section. Pitches in the pitch class E are treated specially, insofar as they are all retained in the available-pitch set even once they lie below the ascending conceptual fundamental. All other pitch classes are gradually and systematically weeded out until only the Es between E_1 and E_7 are left sounding, at which point these are reinforced and released by the final percussive clang.

As the process of *Clang*'s second half unfolds, the texture increasingly resembles a single complex tone synthesized by the ensemble as a whole. This new harmonic order spreads slowly upward from the bass as the conceptual fundamental ascends, so that progressively clearer glimpses of harmonicity emerge amid the waves of random dissonance spawned by the available-pitch procedure. Once the conceptual fundamental attains E_1 it becomes playable, and all available pitches thereafter correspond to harmonics of this *sounding* fundamental. The result simulates a single monumental tone whose continually shifting harmonic spectrum is synthesized by the entire orchestra in cooperation. The attendant sense of emergent unity and solidity is only intensified by the continued pruning of the pitch set, which ultimately leaves only a towering column of Es.

The large-scale trajectory of *Clang* is a broad arc of tension and resolution, moving from the simplicity of a single tone through an increasingly complex welter of different timbres, pitches, and harmonies and finally returning via a different route to a unitary percept. The manner in which apparent chaos gradually cedes to sublime order in many of Tenney's works suggests a transcendentalist undercurrent, even if the composer avoided pronouncements on such metaphysical topics.

8.3 *Spectral CANON for CONLON Nancarrow* (1974)

PLAYER PIANO
3 mins., 30 secs.

Conlon Nancarrow was an American composer who is best known for his series of around fifty studies for player piano. These were composed over the course of forty-five years beginning around 1948, during which time Nancarrow was residing in relative seclusion in Mexico City. These now-classic studies explored highly inventive approaches to realizing and organizing extreme rhythmic complexity, including varieties of ostinato, isorhythm, tempo canon, and acceleration canon (Gann 1995). Tenney first heard Nancarrow's music on their premiere commercial recordings, which were released in 1969 (Tenney 1988b, 35).[5] While in Mexico City in the early 1970s, he took the opportunity to contact Nancarrow in person. Over the course of subsequent correspondence, Nancarrow sent him a complete collection of recordings and scores for the studies, ultimately resulting in publication of the scores, as well as Tenney's extensive analyses of them (1977b).

Tenney's homage, *Spectral CANON for CONLON Nancarrow*, comprises a complex rhythmic canon, recalling the frequent appearance of such devices in Nancarrow's music. The compositional design was refined by Tenney on a teletype terminal and then punched by Nancarrow himself on his own roll-punching machine. Realization was undertaken with assistance from composer Gordon Mumma on a player piano in Santa Cruz, California.[6]

The structure is a canon in twenty-four voices lasting roughly 3.5 minutes. Figure 8.4 provides a graphical score of its opening, with canonic voices numbered in italics at their entrances. Each voice of the canon is assigned a different single pitch, which it repeats undampened again and again. The pitches used are the first twenty-four harmonics of A_1 (55 Hz), to which the required piano strings are precisely retuned. The sequence of interattack durations is identical in all voices, although the higher a voice is pitched, the later it enters—hence the canonic aspect. The duration sequence is monotonically decreasing at first, but once a voice has sounded a specified number of attacks (this number is the same for all voices), the sequence begins to retrograde. Only the lowest-pitched voice finishes its retrograde, the piece ending at the moment when this happens; the higher voices, not having finished their retrogrades, are truncated at that time. Although these pitch and temporal resources are narrowly restricted in themselves, their *interaction* produces complex and surprising results.

The piece opens with A_1 slowly repeated, its constituent harmonics ringing above the low fundamental. As successive voices enter, climbing gradually up the harmonic series, polyrhythms emerge that increase in complexity until

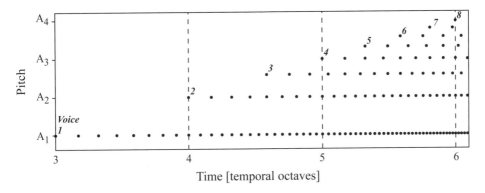

FIGURE 8.4. Graphic score for the opening of *Spectral CANON for CONLON Nancarrow*. Time is measured in units of temporal octaves (~23.5 secs.) relative to the temporal fundamental of voice 1.

the superimposition of many chiming voices becomes a chaotic maelstrom of sound. The strong beat initially supplied by the lowest voice gradually becomes a steady drone as the repetition rate of its undamped tone increases, the sense of unifying pulse temporarily disappearing. Slowly, however, a new and surprising variety of order subtly creeps into the lower voices as rising and falling glissandi begin to sweep progressively higher along the harmonic series, punctuated by simultaneous attacks in multiple voices. These ringing glissandi subsume successively higher pitches until, as their lengthening sweeps finally attain the texture's treble extreme, the piece dramatically concludes with all twenty-four voices sounding simultaneously for the first time. Due to the accurate harmonicity and synchrony of attack, the result is surprisingly perceived less as a chord than as a single tone pitched at A_1, recalling the first pitch heard at the opening. It is as though the constituents of this single complex tone appear torn asunder in the core of the piece but are powerfully welded together again in its concluding gesture.

There exists an unreleased longer (5 mins., 25 secs.) version of Tenney's *Spectral CANON* that was extended and realized by composer Clarence Barlow using a computer-driven player piano while he and Tenney were both teaching at the 1990 Darmstädter Ferienkurse in Darmstadt, Germany. This extended version continues beyond the total simultaneity at the end of the original version, allowing *all* voices to finish their retrogrades, with voices falling silent one by one in the same order in which they first entered. Additional high-register glissandi and simultaneities are heard between the remaining voices as they play out, the thinning textural density allowing surprising treble melodies to gracefully emerge. For reasons of analytical convenience, the following analysis will model this extended version of the piece. The conclusions will straightforwardly apply to the shorter original version as well.

An analytical starting point can be found by observing that the lowest voice in the graphical score of figure 8.4 qualitatively resembles a harmonic series turned on its side, its interattack durations decreasing from left to right just as the pitch intervals between successive harmonics diminish in size as the series is ascended. Indeed, by the composer's own account, composition of the work involved experiments with various juxtapositions of such "durational harmonic series."[7] By analogy with a harmonic series of pitches, it is thus possible to speak of durations within a canonic voice as *temporal intervals*, such as *temporal octaves*. In particular, by direct measurement it can be confirmed that this durational harmonic series is missing its lowest seven "harmonics" (attacks), so that it begins in its "fourth octave." Thus—as Larry Polansky (1984, 223) points out—the first eight sounding attacks occur during a temporal octave of roughly 23.5 seconds, the following sixteen attacks over the course of a similar interval, the following thirty-two attacks similarly, and so forth, as illustrated in figure 8.4. In each voice, the initial seven attacks are presumably omitted from the durational harmonic series on aesthetic grounds, since if they were retained, then the time interval between the first and second attacks would be a full temporal octave of more than 20 seconds.

Voice-entrance times also articulate a durational harmonic series, with the same octave duration. In this case, however, the series begins in its first octave, wherein a single new voice appears, while two voices enter in the second octave, and so forth, as again shown in figure 8.4. Note that, despite the exponentially increasing rate of voice entrances, the pitch of entering voices ascends linearly in time due to the logarithmic narrowing of pitch intervals within the harmonic series (section 7.2). This narrowing, in light of the physical spacing of piano keys and strings, limits the total number of voices possible, and Tenney settled on twenty-four (2000c).[8]

The above compositional features are summarized in the following four conditions, which fully specify the pitch-time structure of the extended *Spectral CANON for CONLON Nancarrow*:

- Numbering the voices from 1 to $N = 24$ beginning with the lowest, the pitch of voice n corresponds to the nth harmonic relative to a fundamental of A_1.
- The rhythm in each voice is identical, apart from its canonic delay, and displays retrograde symmetry, with voice 1 beginning its retrograde at the moment when voice N enters.
- Just as in a harmonic pitch series, wherein the pitch interval from the fundamental to a particular harmonic is given by the logarithm of its harmonic number, the sounding attacks of the forward portion of the attack-time sequence in voice 1 occur at times

$$\{\log_2 8, \log_2 9, \log_2 10, \ldots\}.$$

The time scale used here has units of temporal octaves (not seconds) and a temporal origin located three temporal octaves before the first attack of the

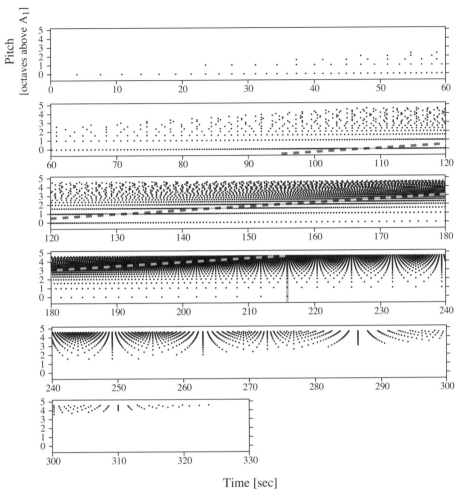

FIGURE 8.5. Complete algorithmically generated graphic score for *Spectral CANON for CONLON Nancarrow* in Barlow's extended 1990 version.

piece.[9] The temporal octave is a constant chosen such that the time interval between the first two sounding attacks is 4 seconds. Thus it is given by

$$\frac{4}{\log_2(9/8)} \approx 23.5 \text{ seconds.}$$

- The entrance of voice n is delayed relative to that of voice 1 by a time interval of $\log_2 n$ temporal octaves.[10]

A complete graphic score of the extended *Spectral CANON* is shown in figure 8.5 as algorithmically generated by the author from the above specifications. The vertical gray line marks the conclusion of Tenney's original 1974 version. Attacks preceding the oblique dashed line are presenting forward durational sequences, while those following it are presenting retrograded durational sequences. For analytical purposes it is convenient, initially, to ignore the fact that the collections of forward and retrograded attack-time sequences overlap in time and to instead treat them separately. I will refer to the forward collection (preceding the dashed line) as SC1 and the retrograde one (following that line) as SC2. Each of these overlapped sections individually exhibits various unique and sometimes unexpected features arising from coordination between voices, including simultaneities, arpeggiations, and polyrhythmic relationships.

Figure 8.4 shows that as successive voices enter at the opening of SC1, increasingly complex polyrhythms appear in the sequence 2:1, 3:2:1, 4:3:2:1 . . . The first sound in the piece is the entrance of voice 1 with eight attacks of A_1 before voice 2 enters with A_2 reiterated on every second attack of voice 1, followed by voice 3 with E_3 on every third attack of voice 1, and so forth. As more voices enter, it becomes more difficult to recognize specific polyrhythms because new voices enter before the preceding rhythmic pattern completes a full cycle.

Figure 8.5 reveals a number of other striking features that are audible in the first 100 seconds of the music. Simultaneous attacks between multiple successive voices sometimes appear (such as near 51 seconds), and these are flanked by descending and ascending arpeggiations ("voice glissandi") through those voices. Figure 8.6 provides an excerpt from the reference score, in which the composer marked the entrances of new voices with dashed vertical lines and simultaneous attacks in adjacent voices with solid vertical lines. To these I have added gray lines that highlight examples of voice glissandi among low voices, as well as simultaneous dyads describing *parabolas* among the upper voices. Distinct parabolic pitch trajectories are difficult to aurally distinguish because of the interleaving of their attacks, but near their vertices they can clearly be heard converging to unisons or consecutive-voice dyads, the latter close intervals being particularly salient features of the texture.[11] During the *Spectral CANON's* rapid and complex middle portion, the irregular sequence of highest-sounding pitches engenders fleeting melodic lines, which are sometimes compound.

SC2 corresponds to the portion of figure 8.5 following the dashed oblique line. Inspection reveals that, like SC1, it involves complexly stratified polyrhythms but that these are of a quite different sort. They include tutti attacks (involving all voices below the dashed line) that gradually grow in height above the lowest voice. The time interval between these simultaneities is subdivided into successively finer fractions by successively higher voices so as to generate a multilayered divisive polyrhythm (1:2:3:4: . . .), the whole of which undergoes a gradual ritardando. Until the conclusion of Tenney's original version at the figure's vertical gray line, not all twenty-four voices participate in this divisive polyrhythm, since some high ones are still presenting forward forms of the durational sequence (in other words, they belong to SC1 and thus fall above the dashed line in figure 8.5). The continuation heard in the extended version of the piece exhibits simultaneities between those upper voices that are still sounding as lower voices one by one conclude their retrogrades.

FIGURE 8.6. Excerpt from the reference score (Byron 1975, 163; 90–100 secs.) to *Spectral CANON for CONLON Nancarrow*, annotated.

Surprising resultant features that gradually emerge after 190 seconds include the long harmonic glissandi that flank the simultaneities. Figure 8.7 reveals that these glissandi are actually multiple on either side of each simultaneity. My ear usually follows the descending curve immediately following each simultaneity, but due to the pervasive sharing of attacks between different glissandi, it is often lured by an ascending curve that is not the last before the next simultaneity. Whichever curve my ear follows, others provide pre- or postechoes.

Over the course of SC1 the music undergoes a gradual progression from stark simplicity to chaotic complexity via concurrent increases in tempo, re-

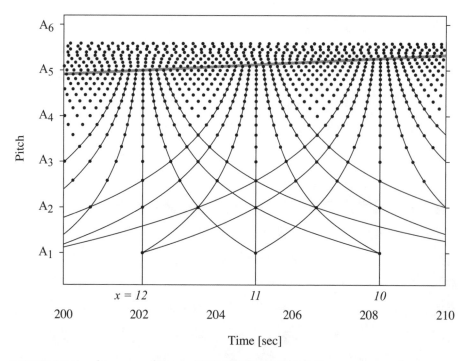

FIGURE 8.7. Graphic score of *Spectral CANON for CONLON Nancarrow* near the conclusion of Tenney's original 1974 version. Voices above the thick gray line are still part of SC1 (so they have not yet begun to retrograde and thus are still increasing in tempo). Total simultaneities among the lower voices are indicated with thin lines, as are segments of selected harmonic glissandi flanking those simultaneities. The horizontal axis is linear in real elapsed time, whose values are indicated in roman type, while the coordinate *x* in italics counts simultaneities backward in time from the end of the extended version.

gistral compass, number of sounding voices, polyrhythmic complexity, and harmonic complexity. In SC2 sensible order is progressively recovered via a different process. Compared to the complex welter of the work's middle portion, the texture seems to simplify as the music draws to a close. This is a product in part of the decreasing reiteration rates of the lower voices, which determine the sensed tempo of the music by demarcating the audible durations that the higher-pitched voices subdivide. Also, the glissandi and simultaneities emerge as gestalts subsuming many individual attacks, so that an audibly complex texture comprising a counterpoint of many brief, rapid, and unpredictable melodic snippets is gradually superseded by a texture comprising larger composite features. The perception of an inexorable process of complexification and fragmentation gradually yielding to a grand order that subsumes all musical features constitutes the large-scale formal arc of the work.

The progressive emergence of this new order is effected by the structural splicing of SC1 and SC2 that occurs in the middle of the piece and that is represented by the oblique dashed line in figure 8.5. The smoothness of the transition is promoted by adherence to a static pitch reservoir and by the very gradual tempo change within each voice, which ensures rhythmic continuity when its retrogression begins. What is perhaps surprising, however, is that simple retrogression within each voice (coupled, of course, with a specific set of canonic lags) produces the formally crucial transition between two very different types of stratified polyrhythm. It turns out that this is a consequence of the specifically logarithmic time dependence of the attack-time sequences, which is inherited from the composer's choice of the harmonic series as his rhythmic model (Wannamaker 2012, 65–66).

In *Spectral CANON*, the structural analogy between pitch and duration induces definite audible correspondences between harmonic and polyrhythmic complexities. In SC1, for instance, the frequency and tempo ratios between any two given voices are equal. This correspondence is audible at the opening of SC1, where polyrhythms of greater/lesser rhythmic complexity can be discerned involving pitch dyads of respectively greater/lesser harmonic complexity. Inspection of figure 8.7 reveals that this correspondence persists in SC2, although it is difficult to hear amid the more complicated texture. Indeed, these detailed correspondences become difficult to follow after the first minute of music. On the other hand, coordination between the steady increases in overall harmonic and rhythmic complexity throughout the opening is also a consequence of the structural pitch-rhythm analogy, and this constitutes an essential feature of the overall compositional design.

8.4 *Harmonium #1* (1976)
for Lou Harrison
TWELVE OR MORE SUSTAINING INSTRUMENTS
7–21 mins.

Following his departure from CalArts, Tenney spent the 1975–76 academic year teaching at the University of California in Santa Cruz. Although he finalized no new compositions there, he began work that would lead to his pivotal *Harmonium* series of pieces. He would also get to know composer Lou Harrison, who lived in nearby Aptos and who had been producing works using just intonation since the 1950s. Tenney would dedicate this first of his *Harmonium* pieces to Harrison.

The economical score to *Harmonium #1* (1976) fits on a single page and lucidly illustrates the essential structural processes common to all eight members of the *Harmonium* series. The complete score is reproduced in figure 8.8 with my added annotations and transparent overlays. It comprises seven sections delimited by double bar lines and enumerated in the figure using roman numerals. Each such section in turn comprises from two to five segments, delimited

FIGURE 8.8. The complete score to *Harmonium #1* with annotations.

by single bar lines. Individual segments enclose a set of available pitches from which performers are instructed to freely and independently choose. Pitch deviations from equal temperament (if any) are indicated above each notehead in cents. Each performer is instructed to execute tones that are 4 to 10 seconds in duration, with a symmetrical swell in loudness from *pianississimo* to the

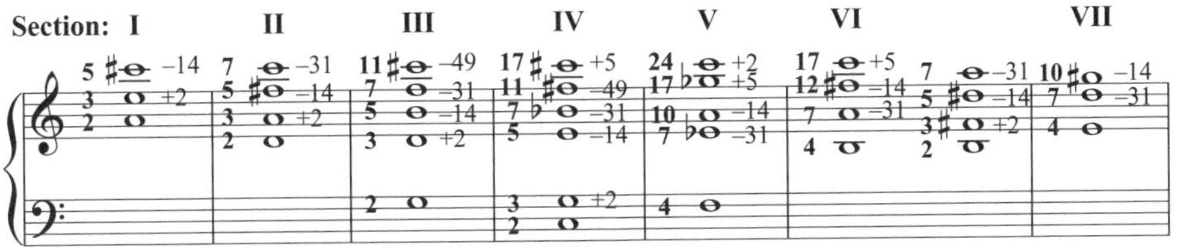

FIGURE 8.9. Milestone harmonies for each section of *Harmonium #1*. Associated harmonic numbers are indicated in bold to the left of each harmony, while any nonzero deviations from equal temperament are indicated to the right in cents.

marked dynamic and back again. After each tone, the performer is to pause before playing another (or the same) pitch. Each segment contains at least one open notehead, indicating a new pitch that was not available in the preceding segment. Filled noteheads, on the other hand, indicate pitches that have been retained. Any performer may initiate the transition to the next segment by introducing a pitch that is new in that segment (as indicated therein by an open notehead), although the instructions stipulate that this should be done such that each section is between 1 and 3 minutes in duration.

The annotations added to the score in figure 8.8 include gray rectangles indicating what I will refer to as *milestone harmonies* and thick gray lines demarcating pitch classes associated with those harmonies. The pitches in each milestone harmony comprise a subset of some harmonic series, but the fundamental of that series changes from section to section. In each case, the harmonics appearing are limited to prime numbers 2, 3, 5, 7, 11, and 17 or higher-octave equivalents thereof. These milestone harmonies are collected in figure 8.9, which indicates in bold type the harmonic numbers of the constituent pitches and the deviation (if any) in cents of each pitch from 12TET. The pitch of each fundamental is absent, but its pitch class always appears in the bass of the harmony.

The sequence of intervals between bass notes follows a tempered diatonic cycle of fifths descending from an A, a tritone being introduced between sections V and VI so that the sequence terminates one step before it would return to its origin. In each of sections I–IV, the bass descends a tempered perfect fifth, permitting the gradual introduction of higher harmonics in ascending registral order. As figure 8.8 shows, the first three introductory segments accumulate prime-numbered harmonics 3 and 5 above the A in the bass. In the ensuing segments, these pitches are replaced, one by one and via smooth voice leading, with pitches belonging to the milestone harmony of the next section. This process culminates with the appearance of the complete new milestone harmony at the beginning of section II. This replacement process is repeated similarly in each successive section until the arrival of section IV, engendering stretches of quasi-canonic imitation between the registrally segregated "voices" visible in figures 8.8 and 8.9. Replacement always begins with harmonic 5, which is lowered to become what will eventually be the seventh harmonic above the new bass. Initially, this lowering gives the impression of a change from major to minor mode, which in each section furnishes a cue that the process of pitch replacement has begun. This process proceeds to harmonic 3 and then higher ones, if present. Finally, the old bass becomes the third harmonic of the new fundamental through an effectively negligible intonational adjustment of 2 cents, while the pitch class of the new fundamental simultaneously appears in the bass.[12]

The accretion of higher harmonics culminates in Section IV. Strikingly, the accumulated pitches are reminiscent of higher chordal extensions familiar from tertian tonal practice: chordal sevenths (harmonic 7), sharp elevenths (harmonic 11), and flat ninths (harmonic 17). The harmony in section IV might thus be interpreted as a just-intoned version of a $C7^{\flat 9\sharp 11}$ chord, although the registral location of the flat ninth in the treble affirms that it is not an alteration of a natural ninth associated with harmonic 9 but that it instead derives from the higher harmonic 17. This milestone harmony also recalls Stravinsky's *Petrushka chord*, a polychordal superimposition of two triads whose roots are separated by a tritone.[13] In this case, however, the intonations of the two triads are not identical: the lower C triad involves the relatively simple intervals between harmonics 2, 3, and 5, while the superposed F-sharp triad involves the more complex intervals between harmonics 7, 11, and 17. In any event, this pitch-class hexachord is a subset of a just-intoned octatonic scale derived from prime-numbered harmonics—a collection that previously appeared in approximated forms in *Clang* (1972) and the *Chorales* series (1973–74), and that would continue to make occasional appearances in Tenney's later work.

Following section IV, the bass ascends by fourths rather than descending by fifths, and the number of available pitch classes begins to decrease. This necessitates changes in the pattern of voice leading, such as the transposition of some lower-numbered harmonics into higher registers. These adjustments first appear in section IV, where the harmonic 17 is lowered to 16, becoming harmonic 24 of the next milestone harmony (an octave equivalent of harmonic 3). Furthermore, the fundamental pitch class of the new milestone harmony thereafter appears at the beginning of each section rather than at the end as previously, the other available pitches then adjusting successively so that the complete milestone harmony appears only at the end of each section instead of at the beginning. Section VI is exceptional insofar as it arrives via a tritone movement in the bass that requires only slight pitch adjustments above it. The remainder of that section is unique insofar as it comprises only changes in registration, by means of which it recovers the intervallic structure of section II and its lower harmonic numbers (as shown in figure 8.9).

While smooth voice leading between colorful just-intoned harmonies may constitute an alluring surface feature of *Harmonium #1*, a deeper musical topic involves certain qualitative transformations in harmonic complexity that oc-

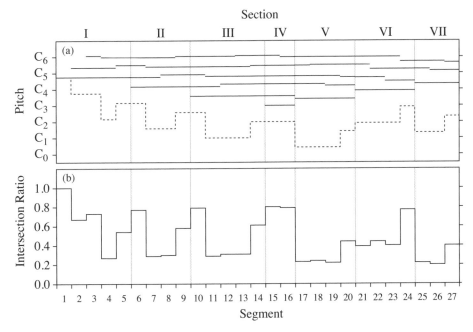

FIGURE 8.10. *Harmonium #1.* (a) Available-pitch sets (solid lines) and GCD pitches (dashed lines) subject to the simplifying approximation that the intervals between successive bass notes are just intervals. (b) The intersection ratio of the sounding pitches with a harmonic series on their GCD pitch.

cur as milestone harmonies are approached and departed. These perceptual transformations are correlated with changes in the intervallic similarity of the chord voicing to the harmonic series. For instance, as shown in figure 8.8, the milestone harmony of section III corresponds to harmonics 2, 3, 5, 7, and 11 of a G_2 fundamental in their correct registral locations, while the pitch sets of the preceding and following few segments are less simply rationalized. This is illustrated in figure 8.10(a), which depicts all available-pitch sets and their GCD pitches (i.e., their *conceptual fundamentals*; section 7.6.1).[14] Figure 8.10(b) shows the intersection ratios between a harmonic series on this GCD pitch and the aggregate of all harmonic partials associated with members of the available-pitch set. As discussed in section 7.6.1, this ratio represents the fraction of a complete harmonic series on the GCD pitch that is collectively represented by the partials of the sounding tones and is thus one measure of the harmonicity of the available-pitch set (i.e., of its similarity to a harmonic series and thus, prospectively, of its toneness).

The unison pitch in the opening segment is the simplest harmony in the piece and furnishes the only occasion on which the GCD pitch of the collection is also a sounding member of that collection. Being precisely a harmonic series on this fundamental, the corresponding intersection ratio is unity. The intersection ratios in the next two segments are somewhat lower, since the fundamental is no longer part of the available-pitch set. In the fourth segment, however, pitches associated with the next milestone harmony begin to invade the available-pitch set, with a resulting plunge in both the GCD pitch and the intersection ratio. Perceptually, this correlates with a sudden increase in perceived harmonic complexity. The intersection ratio begins to recover at the end of section I, since in segment 5 the only pitch of the first milestone harmony that has not been replaced is its bass, which is effectively identical to a pitch in the next milestone harmony. In other words, in segment 5 the new milestone harmony is complete except for its bass, whose subsequent appearance marks the beginning of section II and is accompanied by an upward jump in the intersection ratio. This represents a striking increase in harmonicity and perceptual fusion among the pitches present, resulting in what Tenney described to me in a 2003 conversation as a "making of sudden harmonic sense to the pitches you've been hearing."[15]

This sensible process of harmonic obfuscation followed by clarification is repeated at the boundaries of sections III and IV. Each time, the first appearance of pitches associated with the next milestone harmony induces a palpable disruption of the preceding segment's harmonicity. In sections V and VI, the bass of the new milestone appears first (at the beginning of the section), precipitating this disruption at the outset of these sections, with toneness recuperating only at their conclusions. In section V, due to the unique voicings necessitated by the upward bass motion, the culminating milestone harmony in segment 20 displays much weaker harmonic coherence than do the milestone harmonies in the other sections. This illustrates the significance of voicing choices for harmonic perception. This factor is emphasized even further in section VI, where simple reregistration of the pitches into an intervallic pattern found lower in the harmonic series produces a strong sense of harmonic simplification, as correlated with the upward leap of the intersection ratio in segment 24. A conclusive gelling of the texture is, however, always prevented by the continual flux of pitches and timbres arising from the available-pitch procedure.

Harmonium #1 is an exploration of the special character of the harmonic series as an intervallic structure that is strongly disposed to perceptual fusion. Formally, the remaining members of the *Harmonium* series are variations upon the basic structure of *Harmonium #1*. In the evolution of its intonational details, however, the series incorporates some subtle but far-reaching conceptual developments that signal Tenney's progression beyond the harmonic series as his sole harmonic model and toward his later theory of harmonic space and associated works. This transition was first reflected compositionally in *Harmonium #3* (1980), for which section 9.2 provides an analysis with which the above description of *Harmonium #1* may be compared.

8.5 *Three Indigenous Songs* (1979)

for Lionel Nowak
TWO PICCOLOS, ALTO FLUTE, BASSOON OR TUBA, TWO PERCUSSION
9 mins approx.

    I. No More Good Water (Jaybird Coleman)
    II. Kosmos (Walt Whitman)
    III. Hey when I sing these 4 songs Hey look what happens

Three Indigenous Songs (1979) is the first of three works (appearing over the course of two decades) in which Tenney directly orchestrated acoustical components of American English speech. Its three movements are based upon three different models: (1) Tenney's transcription of the blues "No More Good Water" as recorded by Jaybird Coleman in 1927, (2) a transcription of a recording of Tenney's own voice reading the poem "Kosmos" by Walt Whitman, and (3) Tenney's prior choral setting of an Iroquois text as translated by poet Jerome Rothenberg (1972, 31), entitled *Hey When I Sing These 4 Songs Hey Look What Happens* (1971).[16] The prospects for actually evoking intelligible utterances by means of such "instrumental synthesis" will not seem entirely implausible to those who have heard examples of so-called *sine-wave speech*, in which comprehensible speech is produced using as few as three sine waves whose frequencies track those of the lowest-frequency formant peaks of the spoken model (Remez et al. 1981).[17] Nonetheless, Tenney's goal was not the robust synthesis of comprehensible speech but the exploration of a domain somewhere between that of speech and music, as he indicated in the preface to the score:

> The perceptual space induced by THREE INDIGENOUS SONGS is meant to be somewhere near the threshold between music and speech. Occasionally, perhaps, some semblance of the underlying texts may actually be heard.
>   The first two stanzas of text in the source recording for Movement I are:
>
> > Well there's no more good water
> > because the pond is dry.
> >
> > I walked down to the river
> > then turned around and 'round.
>
> In the music these stanzas are each preceded by freely composed simulacra of the recording's harmonica choruses.

My reconstruction of the composer's working method from his notes is illustrated in figure 8.11. Part (a) of the figure shows measure 7 of the first movement. The text "wa-ter" is provided in the score only as a reference, being neither spoken nor sung in performance; instead, its components—or, more precisely, its *u*, *a*, *t*, and *e* sounds—are musically transcribed. The sounds subjected to

FIGURE 8.11. *Three Indigenous Songs.* (a) Score excerpt (m. 7). (b) Frequency values in hertz and corresponding pitch ranges for the first three vocal formants (labeled F_1, F_2, and F_3) as they appear in the composer's notes. (c) Equal-tempered approximations to harmonic series on C-sharp$_3$ and G$_2$.

transcription are represented on the text staves using symbols of the International Phonetic Alphabet. Consonants are rendered by the percussionists using woodblocks (for *k*, *t*, and *p*), tom-toms with sticks (for *g*, *d*, and *b*), tom-toms with brushes (for *th*, *f*, and *h*), and suspended cymbals (for *s* and *sh*). The pitches of vowels and certain other voiced speech sounds were transcribed from the source recording and appear throughout as the bassoon/tuba part. The flute and piccolos play harmonics of each fundamental that are near the centers of the first three vocal formants associated with the associated speech sound. Flutes are an apposite instrumental choice for these upper parts because the relatively simple sound spectra that they produce suit their role of supplying particular harmonics.

Figure 8.11(b) is adapted from Tenney's composition notes and specifies the locations of the first three formants (labeled F_1, F_2, and F_3) for the vowel sounds ɑ (*a*) and ʌ (*e*) that appear in *water*.[18] These locations are indicated in the figure both as frequencies taken from the acoustical literature and as the nearest corresponding equal-tempered pitches.[19] Each formant location falls within a range whose lower and upper limits are indicated with filled noteheads and whose midpoint is indicated using an open notehead. Figure 8.11(c) (also excerpted from Tenney's notes) shows equal-tempered approximations to the harmonic series above the fundamentals associated with the bassoon/tuba pitches C-sharp$_3$ and G$_2$. With this information at hand it is a simple matter to select harmonics of the appropriate fundamental that fall within the formant regions associated with a given vowel and assign the pitches of those harmonics to the alto flute and piccolos. For instance, vowel ɑ begins on fundamental C-sharp$_3$ so that its sixth and eighth harmonics (G-sharp$_5$ and C-sharp$_6$) fall in the first and second formant regions, respectively, and are assigned to the alto flute and piccolo II. The twentieth harmonic (F$_7$) appearing in piccolo I lies very close to the third formant region.[20] When the fundamental changes to G$_2$, harmonics of that pitch must be selected instead: harmonics 8, 10, and 24 (G$_5$, B$_5$, and D$_7$) fall within the appropriate formant regions. After the tom-tom renders the D (*t*) consonant, the ʌ (*e*) sound appears, the formant regions being shifted to those associated with this new vowel so that now harmonics 6, 12, and 24 of G$_2$ (D$_5$, D$_6$, and D$_7$) appear in the flutes. The fleeting G$_6$ in piccolo II may emulate a *formant transition*, a rapid movement of a formant peak that immediately follows or precedes certain consonants and is important for their correct identification (Parsons 1986, 121–23).

Due to Tenney's selection of sources with strong sonic characters—coupled with his meticulously pursued process of acoustically informed transcription—particularities of the sources are clearly projected onto the resulting music. For instance, the transcribed blues song, the Whitman poem, and the Iroquois chant of *Three Indigenous Songs* all exhibit markedly different characters immediately relatable to their sources. Note, however, that these sources are themselves complex artifacts. Each incorporates aspects inherited from (1) the physics of speech production; (2) general rhythmic, inflectional, and grammatical patterns of the English language; (3) qualities related to the source's cultural origins; (4) the unselfconscious vocal idiosyncrasies of its original author; (5) features intentionally imbued therein by that author; and in some cases (6) corresponding attributes from the contemporary speaker whose voice was recorded for transcription purposes. The list of contributions runs a gamut from the purely impersonal to the most intimately personal, although even the latter factors are ultimately perceived through the alienating lens of spectrum-analytic transcription.

Where much instrumental music depends for its impact on the metaphorical evocation of vocal expressivity, here the evocation is boldly literal. My experience of these pieces is reminiscent of viewing an X-ray: they confront me with the strange and variegated materiality underlying even the most intimate aspects of subjectivity. The music affords the almost surreal spectacle of an ensemble seated upon a stage attempting to reenact before an audience the assembly of these material aspects into a coherent, expressive self. Measures of success and shortfall both contribute to the poetry of the work.[21]

Harmonic Spaces (1980–85)

In Tenney's music of the 1980s, certain distinctive new types of harmonic structure began to appear. These reflected his development of a new model of harmonic relations involving a multidimensional *harmonic-space* lattice and an attendant concept of *harmonic distance* within that lattice. This model provided him with an alternative to that of the harmonic series, which had dominated his thinking about harmony in the 1970s.

A general introduction to Tenney's harmonic theories, including his model of harmonic space, is provided in chapter 7, and the following analyses will assume familiarity with the concepts introduced in that chapter.

9.1 The Harmonic-Space Music

Among the various aspects of Tenney's harmonic theories, the concepts of harmonic space and harmonic distance were those of which he most often spoke, and they were the only ones of which description was published during his lifetime. In contrast, concepts related to toneness that were applicable to his harmonic-series music made appearances in the musicological context of his monograph *A History of 'Consonance' and 'Dissonance'* (Tenney 1988a; section 7.6), but his theories related to them were published only posthumously (Tenney 1979b) (although he personally prepared them for publication near the end of his life). The representation of these ideas in his music, however, is somewhat reversed: manipulation of harmonicity figures pervasively in Tenney's harmonic-series compositions of the 1970s and 1990s, while the concept of harmonic space underpins a smaller number of works that principally date from the first half of the 1980s.

The outlines of Tenney's harmonic-space concept are first discernible in *Harmonium #3* (1980; section 9.2) and persist in the *Harmonium*s composed thereafter (*#6* and *#7*). The new model remains present obscurely but with slowly increasing elaboration in *Chromatic Canon* (1983) and *Band* (1983). Nothing in these developments anticipated, however, the sudden and sophisticated materialization of harmonic space as a basis for Tenney's lengthiest and most complex compositions: *Bridge* (1984; section 9.3) and *Changes: 64 Studies for 6 Harps* (1985). *Water on the mountain . . . Fire in heaven* (1985) quickly followed as an adjunct to *Changes* before Tenney's compositional and research activities were disrupted by events in his personal life (chapter 10). Although he subsequently spoke often of the harmonic-space concept and expressed intentions to make further use of it compositionally, in fact it resurfaced only in *Tableaux Vivants* (1990) and in his final work, *Arbor Vitae* (2006; section 11.4).

Regarding his compositional applications of the concept of harmonic space, Tenney made the following remarks:

> [Harmonic space] provides a kind of field of movement, field of activity. One can conceive of a musical process moving in that space. . . .
>
> The concept is [also] a very useful basis for the design of scales or pitch sets. Because you can sit down and decide you're going to elaborate a structure of pitches or pitch classes, that makes certain things possible, or available, and then work it out, depending on how many pitches you are able to deal with, which depends on what your sound-producing medium is, and how many kinds of relationships you want to be able to hear in the work. So it's a very useful basis for scale design or pitch-set design. (Tenney 1996d, 116)

Tenney's archives contain unpublished reams of such designs, including tables, figures, and multicolored lattice diagrams. Of these, only a small fraction eventually found compositional application.

Whereas Tenney's harmonic-series pieces often feature gradual and continuous processes, his harmonic-space music can be highly articulated and unpredictable. Indeed, listeners more familiar with Tenney's continuous process music may be caught off guard by the rapid harmonic rhythm typical of his harmonic-space pieces. Even if harmonic-series compositions such as *Voice(s)* (1982/1984) and *Glissade*, V: "Stochastic-Canonic Variations" (1982) had insinuated a trend toward greater textural elaboration, they could scarcely prepare a listener for the eruption of formal, executional, and aural complexity in *Bridge* and *Changes*. These lengthy and intricate works were Tenney's first compositions since the early 1960s to be produced with the aid of a computer. They renovated and extended the algorithmic techniques of his early computer-synthesized music (section 4.5), albeit within a medium that was now purely instrumental. In particular, Tenney's new software algorithms of the 1980s introduced stochastic control of harmony and—in *Bridge*—new layers of textural and formal organization. He would thereafter frequently use software as a compositional aid, creating new algorithms for individual pieces or for series of related pieces.

Alongside manifestations of Tenney's new harmonic-space model, works based on the harmonic series and harmonic fusion continued to appear in his output. Indeed, these included some of his most singular expressions thereof, such as *Koan for String Quartet* (1985), a harmonization of his earlier *Postal Piece, Koan* (1971) for solo violin (section 6.3.1).

9.2 *Harmonium #3* (1980)
for Susan Allen
THREE HARPS
4 mins., 16 secs.

In *Harmonium #3*, a new set of compositional and theoretical concerns began to manifest in Tenney's work.[1] Preceding works of the 1970s such as *Clang* and *Quintext*, V: "Spectra for Harry Partch" typically invoked the fusion, fission, and interrelations of components within a harmonic series. Signally, this duality between timbre and harmony—between unity and multiplicity—is not emphasized in *Harmonium #3*. Instead, transitions occur between distinct sets of tones, within which each tone maintains a relative autonomy. Accordingly, a new notion of *harmonic proximity/distance* between pitches begins to assume conceptual and technical centrality, and associated harmonic configurations that are less straightforwardly relatable to the harmonic series appear. The following analysis may be compared with that in section 8.4 of *Harmonium #1*, a work whose structure is closely related but in which the paradigm of the harmonic series still prevailed.

The score to *Harmonium #3* calls for its three harps to individually be tuned in twelve-tone equal temperament (12TET), but harp I must be tuned 14 cents flat, and harp III 14 cents sharp relative to harp II. (For analytical convenience, however, I will take harp III to be the pitch reference with a deviation of 0 cents, with respect to which harp II is 14 cents flat and harp I is 28 cents flat.) This intonational scheme affords a highly accurate approximation in harp II to the pitch class of the fifth harmonic when the pitch class of the fundamental is in harp III, as shown in the third column of table 9.1. However, close inspection of the other pitch classes used reveals that not all of them correspond to the best available approximations to those of low harmonics. In particular, the pitch classes that in *Harmonium #1* would have corresponded to those of harmonics 11 and 17 are both played by harp II, but harps I and III, respectively, would have resulted in smaller deviations (−21 and +5 cents) from the harmonic series.

In fact, although Tenney apparently retained the intervallic spacing of the harmonic series as a model for chordal voicing, the "tritone" and "semitone" pitch-class intervals above the bass were not intended to provide approximations to eleventh and seventeenth harmonics. The rightmost two columns of table 9.1

TABLE 9.1. Approximations to just intervals in *Harmonium #3*

Harmonic ratio class	Deviation (in cents) of harmonic pitch class from				Alternative frequency ratio class	Alternative deviation (cents)
	12TET	*Harmonium #3*	Harp			
17/16	+5	+19	II	(−14¢)	21/20	−2
11/8	−49	−35	II	(−14¢)	7/5	−3
7/4	−31	−3	I	(−28¢)	7/4	−3
5/4	−14	0	II	(−14¢)	5/4	0
3/2	+2	+2	III	(0¢)	3/2	+2
1/1	0	0	III	(0¢)	1/1	0

provide alternative interpretations of the intervals appearing in *Harmonium #3*, expressed as frequency ratio classes. Instead of the 11/8 and 17/16 ratio classes that would have been associated with the eleventh and seventeenth harmonics of 1/1, Tenney instead adopted close approximations to the ratios 7/5 (the "tritone" between harmonics 7 and 5) and 21/20. Now 21/20 = 7/5 × 3/2 ÷ 2/1, so this "semitone" interval class is equivalent to a just 3/2 fifth above the adopted 7/5 tritone. The higher prime factors 11 and 17 are therefore eschewed, and the greatest prime factor appearing in the ratio set is 7. Adopting the terminology of composer Harry Partch, *Harmonium #3* thus employs a *7-limit* tuning system. The restriction to ratios involving prime numbers of magnitude no greater than seven reveals a new interest on Tenney's part in harmonies derivable from collections of relatively simple frequency ratios involving low primes, with more complex relationships (such as 21/20) available as combinations thereof. In 2003 the composer described this development in *Harmonium #3* to me as the beginning of his interest in compact sets in harmonic space, adding that "you can get all the complexity you want from 7-limit."

As voiced in the score, the complete pitch set could in principle be interpreted as harmonics 10, 15, 25, 35, 56, and 84 of their GCD frequency, but such an analytic appeal to harmonicity not only resorts to extraordinarily high harmonic numbers but also does not reflect certain important aspects of the harmony as perceived. First, the collection as a whole does not fuse strongly both because of the great height of these "harmonics" above the associated GCD pitch and because—given the register of the music—that GCD pitch would be infrasonic. Furthermore, this interpretation would fail to capture the relatively simple intervallic connections that *are* audible between the pitches in the set. These are more clearly reflected in figure 9.1, which represents the frequency ratio classes approximated in *Harmonium #3* as points in three-dimensional pitch-class projection space, wherein they occupy a connected and relatively compact region. The 7/5 ratio relative to 1/1 corresponds to the combination of an ascending 7/4 seventh with a descending 5/4 third, 21/20 being arrived at by an additional ascent of a 3/2 fifth, as previously indicated.

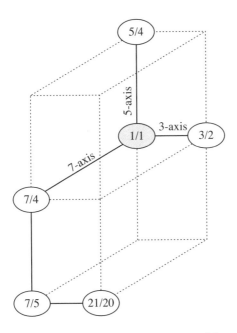

FIGURE 9.1. Representation in pitch-class projection space of the ratio-class set approximated in *Harmonium #3*.

The elegant geometrical representation of the major triad in pitch-class projection space is visible in figure 9.1, outlined by the lattice vertices associated with 1/1, 3/2, and 5/4 ratios. Their geometrical configuration is that of a right triangle with its right angle at lower left. The vertex at 7/5, however, marks the right angle of another such triangle, representing a second just major triad. Thus the hexachord of *Harmonium #3* can be regarded as a just-intoned version of Stravinsky's *Petrushka chord*, a bichord comprising two major triads whose roots are a tritone apart. Unlike in *Harmonium #1*, here the intonation of each triad is identical and maximally simple, and—depending on their voicing—the combination is readily audible *as a bichord* in the music. Additionally, the lattice representation captures a consequence of these particular intonations for voice leading: if the 1/1 "root" descends a 3/2 fifth, the two 3/2 fifths appearing in figure 9.1 produce two common tones as 1/1 and 7/5 become 3/2 and 21/20, respectively. In other words, the root and tritone of the first bichord become the chordal fifth and minor ninth in the second one, each appearing as the same pitch class in the same harp, although possibly in a different register. In Tenney's terminology, the root and tritone of the first bichord are *contained* by the tones of the second bichord in this "downhill" root progression (section 7.7.3).

In practice, 3/2 just fifths are approximated in the music by tempered fifths, the difference of 2 cents being aurally negligible. Over the course of the piece, the bass traverses a complete twelve-note chromatic cycle of such descending

FIGURE 9.2. The first six and the final milestone harmonies of *Harmonium #3*.

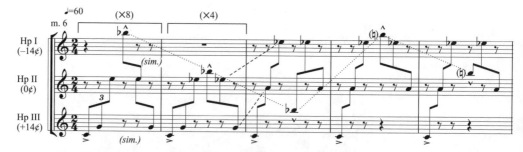

FIGURE 9.3. *Harmonium #3*, score excerpt (mm. 6–10), annotated. Intonations are as marked in the score (+14 cents relative to table 9.1 and figure 9.2).

tempered fifths from G through D with no diatonicizing tritone, as shown in figure 9.2. Alternating upward and downward arpeggiations serve to delineate the harmonies, entailing some challenging hockets between the instruments. Voice leading is often accomplished using a sequence of minimal pitch adjustments constituting microtonal passing tones between the chord tones of successive milestone harmonies. This is illustrated in figure 9.3, where a dotted line has been added to show the incremental voice leading of a B-flat in harp I through all available intermediate pitches to a B-natural 114 cents higher in harp II, thus supplying the 7/5 tritone above a new bass (F) that will shortly appear in harp III. The effect is akin to that of repeatedly tweaking a tuning peg until a desired intonation is finally attained.

From measure 19 onward, the voice leading between milestone harmonies is immediate rather than incremental, and incremental voice leading is instead employed between two different voicings of each milestone harmony. Figure 9.2 shows both voicings for two successive stations of the bass progression (beginning in mm. 19 and 23, respectively). To varying degrees, the final voicing of each milestone harmony is such that the instruments traverse it via a sequence of relatively simpler intervals, and the two triads of the bichord are registrally segregated. This is illustrated in harmonic space by figure 9.4, which compares the ascending traversals of the set in measures 23 and 26.

Uniquely, the final milestone harmony of the piece is closely voiced, as shown in figure 9.2. This voicing is traversed up and down in a particularly rapid hocket, thus assuming a scalar (gapped octatonic) quality instead of a chordal one.

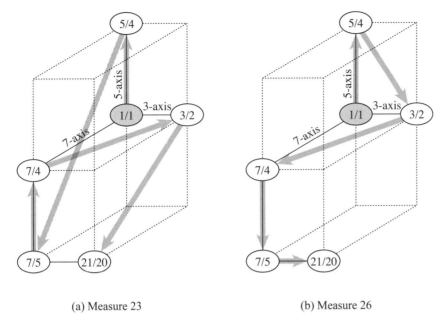

(a) Measure 23   (b) Measure 26

FIGURE 9.4. Ascending traversals of the milestone harmony in measures 23 and 26 of *Harmonium #3*, compared.

The far-reaching significance of the new developments in *Harmonium #3* could be easily overlooked—after all, they *merely* involve tuning part of a hexachord differently from in the previous *Harmonium*s. This small change, however, consolidates all of the elements that would support Tenney's complex large-scale works of the 1980s: just intonation as a reference, a focus on harmonic *proximity* rather than harmonic fusion, the concept of a multidimensional *harmonic space* modeling such proximity relations, a criterion of compactness for sets in that space, and a concept of musical movement within that space (Tenney [1993c/2003] 2015, 380). The composer later recalled: "The idea of harmonic space developed from a purely theoretical standpoint having to do with organizing the world of pitch relations. And once the concept of harmonic space was clear to me, it immediately became extremely useful in composition so that I could then treat harmonic activity literally as movement in harmonic space" (Tenney 1996b, 12).

9.3 *Bridge* (1984)

TWO PIANOS, EIGHT HANDS IN A MICROTONAL TUNING SYSTEM
40 mins.

Like many of Tenney's titles, that of *Bridge* admits more than one interpretation. In one sense, it seems to mark the work as an important personal site of *passage* for Tenney as a composer, leading to a realm of new musical possibilities.

At the same time, it suggests a lasting *connection* between disparate conceptual domains, or between the new and what has gone before it. In a concomitant essay, "Reflections after *Bridge*" ([1984b] 2015), Tenney touched upon all of these senses:[2]

> Since the revolution in aesthetic attitudes wrought by John Cage circa 1951, it has come to pass that virtually anything is possible in music. And yet not everything seems equally urgent or necessary, and, without a sense of necessity, one's musical activities can quickly degenerate into mere entertainment or redundancy. One area of investigation that has that sense of urgency for me now is what I call "harmony"—that is, that aspect of music that involves relations between pitches other than those of sheer direction and distance (up or down, large or small). It has gradually become clear to me that any new development of harmony in this sense will involve more careful considerations of intonation and the design of new tuning systems; the work of Harry Partch has thus taken on a significance quite above and beyond its dramatic (and even heroic) character. It has become, in fact, an indispensable technical point of departure, just as Cage's work has provided us with an essential aesthetic foundation. ([1984b] 2015, 305)

For Tenney, the technical point of departure provided by Partch was primarily a recognition of intonation as a fundamental and potentially renovating consideration for harmonic practice and, more specifically, Partch's identification of frequency-ratio simplicity as a acoustical correlate for perceived harmonic simplicity (or "consonance"; Partch [1949] 1974, 87; see section 7.3). Cage's aesthetic foundation, on the other hand, derived from his reconception of music as "sounds heard." This emphasis on the experience of the listener (rather than on the intent of the composer) would be reflected in Tenney's mature work as a phenomenological orientation (section 1.2.1). Accordingly, *Bridge* was in part intended to demonstrate that a Partchian concern with harmonic relationships can be made consistent with Cage's thinking—and, in fact, can extend it—insofar as such harmonic relationships represent inherent aspects of auditory perception (of "sounds heard") rather than products of convention.

The synthetic project of *Bridge* encompasses not only aspects of Cagean aesthetics and Partchian theory, however, but also a number of Tenney's other characteristic concerns. For instance, its form pivots about an extended gradual transition that proceeds from one sound world to another, recalling the gradual processes prevalent in his music of the preceding decade. A salient difference is that in *Bridge* the process is controlled stochastically rather than deterministically. The computer offers a powerful tool for stochastic composition, and *Bridge* marks Tenney's return to its use as a compositional aid for the first time since his departure from Bell Labs two decades earlier. The piece correspondingly revisits and extends the multileveled hierarchies of temporal gestalts (i.e., of perceived formal groupings) and polyphonic stratification that Tenney had theorized in "Meta/Hodos" (Tenney [1961] 2015; section 3.4) and that last appeared in his computer music of 1962–64 (section 4.5). *Bridge* thereby draws

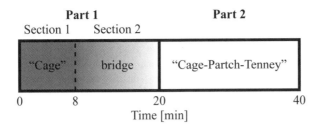

FIGURE 9.5. Formal outline for *Bridge*.

together its composer's involvements with Cage, Partch, harmony, gradual process, the comphuter, algorithmic composition, and formal perception. It even invokes Tenney's personal history as a performer, the composer commenting, "I've written very little for piano in all of my career as a composer, so that I've very seldom had any of my own work that I could perform as a pianist . . . and this has been interesting to me to finally have something that involves me as a pianist" (1984a, 10).

Formally, *Bridge* comprises two large parts, the first of which is subdivided into two sections, as shown in figure 9.5.[3] Part 1, section 1 exhibits the statistically homogeneous (i.e., ergodic) texture that Tenney associated with Cage's music of the 1950s (section 4.2) and that was exemplified in Tenney's earlier algorithmic compositions *Ergodos I* (1963) and *Ergodos II* (1964), both of which were dedicated to Cage. Regarding this first section, Tenney wrote that "the individual elements (single tones and aggregates) are generated independently with respect to all of their characteristics (pitch, duration, dynamic level, aggregate density). That is, there are no constraints on the random process, and the texture is thus similar in many respects to that in many of the works of John Cage since 1951."[4]

Part 1, section 2 provides a gradual statistical transition—a "bridge"—from the musical and conceptual world of Cage in part 1, section 1 to that of Cage, Partch, and Tenney together in part 2. Tenney explained:

> What I'm trying to do in the piece is make a tangible connection from one kind of musical situation to another, from one kind of musical organization to another, and to make the connection in a way that shows them as both parts of the same universe of possibilities, doesn't set them up as opposing poles. One way of making this even more explicit is to say that I'm trying to create a tangible bridge between the musical world of John Cage and another musical world which, though certainly very different in sound to that of Harry Partch, has some aspects in common with that, at least in the sense that it involves a new tuning system and so forth. (1984a, 12)

In contrast with the opening of *Bridge*, part 2 displays both hierarchical temporal gestalt organization and polyphonic stratification (section 3.4). In this last and lengthiest portion of the piece, stochastically generated formal gestalts are distinguishable from one another by virtue of statistical differences in their various musical parameters, including—for the first time in Tenney's work—harmonic content. In particular, part 2 explores a unique nontempered tuning system through a stochastic survey of its harmonic possibilities:

> Now a lot of people are going to listen to that piece and after reading my program notes about it that mention harmony, they will come out saying, I don't know what you mean by harmony. But it really does manifest a concern with harmony . . . , but in a sense rather different from what we are accustomed to meaning by the word. . . . The way I'm realizing that is not by making specific choices, to go from this combination of pitches to that combination of pitches at this moment, you see, but rather setting up a situation where potentially, and eventually, everything could happen. All the possible permutations and combinations of these pitches could occur. They don't, even in 40 minutes, I'm sure, but there are an awful lot of combinations. And they occur in ways that are again stochastically organized. (Tenney 1984a, 11–12)

The last 20 minutes of *Bridge* accordingly unfold a vast array of temporal gestalts possessing varied harmonic qualities. Polyphonic strata and temporal groupings are variously differentiated in register, temporal density, dynamics, articulation, vertical density (pitches per chord), and harmonic character, all of which evolve in time and which contrast with one another sequentially and/or concurrently. In particular, individual gestalts delineate harmonic regions of varied centers, complexities, and rates of change, with qualities accordingly ranging from astringent dissonance to warm diatonicism. While I suspect that Tenney would have neither endorsed nor repudiated specific associations, to my ear the stochastically generated textures project a phantasmagoria of tangentially evoked styles that range from thorny modernism to lyrical romanticism to vernacular musics. Particularly striking passages include those in which polyphonic textures present markedly distinct harmonic regions in different registers. The juxtapositions and superimpositions of contrasting gestalts sometimes evoke the polyphony of quasi-autonomous musics encountered in compositions by Charles Ives, whose music Tenney had studied closely and performed (section 5.2). Tenney's encounter with such Ivesian textures appears to have informed his theories of polyphonic temporal gestalt organization as described in "Meta/Hodos," and those theories would in turn provide the foundation for algorithmically generated formal organization in his own computer music, including *Bridge*. With apologies to composer György Ligeti, it is tempting to describe *Bridge* as a "self-portrait with Cage and Partch (and Ives is in the background)."

9.3.1 Pitch-Class Organization

The prefatory notes in the score to *Bridge* include a detailed description of the just-intoned tuning required. This is represented in figures 9.6 and 9.7, which are reproduced from the score.[5] The two pianos employed are tuned differently

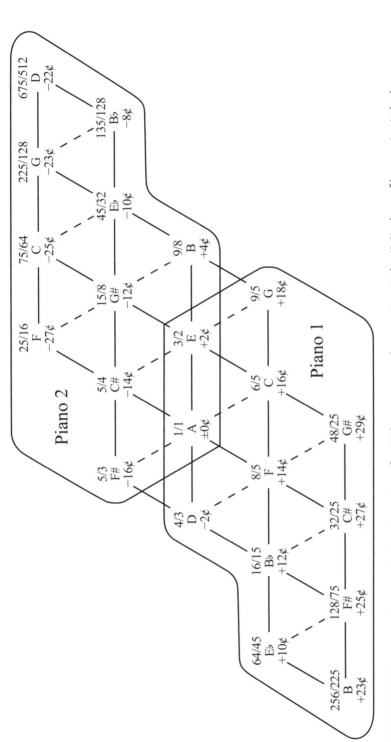

FIGURE 9.6. The twenty-two-tone just tuning system for *Bridge* represented as a region in the (3,5) plane of harmonic pitch-class projection space. Deviations from 12TET are indicated in cents.

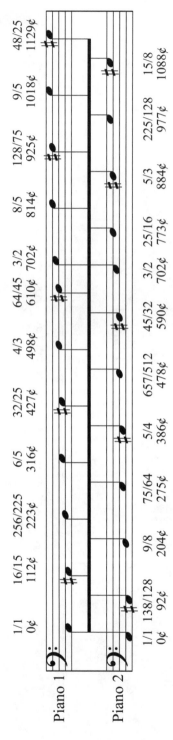

FIGURE 9.7. The twenty-two-tone just tuning system for *Bridge* represented as ascending pitches within one octave. Intervals in cents and frequency ratios are indicated relative to pitch class A.

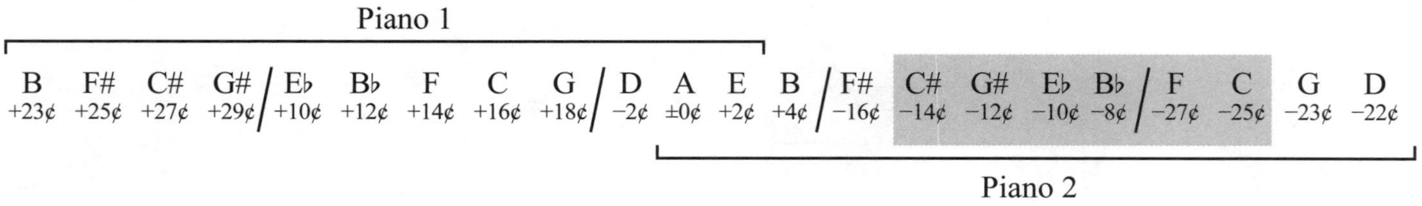

Piano 1

B	F#	C#	G#	Eb	Bb	F	C	G	D	A	E	B	F#	C#	G#	Eb	Bb	F	C	G	D
+23¢	+25¢	+27¢	+29¢	+10¢	+12¢	+14¢	+16¢	+18¢	−2¢	±0¢	+2¢	+4¢	−16¢	−14¢	−12¢	−10¢	−8¢	−27¢	−25¢	−23¢	−22¢

Piano 2

FIGURE 9.8. The twenty-two-tone just tuning system for *Bridge* represented as a "sequence of fifths." All fifths are 3/2s except for four 40/27s, which are indicated by oblique lines.

from each other, sharing only two pitch classes (A and E), so that between them twenty-two different pitch classes are available in each octave. Pitch class A serves as 1/1 and 0 cents for measurement purposes but has no special status within the system.

This tuning makes available pitch-class collections of harmonic complexity ranging from the very simple (including various just intervals and triads) to complex chromatic configurations. This is illustrated in figure 9.6, which represents the available pitch-class set as a region with the (3,5) plane of pitch-class projection space. Horizontal lines (reading from left to right) represent the ratio class of 3/2 just fifths, and solid diagonal lines (reading upward) represent the ratio class of 5/4 just major thirds. Dashed lines (reading downward) consequently represent the ratio class of 6/5 minor thirds. Various harmonically simple pitch-class sets appear as compact regions within the lattice. In particular, just-intoned major triads appear as upward-pointing triangles, and minor triads appear as downward-pointing ones, while major and minor seventh chords appear as small parallelograms with horizontal tops and bottoms.

Reading successive rows of figure 9.6 from left to right beginning at the bottom left of the figure traverses the twenty-two pitch classes of the set via an unclosed "sequence of fifths." This sequence is unwound in figure 9.8. It mostly comprises successions of 3/2 *pythagorean fifths* (702 cents), but there are four 40/27 *ptolemaic narrow fifths* (680 cents) interposed where the sequence passes from one row of figure 9.6 to the next row above it.[6] As in a conventional sequence of tempered fifths, any twelve successive pitch classes constitute a twelve-note chromatic scale, any seven a diatonic scale, and any five a pentatonic scale, although in this tuning system the details of intonation may differ between two scales of the same cardinality depending on the disposition within them of narrow fifths.

In part 2 of *Bridge*, the sequence of fifths shown in figure 9.8 constitutes an autonomous musical dimension within which *harmonic regions* can be defined. Such a harmonic region can be envisioned as a window onto the sequence shown in figure 9.8, possessing a particular location and width and from within which pitch classes are stochastically selected by the compositional algorithm. An example of such a window is represented in the figure using a gray filled rectangle. During the course of part 2, many different such windows appear, each associated with a particular temporal gestalt unit in some particular polyphonic stratum. These windows are not fixed but move smoothly from one location to another in the sequence of fifths over the course of their associated temporal gestalts (generally changing their width as they go). They then disappear, to be replaced by other possibly contrasting windows associated with new temporal gestalts. A broad window might encompass a relatively large "chromatic" collection of pitch classes, while a narrow window might restrict harmonic configurations to a smaller "diatonic" or "pentatonic" set. In this way, the location and width of a harmonic region become factors capable of contributing to the cohesion or segregation of temporal gestalts. Furthermore, multiple different windows associated with gestalts in different polyphonic strata may exist concurrently in different regions of the sequence of fifths, within which they may or may not overlap. For instance, as figure 9.8 shows, each of piano 1 and piano 2 contains a "C-sharp" neighborhood, but while these two neighborhoods would be identical in a tempered cycle of fifths, in this unclosed sequence of fifths they will instead be heard as harmonically distinct (since the two C-sharps differ by 41 cents). Thus harmonic regions can also contribute to the cohesion or segregation of polyphonic strata, facilitating something like an extended just-intoned polymodality. Tenney remarked in an interview:

> Momentarily, if you extract a short passage from the piece, in a given polyphonic part, you could very well identify it as being in A-flat major or something like that.
>
> *But those things were determined by the computer's choices.*
>
> Yes. . . . I had organized it in such a way that that could happen, but I wasn't saying when it's going to be in A-flat. It could go into tonal regions, key regions, at any moment and then could go out of them into another one. But the way it moves among these, well, it's the fastest rate of modulation in the history of music!! (Tenney 1984a, 12)

9.3.2 Formal Processes

This subsection examines in detail the technical means by which the music of *Bridge* was algorithmically generated, treating each of the piece's large formal divisions in turn.

PART 1, SECTION 1

Figure 9.9 provides an excerpt from part 1, section 1 of the score to *Bridge*. Rhythmic notation is proportional, with each system comprising 15 seconds of music divided into three 5-second measures. Notes of three different sorts appear, corresponding to three articulation types: filled unstemmed notes are to be played staccato; stemmed notes are to be played legato, with their duration indicated by the length of a beam; and open notes are to be sustained as long as practically possible by whatever means. When an element comprises multiple pitches distributed among staves, solid vertical lines signify the coordination of attacks, while dashed vertical lines (often used in conjunction with eighth rests) signify coordination of releases. Dynamics are marked where they change, which in this opening section is usually from element to element. The score indicates that the two players at a given piano may distribute their parts however they see fit and that, in the event that an excerpt proves impossible to realize as written, the players may resolve the difficulties using their own discretion. Although the

TABLE 9.2. Maximum available parametric ranges in *Bridge*

Parameter	Part 1, section 1	Part 2
note log-duration	-2-2 (2^{-2} = 0.25 to 2^2 = 4 secs.)	-2-2 (2^{-2} = 0.25 to 2^2 = 4 secs.)
dynamic	*pp, p, mp, mf, f, ff*	*pp, p, mp, mf, f, ff*
articulation	staccato, legato, sustained	staccato, legato, sustained
pitch class	not computed	1–22 (sequence-of-fifths order)
pitch	1–161 (A_0–C_8 in piano 1)	1–161 (but pitch class chosen first)
notes per element	1–4	1–8

texture changes over the course of the work's duration, the notational techniques remain consistent.

Part 1, section 1 exhibits the relatively amorphous *ergodic* form that Tenney associated with Cage's music of the 1950s. Accordingly, it possesses no systematic temporal organization above the level of the single element (i.e., the note or chord). This is because the parametric values for each element were randomly selected without bias from within the maximum ranges available. These maximum parametric ranges are indicated in table 9.2.[7]

On the one hand, this generative procedure imparted to individual elements a particularity and relative autonomy with respect to their qualities. On the other hand, such fixity among parametric distributions precluded the systematic creation of higher temporal gestalt levels via statistical parametric similarity and contrast—in other words, it did not afford the control of longer-term parametric means and ranges that would have been required in order to differentiate clangs, sequences, and so forth. In the same happenstance way that flipping a coin may occasionally yield three tails in succession, groupings of elements may sometimes be perceived nonetheless due to their similarity in some parameter. However, such a grouping is not usually supported by similarity in other parameters and rarely participates in any longer-term statistical trajectory.

PART 1, SECTION 2

Regarding the design of this "bridge" section, Tenney remarked:

> I wanted to be able to create very gradual transitions from one kind of condition to another. For example, in Section 2 of Part I, there is a transition, or a bridge—to use that term in a narrower sense than I mean it in the title, but I meant to include this too—like a bridge passage in traditional music is a transition from one kind of situation to another. But I wanted to create this transition over a period of 12 minutes. The computer is extremely useful with that kind of thing. (1984a, 10)

Over the course of this transition, parametric means and ranges become progressively constrained in value, while changes in them are coordinated in time. These adjustments are effected such that a multilayered hierarchy of temporal

FIGURE 9.9. The opening system of the score to *Bridge*.

gestalt units gradually appears in which various musical parameters contribute to the cohesion and segregation of units in a cooperative manner. *Bridge*, part 1, section 2 thereby grades from the relatively amorphous texture of part 1, section 1 to the stochastic but formally feature-rich texture of part 2. The transformation is illustrated in figure 9.10, which supplies a complete graphical score for the pitch parameter in part 1, section 2. Other musical parameters undergo similar transformations.

At the beginning of the transition, the perceived texture is still that of the preceding section. It is devoid of any systematic polyphonic stratification or temporal gestalt organization, with all musical parameters distributed uniformly over their maximum ranges and changing without constraint from one element to the next. In other words, there exist none of the statistical parametric contrasts that would be necessary in order to systematically delineate either polyphonic strata or temporal groupings. By the end of the section, however, the texture has gradually approached that of *Bridge*, part 2. In particular, it exhibits a variable number of polyphonic strata, with each stratum containing not only discernible clangs but also sequences and—for the first time in Tenney's music—even higher-level algorithmically determined formal units. In particular, elements, clangs, and sequences appear as in *Phases* (1963) and *Ergodos II* (1964), but the formal hierarchy now extends to *segments* as well.

In figure 9.10, segment means are shown with solid lines, sequence means with dashed lines, and clang means with dotted lines. For each clang, a light gray polygon represents the available range within which the pitches of individual notes could be stochastically selected by the compositional algorithm. Darker gray dots represent the pitches of individual notes as actually selected within those ranges. In order to produce statistical trends on various time scales, the musical parameters characterizing each clang, sequence, and segment were derived from probability distributions whose means and ranges varied linearly in time, as shown.

The formal cosmogenesis of part 1, section 2 was accomplished by progressively increasing the maximum number of polyphonic strata permitted at each hierarchical formal level, along with the ranges available for parametric means at the clang, sequence, and segment levels. In particular, the amorphous conditions at the opening of the section can be understood as the result of having multiplied the parametric ranges for clang means, sequence means, and segment means by factors of zero so that their values were constrained to the midpoints of the total available parametric ranges. This left element-level parameters free to be distributed across the entirety of those maximum ranges. Over the course of the section, however, those multiplicative factors were gradually increased away from zero toward one, as shown in figure 9.11. Parametric means and ranges were determined for higher-level gestalt units first, followed by those for their successively lower-level constituent units. Consequently, given the fixity of overall parametric limits (such as the total pitch range of the instruments), over the course of the section the parametric means and ranges available at the various hierarchical levels begin to enter into obligatory trade-offs: those at the lower levels necessarily become more constrained as those at higher levels increasingly vary. Figure 9.10 shows that as the suppression of their ranges is progressively eased, means for clangs, sequences, and segments begin to stray from the midpoint of the total range. The pitch means for clangs lead this process of gradual deviation, so that by the second minute of the section local registral groupings and linear statistical trajectories start to become clear. As pitch means for the higher-level gestalts increasingly wander in turn, larger-scale pitch trajectories become evident until, by the end of the section, segment-level trends have developed.

Figure 9.11 also illustrates certain other significant changes that take place as the section unfolds, including increases in the maximum number of polyphonic strata possible at the levels of elements, clangs, and sequences. Figure 9.10 shows that polyphony accordingly begins to appear as the number of strata is allowed to increase at progressively higher formal levels. The final minutes of the section exhibit a polyphony of registrally segregated gestalt units whose means and ranges are in counterpoint as much as their elements are.

All other musical parameters (harmonic region, duration, dynamic, and articulation) independently undergo similar progressive focusing into definite ranges and trajectories for each temporal gestalt. Consequently, statistical changes coordinated across multiple parameters at gestalt boundaries often cooperatively reinforce the perception of such boundaries. As shown in figure

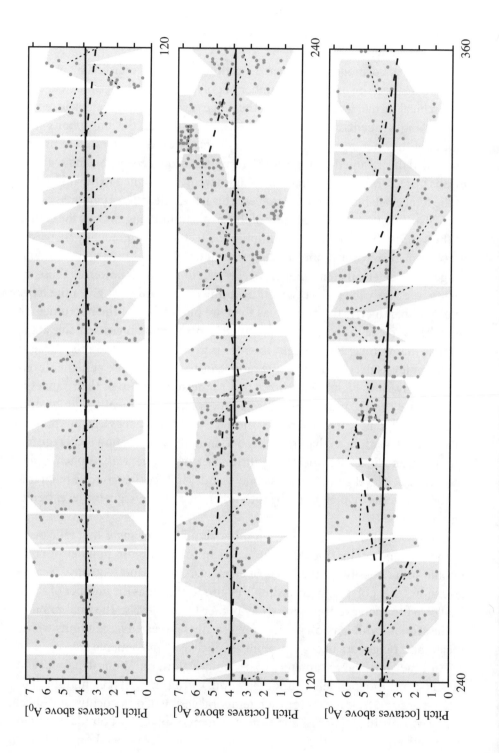

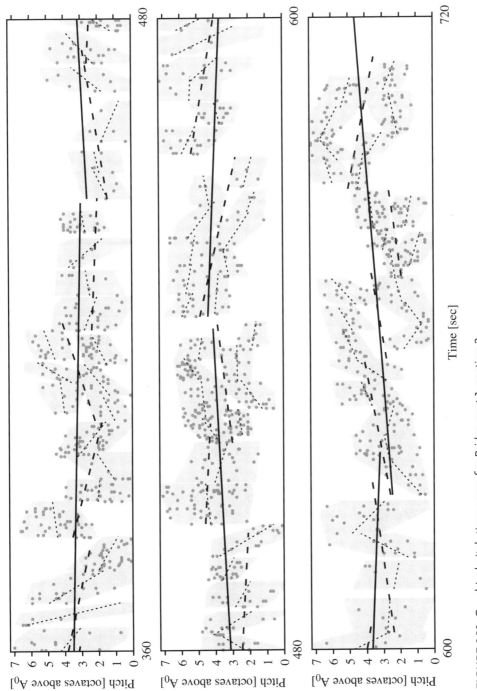

FIGURE 9.10. Graphical pitch-time score for *Bridge*, part 1, section 2.

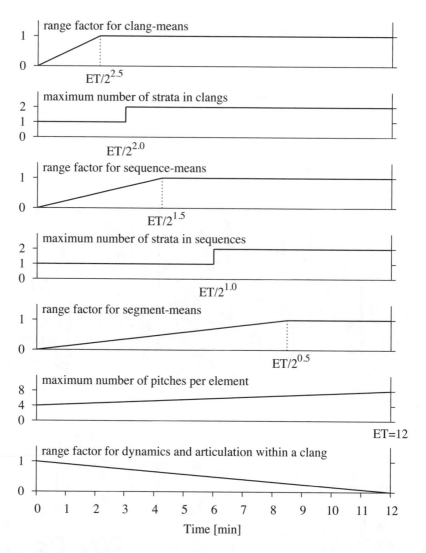

FIGURE 9.11. Variation in parameter range factors and maximum numbers of polyphonic strata over the course of *Bridge*, part 1, section 2. The abscissa represents time elapsed in the section, with ET representing its total duration (12 mins.).

9.11, the range of the random variation applied to the dynamics and articulation parameters at the element level progressively narrows, such that by the beginning of part 2 these parameters are simply equal to the values of their clang means (truncated to integer values), yielding a relative uniformity that supports the internal cohesion of clang units. Finally, figure 9.11 stipulates a gradual increase in the permissible number of notes per element (i.e., chord size) over the course of the section. This increase is visible in figure 9.10 and helps to elaborate the chordal possibilities of the various harmonic regions that emerge.

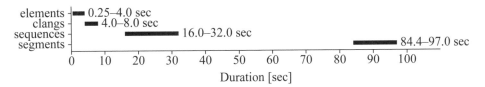

FIGURE 9.12. Duration ranges for temporal gestalt units at various hierarchical levels in *Bridge*, part 2.

PART 2

The full manifestation of a new formal and harmonic organization arrives with the beginning of part 2 and prevails to the end of the piece. The duration ranges for its various temporal gestalt units are illustrated in figure 9.12, the 20-minute duration of part 2 accommodating a total of thirteen successive segments. Clangs, sequences, and segments may all exhibit one or two polyphonic strata, although the total number of concurrent strata is never permitted to exceed four.

The factors potentially serving to segregate temporal gestalts and polyphonic strata from one another in part 2 include differences in the means and ranges of all of the following musical parameters:

- pitch register
- harmonic region in the sequence of fifths
- temporal density (or, reciprocally, interattack duration)
- articulation type
- dynamics
- the number of notes per element (chord size)

Parametric distributions are illustrated in figure 9.13 for the opening of part 2, segment 9. This segment displays a relatively simple texture, featuring two polyphonic strata of sequences. Parametric values for these two strata are separated into the left and right columns of the figure. Parametric means for sequences and clangs as determined by the compositional algorithm are shown with coarsely and finely dashed lines, respectively, while parametric ranges for the elements within each clang are shown as gray filled polygons. The parametric values for individual tones, as randomly selected by the algorithm within these ranges, are indicated with dark gray dots.[8] As was the case at the *end* of part 1, section 2 (but in contrast to part 1, section 1), articulations and dynamics in part 2 are not permitted to vary randomly from one element to the next but instead are simply assigned the current value of the gradually varying clang-level mean and then truncated to an integer value.

Over the course of each temporal gestalt unit at each formal level and for each musical parameter independently, the mean of the probability distribution from which parametric values were randomly selected was made to vary linearly over

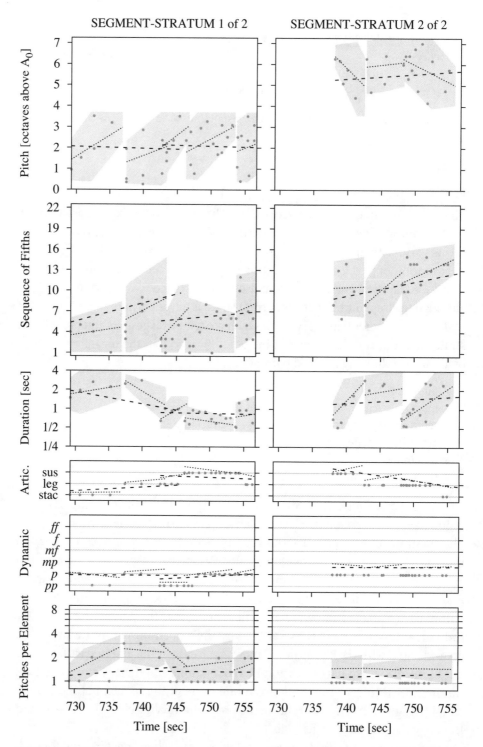

FIGURE 9.13. Parametric values at the beginning of *Bridge*, part 2, segment 9. The abscissa represents time elapsed since the beginning of part 2.

the course of the gestalt, which tended to induce a statistical trajectory in that parameter's values, as shown in figure 9.13. For instance, in the first polyphonic stratum, element duration displays a decreasing trend over the course of the first sequence because the mean durational value for clangs linearly decreases; within some *individual* clangs in this sequence, however, element duration exhibits a decreasing trend, while within others, the trend is increasing. In an interview, Tenney likened the parametric distribution to a target in archery:

> [Iannis Xenakis] points out that the root [of the word "stochastic"] is a Greek word meaning aim, as in aiming at a target. And a good image for the kind of textures that can arise is the pattern of hits on a target. They're clustered around in a certain region, and within that region they are random, but they're not all over the place. . . .
>
> *So in the generation of random numbers, what exactly did the computer determine?*
>
> It determined where the target was. The target moves. The target changes size and moves around, if we're using that image. And in fact there are targets within targets. Regions within regions. It's hierarchical ... (Tenney 1984a, 10)

Comparing the left and right columns of figure 9.13 reveals that the pitch parameter was treated specially insofar as concurrent gestalt units in distinct polyphonic strata were made to inhabit disjunct pitch ranges. Here, stratum 1 is confined to a lower register and stratum 2 to a higher one. In contrast, the corresponding ranges in other musical parameters were freely permitted to overlap. Thus the pitch parameter assumes foremost importance in the perceptual segregation of polyphonic strata, although such segregation may or may not be buttressed by differences in other parameters. Consider, for instance, the music at roughly 742 seconds into part 2, as represented in figure 9.13. Both segment strata are quiet and legato, so that these parameters do not contribute to the discrimination of the strata. Both exhibit low numbers of pitches per element, although the consistent single-note texture of the higher-pitched stratum 2 is noticeably different from that of the lower-pitched stratum 1, which includes occasional trichords and dyads. The greater mean temporal density of the higher stratum is detectable, especially following the onset of its third clang at around 747 seconds. As usual, the strongest factor segregating the two segment strata is pitch register, but this is strongly reinforced by the difference in harmonic region, with the higher-pitched stratum residing significantly higher in the sequence of fifths than the lower-pitched stratum. Indeed, the upper and lower registers seem to inhabit two disparate harmonic worlds, an effect reminiscent of Ives's combinations of simultaneous but independent musics.

Within a single polyphonic stratum *any* parameter may function as the principal inducer of temporal gestalt segregation, although multiple parameters frequently cooperate in that role. Consider the lower-pitched stratum in figure 9.13, which is first heard alone at the outset of the segment before the higher-pitched stratum enters. On the one hand, both of the two successive sequences in this bass stratum exhibit quiet dynamics, a harmonic region mostly confined to the lower portion of the sequence of fifths, large to moderate interattack durations, and a modest number of pitches per element. Thus those parameters serve as factors of cohesion for each of these two sequences. On the other hand, each of the first two clangs exhibits a general upward drift in pitch, but the plunge in mean register at the beginning of the second clang serves to segregate it from the first, as does the increase in the number of pitches per element and the change from staccato to legato articulation. The arrival of the third clang is marked less by registral change than by a clear decrease in the mean interattack duration and a shift in harmonic region.

Tenney made few interventions in the output data from his composing program, so that it accords closely with the published score. His rare local alterations included eliminating or octaviating pitch unisons and conforming articulations or dynamics within a clang where only a single exceptional value occurred. As a general principle, Tenney tended to refrain from ad hoc interventions at the local level, preferring to make global changes to his algorithms whenever their products proved unsatisfactory to him. Asked whether aspects of the music were determined by his personal taste, he replied: "Not in the way of details. The whole design corresponds to my taste in a way: The decision to use a random process is an expression of taste, isn't it? There's a wonderful kind of paradox here, or ambiguity, that that decision implies an acceptance of the detailed results, whether or not those details correspond to one's taste" (Tenney 1984a, 11).

Such acceptance in itself nods toward a Cagean attitude of "letting sounds be themselves." Indeed, Tenney's compositional plans include the following remarks regarding the stochastic control of musical parameters: "All three [major divisions of *Bridge*] will be 'ergodic' in the sense that the absolute means and ranges are fixed (i.e., not 'shaped' at input)—but variously constrained by the gestalt and polyphony controls. Thus all three remain within Cage's *esthetic* domain, [the second two] simply extending it *technically*."[9] Tenney's technical extensions in *Bridge*, however, address dimensions of listening experience that Cage's music (at least up to that time) had not. In particular, Tenney extended the phenomenological aspect of Cage's work by offering as objects of perception not only local "sounds heard" but also hierarchies of temporal groupings, as well as harmonic relations.

9.4 *Koan for String Quartet* (1984)

STRING QUARTET
25 mins.

In *Koan for String Quartet*, Tenney reached back thirteen years to revisit *Koan* (1971) for solo violin from his collection of *Postal Pieces* (section 6.3.1). That earlier solo is a rigorously streamlined process-oriented work in which a cross-string tremolo gradually traverses the registers of the instrument. The quartet version reimagines the earlier piece as the basis for a focused study in harmonicity and thus represents a remarkable outgrowth from Tenney's explorations of the harmonic series. The result is one of the clearest and most striking expressions of his engagement with harmony.

The idea for a quartet version of *Koan* apparently came to the composer during a performance of the solo piece.

> I start[ed] thinking about how each of those intervals that we hear in that piece can have a harmonic interpretation. Each of them understood in a certain way does have a harmonic meaning. But that harmonic sense of the interval, except for a few of the simplest intervals, is out of reach of the listener, any listener, me included. But there is a way to put those intervals in a context in which they can be heard to have that harmonic sense. . . . Again the piece arose out of a kind of problem in the perception of the first piece. (Tenney 1984a, 12)

> The first violin part in this *Koan for String Quartet* is essentially the same as that earlier piece, but here the other instruments of the quartet are used to provide a harmonic context—and thus a harmonic "meaning"—for each of those microtonal intervals, within a fairly complex, just tuning system. The resultant sonorities might be conceived as a complex "chord progression" on various different roots or fundamentals. Some of those sonorities will be quite familiar to the Western ear; others are rather more "exotic."[10]

With respect to harmonic structure, however, the primary technical precedent for *Koan for String Quartet* is not the solo *Koan* but *Glissade*, IV: "Trias harmonica" (1982) for viola, cello, and double bass. As in that earlier work, instrumental lines very gradually diverge in pitch—a rigorous and perfectly predictable process that nonetheless evokes a diverse and surprising sequence of harmonic events. *Koan for String Quartet*, however, differs from both "Trias harmonica" and the solo *Koan* insofar as the moving instrumental lines progress in discrete and precisely stipulated microtonal pitch steps rather than in continuous glissandi. In particular, pitches remain constant throughout the duration of each measure (roughly 5 seconds), changing only from one measure to the next. Thus each harmony persists for long enough to assert its particularity and to permit a degree of contemplation before the next one supersedes it.

The pitches of the first violin part determined those of the other instruments. As in the solo *Koan*, the first violin plays cross-string tremolo dyads throughout, outlining two structural voices. In each section, one of those voices is constant in pitch, while the other rises. The discrete pitches of the moving voice were determined by dividing the interval of a fifth into forty-two equal-tempered steps (using six equal steps per semitone, or 72TET). Then the simplest just-intoned approximation was found for the interval between each step and the fixed voice. That is, a neighborhood half of a step wide on either side of each tempered interval was searched for the just-intoned interval whose reduced frequency ratio was simplest in the sense of having the smallest denominator. This just-intoned interval (rather than the tempered one) was then assigned to violin I.[11]

Figure 9.14(a) provides a schematic pitch-time score for all seven sections of the piece. The two voices of the tremolo in violin I are represented by solid lines, although the discrete pitch steps of the moving voice are too small to be visible in the figure. The other instruments enter in turn: viola in section B, and violin II in section D. The cello discreetly doubles the static pitches of violin I in sections A–E before finally asserting its independence in section F. Figure 9.14(b) represents the corresponding trajectories of the instruments' fundamental frequencies, which by design are evenly spaced at all times (until section F). Thus, once the rationally related frequencies of the violin I tremolo are stipulated, they determine definite rational frequency relationships for all of the other instrumental tones due to the requirement that they be evenly spaced in frequency. (An exception to this even spacing appears in section F, where the frequency difference between the upper violin I line and the violin II line doubles that between other adjacent lines, perhaps in order to reduce the number of occasions on which violin II reproduces the pitch class of some lower tone.) As the preface to the score indicates, on account of the even spacing of the individual instruments' fundamental frequencies, "the pitch sets derived this way can be conceived as subsets of the harmonic partials of [an overall] 'fundamental' which changes from measure to measure." Thus the "harmonic context" of violin I's tremolo, to which the composer alluded, can be understood as a notional harmonic series to which all of the instruments' tones belong. The unheard *conceptual fundamental* (or *GCD frequency*) of this notional harmonic series is the greatest common divisor (GCD) of the instruments' various fundamental frequencies.

As figure 9.14 illustrates, the successive sections of *Koan for String Quartet* subject the "thematic" material of the solo *Koan* to increasingly rich harmonizations. The sequence of harmonic elaborations is represented in figure 9.14(c), in which the frequency ratios associated with selected relatively simple harmonies are marked. As a prospective gauge of harmonicity and toneness—which is one sense of *consonance* or harmonic "simplicity"—vertical bars indicate, for each measure of the score, the value of the intersection ratio between the collection of instrumental harmonics and a notional harmonic series on the conceptual fundamental of that collection. This ratio represents the fraction of a complete harmonic series that is constituted by the aggregate of sounding partials (section 7.6.1). The harmonies display varied intersection ratios, reflecting their varied complexities, and a similar disposition of more and less complex harmonies recurs in each section, as shown in the figure. The simpler a harmony, the better

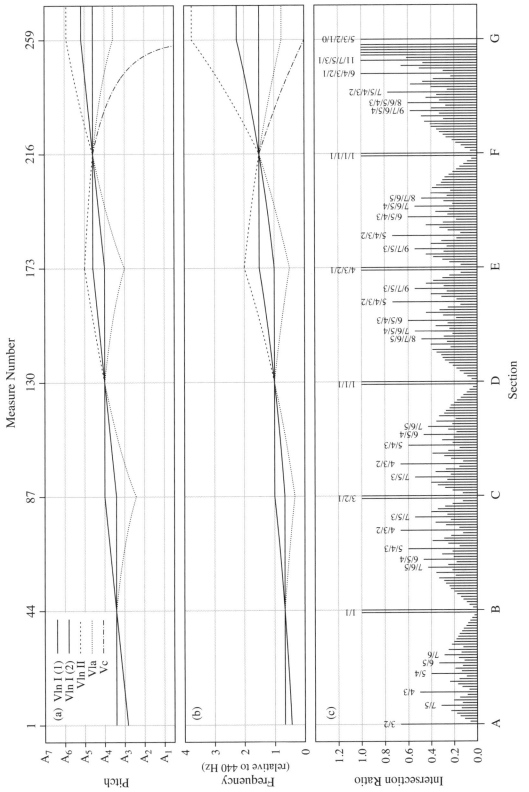

FIGURE 9.14. Pitch contours, frequency contours, and harmonic intersection ratios in *Koan for String Quartet*. The frequency ratios associated with selected harmonies are marked in part (c) of the figure.

it is temporally separated from other comparably simple harmonies, a property that is inherited from the structure of the rational number system (section 7.8). For instance, comparably simple harmonies do not very closely adjoin 7/6, but 5/4 is even more isolated from harmonies comparable in simplicity to itself, although not so well as either 3/2 or 1/1 are thus isolated. This entails that relatively simple ratios are surrounded by ones of relative complexity, as shown. Highly complex ratios, associated with low intersection ratios in the figure, may pass without establishing distinct harmonic identities, or they may be heard as inflections of nearby simpler harmonies, per Tenney's principle of interval tolerance (section 7.3).

Section A provides an exposition of the solo violin tremolo, gradually scanning the intervals between a just fifth and a unison, as in the original solo *Koan*. In this first section, the intersection ratio only assumes its maximum attainable value of one at the final unison.

In section B, the tremolo retrograde inverts so that, despite the resulting changes to the pitches involved, the sequence of intervals simply retrogrades. The viola enters in order to harmonize these intervals from below. The equal spacing of all three fundamental frequencies transforms, for instance, the solo violin's 4/3 of section A into 4/3/2 in section B and its 7/5 into 7/5/3. Intersection ratios either increase or remain unchanged relative to their counterparts in section A because in each measure the addition of the viola tone to the violin tremolo augments the aggregate collection of partials without affecting its GCD frequency. In particular, 3/2 in section A becomes 3/2/1 in section B, which attains the maximal intersection ratio of one, since the GCD frequency of the collection is actually present (and, of course, the sounding harmonic series on that GCD frequency completely intersects itself). Section C in turn retrograde inverts section B, precisely retrograding its sequence of harmonies using higher pitches.

In section D, violin II enters in order to add chord members above the corresponding harmonies of section C, while section E retrogrades through the harmonies of section D.

In section F, the cello's frequency plunges below those of the other instruments. As shown in figure 9.14(a), the stipulation of equal spacing in frequency entails that the cello's fundamental frequency must fall to zero at the conclusion, attaining a vibrationless state. The corresponding pitch trajectory would plunge toward negative infinity, as illustrated in figure 9.14(b), a practical impossibility for the instrument. Although a scordatura extends the range of the cello downward by a just fourth, it thus remained necessary for the composer to transpose the nominal pitches up one octave in measures 256 and 257. This modification is not represented in figure 9.14 but is visible in the score excerpt of figure 9.15. This sudden disruption to the cello's monotonic descent is dramatic in itself, but the final measures of section F possess an additional striking characteristic:

FIGURE 9.15. Score excerpt showing the conclusion of section F from *Koan for String Quartet* (mm. 253–58).

the GCD pitches of the harmonies (the 1s in the ratios) are actually sounded by the cello in measures 251 and 253–55 (and would be in measures 256–57 as well if not for the cello's obligatory octave transposition). This maximizes the intersection ratio in these measures and lends a particularly strong coherence to the harmonies.

In measure 258, where section F concludes and where the nominal frequency value of the cello line would have reached zero, the score contains an abbreviated measure of rest. Section G comprises a single harmony (5/3/2/1) representing the unreached harmonic goal of section F, with the zero-frequency component omitted. (Perhaps it is to be supplied by atmospheric pressure!) The piece concludes as the players gradually move their bows toward and onto their bridges so that tone cedes to noise.

Tenney was aware of the intonational difficulties that the piece would likely present to most performers. The preface to the score contains the following passage:

> Many of the intervals and chords which are called for in this piece will be unfamiliar to the players, and a set of electronic tuning devices with meter-display of cents-deviations from tempered pitches . . . will probably be necessary to achieve the accuracy of intonation desired here (although even this will not be of much help—except perhaps in rehearsals—to the first violinist, whose tones are too short to register on the meter). It should be possible, however, to tune the pitches in certain measures strictly "by ear" (generally those measures in which the ratio-terms—shown "boxed" in the score—involve prime numbers no higher than 7).

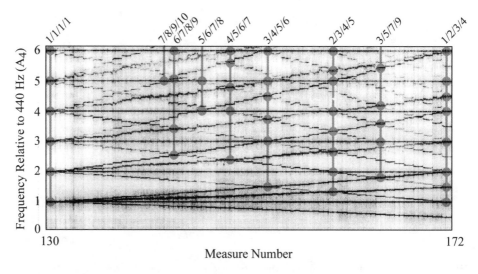

FIGURE 9.16. Annotated spectrogram of *Koan for String Quartet,* section D (mm. 130–72), as performed by Quatuor Bozzini.

The score excerpt in figure 9.15 shows one such boxed frequency ratio above measure 253, as well as unboxed ratios for other measures. The deviations of pitches from 12TET are indicated in cents above the noteheads. Also, beside each note are indicated both its frequency ratio and its pitch interval in cents relative to the fixed pitch in violin I's tremolo.

Despite the significant intonational challenges, highly accurate performances of *Koan for String Quartet* are possible. Figure 9.16 provides a spectrographic analysis showing the evolving registral distribution of sound energy in section D from a live recording of the Quatuor Bozzini performing solely by ear without the aid of electronic tuners.[12] The discrete pitch steps of the instrumental parts are plainly visible. The lowest four frequency contours (fanning outward from 440 Hz) represent the fundamentals of the instrumental tones and thus reproduce the representation of section D shown in figure 9.14(b). Higher harmonics of the tones are visible fanning outward from multiples of 440 Hz. Since the frequencies are rationally related by design, many coincidences between harmonics occur. Some of them are marked using transparent dots superimposed on the spectrogram, with associated ratios labeled above the figure. Such harmonic coincidences are more numerous and lower in register when the fundamental frequencies exhibit relatively simple rational relationships. As moving partials converge to unisons, acoustical beating between them slows and then ceases, providing a vivid cue to the arrival of a relatively simple harmony.

The previously remarked disposition of simple ratios within neighborhoods dominated by relatively complex ones engenders an inherent drama to the unfolding music. While the progressive abatement of acoustical beating may herald the arrival of a relatively simple harmony, the sudden harmonic simplification and fusion at the advent of that harmony has a striking and visceral quality of its own. A baseball player knows the tangible feeling of having hit the ball with the "sweet spot" of the bat, and in a faithful performance the emergence of a simple rational harmony elicits a similar sense of physically satisfying accuracy. Moreover, as the fullness of the harmonization increases, this sense of distinctive harmonic identity—of being intonationally "spot on"—spreads in varying degrees to an increasing number of chords. These include harmonies that are quite unlike those in the familiar tempered vocabulary, and their recognizable particularity advances a more convincing case for a perceptually grounded expansion of harmonic practice than any theoretical argument could do.

CHAPTER 10

Transition and Tradition
(1986–94)

After the focused explorations of complex harmonic ideas in *Bridge* (1984), *Koan for String Quartet* (1984), and *Changes* (1985), Tenney's production in the second half of the 1980s became more sporadic and diverged in an array of directions whose multiplicity defies encapsulation. The reasons for this diffusion were several, but first among them was surely the fact that over the course of twelve months, beginning in autumn 1985, his personal life was upended by tragedy. After the happy birth of a son, Nathan, in 1983 and a daughter, Adrian, in 1985, Tenney—long a heavy smoker—was diagnosed with lung cancer in October 1985. He would survive only after the surgical removal of a lung. Staggeringly, just weeks thereafter his wife, Ann Holloway, would be diagnosed with a cancer to which she would succumb in September 1986. For a time, the grieving Tenney would shoulder sole responsibility for the care of his two young children.

The middecade calamities in his personal life and his intensified parental obligations arrested the focused theoretical program that Tenney had been pursuing in the early 1980s, and he would not attempt to pick up its threads again until the late 1990s. His compositional productivity also flagged, and for more than a year and a half he produced no new pieces. In 1987, however, Tenney began a new relationship with artist manager Lauren Pratt, and their marriage the following year would become the longest personal partnership of his life.[1] The relationship buoyed Tenney, and his creative output began to resurge. He would dedicate *Rune* (1988) for percussion ensemble to Pratt, "who made it all possible again."[2]

The revitalization of Tenney's compositional activity happily coincided with an increase in the number of requests and commissions that Tenney was receiving for new pieces. These contributed to the heterogeneity of his output during these years by occasioning pieces suited to particular ensembles or performers, for some of whom music in just intonation would not have been well suited. Such works included *The Road to Ubud* (1986) for gamelan and prepared piano, *Rune* (1988) and *Pika-Don* (1991) for percussion ensemble, and *Cognate Canons* (1993) for solo percussionist with string quartet. Among these there also appeared an apparently unique example of a patently nostalgic work, *Three New Seeds* (1991), which revisited the techniques and style of Tenney's early *Seeds* (1956/1961). There also materialized a rare outcropping of overtly political works, which had been virtually absent from his output since the mid-1960s. *Pika-Don* (1991) was composed for the University of New Mexico Percussion Ensemble in Santa Fe, a location that recalled for Tenney his youthful fascination with the first nuclear weapons tests near Alamogordo, not far from where he was born. It was followed by a second (and last) openly political piece, *"Ain't I a Woman?"* (1992), an orchestration of speech based on a text by nineteenth-century abolitionist and feminist Sojourner Truth.

While long-standing, Tenney's characteristic practice in his music of homage to other composers becomes especially conspicuous after 1990. These appreciations appear most noticeably as explicit dedications to other artists but also as adaptations or abstractions of their techniques, as in the tempo canons of *Cognate Canons* (1993, dedicated to Conlon Nancarrow) and the ergodic texture of *Ergodos III* (1994, in memoriam John Cage). Such tributes reflect Tenney's continuing investment in his particular conception of an experimental music tradition (section 5.2).

While Tenney's works of this era embraced a diversity of concerns and often exhibit unique forms not found elsewhere in his output, they also include certain striking new incarnations of longstanding interests. These included the available-pitch procedures of *Critical Band* (1988; section 10.1), whose gradual harmonic unfolding traces a line from the unison *Klangfarbenmelodie* of the second movement of *Seeds* and *Swell Piece No. 2* (1971) through the acoustical beating of *Beast* (1971) to the harmonic-series music of *Clang* (1972) and beyond. On the other hand, the stochastic sound masses of *Flocking* (1993; section 10.2), *Ergodos III* (1994), and the later *Last Spring in Toronto* (2000) seem to concentrate certain ideas from "Meta/Hodos" ([1961] 2015) in order to produce a heightened awareness of macroscopic formal grouping and shape.

10.1 *Critical Band* (1988)

FOR ANY SIXTEEN OR MORE SUSTAINING INSTRUMENTS
17 mins.

At a rehearsal of *Critical Band* in preparation for its 1988 premiere, composer John Cage approached the ensemble to inquire what piece they were playing.

According to the director, upon being informed, "he smiled and looked up at the ensemble and then back at me and said softly, 'That is the most beautiful piece of music I have ever heard'" (Franklin 2006, 249). Cage had long regarded harmony as a form of conventional artifice to be avoided (Cage [1954] 1961, 152), but following this experience, he told Tenney, "If this is harmony, I take back everything I ever said; I'm all for it" ([1989a] 2000, 247). Cage expanded further in a 1990 radio interview:

> I have a feeling now for harmony. . . . I'm surprised at almost all the ideas that come to my head because they have to do with harmony. . . .
>
> *And when did you discover your affinity to harmony?*
>
> Naturally I had to have help because my experience led me to believe that I had no feeling for harmony, so that I needed help.
>
> *You had to take lessons in harmony?*
>
> Yes and it happened without going to school. . . . I went to a festival called New Music America in Miami and there was a beautiful piece . . . by James Tenney. . . . It began with the sound of an accordion playing one note—not playing many notes, just one note. Then another instrument played the same note. Some people in the audience continued to talk because there had been an intermission and they thought, "Oh, they're playing the same note, so we don't have to listen. They must be tuning their instruments" [*laughs*]. So they went on talking. It occurred to me that they weren't tuning and so I listened carefully. They played the same note for quite a while, not all together but each one in his turn. And then shortly one of the tones was a little bit flat and the next one was a little bit sharp—microtonally. Then a little bit of time passed with this kind of sound and it began to get wider—the difference between the sounds that came from the instruments. And it lasted for half an hour. Finally, the distance between the sounds was very great and you had the feeling that sound was stretching itself. It was as though sound was a person stretching and reaching as far as he could from the low to the high. It was just perfectly beautiful. It was the first piece which gave me the experience of a harmony which I could understand or experience and love. Because, you see, years ago I told Schoenberg that I had no feeling for harmony, and he said, "Well, you'll never be able to write music," and I said, "Why not?" and he said, "Because you'll come to a wall, and you won't be able to get through." And this piece of Tenney gave me the sense that there was no wall at all—that sound is by its own nature harmonious. . . . Harmony is just sounds coming together at the same time. (1990a)[3]

In his late "number pieces," Cage demonstrated a renewed interest in combinations of tones, particularly in his "anarchic harmony" of randomized pitch collections (Swed 1993). Following the profound influence of Cage's music and thought on Tenney's work during the previous decades, influence thus flowed in the opposite direction—from Tenney to Cage—during the late 1980s. Accordingly, Cage included the following lines in his 1989 mesostic, "The Readymade Boomerang," a copy of which he sent by mail to Tenney.[4]

```
                    alTernatives
                    to Harmony
                    lifE spent finding them   beating my head
          against a wall   now haRmony
                    has changEd
                    its nAture   it comes back to you   it has no laws
there is no alternative to it   how Did that happen
          first of all james tenneY   his varèse-given vision
```

The title of *Critical Band* refers to a psychoacoustical quantity known as the *critical bandwidth*, which is the frequency bandwidth within which the waveforms of two concurrent pure tones with distinct frequencies will interact in the ear (Moore 2013, 68–71). Two components whose frequencies fall within a single critical bandwidth will be heard as a smooth unison if they precisely coincide; otherwise, they will evoke a sensation of *roughness* due to their beating (section 7.5). On the other hand, two components separated in frequency by more than a critical bandwidth will be heard as two autonomous tones that do not beat against one another (Roederer 2008, 34–42). While in actuality the edges of a critical band are not crisp, so that the perceptual segregation of two tones occurs gradually as the interval between them increases, above A_4 (440 Hz) the interval corresponding to a nominal critical bandwidth is between a minor third and a major second, expanding at lower frequencies.

As reflected in Cage's description of the premiere, the formal scheme of *Critical Band* involves a progressive enlargement in overall pitch range, beginning from unison and gradually expanding to three octaves. Initially, the fundamental frequencies of all tones reside within a single critical bandwidth of one another so that they are not audibly distinct. As they begin their gradual registral divergence, they instead produce sensations of beating and roughness as they diverge. Over the course of the piece, as the registral range gradually expands and the separation between pitches exceeds a critical bandwidth, sensory roughness subsides and the sounding tones become clearly distinct, assuming various harmonic relationships to one another.

The opening of the score is shown in figure 10.1. An available-pitch procedure is employed. The piece comprises thirteen sections, delimited in the score by bar lines, with each section introducing at most two new available pitches, one above and one below the previous available-pitch set. Players freely choose their pitches from those available for the current section, although when a section introduces more than one new pitch, the higher one is to be sounded first. Performers are instructed to sustain each pitch that they select for roughly the duration of one breath in wind instruments or one upbow-downbow pair in

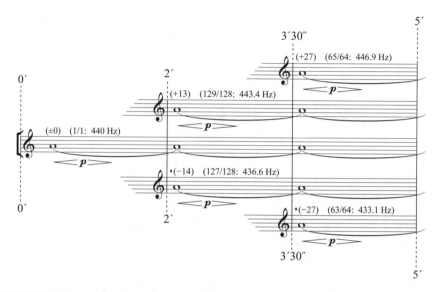

FIGURE 10.1. Excerpt from the opening of the score to *Critical Band*.

strings. Performance arises out of the tuning of the ensemble to A_4, so that the audience often becomes aware that the piece has begun only after the fact.

The score indicates pitch deviations in cents from equal temperament, as well as frequency ratios relative to 440 Hz and the absolute frequency in hertz of each tone. Electronic tuners can be used in order to achieve the stipulated pitch intonations, but Tenney maintained that ultimately it was desirable and possible to achieve the required tunings by ear:

> I developed techniques, when I was coaching ensembles, to work on it. For example, in the beginning [of *Critical Band*], when the second pitch comes in, the player on that second note has to count the rate of the beats that are produced between the new note and the first note to know that the pitch is right. So there are a number of techniques and technologies that we may have to call on to develop this. But the most important thing, finally, is that we can learn to hear a lot of it. These other things can be aids to hearing, but finally, finally we're going to be able to hear these subtle differences that have been trained out of us in standard conservatory training that is piano based. (1996c, 4)

Figure 10.2 provides a complete graphical representation of the available-pitch sets in each section. The gray-shaded region in the figure approximates the psychoacoustical critical bandwidth about A_4.[5] The available-pitch sets initially undergo gradual expansion in range about A_4, beginning with the accumulation of five pitches and continuing as the intervals between adjacent tones begin to progressively increase from one section to the next. As illustrated, until section 6 the entire available-pitch set falls within a single critical bandwidth so that

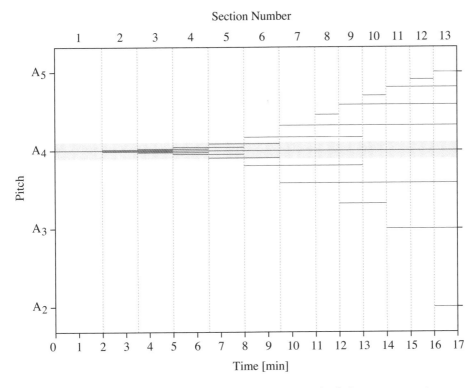

FIGURE 10.2. Available-pitch sets in *Critical Band*. The gray-shaded region approximates the psychoacoustical critical bandwidth around A_4 (440 Hz).

sounding tones are not audibly segregated but instead combine to produce shifting timbral colorations and acoustical beatings of gradually increasing sensory roughness. Beginning in section 6, some tone pairs are separated in pitch by more than a critical bandwidth and are heard as autonomous (especially if some tones in the middle of the set are momentarily not sounding), but not until section 10 do most *adjacent* pitches decisively occupy separate critical bands. Thereafter, most tones are heard as autonomous, so that they exhibit various harmonic relationships as instruments enter and exit. Thus the formal trajectory of the work involves a gradual perceptual transition from a nonharmonic regime to a harmonic one.

In order to elucidate the structure and progression of the available-pitch sets, table 10.1 recasts them as sets of fundamental frequencies. The spacing of table rows approximates a linear vertical frequency axis, although the table is broken into two parts (left and right) with different vertical scales for reasons of space. The possibly infrasonic *conceptual fundamental* or *GCD pitch* of each frequency set (i.e., its greatest common divisor) is indicated at the bottom of the table, with a dash appearing wherever it has not changed from the previous

TABLE 10.1. Available fundamental-frequency sets in *Critical Band*, with each frequency expressed as a multiple of the conceptual fundamental (GCD frequency) of the current set

						Section						
1	2	3	4	5	6	7	8	9	10	11	12	13
												8
											15	
										14	14	7
									13			
				34				12	12	12	12	6
							11					
			66	33		10	10	10	10	10	10	5
		130	65		18	9	9	9				
	129	129			17							
1	128	128	64	32	16	8	8	8	8	8	8	4
	127	127			15							
		126	63		14	7	7	7				
			62	31		6	6	6	6	6	6	3
								5	5			
				30						4	4	2
												1
A_4	A_{-3}	—	A_{-2}	A_{-1}	A_0	A_1	—	—	—	—	—	A_2
440	3.4375		6.875	13.75	27.5	55						110

Conceptual fundamental [Hz]

section.[6] In each column, the available fundamental frequencies are expressed as multiples ("harmonics") of the current conceptual fundamental frequency.

The table shows that, beginning in section 4, the set of available frequency values for the current section is derived from that of the previous section by deleting the odd-numbered multiples of the previous fundamental; the three remaining even-numbered frequencies are then divided by two in order to express them as multiples of a new fundamental frequency that is one octave higher than the last. The new set is completed by adding one new multiple above and one below the three inherited from the preceding set. This procedure is repeated four times, with A_4 consecutively reinterpreted as the 128th, 64th, 32nd,

16th, and finally 8th harmonic of a fundamental that rises by octaves from an infrasonic A_{-3} to a potentially audible but unplayed A_1.

Beginning in section 8, a different process unfolds in which the conceptual fundamental remains at A_1. The total number of available frequencies undergoes a net increase from five in section 7 to eight at the conclusion. The upper bound of the available frequency set ascends stepwise from the eleventh through (in section 12) the fifteenth harmonic of the A_1 fundamental, while the lower bound descends stepwise (at half the pace) from the sixth through the fourth harmonic. During the course of this process, odd-numbered harmonics are pruned from the set so that, at the final section, only even-numbered harmonics of A_1 remain, and these are expressible as harmonics of A_2 via division by two. With the addition of A_2 itself as an available frequency in the concluding section, the conceptual fundamental of the available set, for the first time, actually sounds.

Whereas the process in sections 1–7 of symmetrical expansion in frequency carried the work's frequency structure to the point where harmonic relationships between autonomous tones emerged, the process inaugurated in section 8 carries the expansion forward into an exposition of the harmonic world thus entered, in particular, of the intervals in the harmonic series. As the music draws to a close on the eight lowest partials of the series, the formal trajectory of the work is revealed as a gradual progression from one perceptual unity to another—from a literal unison, through radiating harmonies, to the fusion of an orchestrated harmonic series.

10.2 *Flocking* (1993)

for Gertrud Schneider and Tomas Bächli[7]
TWO PIANOS TUNED A QUARTER TONE APART
13 mins.

The solemn formal processes of *Flocking* (1993), *Ergodos III* (1994), and *Last Spring in Toronto* (2000) seem to distill the ideas of "Meta/Hodos" (section 3.4) to a stark essence: sonic shapes splashed onto a canvas of silence, from which they quickly fade. These works solicit an unaccustomed shift in the balance of attention away from the local events and continuities that constitute the usual focus of listening and toward macroscopic groups and shapes. It is almost as though the fundamental musical unit of the "note" had been partially relocated to this higher temporal gestalt level, occasioning a similar adjustment of aural focus. It is tempting to speak of an elevation of form relative to content, although Tenney would surely have said that they are the same thing apart from the temporal scale that is under consideration. Local elements, however, regain a curiously transformed aural vividness precisely in their roles as the integral determiners of larger gestalts. Relative uniformity in timbral, textural, and rhythmic characters serves to isolate as topic these macroscopic morphologies delineated in pitch, dynamic, and temporal density. As in much of Tenney's music, there can emerge a sense that one is "listening to listening" by self-consciously contemplating the experience of hearing and the perceptual structures emergent therein.

Beginning with *Rune* in 1988, Tenney sometimes integrated the processes of algorithmic composition and score production in a single computer program. In the case of *Flocking*, the program code produced no output data other than the work's graphically notated score, which rolled directly out of Tenney's printer as it was determined by the algorithm. Figure 10.3 shows the eighth page of the result. Its stippled groupings perhaps evoke not only the avian "flocking" of the title but also the word's less commonplace meaning of powdered material used for producing a pattern on wallpaper or cloth.

Both pianists read from the same score. The rhythmic notation is proportional: each page represents a duration of 60 seconds, with time increasing from left to right. Individual piano tones (elements) are indicated by small black filled squares. Four different sizes of square appear, increasing in size with the intended dynamic, which ranges from *pianissimo* to *fortissimo*. Pitch increases from low to high on the page, which is understood to span the range of the instruments, but a graduated pitch scale is not provided. The preface to the score indicates: "No effort needs to be made to play each note precisely, but rather simply to render the general characteristics of the various textures, and their gradual evolution in time." Each piano is tuned in 12TET, but one instrument is tuned a quarter tone higher than the other. The tempered quarter-tone intonation (24TET) thus cooperatively realized by the two pianos is not a typical tuning system in Tenney's music, since it is of limited aid in the approximation of simple just intervals. In *Flocking* it defamiliarizes the instruments' timbres and intervals and prevents incidental pitch-class coincidences between them, but it serves no other harmonic purpose. Articulations are to be staccato throughout, although the pianists are permitted to use the damper and sostenuto pedals "in some agreed-upon, coordinated way" and to employ the una corda pedal, pizzicati, and striking of the strings in addition to the keyboard. Quite varied realizations are thus possible. Following an energetic North American premiere that found filmmaker and improvising pianist Michael Snow in the audience, I overheard Snow ask Tenney—to the composer's delight—whether he ever listened to bebop pianist Earl "Bud" Powell.

Activity is initially dense but quiet and restricted to the middle registers of the instruments. The texture is formally almost featureless due to its uniformity in pitch, dynamic, and durational distribution. Over the course of the second minute, however, distinctive features begin to emerge, delineated by parametric contrasts that are initially modest but that gradually increase in magnitude. By the seventh minute, distinct aural gestalts (clangs)—each a few seconds long—pervade the texture, as shown in figure 10.3. These groups of tones are

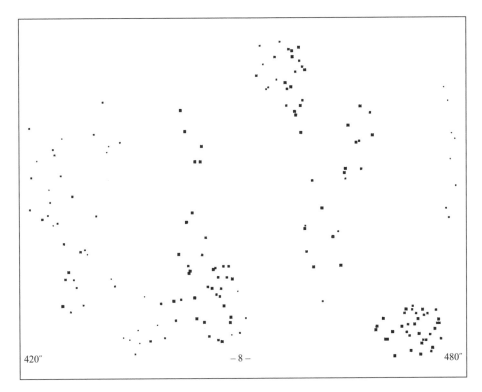

420"   — 8 —   480"

FIGURE 10.3. A page from the score to *Flocking*.

sharply distinguished by differences in register, dynamic, and attack density. For instance, the figure shows that around 460 seconds a loud, high-pitched, and rapid clang gives way to one that—although also loud—is lower pitched and relatively sparse. Such parametric contrasts may be further emphasized by the performers' choices of pedaling and timbre. The statistical attributes in which perceptually meaningful contrasts may appear include not only parametric means but also parametric ranges. Around 470 seconds, for instance, a loud, low-pitched clang about one octave wide gives way to a quieter, higher-pitched clang about three octaves wide. The coherence of such aural gestalt groupings due to their internal parametric consistency and their segregation from adjacent groupings due to parametric contrasts produces the "flocking" of musical elements to which the title alludes.

Figure 10.4 shows the evolution of parametric ranges over the course of the music as determined from the computer code for Tenney's compositional algorithm.[8] Light gray filled regions represent allowed ranges for the parametric means of clangs. The boundaries of these gray regions have the same functional form for each parameter: the ascending portion of a raised cosine function attaining its maximum value at 8 minutes, followed by the descending portion of another raised-cosine function of shorter period. (This curve is symmetrically

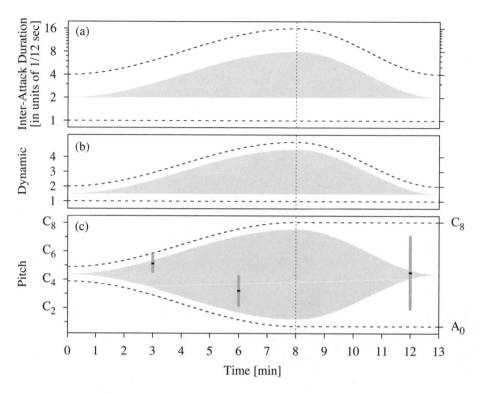

FIGURE 10.4. Parametric ranges as a function of time in *Flocking*. Vertical bars in part (c) of the figure illustrate the computation of element ranges at three different times.

reflected about the middle of the keyboard to derive the range for clang means in the pitch parameter, as shown in part (c) of the figure.) The formal pivot at 8 minutes divides the music at eight-thirteenths of its total duration, which closely approximates its golden section. The precise location of this division, however, is aurally undetectable due to the continuity of the parametric evolutions. For elements (i.e., for the individual piano tones of which clangs are comprised), the maximum parametric ranges are represented in the figure by dashed lines above and below the gray filled shapes. In most instances, these element-level bounds reside at constant distances above and below the clang-mean distributions; the pitch bounds for elements in the latter portion of the piece are an exception to this rule, residing instead at the absolute limits of the standard piano keyboard.

The algorithmic process by means of which parametric values are selected is illustrated for the pitch parameter in figure 10.4(c) using vertical bars associated with notional clangs at three different time values.[9] The procedure is "top-down," determining parameters first for clangs and then for their constituent elements. The computations proceed similarly for the interattack duration and dynamic parameters. For each new clang, a total duration is randomly selected without bias in the range of 2–6 seconds, and it is appended to the immediately preceding clang without interruption. The mean parametric value for the new clang is then selected without bias from within the light gray filled shape in the figure, as represented therein by a short black horizontal line. The range within which each clang's element parameters are chosen is randomly determined subject to certain constraints. These constraints are that this range (a) is symmetrical about the clang mean value, (b) lies within the upper and lower bounds on element values (represented by the dashed curves in figure 10.4), and (c) is wider than a stipulated minimum (which, for the pitch parameter, is one octave).[10] Examples of such ranges are represented by the dark gray bars in the figure. The parametric value for each individual element in the clang is then randomly selected without bias from within this dark gray range. Pitch and dynamic values are truncated (rounded down) to the nearest integer. The individual interattack durations for elements—determined in accordance with figure 10.4(a)—are concatenated until the current clang duration is full, at which time the whole process is repeated for the next clang.

Figure 10.4 shows that the music begins with clangs that are quiet and rapid, with elements that are uniformly distributed within the middle octave of the instruments. The parametric similarity of these opening clangs renders their temporal boundaries imperceptible, so that the effect is one of continuous random muttering. As the piece unfolds, the prospects increase for louder, slower, higher, lower, and more internally variable clangs. The greatest diversity of possibilities is attained at the 8-minute mark, where varied clangs of contrasting tempo, dynamic, register, and range are juxtaposed. In contrast with the increase in musical density commonly featured during the approach to a climactic point, an expansive and varied texture sets in as longer and slower clangs appear alongside the sort of rapid configurations that were characteristic of the work's opening. As the music proceeds toward its conclusion, the dynamic and rhythmic conditions of the outset gradually return, and the pitch mean is progressively again restricted to the middle octave of the keyboard. However, the disposition of pitch ranges contrasts with that found at the opening insofar as the bounds on element pitch values (the dashed curves in figure 10.4[c]) no longer track those for pitch means (the edges of the light gray filled shapes). Thus mean pitch value—previously a major factor in the discrimination of different clangs—gradually ceases to play any role, while distinctions between the pitch ranges of successive clangs become the principal factor distinguishing them. The results occasionally recall the opening, but the diversity of broader ranges lends a more expansive and, perhaps, reflective quality.

Although a concept of form as the product of unfolding process is fundamental to most of Tenney's mature music, and while the concept of organicist growth to form was particularly influential on his early thinking (section 4.1), in general he refrained from citing specific metaphors for his music. An exception is provided by the (currently unpublished) *Orchestral Study: The "Creation*

Field" (1974), whose subtitle invokes nonstandard cosmological models that are also paralleled in its form. As far as I know, however, Tenney nowhere else explicitly invoked such musical allusions to cosmology. To my mind, at least, cosmological metaphors are nonetheless readily summoned by certain of his late works, including *Flocking* (1993), *Last Spring in Toronto* (2000), *To Weave (a meditation)* (2003), and *Arbor Vitae* (2006). In 2004 an interviewer queried:

> *So James Tenney, you are a teacher, a performer, a composer, a theorist—anything else?*

> I used to joke that I'm an amateur cosmologist [*laughs*] because I've always been interested in science. (Tenney 2004b; also see Polansky 2007)

In the late 1950s, as part of his master's program at the University of Illinois, Tenney studied the still novel science of information theory in courses taught by his supervisor, Lejaren Hiller (a chemist by training). The experience made a strong impact on the young artist (Tenney [1964] 2015, 97; 2000f). In information theory, *entropy* is the average rate at which information is produced by a random message source, while in thermodynamics, the related concept is a measure of the degree of disorder in a physical system. The second law of thermodynamics states that the overall entropy (disorder) of an isolated physical system can never decrease, entailing a particular directionality for time (sometimes called "the arrow of time"). This has spawned such hypothetical projections as that of the *heat death of the universe*, according to which all matter and energy will tend in the long run to a static and maximally disordered condition. On a more mundane scale, the implications of the second law can be observed in the gradual diffusion of a droplet of colored ink into a glass of water. Such a process progresses irreversibly from initial concentration through complex evolving figurations to a final uniform dispersal.

Flocking's registrally restricted opening texture readily suggests a constrained and formless but energetic primordial state. Amid the ensuing gradual parametric liberation, a turbulent formal complexification unfolds. This begets differentiated and dynamic gestalts that cohere around parametric similarities and segregate via parametric contrasts. At the conclusion, these figures become diffuse and registrally centric, although Tenney eschews a complete textural "heat death" by preserving variation in registral width. If aspects of this progression seem to court cosmological metaphors, it may only be that cosmology furnishes a tempting poetic analogue to many natural and social processes. The actual medium in which the diverse forms of *Flocking* proliferate is, of course, the perceiving consciousness of the listener as animated by the music.

CHAPTER 11

Spectra and Diaphony
(1994–2006)

The 1990s brought a measure of increased international recognition to Tenney's work, especially in Europe. This was bolstered when, after an absence of thirty-two years, John Cage returned in 1990 to teach at the Darmstadt International Summer Courses for New Music in Germany and brought Tenney with him. A subsequent 1993–94 residency in Berlin further raised Tenney's European profile. By middecade, he was receiving a daunting volume of commissions and requests for new pieces. Partly in response to this increased demand, series of works would begin to feature among his output, including the *Spectrum*s 1–8 (1995/2001), the *Diaphonic* series (1997; section 11.3), and *Seegersong*s *1* and *2*. Such series comprise multiple distinct instantiations of a single general conception and design.

In the fall of 2000 Tenney returned after an absence of two and a half decades to again teach composition at the California Institute of the Arts (CalArts) in Valencia, California. The move was motivated in part by considerations of job security in light of Canadian retirement laws as Tenney turned sixty-five years of age—particularly since he was still supporting a family that included a new son, Justin, born in 1993. Understandably, he also felt a certain satisfaction in being invited to return to an endowed chair after the ephemerality of his previous position there.[1]

11.1 Dissonant Counterpoint and Statistical Feedback

A particular concern for Tenney during the late 1990s would be an integration of the harmonic-series structures that appeared in his music of the 1970s with the seemingly incompatible practice of American *dissonant counterpoint*.

Dissonant counterpoint was a radical compositional technique first developed in the second decade of the twentieth century by theorist-musicologist Charles Seeger in collaboration with his composition student Henry Cowell (Spilker 2011). Manifestations of the technique appear vividly in the compositions of Ruth Crawford (Seeger) circa 1930, but also in certain works by John J. Becker, Johanna Beyer, Vivian Fine, Lou Harrison, and Carl Ruggles, the last of whom was mentor to a young Tenney in the 1950s (section 2.3). Seeger portrayed the technique as a progressive musical response to the predominance of homophony in the preceding era of Western music. Assuming that reflexive hearing of traditional tonal relationships was strongly habituated, he wrote that "it becomes necessary to cultivate 'sounding apart' rather than 'sounding together'—diaphony rather than symphony" (Seeger 1930, 28). To this end, the technique of dissonant counterpoint as described by Seeger emphasized dissonance over consonance, assiduously refuted tonal references both within and between voices, prescribed regular pitch-class circulation, promoted complex rhythmic relationships between voices, and was extensible in principle to dynamics and other parameters of music.

Galvanizing for Tenney was his reading in the 1990s of Seeger's "Manual of Dissonant Counterpoint" ([1931] 1994), which had been cowritten with Crawford and completed in 1931 but which was not published until 1994 (Tenney 2001; Spilker 2013). By 1997 Tenney was teaching his students about dissonant counterpoint technique. He was also attempting to synthesize it compositionally with his own prior interest in harmony, although he saw in this project a particular technical challenge:

> [In my teaching, I'm] seeing as various manifestations of the same phenomenon . . . some of the most dissonant and complex work of Ives, the music of Ruggles, Dane Rudhyar, Ruth Crawford Seeger, and the theoretical writings of Charles Seeger. I'm connecting all this and the music of [Edgard] Varèse and Stefan Wolpe. I see them as various manifestations of the same phenomenon, which is the taste for dissonance, and at the same time a taste for complexity of other kinds, rhythmic complexity. Right now I'm interested in integrating that dissonant, contrapuntal idea in my own work along with the new insights I have about harmony. This is a difficult problem, because in its nature, when you're working with harmony, unless you work very hard to avoid it, it's easy for things to start sounding sweet [*laughter*]. (Tenney 1997)

His approach to this problem would invoke, on the one hand, the relatively complex harmonic relationships available between higher members of the harmonic series and, on the other hand, an algorithmic approach to the suppression of close pitch-class repetition.

The avoidance of close pitch-class repetition—especially within any single voice—is a key feature of dissonant counterpoint technique as developed by

Cowell and Seeger, who prescribed that no pitch class should be repeated until several others had intervened (Cowell [1930] 1996, 41–42; Seeger [1931] 1994, 174). Avoidance of proximate pitch-class repetition had already appeared as a feature of Tenney's early instrumental and computer music. In 1964 he had written: "Since my earliest instrumental music (*Seeds*, in 1956), I have tended to avoid repetitions of the same pitch or any of its octaves before most of the other pitches in the scale of twelve have been sounded. This practice derives not only from Schoenberg and Webern and twelve-tone or later serial methods but may be seen in much of the important music of the century (Varèse, Ruggles, etc.)" (Tenney [1964] 2015, 120). Moreover, Tenney had already used simple algorithmic means to prevent close pitch or pitch-class repetition in some of his computer music pieces of the 1960s, such as *Stochastic String Quartet*, *Dialogue*, and *Music for Player Piano*. His music of the 1990s, however, achieved this avoidance using a more sophisticated stochastic technique sometimes referred to as *statistical feedback*, wherein statistics regarding the past values of some random quantity are used to modify the probability distribution from which that quantity's next value will be selected (Ames 1987b, 1–3). In Tenney's music, this approach first appeared in *Changes* (1985) ([1987a] 2015, 345). It recurred (albeit in rudimentary form) in *The Road to Ubud* (1986) and then in *Tableaux Vivants* (1990). From 1995 onward, however, Tenney would employ the technique regularly whenever he made use of computerized algorithms for composing. It was epitomized in a set of pieces that I will refer to as Tenney's *Diaphonic* series, which includes *Diaphonic Study* (1997), *Diaphonic Toccata* (1997), *Diaphonic Trio* (1997), *Seegersongs 1* and *2* (1999), *Prelude and Toccata* (2001), and *To Weave (a meditation)* (2002). The procedure and generalizations thereof have been analyzed in detail by Larry Polansky, Alex Barnett, and Michael Winter (2011), who have dubbed it "the dissonant counterpoint algorithm."

The essence of Tenney's dissonant counterpoint algorithm was that whenever a particular pitch class (pc) was stochastically selected, then the probability of its selection was strongly suppressed, gradually recuperating over the course of some fixed number of subsequent selections. In other words, the probability that a particular pc would be selected twice in immediate succession was small or nil, but the probability that it would be selected recuperated progressively as the number of other subsequently selected pcs grew. The algorithm for the monophonic *Seegersongs 1* and *2* (1999) provides a characteristic example of the procedure. The probability weights for all twelve pcs were initialized to one.[2] Whenever a particular pc was subsequently selected, however, its probability weight was set to $2^{-10} = 1/1{,}024$, strongly suppressing the probability of its immediate reselection. With each subsequent random selection, this probability weight was doubled either until the suppressed pc was selected again (and its probability weight accordingly reset to 1/1024) or until its probability weight had (after the selection of ten other pcs) returned to unity. Figure 11.1 provides

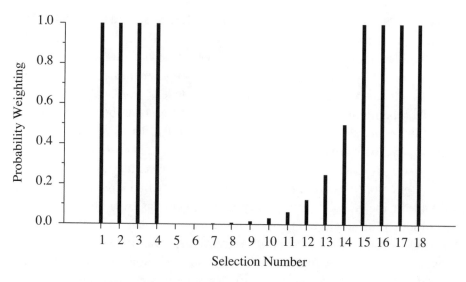

FIGURE 11.1. Recuperation over time of the probability weight for a single pitch class after its suppression via statistical feedback at selection number 5.

an invented example showing the changes in time of the probability weight for a single pc chosen for the first time as the fifth pc of the piece and then not selected again until after the eighteenth pc selection. At any instant in the midst of the compositional computations, the probability weights of the sundry pcs included some that were in various stages of recuperation from suppression and others that were of the nominal unit value. At any given moment, the number of different pcs with a substantial probability of selection depended on the strength of suppression and the rate of recuperation used for the particular piece, but often it was only a few.

In polyphonic pieces such as *Diaphonic Study* (1997), Tenney used statistical feedback to prevent close pitch-class repetition not only *within* each voice but also *between* different voices. To this end, once a pitch class had been selected in a particular voice, its probability of selection was temporarily suppressed in *all* voices. Furthermore, the use of statistical feedback was extended to promote another feature typical of classic dissonant counterpoint: the projection of dissonance *between* distinct polyphonic voices. Whenever a pc was selected to appear in a particular voice, this dissonation between voices was promoted by temporarily increasing the selection probability of pcs adjacent to it *in all other voices*. In other words, in all other voices and for all pitches differing from the currently selected pitch by a semitone interval (or some octave equivalent thereof), the probability of selection was temporarily increased, gradually returning to normal over the course of subsequent selections.[3]

Tenney frequently combined the pitch-class probability weights determined by the dissonant counterpoint algorithm with other probabilistic constraints on pitch. Such combinations were straightforwardly achieved by simply multiplying the weights associated with each constraint. In the *Seegersongs*, for instance, in addition to the probabilistic constraints on pitch class imposed by the dissonant counterpoint algorithm, pitches were selected only within a registral window that gradually varied in time. In order to combine these two constraints—one on pitch class and the other on pitch—a probability weight function for pitch was defined whose value was uniform and nonzero within the registral window but zero outside of it. For each pitch value within the fixed overall pitch range of the piece, this registral weight was then multiplied by the separate weight associated with its pitch class as computed by the dissonant counterpoint algorithm. This product of two weights thus furnished a single new probability weight for the associated pitch that captured both the registral and pitch-class constraints. Thus the technique of statistical feedback furnished a powerful and flexible approach to combining multiple parametric constraints.

11.2 *In a Large, . . .* (1994–95)

In a Large, Open Space (1994)
TWELVE OR MORE SUSTAINING INSTRUMENTS
variable duration

In a Large, Reverberant Space (1995)
TWELVE OR MORE SUSTAINING INSTRUMENTS
variable duration

Among Tenney's late works, *In a Large, . . .* is simultaneously the most economical in its design and the most consequential for his subsequent compositional direction. It would galvanize his return to the harmonic series as basic harmonic material but with a new focus on the dissonant relationships available in its upper reaches. This watershed development would reverberate in a succession of subsequent pieces, including the *Spectrum* series (1995/2001), *Diapason* (1996), and the *Diaphonic* series of pieces (1997).

    In a Large, . . . exists in two nearly identical versions: *In a Large, Open Space* and *In a Large, Reverberant Space*. Both call for the musicians to be dispersed throughout a performance space about which the audience is free to move, and in both cases all performers independently and repeatedly select their pitches from the same unchanging pitch set, which is a harmonic series.

    The score to *In a Large, Open Space* is shown in its entirety in figure 11.2. Tenney remarked, "I don't know why, but my image of that piece is always of a football field. With nobody in the stands [*laughs*], people walking around on the field" (1996b, 10). In practice, *In a Large, Open Space* has often been played in enclosed spaces about which the audience can freely move. Inspired by a visit

In a large, open space, within which the audience is able to move freely, for any 12 or more sustaining instruments.

James Tenney, Berlin, 1994

The musicians should be distributed in the space as widely and evenly as possible, with instruments of lower tessitura located more centrally, higher ones more peripherally. Each player plays one after another of the "available pitches" within the range of his/her instrument (see the notation below), very quietly *(pp)*, with a soft attack, for some 30 to 60 seconds. After a breath or short pause, another pitch is chosen (generally trying to avoid duplicating a pitch already sounding on another instrument), and the same process is repeated, again and again, for the duration of the performance or installation.

Available pitches for **In a large, open space.** The numbers above each notated pitch indicate deviations from the tempered pitch in *cents* (hundredths of a tempered semitone). In order to achieve the required accuracy of intonation, players of instruments with variable intonation should be equipped with an electronic tuning device. Instruments of fixed pitch (e.g. accordion, vibraphone (arco), etc.) may play only pitches which differ by no more than 5 cents from the tempered pitch.

FIGURE 11.2. The complete score to *In a Large, Open Space* (1994).

to the Minoritenkirche in Krems, Austria, the score to *In a Large, Reverberant Space* differs only insofar as the first sentence of the instructions reads: "The musicians should be distributed in the space as widely and evenly as possible, with instruments of higher tessitura located nearer to the entrance to the space, lower ones more distantly."

The score describes the presentation of *In a Large, . . .* as a "performance or installation." Criteria that would distinguish one from the other are not made explicit. Perhaps a "performance" might have declared durational limits such that a listener might expect to stay for its entirety, while an "installation" would not. The score includes no prescription for beginning, ending, or determining the duration of a presentation. At the premiere, following a change of mind in midperformance, Tenney distributed written instructions to all of the players, one by one, in descending registral order indicating that, after receiving the instruction, they should play for approximately one more minute and then stop (1996b, 9). More commonly, prearranged visual cues or a predetermined total duration have been used.

In a Large, . . . bears certain features more often associated with sound installations than with concert pieces, leading composer Richard Glover to describe it as a "performed installation" (Glover and Harrison 2013, 29–40). These features include its (typically) extended duration, the statistically stationary character of the musical texture, the spatially immersive quality of the listening experience, the lack of a preferred audience location or orientation, and the freedom of the audience to enter, exit, and move about the space at will.

Tenney remarked, "My intention was to create a situation in which the listener, to a great extent, determines his or her own experience of the music" (1996b, 9). This aspect of *In a Large, . . .* relates it to such earlier pieces as *For Ann (rising)* (1969) and various texturally dense works including *Saxony* (1978) and *Voice(s)* (1982/1984), wherein each listener's experience of the music is to a significant degree determined by their individual decisions regarding how to direct their attention. With *In a Large, . . .* choices regarding aural focus again play a significant musically constitutive role, since generally there are more discriminable sources (and hence intervals, timbres, and locations) than can be attended simultaneously. Additionally, the fact that listeners can independently enter and traverse the space while the performance is ongoing empowers their active exploration of different listening locations and orientations. By moving, they can compare the acoustics at different spots, vary the constellation of source locations, and adjust the "mix" of different instrumental timbres and registers by moving closer to some performers and away from others. While many listeners may choose to migrate between discrete locations—pausing to attend at each as though exploring an art gallery—with care it is also possible to listen while moving, thus experiencing controlled cross-fades between different sound states.

Listeners are free to approach individual performers and to peruse the score from which they are reading. This transparency and intimacy provide opportunities for musical insight and empathy, as the listener observes the performer's care in the selection and tuning of pitches (Tenney 1996b, 9–10). Reading the score will furthermore confirm that there are no predetermined formal trajectories and no expressive meaning to be deciphered in the particular order of musical events. This awareness may encourage the attention of audience members to their current sonic environment and to their autonomous role in constituting the musical experience through directed listening and movement. Indeed, to explain the significance of transparency with respect to process in performances of *In a Large*, . . . Tenney invoked a post-Cagean listener-centered perspective: "It has to do partly with what I take to be the essence of Cage's revolution. He once wrote 'Sounds we hear are music.' I continue to think that this is a remarkable formulation, a remarkable definition, in a number of ways. One thing that needs to be understood about it is that it shifts the focus of the musical enterprise from the feelings and thoughts and so forth of the composer to the experience of the listener: this becomes the central point of the whole exercise" (Tenney 1996b, 9).

As shown in figure 11.2, the shared available-pitch set comprises the lowest thirty-two harmonics of F_1. Tenney observed that the F_1 "fundamental" of this set is so low that "among sustaining instruments, only the contrabass, the tuba, the contrabassoon, and the contrabass clarinet can play it" (Tenney 1996b, 10). Even for those few instruments F_1 remains just one pitch choice among many, so that in performance there are many occasions when this rationalizing fundamental pitch is not sounding. As musicologist Bob Gilmore pointed out, this is equally true for other low harmonic numbers: "The lower partials therefore have no necessary prominence in the texture, nor are they continuously present; the effect of this is to free the music from its quasi-tonal anchor (the fundamental of the series) and to yield a perceptually more complex harmonic fabric, in which microtonally dense simultaneities from the upper reaches of the series can occasionally dominate the aural surface."[4] Together with the requirements that there be at least twelve instruments in use and that players attempt to avoid reproducing pitches that are already sounding, the limited availability of low partials entails that complex harmonic relationships from higher in the series will almost always be present, and sometimes exclusively so. This fact distinguishes *In a Large*, . . . from earlier pieces such as *Quintext*, V: "Spectra for Harry Partch" (1972), *Saxony* (1978), and *Voice(s)* (1982/1984). While those earlier works also use pitch sets derived from the harmonic series, they introduce higher partials progressively and abate or rationalize complex dissonances with a strategic return to lower partials or by introducing the collective fundamental. In contrast, throughout *In a Large*, . . . all pitches in the set are continually available to the performers, so complex harmonic configurations may prevail at any time and in practice tend to be a feature of the texture almost throughout.

Although the audience can move freely, the stipulated spatial arrangement of instruments imposes a degree of what might be called an *architectural* structure on the listening experience (as opposed to a determinate temporal one). The score for *In a Large, Open Space* indicates that instruments of lower register should be located near the center of the space so that higher partials and the more complex harmonic relationships available among them will be relatively salient as the listener approaches or leaves the performance area, while lower partials will be (on average) more prominent in the middle of that area. Thus the perceptual rationalization and synthesis of the ensemble of sounding pitches as harmonic partials will tend to be more pronounced near the center of the space. A similar effect occurs in *In a Large, Reverberant Space* as listeners move away from the entrance and into the interior of the chamber.

It is possible to follow instrumental entrances as melody, although the stipulation of long tones and "soft attack" promotes harmonically oriented listening. The score indicates that performers should sustain each selected pitch for 30 to 60 seconds, with only a "breath or short pause" between tones. Thus, the average temporal overlap between a pair of concurrent pitches permits many opportunities for listeners to focus on particular harmonic relationships. On the other hand, with an ensemble of twelve performers, if each player takes, say, 60 seconds in total to play one pitch and then to choose their next one, a new attack will be heard every 5 seconds on average, and that average attack rate will increase proportionally as the number of performers increases. Thus the total collection of sounding pitches is in clear but gradual flux.

The requirement that performers should be "distributed in the space as widely and evenly as possible" supports the discriminability of sound sources via localization. Together with the stipulation of a common dynamic, dispersal of sources also promotes dynamic balance between the instruments when the listener is not close to any one player—in other words, it tends to afford a variety of listening locations where the loudness levels of multiple sources are comparable to one another so that harmonic relationships between them are easily heard.[5] Reverberation in a performance space will tend to further support dynamic balance among tones and also to partially obscure source locations, since hard surfaces reflect sound energy around the space rather than allowing it to escape. Consequently, instruments far from the listener would tend to be heard less well on Tenney's imagined football field than in a cathedral, and closer instruments would correspondingly predominate more strongly, so that the composite sound would be even more sensitive to the listener's location. On the other hand, source location would tend to be clearer on the field.

While the particular choices of the listener and performers substantially determine the experiential form of *In a Large, . . .*, I think that the crucial tension animating the music derives from the choice of the harmonic series as available-pitch set. In a late essay concerning the multidimensional character of pitch perception, Tenney wrote: "Regarding the nature of auditory perception, it is often useful to think about the evolution of hearing, and I would invoke the image of a primitive hominid trying to survive in the savannah (our ears, after all, surely evolved as a means of survival, not for musical ends). What would the auditory system of this primitive hominid need to be able to do?" ([1993c/2003] 2015, 368). After proposing an auditory mechanism dedicated to rapid pitch-contour detection (useful for quickly detecting acoustical changes in the environment), Tenney posited a second, necessarily slower mechanism useful for discriminating acoustical sources: "[The first mechanism] won't help in the determination that the several harmonic partials in the sound of [a] lion's roar are actually coming from just one lion. For that, something else is needed—a mechanism that can detect any correlations among individual partials in the signal and thus determine when two or more widely separated frequencies are so closely related (in some respect) that they are likely to have been produced by the same sound source" (370–71). In particular, this second mechanism would participate in the determination of harmonic relatedness, the perceptual grouping of harmonically related sound components, and the association of such a grouping with a unique source (and, conversely, the discrimination of that source from other sources). In nature, such determinations regarding source integration or discrimination would generally be supported by additional acoustical information, indicating the spatial location from which the various sound components arrive, their onset synchrony or asynchrony, and any coordination between the modulations of sonic parameters. What in part makes the experience of *In a Large, . . .* fascinatingly ambiguous is that tones all drawn from a single harmonic series—an auditory cue to their having a *common* source—persistently exhibit different perceived locations and temporal variations, which are cues to their having *distinct* sources. If the impression of multiple sources dominates, a stubborn insinuation of oneness still tugs at the ear. Even when the texture is briefly static, perception can shuttle unstably between fusion and fission, and voluntary shifts between the two can sometimes be accomplished by attending more or less narrowly within the texture. At other times, coalescence can prevail among certain components while others enter into provisionally separate harmonic constellations of discrete pitches. In this liminal perceptual state, the question of sonic unity versus multiplicity is posed anew with each shift in listening attention and with each instrumental entrance.

11.3 *Diaphonic Study* (1997)

STRING QUARTET AND PIANO
18 mins.

Diaphonic Study (1997) was the first of a series of pieces inspired in part by the twentieth-century American style of atonal part-writing known as *dissonant*

FIGURE 11.3. The harmonic scale used in *Diaphonic Study, Diaphonic Trio*, and *Prelude and Toccata.*

counterpoint. Diaphonic Study was followed by the related *Diaphonic Toccata* (1997), *Diaphonic Trio* (1997), *Seegersongs 1* and *2* (1999), *Prelude and Toccata* (2001), and *To Weave (a meditation)* (2003). All of these pieces were composed using an algorithmic technique known as *statistical feedback* to emulate certain aspects of dissonant counterpoint style. These were the avoidance of close pitch-class repetitions and the promotion of dissonant relations between voices. Details regarding dissonant counterpoint and Tenney's statistical-feedback algorithm are included in section 11.1.

The term *diaphonic* appearing in Tenney's titles refers both to an ideal of polyphonic "sounding apart" as articulated in the writings of Seeger on dissonant counterpoint (Seeger 1930, 28) and to the titles of the four *Diaphonic Suites* (1930), composed by Ruth Crawford. In *Diaphonic Study*, Tenney undertook accommodation of diaphony with harmony (in his nontonal sense of the word) through the combination of three techniques. The first of these was the use of a twelve-note *harmonic scale*, depicted in figure 11.3. This scale comprises selected pitch classes (pcs) appearing in the fifth octave of a harmonic series with fundamental F, but these are repeated in all octaves. It thus draws upon relatively high reaches within the series and the wealth of complex and dissonant harmonic relationships available there, which had been previously highlighted by *In a Large, . . .* (1994–95). The piano is retuned to this scale and serves as an intonational reference for the other instruments. Second, Tenney created a computer algorithm that, among its other operations, stochastically selected pcs from this scale while using statistical feedback in order to deter close pitch-class repetition and to promote dissonance between voices (section 11.1). The third technical component involved a formal process that Tenney had employed in a number of earlier works, beginning with *Clang* (1972). This was the raising of a *conceptual fundamental* (or *GCD pitch*) through successive octaves from one formal section to the next, with attendant deletion from the texture of all pitches not corresponding to harmonics of the new fundamental (section 8.1).[6]

The harmonic filtering process is illustrated in figure 11.4. Each of *Diaphonic Study*'s six successive 3-minute sections corresponds to a different pitch set from which Tenney's compositional algorithm stochastically assigned pitches to instruments. Available pitches are represented by horizontal lines, whose uneven spacing reflects that of Tenney's nontempered harmonic scale. The conceptual

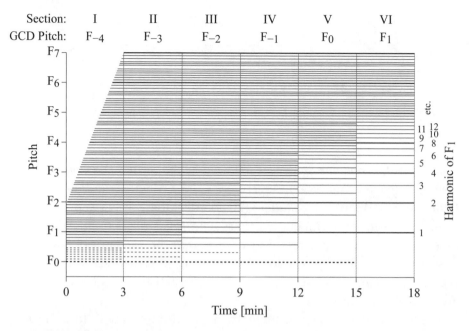

FIGURE 11.4. Pitch sets in *Diaphonic Study*.

fundamental of each pitch set is indicated at the top of the figure. In the first section, instruments enter in ascending registral order as the compass of the pitch set expands upward. All pitches initially correspond to harmonics of an infrasonic F_0, although any pitches selected below C_1 (indicated using dashed lines in the figure) are in practice voiced an octave higher, thus respecting the limits of the keyboard. With each octave ascent by the conceptual fundamental, pitches that do not correspond to harmonics of the new fundamental are deleted from the available set.

The transitions between sections are so continuous as to be undetectable by ear, but in the bass register a change in harmonic character becomes increasingly audible following the work's midpoint. Temporal density and dynamic peak at the golden section of the piece as shown in figure 11.5, thus emphasizing the transition to section V, where the harmonic direction becomes clear. As shown in figure 11.4, harmonic simplification spreads upward from the bass in the final sections until the conceptual fundamental of the pitch set finally sounds as F_1 in section VI. Low pitches and sometimes high ones enter into intelligible relationships underpinned by their common affiliation with the conceptual fundamental, but the continually cycling pcs drawn from the "chromatic" upper reaches of the available set at most flirt with such rationalization. A "dissonant counterpoint" thus persists as a component of the texture even as musical activity subsides to a conclusion.

Musical details were determined using a simplified version of an algorithmic approach that Tenney developed in his computer music of the early 1960s

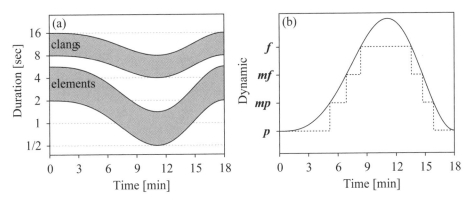

FIGURE 11.5. The evolution of (a) durational ranges and (b) dynamic values over the course of *Diaphonic Study*. Dynamic values following quantization are illustrated using a dashed line.

(section 4.5) and to which he often returned beginning in the mid-1980s. In his computer algorithm, the composer treated the ensemble as comprising six monophonic voices, corresponding to the instruments of the string quartet plus piano left hand and piano right hand. The formal hierarchy comprises only two levels: individual tones (*elements*) and short quasi-legato groupings of tones (*clangs*) terminated by rests. Clang durations within each instrumental part were determined independently from those in other parts and were randomly selected within the time-varying range indicated in figure 11.5(a). One in three clangs (on average) was then randomly replaced by an equivalent period of rest, although within any single part two consecutive clangs of rest were not permitted. Elements were assigned durations randomly selected within another range (also shown) and concatenated to fill the previously determined clang duration. Each element was assigned a pitch that was within the associated instrument's range and that was selected from the current available-pitch set by the stochastic feedback algorithm. Once the specification of a particular clang was finished, the algorithm would proceed to generate a new clang in whichever part was furthest from completion. As shown by the score excerpt in figure 11.6, rhythm is proportionally notated, the elements of each clang are beamed together, and each notehead in the string staves is accompanied by a deviation in cents from 12TET. Breath marks indicate the beginnings of rests, and tick marks between staves appear every 3 seconds.

Tenney's *Diaphonic* compositions epitomize the penchant for synthesis detectable in much of his work. Within an idiosyncratic new formulation, these pieces draw together threads from his dissonant student works and studies with Carl Ruggles, the formal theories of "Meta/Hodos," his algorithmic computer music of the 1960s, the gradual processes and harmonic-series textures of his music in the 1970s, and his interest in stretching the limits of perceptible harmonic relationship.

FIGURE 11.6. Excerpt from the score to *Diaphonic Study* (11'30"–11'39").

11.4 *Arbor Vitae* (2006)

STRING QUARTET
13 mins.

In a stratospherically high register, faint sounds—almost as much bow noise as tone—emerge from silence like gleams of light in a vast dark space. Sustained artificial harmonics follow quietly one after another without interruption, their delicacy only making the enveloping emptiness seem more present. Unaccustomed as the ear may be to listening for harmony in this register, it might not immediately apprehend that many of the wispy intervals appearing are simple, closely voiced, and consonant. Just-intoned versions of triads and seventh chords emerge, sometimes including sharp elevenths or strange transitional tones. Gradually, pitches begin to creep downward as attack density and dynamic almost imperceptibly begin to increase and more complex harmonic configurations start to appear. These now involve various seconds, sevenths, ninths, and more exotic intervals. Sometimes pitches seem to disorientingly change harmonic allegiances, participating first in one grouping and then in another as attendant pitches appear or disappear. As the music expands into the bass register, natural harmonics and stopped notes emerge. Attack density and dynamic increase as widening voicings project harmonies of diverse complexity. Simple configurations appear only to be subsumed into complex ones, while complex ones sometimes cede to simpler, more familiar sonorities. Often, multiple harmonies seem to coexist, delineated by register, entrance timings, and/or internal coherence. A climax of density and dynamic finds voicings closing into the bass, the rich dark tones of the instruments' lower strings predominating as cello and viola come to the fore. Almost unnoticed, the pitch trajectory changes direction, rising through shifting harmonies of varied dissonance made more vivid by close voicings. At its close, the music returns to the gossamer high-register tones of its opening without relinquishing the mercurial harmonic complexity acquired over its course.

For almost two decades Tenney had contemplated a return to composition using his concept of harmonic space and associated lattice models of pitch relations (section 7.7). In the mid-1980s, these ideas had provided the theoretical foundation for his monumental *Bridge* (1984) and *Changes* (1985), and he often evoked them in scholarly contexts throughout the rest of his career. With the exception of *Tableaux Vivants* (1990), however, his later harmonically oriented compositions instead invoked models based on the harmonic series. Not until *Arbor Vitae*—his final work—would harmonic space per se again figure centrally in Tenney's compositional designs. The result is a unique work that is at once strange, uncompromising, elemental, and powerfully evocative of the tacit spiritual undercurrent in all of his music.

Tenney had begun work on *Arbor Vitae* in 2005, producing detailed notes, sketches, and computer code for the compositional algorithm. In May 2006, however, his progress on the piece was interrupted when he was diagnosed with advanced cancer and began chemotherapy. During the following months, an enervated Tenney was visited by composer-theorist Michael Winter, a former student, who offered to assist him in the completion of *Arbor Vitae*. With Winter's assistance the piece was completed less than two weeks before Tenney died on August 24. In my last exchange with the composer, he expressed particular pride in it. It was premiered the following December by the commissioning Quatuor Bozzini at a festival commemorating Tenney and his work. Winter (2008) has published a detailed account of the history, structure, algorithm, and realization of *Arbor Vitae* that remains the most complete resource available to readers who are interested in this complex work. The following summary treatment draws upon both Winter's article and Tenney's archival notes.

The harmonic trajectory of *Arbor Vitae* systematically unfolds a highly structured collection of thirty-five pitch classes, exposing fluid harmonic relationships that slowly progress from the relatively simple to the complex and polytonal. The

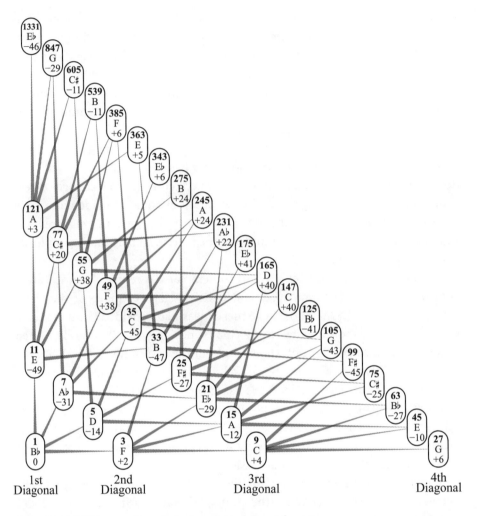

FIGURE 11.7. The complete pitch-class set used in *Arbor Vitae*.

pcs appearing and the interrelations between them are represented in Tenney's notes and in figure 11.7 as a quaternary tree structure—the "arbor" of the work's title. Each location or *node* in the tree represents a different pc and is labeled two ways in the figure: once in boldface with its ratio class relative to the *global root* of B-flat (ratio class 1/1, located at lower left) and again as a pc letter name with a deviation from 12TET indicated in cents.[7] Each ratio class differs from those immediately connected to it in the figure by one of the prime factors 3, 5, 7, or 11. Multiplications by these factors are respectively associated with gray lines tapering outward (i.e., upward and/or rightward) from a node, reading these lines counterclockwise from the lowest. For instance, successive powers of three appear across the bottom of the figure. Even the pcs most remote from the original 1/1 might thus be construed as corresponding to the pcs of "prime

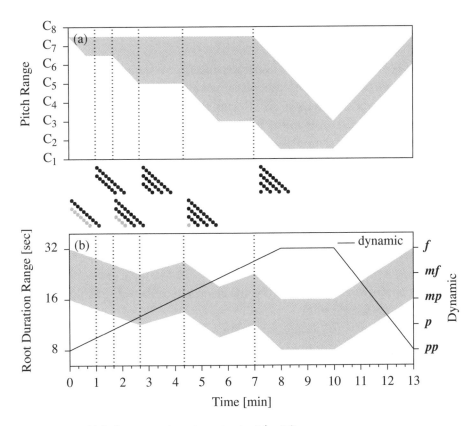

FIGURE 11.8. Global parametric trajectories in *Arbor Vitae*.

harmonics of prime harmonics of prime harmonics" of the originary B-flat. The concept of rootedness invoked here thus correlates with Tenney's concept of harmonic containment (section 7.7.3), wherein pcs above and to the right of the global B-flat root appear within its harmonic series, while that B-flat does not appear in theirs. Crucially, however, since the same set of multiplicative prime factors is associated with each ramification in the tree, any node can be regarded as a *local root* or *local 1/1* for the nodes connected to it via outgoing lines. This fact enables the polyharmonies sometimes audible in the music.

As shown in figure 11.7, the ratio classes appearing in *Arbor Vitae* can be arrayed in what Tenney called *diagonals* according to the number of prime factors they possess. For instance, all ratios in the third diagonal comprise two prime factors.[8] At the outset of the piece, only pcs residing on the rightmost "fourth diagonal" are heard, with successive diagonals to its left added one by one over the course of the first seven minutes of music. This process is depicted in figure 11.8 using a sequence of six dot arrays iconically representing the sets of diagonals active at various stages in the piece. The left edge of each dot array is aligned with the time value at which its particular structure begins to guide the operation of the pc-selection algorithm. These time values tend to be coordinated with other parametric changes, as indicated by dashed verticals in the other parts of the figure.

As the dot arrays of figure 11.8 illustrate, once a pc became available for selection by the composing algorithm, it remained available, so that the reservoir of available pcs never decreases in size during the piece. By stochastically selecting pcs from that reservoir in the following fashion, the algorithm produced a succession of local harmonies of widely varying complexity. Now and again the algorithm stochastically selected a new pc from the leftmost active diagonal to serve as a structural harmonic root. Sounding pcs (which Tenney called *branches*) were then selected from nodes that could be reached from that root via some connected sequence of outgoing lines in figure 11.7. Depending on the section of the piece, the root itself may or may not also have been selectable as a branch (and thus permitted to sound). Where the root itself was not thus selectable as a branch, it is represented in figure 11.8 using a gray rather than a black dot; as shown, such unheard roots always became permissible branches at the following formal stage.

Each root persists for a duration value randomly selected from within the gray filled region of figure 11.8(b). These root durations are short enough that a number of different roots appear between changes to the active diagonals but are also long enough that multiple branches are heard during the tenure of each root. The distribution of interattack durations for branches was made identical in shape to that shown in figure 11.8(b) for root durations but was scaled so that between five and twenty-two branches sound per root throughout. Thus the average attack density and the average "harmonic tempo" of root changes progress in tandem toward a sustained maximum near the golden section of the form, decreasing thereafter. The climactic section is further marked by a dynamic peak and the ensemble's farthest excursions into the bass register.

Arbor Vitae thus unfolds in stages of increasing harmonic complexity, as depicted in figure 11.8, although the transitions between stages are seamless to the ear. At the opening, pcs stochastically selected from the third diagonal furnish a succession of roots. Pcs on that diagonal are not yet permitted to sound, however, and are accordingly depicted using gray filled dots in the leftmost dot array of figure 11.8. On the other hand, pcs on the fourth diagonal are available branches (i.e., they are available to sound) and are therefore represented using black filled dots. Because the branches of a particular root are necessarily proximate to one another at this early stage, their ratios exhibit simple rational relationships, resulting in the relatively consonant harmonies of the opening. The attendant root progressions, on the other hand, are more intervallically varied because a relative diversity of more and less complex intervals appears among pcs on the third diagonal.

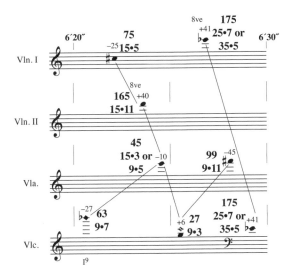

FIGURE 11.9. Annotated score excerpt from *Arbor Vitae* (6'20"–6'30"). Redrawn after Winter (2008, 137, figure 5) with permission.

At the second stage of harmonic evolution, each root selected on the third diagonal becomes potentially available to sound, as indicated in the second dot array in figure 11.8. In other words, whatever the currently selected root on the third diagonal happens to be, it becomes an available branch alongside those on the fourth diagonal to which it is connected. At this stage, the presence of roots—when they are stochastically selected to sound—reinforces the harmonic sense and coherence of successive pc constellations. In the next two stages, roots—first unheard and then heard—are drawn from the second diagonal. Branches connected to a root can now extend not only to the adjacent third diagonal but also to the fourth, potentially resulting in more complex and dissonant harmonies containing members farther removed from the current root. Finally, in the last two stages, the global B-flat root is introduced. The total pc collection then stabilizes as its many harmonic possibilities are stochastically explored in the remainder of the piece.

In these late stages, the harmony sometimes takes on a polychordal or polytonal character. This is illustrated in the annotated score excerpt in figure 11.9, which is redrawn from Winter (2008, 137, figure 5). Following Winter's analysis of this passage, boldface numbers represent ratio classes and selected factorizations thereof in order to clarify the harmonic relationships between pitches, while lines between noteheads delineate simple harmonic groupings. Figure 11.10 provides an alternative depiction of the pcs appearing in this passage as gray filled nodes within a subset of the complete tree previously shown in figure 11.7. Gray filled nodes thus represent sounding pcs, while white filled

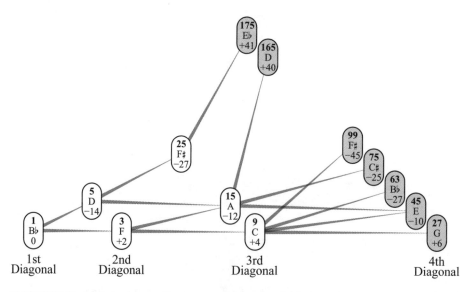

FIGURE 11.10. A pitch-class collection appearing in *Arbor Vitae* (6'20"–6'30").

nodes represent pcs that are structurally significant but not sounding; indeed, the current root on B-flat is not yet permitted to sound at this stage in the piece. Although this B-flat is the structural root relating all of the sounding pcs, not only is it unheard, but its relationship to the actually sounding pcs is sufficiently remote that harmonic groupings relatable to other temporarily *effective* roots may be heard instead. A late arriving E-flat +41¢ furnishes an exotic outlier. A principal harmony comprises ratio classes 3, 5, 7, and 11 relative to an unheard root on C +4¢ (ratio class 9). This appears alongside another harmony comprising ratio classes 3, 5, and 11 relative to an unheard root on A −12¢ (ratio class 15). These two configurations are linked by a shared E −10¢, reflecting the fact that its ratio class of 45 can be factored as either 9 × 5 or 15 × 3, as shown in figure 11.9. Such instances of polyvalency—in which a sounding tone might participate in more than one harmonic configuration—often serve to consolidate polyharmonies in this fashion, but they also contribute to another experience characteristic of *Arbor Vitae* wherein individual tones are heard to change their apparent harmonic identity and relationships over the course of their duration in response to the entrance and/or exit of other contextualizing pitches.

Stochastic selection of roots and branches was conditioned by the initialization of their probabilities and a statistical feedback mechanism that promoted the subsequent circulation of all possibilities (section 11.1). The initial selection probability for each root was made a decreasing function of its ratio class, so that whenever root selection progressed to a new diagonal the selection of roots with relatively small ratio classes relative to the global 1/1 (B-flat) would be initially privileged. Once a particular root was selected, however, its selection probability was nulled to prevent selection of the same root twice in a row, with its probability progressively recuperating over the course of the next four root selections. In practice, the selection of branches associated with a particular root involved the multiplication of its ratio class by a sequence of multipliers stochastically chosen from the set {1, 3, 5, 7, 11}. One was allowed as the first multiplier only if the root itself was permitted to sound; otherwise, some higher multiple of its ratio class would necessarily result. A single multiplier was applied to roots on the third diagonal, resulting in branches connected to it on the fourth diagonal (or, possibly, the root itself, if one was permitted as the multiplier). Two multipliers were applied to roots on the second diagonal, resulting in branches that were connected to it on the third and fourth diagonals (or the root itself, if permitted). Finally, three multipliers were applied to the originary B-flat root once the first diagonal became active, ultimately making pcs on all diagonals potentially available.

The selection probabilities for multipliers were initialized to decrease with the magnitude of the multiplier, promoting relatively simple initial harmonic relationships of branch to root. Once a branch had been fully determined, however, the probability of the most recently selected multiplier was nulled, thereby ensuring that the next branch would be a different one because that multiplier would not appear in its ratio class. Multiplier probabilities were updated following each branch determination such that a nulled value gradually recuperated over the course of the next three branch selections. Upon selection of a new root, however, all multiplier probabilities were reset to their initialization values, providing an expository function wherein branches with relatively close harmonic relationships to the new root would again statistically tend to appear before more distantly related ones. In particular, during the latter half of *Arbor Vitae*, in which the B-flat is selected again and again as root, the harmony can be heard repeatedly returning to its neighborhood before reaching outward once again to more distant relationships.

Once selected by the compositional algorithm, pcs were randomly assigned a register falling within the gray filled region of figure 11.8(a), resulting in closely voiced harmonies at the work's opening and conclusion but permitting wide voicings near its middle. Each resulting pitch was allocated to an individual instrumental part, with each instrument sustaining its pitch until assigned a new one. Transitional harmonies thus result from certain branches sustaining beyond the onset of the next root. To the extent that ranges permitted it, pitch assignments were randomly circulated among instruments while avoiding close repeated attacks within a part. At the opening, each instrument thus sounds one out of every four branches on average, but once pitches begin to fall below the range of the violins, then the viola and cello attack noticeably more often, to emphatic effect.

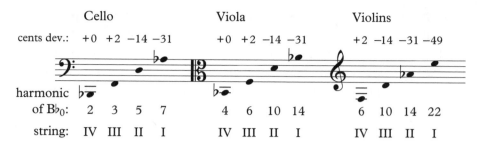

FIGURE 11.11. The string scordatura used in *Arbor Vitae*.

In the score, notes are accompanied by cents deviations from 12TET, and vibrato is proscribed in order to clarify intonation. A scordatura is stipulated, as shown in figure 11.11, permitting numerous required pitches to be realized as natural harmonics. These are indicated using roman numerals for string number with a superscript for harmonic number, as shown beneath the first cello note in figure 11.9. Nonetheless, many carefully intoned artificial harmonics and stopped tones are also required, usually necessitating the use of electronic tuners in rehearsal. Rhythmic notation is proportional, using stemless noteheads on otherwise conventional staves, and all players read from score.

Arbor Vitae merges a number of Tenney's long-standing concerns and techniques in a novel fashion. As in both his early algorithmic compositions of the 1960s and his gradual process music of the 1970s, its rigorous and undramatic processes foster a formal organicism that, in this instance, the title itself also evokes. As usual, these processes also promote variety within a carefully delineated musical domain and reflection by the listener on their own perceptions and perceptual processes. Here the focus is upon harmonic perception specifically, the principal topic with which Tenney had concerned himself for more than three decades. In keeping with his long-standing penchant for multiple entendres, it is tempting to discern in the title a subtle allusion to a life spent among these roots and branches.

CHAPTER 12

A Tradition of Experimentation

Following a 1990 lecture by Tenney, a young attendee inquired, "What advice do you give composers who operate in a postexperimental model?" Tenney prefaced his response with a terminological critique: "There is no such thing as postexperimental. . . . My sense of 'experimental' is just ongoing research. So I don't understand 'postexperimental'" ([1990] 2015, 361).

Attempted characterizations of *experimental music* have taken a variety of forms (Cage [1959] 1961, 69, 73; Nyman 1999, 1–30; Gilmore 2014; Gottschalk 2017, 1–39). Perfunctory versions sometimes frame it as a sociohistorically specific phenomenon with respect to which the concept of a "postexperimental" era might indeed be intelligible. Such versions arrogate the broad descriptor *experimental* to particular scenes for which more precise designations are formulable (e.g., "the 'New York School' of musicians associated with John Cage"). Other explications cite the frequent appearance of certain techniques (such as indeterminacy and/or generative processes) or style features (such as the avoidance of narrative expressivity or the reservation of an expanded creative role for performers and/or listeners). On the other hand, Tenney's particular characterization of experimentalism as "ongoing research" differs insofar as it asserts an underlying exploratory ethos amenable to diverse situationally contingent manifestations.

Elaborating upon this investigative orientation, Tenney asserted:

Once you've fully explored an area, then the only reason to go back to it is just to take advantage of the expertise that you've gained or the reputation that you've gained, and that's not really very deeply satisfying. What you want to do is find out what it is that you don't know how to do and proceed in that direction. To me, that's the fundamental meaning of Cage's term experimental music, which I define as doing something [where] you're not sure what the result's going to be because you haven't done it before. Nobody's done it before, right? (2005b)

He was predictably dismissive of the perennial cynicism that holds the potential for discovery to be exhausted, countering, "I was looking up at the clouds in the sky and I thought, that cloud has never been seen before, ever, in the history of the earth" (2005b). On another occasion he remarked, "The complaint that 'it's all been done before,' does not express a new despair. It has probably always been felt by a majority of aspiring artists, just as it has repeatedly been shown to be untrue by a small minority of artists—those who are remembered. No work or body of works is, or can possibly be, the 'last word.' Human creativity is far too prodigious and unpredictable for that ever to be so" (Tenney 1995b, 4).

Indeed, although I know of no thorough census, as far as I can ascertain there exists today a greater number of artists, ensembles, venues, and new recordings dedicated to "experimental music" than ever before. Its practitioners hail from diverse geographical, cultural, and stylistic points of origin and produce work exhibiting a vast range of concerns (Gottschalk 1970; Piekut 2014). I have already noted Tenney's characteristic practice of dedicating works to elder composers (section 5.2), but as evidence of the continuing vitality of an experimental aesthetic and the durable significance of his contribution to it one might in turn adduce the flow of dedications that began to proceed in the opposite direction in the 1980s. Works acknowledging Tenney began as a trickle from associates and students, but since his death their volume has swelled internationally and continues to grow. At the time of this writing, they total more than fifty such compositions of which I am aware.[1]

Acoustics, Sensation,
and Logarithmic Models

The investigation of correlations between objective acoustical quantities and subjectively perceived sensations falls within the scientific domain of psychoacoustics. In many cases, the details of such correlations remain topics of active research, and they remain complex and only partially understood even if the range of possible acoustic stimulus types is restricted to conventionally musical ones.

A venerable approximation to certain correlations between the physical and the psychological is Fechner's law, which asserts that the magnitude of sensation is proportional to the logarithm of the magnitude of physical stimulus. It is arguably misnamed insofar as its accuracy varies considerably depending upon the specific sensation to which it is applied. Restricting attention to typical pitched musical stimuli, Fechner's law applies accurately to the relationship between subjectively perceived pitch height and the frequency of physical vibration that evokes it. It holds well over the range of frequencies to which the ear is sensitive, which is about 20 Hz to 15 kHz in adults. The logarithmic relationship of pitch height to frequency is illustrated in figure A.1, using a linear frequency graduation along the bottom border and indicating the frequencies corresponding to various members of pitch class A along the top border, with pitch A_4 tuned to a frequency of 440 Hz.

The octave, being an interval between pitches, is a psychological rather than a physical entity. While its correspondence to the frequency ratio 2/1 is often casually recited, the implication that a given pitch difference corresponds not to a particular frequency difference but to a particular frequency *ratio* has subtle and important consequences. As the grid lines of figure A.1 show, the frequency

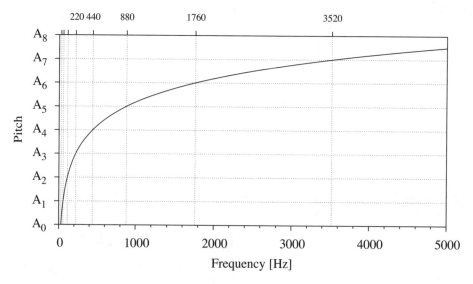

FIGURE A.1. Subjective pitch as a function of objective frequency ($A_4 = 440$ Hz).

difference corresponding to an octave increases with register, the separation between successive vertical grid lines repeatedly doubling as the figure is traversed rightward. This correspondence of a particular pitch interval to a particular frequency ratio holds for all intervals and accords with Fechner's law. In particular, given a pitch interval i between two pitches p_1 and p_2 associated with respective frequencies f_1 and f_2, Fechner's law can be expressed as

$$i = p_2 - p_1 = \log_2\left(\frac{f_2}{f_1}\right)$$

where the choice of a base-2 logarithm yields a result in octaves. (The computed interval can be converted to a value in semitones if it is multiplied by twelve, or in cents if it is multiplied by a further factor of one hundred.) The operation of the base-2 logarithm is effectively to express its argument as a power of two and return the exponent thereof; for instance, if the frequency ratio is exactly a power of two with integer exponent, then a corresponding integer number of octaves will be returned. The inverse conversion of a pitch interval to a frequency ratio involves reversing the logarithmic operation via exponentiation; in other words, it involves raising two to a power equaling the interval (assuming that the interval is expressed in octaves):

$$\frac{f_2}{f_1} = 2^i.$$

From the general mathematical properties of logarithms there arises a calculus of frequency ratios that is parallel to but distinct from that of intervals. Table

TABLE A.1. Correspondences between pitch and frequency and between arithmetic operations involving each

Psychological quantities		Physical quantities	
Pitch interval	i	Frequency ratio	$\dfrac{f_2}{f_1}$
Sum of pitch intervals	$i_a + i_b$	Product of frequency ratios	$\dfrac{f_{2a}}{f_{1a}} \times \dfrac{f_{2b}}{f_{1b}}$
Difference of pitch intervals	$i_a - i_b$	Quotient of frequency ratios	$\dfrac{f_{2a}}{f_{1a}} \div \dfrac{f_{2b}}{f_{1b}}$
Inversion of pitch interval	$-i$	Reciprocal frequency ratio	$\dfrac{f_1}{f_2}$

A.1 collects expressions for some of the most useful correspondences between pitch intervals and frequency ratios and between arithmetic operations involving them.

Fechner's law applies less robustly to other aspects of auditory sensation. The relationship between subjective loudness and acoustic signal intensity is roughly logarithmic for comparisons between similar signals whose intensities are not too low and whose waveform amplitudes differ only by a constant multiplicative factor (Moore 2013, 144–45; Heller 2013, 431–34). Comparisons of otherwise dissimilar sounds, however, can be significantly affected by aspects other than acoustic intensity, such as differences in their registers, timbres, attack characteristics, and durations. Nonetheless, a logarithmic scaling of intensity is often adopted as a pragmatic approximation to perceived loudness, with sound engineers routinely employing a logarithmic *decibel* scale of signal intensity.

Characterization of the relationship between objective (clock) time and subjective judgments of duration is even more fraught, being susceptible to an array of contextual factors, as a visit to the dentist's office will usually confirm. Listeners at least commonly agree that the salience of a fixed durational difference decreases as the absolute durations involved increase; thus the perceived difference between two events whose respective durations are 1 and 2 seconds seems more salient than that between two events whose durations are 10 and 11 seconds. In an early essay, Tenney remarked:

> Both Abraham Moles and before that [Karlheinz] Stockhausen have suggested that the relation between physical and psychological duration corresponds approximately to a *logarithmic* relation . . . although there is not, as far as I know, any conclusive experimental evidence to substantiate this assertion. There is, however, an introspective basis for it that rests on the observation that one's perception of duration is generally in terms of *proportions*, rather than absolute values or absolute differences. *Rhythmic perception*, at least, is directed to the

relative proportions of one duration-value to another—and the appropriate measure of such proportional relations is on a logarithmic scale. (2015, 416–17)

Tenney made explicit compositional use of logarithmic scaling on various occasions, especially in his computer music. If he used an algorithm to determine note parameters by stochastic means, instead of selecting parametric values directly, the algorithm would often select log-parameter values. For example, log-duration values might be selected from a uniform distribution with a given range, but—for purposes of sound synthesis—each selected value would then be converted to an actual duration by exponentiation, the intent being to thereby achieve a distribution of *subjective* durations that would seem fairly uniform. Depending on Tenney's practice in a given work, graphs of frequencies, intensities, and durations in this book at times employ logarithmic ordinates (vertical scales) graduated either nonuniformly in some musical parameter or uniformly in its associated log-parameter. Sometimes both graduations are supplied for comparison, as on the left and right borders, respectively, of figure B.1(b).

Spectrographic Analysis

A spectrogram, for present purposes, is a visual representation of the energy content of a signal as a function of both frequency and time. In music-analytic applications, spectrograms can sometimes furnish useful representations of acoustic signals because certain of their visible features correspond to audible ones afforded by the auditory system, which also performs a joint temporal and frequency analysis of sounds. This section illustrates the application of spectrographic techniques to the analysis of audio signals. Concomitantly, it assembles a basic lexicon of sonic types and attributes relevant to Tenney's music.

A spectrogram is shown in figure B.1 for a succession of eight audio signals separated by silences with time increasing linearly along the abscissa (the horizontal axis). The same spectrographic data are depicted twice: first in figure B.1(a) using an ordinate (a vertical scale) along which frequency increases linearly and again in figure B.1(b) using an ordinate along which pitch increases linearly. (Appendix A discusses the logarithmic relationship between frequency and pitch.) In this figure, the signal energy at a given frequency increases with gray scale intensity, blackness representing zero. (This mapping could also be inverted so that whiteness represents zero.)

The signals represented in figure B.1 are as follows:

i. A sine wave with a constant frequency of 1 kHz, eliciting a pitch of roughly B_5. A sine wave is a signal all of whose energy resides at a single frequency, so that its spectrogram comprises a single line. It could be described as a lone harmonic.

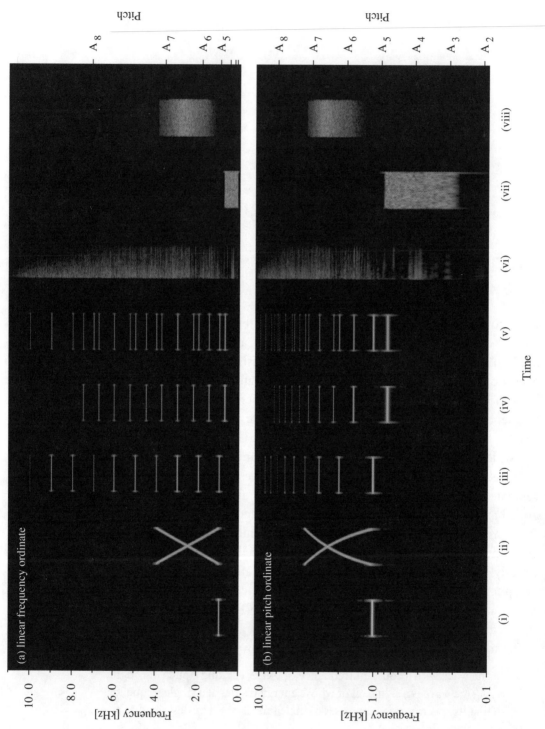

FIGURE B.1. Spectrogram of a succession of eight audio signals of different types separated by silences. The same spectrographic data is shown twice, using (a) an ordinate that is linear in frequency and (b) an ordinate that is linear in pitch.

ii. Two sine wave glissandi crossing. The glissandi follow trajectories that are linear in frequency and that therefore appear concave downward in pitch (cf. figure A.1). Conversely, trajectories linear in pitch would have appeared concave upward in frequency.

iii. A single *harmonic complex tone* possessing a *harmonic spectrum* and comprising, in this example, a total of ten harmonic partials (or, informally, *harmonics*), which are visible in the spectrogram as ten distinct lines. Harmonic complex tones are produced by most musical instruments of definite pitch and are present in speech as vowel sounds. As shown in figure B.1(a), the frequencies of harmonic partials are all integer multiples of the lowest frequency among them, which is called the *fundamental frequency* (or, informally, the *fundamental*). Thus successive partials are equally spaced in frequency. In this example, the fundamental frequency is 1 kHz, so that the harmonics illustrated have frequencies 1, 2, 3, 4, 5, 6, 7, 8, 9, and 10 kHz. In contrast, however, the lower part of the figure shows that, due to the logarithmic relationship between frequency and pitch, the *pitch intervals* between harmonics progressively narrow as their sequence is ascended. In this example, the amplitudes of the harmonics decrease moderately with increasing register, the brightest spectral line being the fundamental. Within the range of fundamental frequencies in customary musical use, harmonic complex tones tend to perceptually *fuse*; in other words, they are usually perceived by listeners not as a collection of distinct harmonics but as a unified gestalt. This gestalt exhibits a unique pitch associated with its fundamental frequency. Higher harmonics are not usually heard individually, although their relative strengths contribute to the perceived timbre of the gestalt. With sufficient time and close attention, however, listeners can *hear out* (i.e., discern individually) some of the individual partials within a harmonic spectrum.

iv. A second harmonic complex tone, again comprising ten partials, but with a fundamental frequency of 0.75 kHz. Thus, in figure B.1(a) the partials—being multiples of this lower fundamental—are more narrowly spaced than those of the previous example. Figure B.1(b), on the other hand, shows that although the pitch of the fundamental is lower, the sequence of pitch intervals between harmonics is identical to that observed in the previous example. In other words, the sequence of pitch *intervals* above the fundamental of a harmonic spectrum is independent of the pitch of that fundamental. This interval sequence is known as the *harmonic series*. A more extensive discussion of the harmonic series and its perceptual correlates is provided in section 7.2.

v. A combination of signals (iii) and (iv): two complex tones with a frequency ratio of 4/3 between their fundamentals, corresponding to the pitch interval of a just perfect fourth. Note that the complicated pattern of spectral lines engendered by the combination of harmonics makes determination by eye of the number of and relationship between complex tones complicated, although it is still possible with careful inspection. The difficulty is compounded if the ordinate is pitch rather than frequency, since the harmonic spacing is not uniform. As the number of tones and the complexity of their relationships increase, the task of visually discriminating them becomes more challenging.

vi. The initial portion of a single stroke on a China-type crash cymbal. Multidimensional oscillators such as cymbals, gongs, bells, and membranes produce *inharmonic spectra* whose partials are not integer multiples of any fundamental frequency. Complexes of inharmonic partials perceptually fuse much less readily than harmonic complexes, accounting for the common evocation of multiple concurrent pitches by a single bell or gong stroke. The pattern of frequency relationships between the inharmonic partials produced by such sources is generally complex, and the density of partials usually increases much more rapidly with increasing register than is the case for a harmonic spectrum, as shown in the figure. The evolving spectrogram reflects the dynamic evolution of the cymbal spectrum, in which high partials fade relatively quickly, while a slow amplitude modulation (in other words, ringing) in the lowest partial is represented by banding in figure B.1(b).

vii. A broadband noise. Unlike the previous signals, the energy in a broadband noise does not reside in discrete frequencies that would appear as lines in a spectrogram but instead is distributed across a continuous range of frequencies. This range is characterized by its *center frequency* (CF) and its *bandwidth* (BW). In this example the center frequency is 500 Hz, while the bandwidth is roughly 600 Hz, so that the noise band spans roughly 200–800 Hz. The signal depicted in the figure could be described as a *narrowband* or *bandpass* noise due to its relatively narrow bandwidth. Other types include *white noise* (in which energy is equally distributed across all audible frequencies), *pink* or *lowpass noise* (in which bass energy predominates, this being the most common type in nature), and *blue* or *highpass noise* (in which treble energy predominates). Any noise whose spectrum is not flat may be described as *colored*. If its bandwidth is sufficiently narrowed, a noise band may begin to evoke pitch. Examples of broadband noises in nature include the sounds of traffic, ocean surf, sibilants, ventilation, and gas combustion. Broadband noise signals can have durations ranging from brief impulses (such as a snare drum stroke, a hand clap, or an unvoiced stop in speech) to continuously sustained sounds (such as surf noise, rain sticks, and sibilants). The acoustical waveforms associated with broadband noises are random or quasi-random.

viii. A second example of a broadband noise with a higher center frequency of 2.5 kHz and a bandwidth of 3 kHz. Note, however, that while the bandwidth is much greater in frequency units than that of the preceding example, it is actually narrower as a pitch interval, which is the more perceptually meaningful measure. It may be noted that, in practice, the *rolloff* in energy at the upper and lower edges of the noise band is not immediate but gradual, so for purposes of bandwidth computation its edges are taken to correspond to the frequencies at which the energy density is half (−3 decibels) relative to its maximum. Moreover, the rolloff may be more or less rapid, as illustrated in sections (vii) and (viii), respectively, of figure B.1.

Most spectrograms appearing in this book use a pitch (log-frequency) ordinate rather than a frequency ordinate, since this produces a more straightforward correspondence between visible spectrographic features and aurally perceived ones. Occasionally, however, a linear frequency axis is used where it clarifies acoustical structures of interest, such as the uniform spacing in frequency of harmonic partials. In either case, as in figure B.1, a second nonuniformly graduated axis may be included in order to indicate values of the alterative ordinate.

Although many technical details regarding spectrographic analysis can be skirted here, two already demand comment in connection with figure B.1. First, spectrography involves an inherent trade-off between resolution in time and resolution in frequency; in other words, increasing temporal resolution unavoidably decreases frequency resolution. In this book it has always been possible to make this trade-off such that the available resolution in each dimension is adequate for analytical purposes, but its effects are often visible in figures nonetheless. Frequency resolution is constant on a linear frequency ordinate, but on a log-frequency (pitch) ordinate the vertical resolution will consequently decrease toward the bottom of the spectrogram. This decrease is visible in figure B.1(b), wherein the lines associated with lower harmonics appear broader than those of higher harmonics. Second, in both parts of figure B.1, short vertical lines delimit most of the horizontal lines representing harmonics. These verticals appear in association with signal transients that are rapid compared to the time resolution of the spectrogram and usually correspond to artifacts of spectrographic analysis rather than audible features in the signal.

As analytical tools, spectrograms are sometimes ill-suited to traditional Western music or other styles in which relationships between pitches are of central importance. For such music, the depiction of all harmonics comprising each complex tone not only is superfluous but also can obscure the more significant relationships between fundamentals. Conventional musical notation, or an adaptation thereof, may furnish a more lucid and economical representation in such cases. On the other hand, spectrograms sometimes provide a useful representation of music in which sonic features incompletely captured by conventional notation play a significant role, such as electroacoustic or instrumental music in which noise bands, indefinitely pitched elements, spectral transformations, and relationships among sound components (such as harmonics) are important. Much of Tenney's mature music falls in this latter category, so that computerized spectrographic analysis often furnishes a useful tool for its analysis, despite the fact that he himself made no recourse to it.[1]

Notes

Preface

1. James Tenney, interview with Brian Karl, 1993, quoted in Tenney 1996b, 11.

2. The borrowing is from philosopher John Searle, who was applying the analogy to consciousness.

1. Introduction

1. Also Jane Wodening, email message to the author, August 10, 2019.

2. "Sounds one hears are music" (Cage 1967, 165).

3. Wishing to avoid connotations of importance, in the 1980s Tenney would come to prefer the term *holarchical* to *hierarchical* when discussing formal perception (1984a, 10).

4. The flight that Tenney recalled here was likely part of a round trip that he made between New York and California in February 1963, not long after completing his first algorithmic compositions at Bell Labs. JTF 1998-038/007 (03).

5. Tenney made further remarks regarding intonational challenges and neural plasticity in an interview with Gayle Young (Tenney 1996b, 12–14).

2. Early Works and Influences (1934–59)

1. Late in life Tenney would more than once draw a connection between the personal trauma of his parents' separation and an important aspect of his artistry: a penchant for synthesis.

Your music reconciles so many things that people don't think belong together, but yet seem completely natural when you combine them.

I think it goes back to my childhood and my experience with my parents who were always at loggerheads and I was always trying to get them together. I like that idea of seeing that some of these things that we think of as [being] in diametric opposition, are not really. (Tenney 2005b)

Tenney repeated this assertion in a 2005 newspaper interview, in which he remarked, "It's a personal characteristic that derives from the fact that my parents fought all the time, and I was always trying to bring them together" (Midgette 2005; similarly in Tenney 1987c).

2. See Tenney (1984c, 2; 1988b, 1); Brakhage (1987, 470); Smigel (2012, 63). See also James Tenney, Fulbright proposal for study abroad, 1959, electronic file, JTF (unprocessed).

3. Tenney's original score for *Interim* represents his principal contribution to Brakhage's early films, but there were others. By his own account, his inexperience with orchestration doomed the recording of a more ambitious score for flute, piano, and strings to accompany Brakhage's *Unglassed Windows Cast a Terrible Reflection* (1953) (Tenney [2003a] 2005, 58–59). Tenney also contributed to a raucous collectively improvised soundtrack for *Desistfilm* (1954), in which he also acted. Smigel (2017a) provides a discussion of these projects, as well as the handful of later collaborations between Brakhage and Tenney.

4. Tenney recalled that in the early to mid-1950s he read published writings by Arnold Schoenberg, Ernst Krenek, René Leibowitz, Dika Newlin, Josef Rufer, and Edgard Varèse (1988b, 2–3).

5. Stan Brakhage to James Tenney, March 20, 1953, JTF 1998-038/001 (12). Further details are provided in Smigel (2012, 65–66, 92n22).

6. A fuller account of the interactions between Brakhage, Schneemann, and Tenney in the 1950s and 1960s is available in Smigel (2012).

7. Decades later, Schneemann (2009) recalled that Tenney's departure from Juilliard was hastened by losing his scholarship after mistaking the date and sleeping through a required recital!

8. James Tenney to David Camesi, Fine Arts Department, California State College Dominquez Hills, July 30, 1974, electronic file, JTF (unprocessed).

9. The movements of *Seeds* completed in 1956 are numbers I, II, III, and V in the final set. Those four were first performed in the summer of 1956 at the Bennington Composers' Conference in Vermont. A recording of that early performance furnished music for choreographer Paul Taylor's dance *Tracer* (1962) with designs by Robert Rauschenberg, which was performed in various cities in Europe and North America between 1962 and 1964 and which has recently been reconstructed by dance scholar Kim Jones (Michael J. Solender, "The Hunt for Lost Choreography," *New York Times*, August 28, 2016). Finished in 1961, the remaining two movements (IV and VI) began life in 1960 as movements of a never-completed string quartet (JTF 1978-018/002 [13]). In 1991, Tenney composed a retrospective *Three New Seeds*, numbering them VII, VIII, and IX, as an extension to the original six (volume 2, section 8.5).

10. An unpublished set of performance notes for *Seeds*—apparently dating from the early 1960s—includes the subtitle "Six Sennets" (James Tenney, n.d., "Seeds for Six Instruments," unpublished performance notes in manuscript, JTF [unprocessed]). A *sennet* was a short trumpet fanfare used in Elizabethan drama to mark the entrance

or exit of an actor or group of actors. Perhaps Tenney learned this at high school in Denver, where he acted in Shakespearean drama. Several movements of *Seeds* indeed open with annunciatory gestures distantly recalling the beginning of *Intégrales* or the second movement of *Octandre* by Varèse, although perhaps the subtitle also asserts Tenney's personal sense of having arrived at a more mature artistic level.

11. *Seeds*, movement II invites comparison to such other twentieth-century "one-note" pieces as Elliott Carter's Eight Etudes and a Fantasy, movement VII (1950), for wind quartet and Giacinto Scelsi's Quattro Pezzi (1959) for orchestra.

12. Analyses of the later movements in *Seeds* are available in Polansky (1984, 135–43).

3. Tape Music and "Meta/Hodos" (1959–61)

1. Tenney added, "There was a primitive electronic studio at Columbia University, but it was not accessible to students. Only Otto Luening and some invited guests could use it; it was not part of the teaching program" (Pritchett et al. [1995] 2001, 199; see also Hiller 1963, 99).

2. Tenney later remarked that as a teacher Gaburo exerted no influence upon his music but that they became good friends (1996d, 119–20).

3. Images of equipment in the studio are available in Hiller (1961, 40).

4. Judging by comparison of the system diagrams in Hiller (1961, 40; 1963, 109), amplitude-envelope control was added to studio facilities after Tenney's departure.

5. Tenney later recalled that "at a party once Claes Oldenburg introduced Andy Warhol to me and he said to Andy, 'Jim is interested in Elvis Presley too.' The whole pop art movement was happening, which I didn't know about until I had already done *Blue Suede*" (Tenney 2000f).

6. JTF 1978-018/001, 1978-018/002, 1998-038/021 (4); Smigel (2017b, 7).

7. The spectrograms in the figure are derived from Tenney's archived work tapes for *Collage #1 ("Blue Suede")*. JTF 1998-038/025 (02).

8. Although it is undetectable by ear, an exact retrograde in track III of *"Blue Suede"* begins near the entrance of track IV, the axis of retrograde symmetry being masked by the second group of reverberant "explosions" on the entering track. This retrograde continues until, circa 169 seconds, it exhausts the previously accumulated track III audio. The remainder of track III comprises a sui generis concatenation of source snippets.

9. The designation "reverberant 'explosions'" is Tenney's (James Tenney, email message to Tom Erbe, October 25, 1990, electronic file, JTF [unprocessed]).

10. According to Tenney, "John Oswald once called me up and said, 'I'd like to refer to *"Blue Suede"* as the first plunderphonics work.' I said, 'I don't like that term.' [*laughs*] But it's become so widely accepted that I've even accepted it. So I guess it was" (2005b). In particular, *"Blue Suede"* evokes Oswald's concept of the *macrosample*, in which all (or, in this case, a substantial amount) of a single preexisting recording is manipulated rather than snippets of multiple recordings (Cutler [1994] 1992, 9).

11. John Oswald, email message to the author, November 17, 2017.

12. The perceived "vulgarities" to which Brakhage alludes presumably include the apparent exclamation "fuck fuck," which surfaces in *"Blue Suede"* at 1'52". Brakhage, a friend of Tenney's since youth, seized upon the emergent sexual connotations of *Col-*

lage #1 ("Blue Suede"), adopting it as the soundtrack to a film in which a submerged sexual dynamic is likewise revealed: *Christ Mass Sex Dance* (1991) (Smigel 2017a, 123).

13. Carolee Schneemann, interview with the author, August 4, 2017, Springtown, NY.

14. Köhler had gone so far as to posit such auditory parallels to visual gestalt-organizing principles: "One can easily show that the factors on which grouping depends in time are about the same as those on which it depends in space. Suppose that I knock three times at short intervals on my table, and that after waiting for a second I repeat the performance, and so forth. People who hear this sequence of sounds experience groups in time. . . . In the present example, the operating principle is that of proximity in time, which is, of course, strictly analogous to the principle of proximity in spatial grouping" ([1929] 1959, 151). However, his theories were otherwise essentially confined to the visual modality.

Schneemann recalled that such parallels between modalities provided a common framework for dialogue between Tenney as musician and herself as visual artist: "The unit, the concept uniting those disparate aspects is gestalt. So that's something that was like a binder for both of us and our influences coming in and out: that the gestalt was inclusive of fragmentation, and inclusive of both an audio and visual relation when you're examining disparate parts" (interview; see also Schneemann 2014, 42–43).

15. For simplicity, the elements shown in figure 3.4 all have unique parametric values, but compounds comprising sounds with concurrent onsets (such as chords) may also constitute elements (elementary temporal gestalts).

16. In "Meta/Hodos" Tenney described state as a "nonformal aspect of the sounds or sound-configurations" ([1961] 2015, 61), but he later characterized state as one of the "three distinct aspects of form" ([1970] 2015, 150–51; [1975a] 2015, 171), as I have done here in order to simplify the exposition. In "Meta/Hodos," he also introduced the concepts of movement and figure as "dynamic" aspects of form associated with the "static" aspects of shape and structure, respectively ([1961] 2015, 79–80), an elaboration that likewise disappears from his later formulations.

17. Tenney usually employed the term *shape* to refer to parametric changes in time, and that is the sense in which it is used in this book, but he also entertained the possibility of shapes related to changes in pitch register in Tenney ([1975a] 2015, 171).

18. The special character appearing in the title of "Meta/Hodos" is the overstrike of a hyphen and a forward slash, which Tenney originally produced on a manual typewriter. In the quoted etymological entry, it represents the conjoining of two roots, *meta* and *hodos*, in the modern English word *method*.

19. "Meta/Hodos" subsequently provided important theoretical underpinning for aspects of the music programming language HMSL (Hierarchical Music Specification Language), developed by Phil Burk, Larry Polansky, and David Rosenboom (Polansky and Rosenboom 1987).

4. Computer Music and Ergodicity (1961–64)

1. Engineer John R. Pierce is remembered as codeveloper of pulse-code modulation (PCM), which remains the standard signal representation in professional digital audio applications, as well as for coining the word "transistor" and for developing the first

communications satellites. He maintained a lifelong interest in computer music and psychoacoustics (Mathews 2003).

2. A chronology of computer music developments is available in Dean (2009, 557–84, updated at https://doornbusch.net/chronology, accessed August 1, 2019). Computer syntheses of popular tunes had been made as early as 1951 at a number of locations. A handful of brief computer synthesized compositions were created in the late 1950s at Bell Labs, the earliest of which were *The Silver Scale* (1957) and *Pitch Variations* (1957), composed by Newman Guttman, a psychologist (Wood and Pierce 1991). The engineers at Bell Labs produced a number of short early pieces as well, including *Stochatta* (1959) by John Pierce and *Numerology* (1960) and *The Second Law* (1961) by Max Mathews. Music theorist David Lewin was the first music professional to write for the system, composing *Study No. 1* (1961) and *Study No. 2* (1961) via postal correspondence with the lab (Kahn 2012, 143–44n6; Mathews 1968, 5).

3. *Complete Works of Edgard Varèse*, volume 1, EMS Recordings, EMS401, 1951. Includes *Intégrales* (1925), *Density 21.5* (1936/1946), *Ionisation* (1931), and *Octandre* (1923). Frederic Waldman, conductor.

4. James Tenney to Edgard Varèse, October 11, 1959, Sammlung Edgard Varèse, Paul Sacher Stiftung, Basel, Switzerland.

5. Carolee Schneemann, interview with the author, August 4, 2017, Springtown, NY.

6. Harold C. Schonberg et al., "A Long, Long Night (and Day) at the Piano: Relay Team of Pianists Plays through the Night," *New York Times*, September 11, 1963, Music sec.

7. See James Tenney, curriculum vitae, October 1968, JTF (unprocessed).

8. After moving to California in 1970, Tenney would include Cage's work in his teachings, but their personal contacts would become occasional. Notably, Tenney would participate with Cage in the American premiere of Cage's *Lecture on the Weather* (1976) on October 16, 1977, at the Albright-Knox Gallery in Buffalo, NY (James Tenney, performances of others' music, as pianist and conductor 1956–74, JTF, unprocessed; curriculum vitae, September 1981, JTF, unprocessed).

9. In its standard mathematical sense, *ergodicity* is a property of certain random processes, that is, of certain sources of random sequences. Claude Shannon, in information theory's foundational article, framed the concept as follows: "Although a rigorous definition of an ergodic process is somewhat involved, the general idea is simple. In an ergodic process every sequence produced by the process is the same in statistical properties. . . . Roughly, the ergodic property means statistical homogeneity" (1948, 390–91). Thus Shannon and standard mathematical usage apply the term *ergodicity* to a source capable of producing diverse sequences of random outcomes, not (as Tenney does) to a single sequence produced by such a source. However, Shannon does observe ("roughly") that the ergodic property entails statistical homogeneity in any particular sequence produced by such a source.

An additional implication that Tenney sometimes attached to the term *ergodic* was that "all the [parametric] ranges were as wide as they could physically be given the sound generating system" (1996d, 62), although in other instances he entertained the possibility of ergodic textures with restricted ranges ([1970] 2015, 157).

10. Tenney here recalled that he asked for a random noise generator to be added to the system, but, confusingly, at least one UGEN with random output (RAND) had already

been described in Mathews's article "An Acoustic Compiler for Music and Psychological Stimuli" (1961, 694), which was submitted and published before Tenney's arrival at Bell Labs. Based on his further remarks in an interview with Douglas Kahn (Tenney 2000f), it appears that what Tenney probably requested was not the addition of a new UGEN but the design of the controllable audio noise generator used in *Analog #1 (Noise Study)* (1961), which comprised a combination of existing UGENs.

11. Even in mid-1963, as he was about to begin exploring ergodicity, Tenney expressed reservations regarding what he perceived to be normative aspects of Cage's aesthetic (Smigel 2012, 80–81). Apart from a handful of theatrical and political works in the second half of the 1960s, however, the particular shift in Tenney's compositional aesthetic from an espousal of expressive dramatic design to a post-Cagean listener-centered exploration of perception would prove to be lasting.

12. Until the advent of MUSIC V in 1966, Mathews's MUSIC systems were hardware dependent. Thus, overall, the update from MUSIC III to MUSIC IV was motivated less by plans to introduce new functionality than by the upgrade from an IBM 7090 computer to an IBM 7094 (Roads and Mathews 1980, 17; Roads 1996, 789).

13. MUSIC III ran on an IBM 7090 computer and afforded a maximum sampling rate of 20 kHz (Mathews 1961, 678). However, most of Tenney's computer-synthesized music appears to have used a sampling rate of 10 kHz, which agrees with the rate used in the acoustical experiments reported in Mathews et al. (1965), in Mathews (1963, 553), and in a 1968 lecture by Tenney (1968b, 29). This rate theoretically permitted the representation of signal frequencies up to half thereof (5 kHz), but in practice the output antialiasing filter would have had to roll off below that frequency, and most of Tenney's audio was restricted to frequencies below 4 kHz (roughly corresponding to pitch C_8 at the top of the piano keyboard). The lower sampling rate reduced both the time required for computation and—perhaps most importantly—the cost, which could be considerable (Mathews 1961, 689; 1963, 553). The signal energy up to nearly 10 kHz in *Fabric for Che* (1967) may represent the exceptional use of a higher sampling rate, or it may be a product of tape-speed manipulation.

14. Mathew's paradigm of modular interconnection has now been rendered visible in graphical audio-programming languages such as Max/MSP (the "Max" part of the name is an homage to Mathews). In such languages, instrument construction involves the interconnection of graphical units much as depicted in figure 4.2. In the MUSIC-N era, however, such graphical representations appeared only on paper in instrument designs or descriptions, while UGENs and their inputs/outputs were specified in practice as lines of text (computer program code).

15. In Tenney's implementation, noise bands were usually generated by means of random amplitude modulation (AM) of a sinusoidal carrier signal. This was effected by connecting the output of a random number generator UGEN to the amplitude control input of an audio-frequency sinusoidal oscillator UGEN. If the rate of random number generation was sufficiently high, then the resulting output from the oscillator UGEN was a noise band of center frequency corresponding to the frequency of the sinusoidal oscillator, of amplitude determined by the amplitude of the random UGEN, and of bandwidth determined by the rate at which the random generator's output changed its value. Temporal variation in each of these parameters was made possible via connections to

the outputs from other UGENs (Tenney [1964] 2015, 100). This appears to have been the technical approach to audio noise generation that Tenney used in all of his own computer music with the exception of *Fabric for Che* (1967) and, possibly, *Entrance/Exit Music* (1962). An alternative approach to generating audio noise manifested therein involved the random frequency modulation (FM) of the sinusoidal carrier. Tenney described in detail the implementation of both techniques, as well as a combination thereof, in the article "Sound-Generation by Means of a Digital Computer" (1963, 42–46).

16. Another area of Tenney's timbral research at Bell Labs concerned the amplitude envelopes of tones, in particular, attack durations (Tenney 1962). In this case, however, he ultimately decided that, for his own musical applications, intuition provided the best guide (Tenney [1964] 2015, 110–11).

17. In practice, the rate and depth of each particular modulation type were typically made functionally dependent upon one another.

18. Composing subroutines were written in FORTRAN, a computer programming language developed in the 1950s.

19. Tenney distinguished his meaning for the word *stochastic* from that of Xenakis. Whereas Xenakis (1958) used the term to denote music governed by the laws of probability, Tenney (2007, 32) used it to describe music composed using constrained random processes.

20. Comparison of figure 3.4 with figure 4.4 shows how Tenney's imposition of mean parametric trends in his computer music augments the analytical formalism of "Meta‡ Hodos" with a composerly prescription for producing a particular species of formal *shape*. On the other hand, in his computer music of the early 1960s, a concern for variety in *state* and *shape* predominated over interest in *structure* (in the sense of relations between parts), especially at lower hierarchical formal levels. This in part reflects the influence of John Cage, in whose music structure, in that sense, played little role in the 1950s and 1960s. In Tenney's later output, however, such works could appear alongside others pervaded to an extraordinary degree by structural relations.

21. In his computerized composing algorithms, Tenney commonly (although not invariably) made the parametric ranges for low-level gestalts as wide as possible subject to two constraints: (1) that those ranges at all times be symmetrical about the (generally time-varying) mean determined for the parameter, as they must be if the PRNG produced symmetrically distributed values, and (2) that those ranges not stray outside the range previously determined for the parent (the next higher level) gestalt. These constraints are exemplified by the dark gray clang-ranges shown in figure 4.4(b). At the highest hierarchical level, parametric ranges would be supplied as input data; in the maximally simple case of *Ergodos II* (1964), for instance, they were made constant and equal to the maximums possible in the synthesis system. The frequent default to maximum available range at various hierarchical levels seems to reflect Tenney's declared predilection at the time for maximum variety (given that hierarchical gestalt creation was to take place at all).

A refined consideration involved keeping the parametric means at one hierarchical level from too closely approaching the boundaries of the parametric range at the next higher level. For example, consider, with reference to figure 4.4(b), that if a clang mean had very closely approached the boundary of the sequence-level distribution, then the symmetry of the clang-level distribution about that mean would have entailed that its range would have to have been made very narrow in order to remain within the range of the parent sequence. Tenney prevented such close approaches in order to ensure that ample parametric range would always be available at all hierarchical gestalt levels. Tenney analyzed such trade-offs between parametric ranges at different hierarchical levels quantitatively in "META Meta/Hodos" ([1975a] 2015, 175–76).

22. Tenney added that, to a lesser extent, the sounds of ocean surf also manifested in *Noise Study* but that he avoided their periodic character. In particular, the sudden onset of the notch envelope in figure 4.6(b) might be heard to recall the crash of breakers.

23. In signal engineering, the word *analog* (as opposed to *digital*) denotes a continuously variable physical quantity. Incidentally, Tenney never composed an *Analog #2*.

24. Tenney's titles are often multiple entendres, so perhaps the title *Noise Study* evokes both of these senses: the first in order to refute the purported unmusicality of his particular materials, and the second as an allusion to his epiphanic aural *study* of the tunnel sounds that initially served only to frustrate attempts at conversation.

25. Whatever the reason, *Noise Study* seems to enjoy a durable appeal, recently inspiring software re-creations (Zavagna et al. 2015) and hardware synthesis modules. (The tELHARMONIC module coded by Tom Erbe for MAKENOISE includes synthesis capabilities inspired by Tenney's *Noise Study*.)

26. Appendix B provides a brief general introduction to the spectrographic analysis of audio signals.

27. Figure 4.5(b)–(f) are redrawn after Tenney's published sketches for *Noise Study*. Marked times correspond to elapsed time in the 2003 compact disc recording commercially released on *New World Records* 80570-2. The ordinates for note duration, bandwidth, and pitch range are roughly evenly graduated on a logarithmic scale, with the exception that the low end of the bandwidth scale decreases more quickly to reach the $\frac{1}{100}$ value (thus making available some very small bandwidths that evoke clear pitches). The gradations of the intensity scale were not directly applied to signal gain but were mapped to gain via one of three different transformations (dubbed "a," "b," and "c" in Tenney [1964] 2015, 102) selected according to the register of the voice and its desired relative loudness. The apparent purpose of these multiple mappings was to nonlinearly boost low-amplitude low-frequency components on account of the ear's relative insensitivity to them. They thus served a role related to that of the "loudness" switch on some commercial stereo amplifiers.

In figure 4.5(b), (c), and (d), the gray-filled regions delimit the range within which parametric values were randomly selected, but Tenney was not explicit about the meaning of the subdivision of these regions in parts (b) and (c) of the figure. Also uncertain is the reason why the duration of *Noise Study* slightly exceeds that indicated in Tenney's plans, as reflected by the extension of the spectrographic image to the right past the other parts of the figure. One possibility is that the final notes—having begun before the end of the planned total duration—were simply allowed to complete their final chosen durations.

Faint *sidebands* are often visible above and below main noise bands, as is the case about the high-frequency noises near 105 seconds in figure 4.5(a). Such sidebands are inherent products of the noise generation algorithm.

The frequency trajectories realized by the computer are linear, so that the corresponding trajectories in pitch (or log frequency) are concave downward, as shown in figure 4.5(a), and this nonlinearity is sometimes audible in long glissandi (see appendix A).

28. The *golden section* is the division of a duration or distance such that the whole is to the greater part as that greater part is to the smaller part. The ratio of the whole to the greater part is $\phi = (\sqrt{5} + 1)/2 \approx 1.618$, which is known as the *golden ratio*. Conversely, the ratio of the greater part to the whole is $\Phi = \phi - 1 = 2/(\sqrt{5} + 1) \approx 0.618$, a value that is sometimes called the *golden ratio conjugate*. Especially after 1970, the golden section often furnishes a formal pivot in Tenney's music, as he remarked in an interview with Libby Van Cleve (1996c, 18). Tenney related his use of such formal skewing to the experience of driving, in which returning from a destination always seemed to him to require less subjective time than traveling to it, perhaps because navigation was easier upon return (1996d, 60). Various analysts have (often controversially) asserted a formal role for the golden section in music by Bartók, Debussy, and other composers (Kramer 1988, 303–21).

29. Tenney (1988b, 35) indicated that he only became familiar with Nancarrow's music later through the first commercial recordings of it released on the Columbia Masterworks label in 1969.

30. As Tenney noted, few naive listeners will detect the canonic aspect of *Noise Study*, although the convergence point nonetheless effects a clear formal pivot. In contrast, the recognition and musical effect of convergence points *as such* in Nancarrow's canons are usually supported by his use of pitch motives possessing a succinct and memorable delineation that diffuse noise bands lack.

31. In an August 4, 2017, interview, Schneemann recounted a triumphal homecoming by Tenney, who—after long seeking the key to alleviating the mechanical quality of computer music—exclaimed, "I've got it, I've got it, it's rubato!" In another telling, Schneemann substituted the word "breath" for rubato (Smigel 2017b, 10). Although the date of this event is uncertain, among Tenney's electronic music, *Phases* seems to achieve particularly breath-like rhythmic and gestural qualities.

32. The design for the software instrument used in *Phases* is published in Tenney ([1964] 2015, 125). PLF*n* was Mathews's designation for a composing subroutine called by the MUSIC-N program to algorithmically determine note parameters (78–94); *n* could range from 1 to 15. The PLF numbers indicated herein are Tenney's and serve to distinguish the various composing subroutines that he successively produced.

33. JTF 2010-050/011 (06). Indicated timings conform to the intended total duration of 12 minutes in Tenney's sketches for *Phases*. The commercially released audio recording has a duration of 12 minutes, 20 seconds, so listeners should be aware that events transpire about 3 percent later in the commercial audio than indicated here.

For most parameters, random parametric selection was made on a logarithmic scale. For example, possible log-frequency values (pitches) were uniformly distributed within a computed range, with selected log-frequency values subsequently converted via exponentiation to frequency values for use by the software instrument (see appendix A).

34. JTF 2010-050/011 (06). Tenney's model of temporal gestalt grouping and polyphony is discussed in section 3.4.

35. This interplay in *Phases* between registrally fixed and linearly mobile gestalts is reminiscent of the interplay between noise bands with fixed and moving center frequencies in *Analog #1 (Noise Study)* (1961), as described in section 4.6.

36. Although the numeric input data for *Phases* appear to be lost, Tenney published the large-scale oscillatory trajectories of selected parameters in "Computer Music Experiences, 1961–1964" ([1964] 2015, 126). These are redrawn in figure 4.9. The variations in some other parameters can also be followed by ear and in spectrograms, such as the gradual decrease in mean frequency envelope ("pitch ornament") range over the course of figure 4.8(a).

37. However, cf. section 5.3 regarding Tenney's earlier connection of Wilhelm Reich's writings to the form of *Phases*.

5. Performance and the Social (1964–68)

1. The Judson group included influential dancer-choreographers Trisha Brown, Lucinda Childs, David Gordon, Deborah Hay, Fred Herko, Steve Paxton, Yvonne Rainer, Arlene Rothlein, and Elaine Summers, musicians Philip Corner and Malcolm Goldstein, and visual artists Robert Morris and Robert Rauschenberg, among others (Banes 1983).

2. Documentation of Tenney's diverse downtown New York involvements in the 1960s are found in JTF, especially in James Tenney, performances of others' music, as pianist and conductor, 1956–1974, JTF (unprocessed). Video documentation of the 1964 *Originale* performance is available as Peter Moore, Barbara Moore, and Karlheinz Stockhausen, *Stockhausen's "Originale": Doubletakes* (New York: Electronic Arts Intermix, 2017).

3. Reflecting more than two decades later on the model of radical creative individualism seemingly exemplified by the composers he regarded as most important, Tenney described his fear that such a model risked creating a sense of isolation among emerging artists influenced by it (1984c, 20). Such a concern appears to have been one motivation underlying his own earlier tradition-building efforts.

4. A listing of program information for all twelve Tone Roads concerts is available in Arms (2013, 92–97). A number of the original programs and posters from Tone Roads concerts are reproduced in Corner (2007).

5. Tenney, performances of others' music, JTF (unprocessed).

6. Peter Garland in "Tenney remembrances," 2016, electronic file, JTF (unprocessed). Also see Mosko and Tenney (2004).

7. James Tenney to John Cage, October 1967, folder 1, box 13, John Cage Notations Project Collection, Northwestern University Music Library Repository, Evanston, IL.

8. In the same interview, Tenney elaborated:

> The idea of its being a movement was pretty much in the minds of George Maciunas and Henry Flynt and a few people like that. . . . There are two ways these things get, as I said, crystallized into movements. One is the naming, which of course is essential—and most of the time the names are provided by critics, usually with negative intent. But frequently—and this seems to me a kind of European thing—there's also the idea of the polemic and initiating a new movement. That's a very European notion, I think. So somehow George Maciunas's European background strikes me as relevant: That was the

way you did it. Whereas Americans are much more individualistic. Later on, if it's going to be useful to be attached to a movement, fine—I'm not going to go argue with anybody about it. But the reality is, it's a very fluid confluence of individuals. That's really how it can have been so lively and vital.

As a received historical construct, however, the membership of Fluxus had been affected by Maciunas's activities of recruitment and exclusion. Schneemann asserted, "Fluxus is my group: we all came up together and we lived inside each other's pockets for fifteen years," but she has not been regarded as a member nor even generally associated with it, perhaps because "Maciunas sent an excommunication directive in regard to my work '65? '66?" (Stiles 1993, 98n80). Schneemann commented further in her statement "Fluxus" (Bonito Oliva 1990, 89). This rift was purportedly precipitated by the sensuality of Schneemann's *Meat Joy* (1964). A discussion of the exclusion by Maciunas of Schneemann and others from Fluxus can be found in Kubitza (2009).

9. Brecht's mailings of event scores bring to mind Tenney's mailout of his *Postal Pieces* a decade later. The history of American postal art extends to earlier dates, however, being particularly associated with artist Ray Johnson's work beginning in the mid-1950s (Crane and Stofflet 1984).

10. In a personal letter to Tenney postmarked June 15, 1962, Brecht expressed this same interest in the totality of experience: "*META/HODOS* [*sic*] is interesting. Will enjoy talking to you about it. Though I am not fully through it, I feel already that we accept (each of us) different limitations. That is, for me, the field nature of sound is only a preliminary step to accepting the field nature of experience" (n.d., JTF 1998-038/001 [09]).

11. An early mockup of *Chamber Music* (1964) bore the Brechtian title *Chamber Music Events*. A subsequent unfinished multimedia work—also dating from the summer of 1964—was to be entitled *Thrice 99 (Events)*.

12. JTF 1998-038/007 (03).

13. Regarding such extreme economy of means, Brecht, drawing on his background as a research chemist, remarked, "In science, you use Occam's Razor. Between two equally valid hypotheses you choose the simplest. It's a question of doing the most with the least energy" ([1973] 1978, 86). Tenney's own enduring fascination with science and his early studies in engineering at the University of Denver may have supported an Occamist inclination toward economy and simplicity in his work as well.

14. Further discussion of the importance of Artaud and Reich in Schneemann's work can be found in Elder (1997) and Archias (2017, 77–121).

15. James Tenney, "On negentropy," letter to Charles Kelley, editor of *The Creative Process: Bulletin of the Interscience Research Institute*, 1966 (unsent), JTF (unprocessed). Tenney comments on this proposal in Tenney (2000f).

16. James Tenney to John Cage, September 13, 1963, folder 1, box 13, John Cage Notations Project Collection.

17. Program and materials for "Judson Dance Theater—a Concert of Dance #8, June 25, 1963," including original drawings/scores for Philip Corner's *Flares*, folder 39, box 3, series A: Arts, subseries 2: Judson Dance Theater, Judson Memorial Church Archive, Fales Library and Special Collections, New York University, New York, http://dlib.nyu .edu/findingaids/html/fales/judson/dscaspace_ref15.html#aspace_ref227 (accessed August 1, 2019).

18. The performance instructions for *Choreogram* are published in Bischoff and Garland (1972, 34–37). However, the version published therein omits an important clause that is present in the archived version and without which some of the remaining instructions are unintelligible. The omitted text is "a condition or set of conditions in which he will remain silent, and" ("Choreogram," JTF 1978-018/005 [02]). This text has been restored in the quotation appearing here.

19. JTF 1998-038/007 (03).

20. JTF 1998-038/007 (03). Also Kahn (2013a, 130–31).

21. Intriguingly, in a letter to filmmaker Stan Brakhage written eight months before the composition of *Choreogram*, Tenney had hypothesized an underlying cognitive faculty receptive across media: "Our perceptions of the two (sound and film) may have this in common: that they both involve a kinesthetic response, a neuromuscular reaction, 'imitating,' in some abbreviated, attenuated, perhaps 'symbolic' way, the perceived process" (Brakhage, Tenney, and Markopoulos 1963, 90). Although Tenney was writing about music and film, his conjecture might be straightforwardly extended to posit a common kinesthetic basis upon which music and dance conduct their perennial dialogue.

22. Peter Garland, email message to Lauren Pratt, August 28–September 6, 2006, JTF (unprocessed). In addition to the swirling of noisy glissandi, there is a musically significant technical correlation between the conclusion of *Poème électronique* (8'08"–8'23") and *Fabric for Che*: in both, the glissandi are nearly linear in frequency and thus concave downward in pitch (as discussed below).

23. James Tenney, unpublished note dated November 21, 1967, accompanying "Tenney—Fabric—work-tapes reel A," JTF 1998-038/044 (01). Until sometime in the 1990s, Tenney appears to have consistently applied an acute accent to the final letter of the title, writing *Fabric for Ché*. Ernesto "Che" Guevara's nickname, however, derived from a Spanish interjection, *che* (common in the Southern Cone), which does not take a diacritic, and surviving examples of Guevara's signature show that he did not use one. According to Tenney's wife, Lauren Pratt, upon discovery of his error Tenney removed the diacritic, as I have done (conversation with the author, September 2018).

24. Further details regarding the controversy surrounding the premiere of *Fabric for Che* are available in Tenney (2000f).

25. Tenney's notes indicate that in March 1964 he had been working toward an unfinished piece to be titled *Ergodos III ("Continuum")*, and the marking *"Continuum"* also appears among his notes regarding *Fabric for Che*, so apparently his interest in a piece exploring sonic continuity had been gestating for some time (notes on computer music, JTF [unprocessed]; also unpublished note dated November 21, 1967, accompanying "Tenney—Fabric—work-tapes reel A").

26. With the exception of *Entrance/Exit Music* (1962), *Fabric for Che* appears to be the only piece in which Tenney explored random frequency modulation (FM) specifically as a source of noise sounds in his own music, although he had described its features in his technical writings (Tenney 1963, 42–46; [1964] 2015, 108–9). In his earlier computer music, random amplitude modulation (AM) was Tenney's preferred technique for generating broadband noises ([1964] 2015, 100, 115, 124), while relatively subtle FM (both periodic and random) was instead employed in the pursuit of naturalistic vibrato (104–8).

27. Tenney's sketches indicate that the planned duration of *Fabric for Che* was 10 minutes. The commercially released audio is 10 seconds shorter, apparently due to the tape speed, not editing. For simplicity, this analysis treats the duration as equaling the intended 10 minutes, so sound events in the commercial release may appear about 2 percent earlier than in the figures shown. Also, although *Fabric* comprises two-channel audio, the stereo distribution of its musical features is not addressed here.

6. Process and Continuity (1969–71)

1. According to Tenney's personal 1974 list of performances, he performed in the March 1967 premiere of Steve Reich's *Four Pianos* (an early version of *Piano Phase* [1967]), as well as the May 1969 premieres of *Pendulum Music* (1968) and *Four Log Drums* (1969). He also performed Philip Glass's *Music in Fifths* (1969) (premiere), *Music in Eight Parts* (1969), and *Music in Similar Motion* (1969) with the composer and his ensemble in January 1970. See Tenney, performances of others' music, JTF (unprocessed); see also Polansky (1984, 287); Reich (1988, 279); Chapman (2013, 247–51).

2. Tenney met his second wife during a brief involvement through Philip Corner in April 1968 with the OM Theater-Workshop, directed by Julie Portman in Boston. Corner was supplying music for a production by the workshop (Corner 1995, 91; Sainer 1997, 65, 70–71).

3. Following interim teaching stints in the summer of 1970, first at the University of California Santa Barbara and then at Stanford University, Tenney assumed a faculty position at the California Institute of the Arts (CalArts), teaching there until mid-1976. In 1970 CalArts occupied a temporary campus in Burbank, California, relocating in 1971 to its current location in Valencia, California, about thirty-five miles north of Los Angeles. A number of Tenney's friends and acquaintances from New York also moved westward to assume positions at the new institution (mostly for brief durations). These included Clayton Eshleman, Dick Higgins, Alison Knowles, Allan Kaprow, Nam June Paik, and Emmett Williams, among others. On the music faculty and staff he found himself among composers and performers Harold Budd, Ingram Marshall, Stephen L. "Lucky" Mosko, Charlemagne Palestine, Mel Powell, Barry Schrader, Morton Subotnick (an acquaintance since the 1950s in Denver), Leonard Stein, Serge Tcherepnin, and Richard Teitelbaum (Marshall 1975). Tenney's students during this five-year sojourn at CalArts included John Luther Adams, John Bischoff, Thom Blum, Michael Byron, Peter Garland, Earl Howard, Carson Kievman, John King, Carey Lovelace, David Mahler, Denman Maroney, David Simons, Chas Smith, and Carl Stone.

4. James Tenney to Carolee Schneemann, November 16, 1971, in Schneemann (2010, 183).

5. Among the attractions of straightforwardly audible processes, Reich, in his classic early essay "Music as a Gradual Process," cited an egalitarian demystification of the composer's role that attends an easily discerned and comprehended process: "James Tenney said in conversation, 'Then the composer isn't privy to anything.' I don't know any secrets of structure that you can't hear. We all listen to the process together since it's quite audible, and one of the reasons it's quite audible is, because it's happening extremely gradually" ([1968] 2002, 35). Although it was Tenney who articulated to Reich

this aspect of easily comprehended musical processes, it does not seem to have provided a major attraction for Tenney himself (nor, indeed, for Reich in his later work, which is less straightforwardly processual overall; Reich 1987, 547). The quoted conversation between Reich and Tenney took place on July 21 and 22, 1968, near Taos, New Mexico, and is partially preserved on audio tape in Tenney's archives, JTF 1999-038/047 (06).

6. Tenney's personal work lists from the 1970s sometimes refer to *Beast, Koan, Cellogram, Having Never Written a Note for Percussion,* and *August Harp* as "Five Koans" for their respective instruments, although only the solo violin scorecard bears that title.

7. An ergodic form might be regarded as a special limiting case of ramp form in which musical parameters are selected from random processes whose global means and ranges are constants. On the other hand, an ergodic form with maximally restricted range is a constant determinate value.

8. James Tenney, liner notes to audio cassette accompanying *Musicworks* 27 (Spring 1984), special issue, "James Tenney." Tenney's use of electronics after *For Ann (rising)* was limited to live tape-delay effects in *Symphony* (1975), *Saxony* (1978), *Glissade* (1982), and other pieces and to prerecorded speech in *Pika-Don* (1991).

9. Unbeknownst to Tenney, Risset had been creating Shepard tone–like signals and using them to quite different musical effect in his computer-music compositions *Computer Suite from Little Boy* (1968) and *Mutations* (1969). In fact, exploitation of pitch circularity and effects resembling Shepard tones to varying degrees have a long history in Western music; a survey of European examples is available in Braus (1995).

10. In 2013 I was surprised to find in the library of the California Institute of the Arts an audio cassette dated March 30, 1970, with recordings of *For Anne (rising)* [sic] on side A and its retrograde, titled *For Anne (falling)*, on side B. The spelling of "Anne" with an "e" reflects the initial dedication of the piece to Tenney's second wife, Anne Christine Tenney. Tenney's curricula vitae to 1975 consistently include the "e" in the title, but by 1981 it was consistently omitted, suggesting that he may have rededicated the piece to his third wife, Ann Holloway, whom he married in 1975. The spelling of Tenney's piano rag "Raggedy Ann(e)" (1969; volume 2, section 10.1) underwent the same pattern of changes.

11. Audio cassette accompanying *Musicworks* 27 (Spring 1984).

12. Appendix B provides a brief general introduction to the spectrographic analysis of audio signals.

13. Tom Erbe, email communication with the author, January 23, 2019. Tom Erbe's accurate computer-generated version of *For Ann (rising)* was released on Artifact Records ART 1007 (1992) and rereleased on New World Records 80570-2 (2003). More recently, Erbe has published a software patch that generates the piece at http://tre.ucsd.edu/wordpress/?p=131 (accessed August 1, 2019). This patch permits three options for the interval between glissandi: the tempered minor sixth of the original, a just-intoned 8/5 frequency ratio, and a frequency ratio equal to the golden ratio, $\Phi = (\sqrt{5} + 1)/2 \approx 1.618$. Tenney had long proposed the golden ratio as a potentially interesting alternative because it causes certain aural combination tones (including the first-order difference and sum tones associated with adjacent glissandi) to coincide with glissandi acoustically present in the recording. Readers can judge for themselves using Erbe's patch, but the small change in ratio does not significantly affect my experience of the piece.

14. Musically trained listeners who would readily identify a static minor sixth com-

monly report difficulty in determining by ear the interval between adjacent glissandi in *For Ann (rising)*. In a 2003 conversation with me, Tenney related this surprising difficulty to his theory that the ear possesses a rapid mechanism for tracking pitch contour but a separate mechanism for determining harmonic relations, and that the latter slower mechanism requires relative pitch stability. Tenney discussed these two posited mechanisms in Tenney ([1993c/2003] 2015, 372).

15. Regarding the earliest examples of the classic Shepard tone, Tenney remarked:

Nobody seems to realize that I generated that tone for Roger Shepard. He was working at Bell Labs right down the hall and he came to me and said, "Do you think we can do something in sound with a computer like that M. C. Escher staircase?" And I said, well, I bet we could. So I generated it for him. The first version was step-wise and in that way was actually more like the Escher. It wasn't continuous. The complements are an octave apart, which merge into a single pitch percept. There's always a sense of only one pitch class at a moment. Because it is fading in at the bottom and fading out at the top there is always something there in the middle. (2000f)

16. His subversive intent notwithstanding, near the end of "Meta∤Hodos" Tenney in fact came close to addressing the conditions of *For Ann (rising)* in his comments on monomorphic sequences and the "arbitrary or subjective" perceptual subdivision of *Three Places in New England*, III ("The Housatonic at Stockbridge") by Charles Ives (Tenney [1961] 2015, 82–83).

17. By "the 'operatic era,'" Tenney means the period in Western music from about 1600 to 1950 (Mumma et al. [1995] 2001, 173–74; see section 1.2.1).

18. Tenney's listing of planned scorecards underwent successive revisions regarding its length, contents, titles, and ordering, originally including settings of texts by Stan Brakhage among other entries. According to Tenney's list of intended recipients, one or more scorecards were mailed to Eleanor Antin, Robert Ashley, Larry Austin, David Behrman, Stan Brakhage, Bob Brown (presumably ethnomusicologist Robert E. Brown), John Cage, Joel Chadabe, Barry Chamberlain, Alan Chaplin, Sam Charters, Barney Childs, Bill Douglas, Nick England, Morton Feldman, Kenneth Gaburo, Philip Glass, Dick Higgins, Marvin Hayes, Lejaren Hiller, Allan Kaprow, Robert Kelly, John Kirkpatrick, Daniel Lentz, Alvin Lucier, Ted Enslin, Max Mathews, John Mizelle, Conlon Nancarrow, Lionel Nowak, Nam June Paik, Eliane Radigue, Steve Reich, Jean-Claude Risset, Dane Rudhyar, Leonard Stein, Morton Subotnick, Bertram Turetzky, Richard Teitelbaum, and Tenney family members, among others (James Tenney, *Postal Pieces* mailing list, n.d., JTF, unprocessed). Other scorecards were given to recipients in person. The set of cards was produced with the help of Alison Knowles and Marie McRoy at the California Institute of the Arts.

19. JTF 1978-018/003 (01). Tenney's "manifesto" goes on to express warm appreciation toward the individual dedicatees, those who helped with production of the set, and "Christine who suggested it in the first place," a reference to Tenney's second wife, Anne Christine Tenney. Tenney first drafted *Valentine Manifesto* on October 21, 1971, revised it January 8, 1973, yielding the version quoted here, considered sharing it again in 1977, but ultimately never posted it. His original plan was to "print it in the shape of a heart, but with the letters very close together—densely packed—then have the whole thing reduced to the point that the words would be just barely legible" (unsent letter

dated July 15, 1977, in the same archival file). It was to be dedicated to "no-one/every-one." *Valentine Manifesto* was finally published in 2016 by the Estate of James Tenney.

20. Tenney's rejection of *drama* seems to invoke a specific sense of the word—after all, it would be difficult to deny that *Having Never Written a Note for Percussion* (1971) is *dramatic* in the sense of being affecting and even surprising. The sense of *drama* to which the above quotation alludes seems to be that of narrative involving conflicts and emotions told through action and dialogue. Conspicuously, the continuity that is typical of Tenney's music in the early 1970s eschews articulation on the timescale of such drama's most basic formal unit: the utterance. Moreover, drama typically engages the audience in continually testing their expectations against unfolding narrative events, so Tenney's disavowal represents in part the rejection of a cognitive framework based on expectation. Gradual, predictable continuity frustrates a listening strategy based on such testing because the listener quickly concludes that ongoing revision of narrative-bound expectations will not be required. It also, however, occasionally prepares exceptional surprises, such as when the high frequencies of *Having Never*'s climax precipitously overwhelm the ear (section 6.1.1).

21. James Tenney, program note for *Koan*, electronic file, JTF (unprocessed).

22. This phenomenon is related to the *trill threshold* discussed in the literature on auditory scene analysis (Stainsby and Cross 2009, 54).

23. *Combination tones* are nonacoustical pitched percepts generated by nonlinearities in the auditory system (Roederer 2008, 43–46). Their frequencies are equal to integer combinations of the frequencies of the acoustical tones. For two acoustical tones of frequencies f_1 and f_2 with $f_2 > f_1$, prominent combination tones include the *(quadratic) difference tone* at frequency $f_2 - f_1$, which falls as unison is approached, and the *cubic difference tone* at frequency $2f_1 - f_2$. The cubic difference tone is often particularly audible following the final unison in *Koan*, since it falls in contrast with the rising and static tones emanating from the instrument.

24. Appendix B provides a brief general introduction to the spectrographic analysis of audio signals.

25. Higher harmonics become particularly audible as two complex tones approach unison because the rate of acoustical beating between their corresponding harmonics increases with harmonic number. Thus the salience of audible beating between lower harmonics subsides before it does so between higher ones (see volume 2, section 5.4.4).

26. See figure 7.5 on [1/1, 3/2] for a representation of salient harmonic dyads in this interval. As always, sufficiently complex ratios, corresponding to low intersection ratios in the figure, may not establish independent identities, either passing without eliciting a sense of particularity or being heard as inflections of nearby simpler ratios, per Tenney's principle of interval tolerance (section 7.3).

27. *Having Never* was recorded by Sonic Youth (on *Goodbye 20th Century*, Sonic Youth Records SYR 4 1999) and Rrose (on *Rrose Plays James Tenney—Having Never Written a Note for Percussion*, Further Records FUR099 2015).

28. Strictly speaking, Tenney's confession in the title to *Having Never Written a Note for Percussion* is only accurate if one excludes from his oeuvre certain early unacknowledged works from 1955–56 composed while studying with Chou Wen-chung in New York.

29. Appendix B provides a brief general introduction to the frequency structures and spectrographic analysis of audio signals.

7. Interlude: Harmonic Theory

1. As here, Tenney often asserted that harmonic practice (in his sense of the term) had ceased to evolve sometime around 1910 ([1983] 2015, 297; [1984b] 2015, 305–6; [1990] 2015, 351–52; [1996a] 2015, 395). On other occasions, however, he commented that it had been developed somewhat further in jazz (Tenney 1997), and he expressed a corresponding interest in jazz harmony (1996d, vi) that appears to be most clearly reflected in his *Changes: 64 Studies for 6 Harps* (1985; Tenney [1987a] 2015, 342). In particular, he recalled listening intensively in the 1970s to recordings of Thelonious Monk: "I've still got those recordings because I felt—and this I can't be any more specific about—because I felt that very few people were doing anything new harmonically after 1910, but I think maybe Monk was" (Tenney 2007, 33).

2. Polansky (1984, 191) suggests that the pitch-class pentachord of *Hey When I Sing* is related to the first five odd-numbered harmonics of a C. If that is correct, then this represents the earliest invocation of the harmonic series as an intervallic resource in Tenney's music.

3. Notably, Tenney did not consider the practice—by composers such as Ferruccio Busoni, Charles Ives, Alois Hába, and Julián Carrillo—of evenly dividing the octave into quarter tones or other like microintervals to provide a suitable avenue for expanding harmonic practice. Regarding such temperaments, Tenney wrote:

> The music that was written in such tuning systems still required other "organizing principles" in order to maintain coherence. The failure of this music to solve the specifically harmonic problem was not due to any lack of skill, talent, or vision on the part of these composers. These qualities most of them had in abundance. Their great expectations of what might be accomplished by such subdivisions of the 12-set [the set of pitch classes available in 12TET] were, however, the result of a misunderstanding of the basic nature of the 12-set itself. That is, this pitch set is not simply a useful or convenient (much less arbitrary) "division of the octave." More essentially, it is a pitch set that approximates certain just intervals . . . fairly well. . . . And the 12-set evolved historically in precisely that way. (Tenney [1984b] 2015, 306)

Accordingly, when Tenney did make use of fine equal divisions of the octave, it was because they furnished improved approximations to particular *just* intervals rather than for the intervallic resources they afforded overall (section 7.3). *Flocking* (1993)—a work in 24TET but concerned with gestalt perception rather than harmony—represents the unique instance in which Tenney used a fine equal temperament otherwise.

4. Elsewhere I have described invocation of the perceptual duality between aggregate timbre and the qualities and interrelations of individual components as a frequent characteristic of so-called *spectral music* (Wannamaker 2008b, 92).

5. Although Tenney considered an explanation of the phenomenon of octave equivalence essential to any complete theory of harmony, it is the harmonic relation regarding which he wrote and commented least. His notes suggest that he never arrived at an explanation of it that was entirely satisfactory to him. He rejected the sometimes-heard argument that

> the octave is the "first" (or "most," or "best," etc., with respect to some property) among the set of rational intervals. . . . Such "explanations" have never seemed convincing to me . . . because of what I perceive as a *categorical* difference—a difference in kind, not

just in degree—between the octave-relation and all other harmonic relations. A tone at the perfect fifth (or twelfth) above another is not just "a little less equivalent" to it than the octave is. The former is not "equivalent" at all, even though it is, say, only a little less consonant, its frequency ratio only a little less simple, etc. (Tenney [1979b] 2015, 266)

6. Additional harmonic relations have been contemplated in more recent literature that admits roles for long-term memory. A survey can be found in Parncutt and Hair (2011).

7. A concise review of psychoacoustical research on harmonic fusion is available in Deutsch (2013, 302–4).

8. A ratio is said to be *reduced* or *in lowest terms* if its numerator and denominator have no common divisors greater than 1. Thus 2/1 is reduced, while 4/2 is not, although 4/2 could be (and customarily is) reduced to 2/1 by eliminating the common factor of 2 from its numerator and denominator.

9. Given the prevalence of the acoustical harmonic series in human and animal vocalization, Tenney viewed this specialized auditory response as a survival-driven evolutionary adaptation, serving to integrate sound components originating from a single source into a single aural image for purposes of source identification and tracking. Tenney elaborates on this evolutionary perspective in Tenney ([1993c/2003] 2015, 368–71; see also section 11.2).

10. While a form of major triad can be located low in the harmonic series among harmonics 4/5/6, no approximation to the common minor triad can be found so low in the series. The lowest candidate is 10/12/15, whose root does not correspond in pitch class to the fundamental of the series, while the lowest candidate whose root does thus correspond is 16/19/24. The judgment of most musicians would be that the harmonic complexity of the minor triad should be much closer to that of the major triad than these higher rational relationships would imply.

11. The fourth chapter of Partch's book *Genesis of a Music* ([1949] 1974) is entitled "The Language of Ratios."

12. In other words, Tenney's tolerance postulate entails that effectively, from a perceptual standpoint, there are no irrational frequency relationships. For instance, the frequency "ratios" corresponding to tempered intervals have algebraic irrational values, but according to Tenney their harmonic identities are perceived categorically as versions of nearby just intervals (whose frequency ratios are rational-valued).

13. Interestingly, models of consonance perception involving mode-locking between coupled neural oscillators exhibit tolerance ranges surrounding simple frequency ratios (Shapira Lots and Stone 2008, 1432).

14. For the purpose of approximating desired just intervals, Tenney first adopted 84TET in *Harmonium #6* (1981), retaining it in *Glissade* (1982) and *Two Koans and a Canon* (1982). In an unpublished note to himself from around that time, Tenney proposed to retroactively apply his 84TET notation to improve the approximations to just intervals in *Clang* (1972), *Quintext*, I and III (1972), *Symphony* (1975), *Saxony* (1978), and all of the existing *Harmonia* (1976–81) except #5, before the next time they were performed. These revisions were never carried out, however (JTF 2010-050/002 [10]). Tenney subsequently began to use 72TET rather than 84TET. When in 1984 he revised an early (1982) version of *Voice(s)*, he updated the notation from 84TET to 72TET, and

72TET subsequently appeared in *Changes: 64 Studies for 6 Harps* (1985), *Water on the Mountain . . . Fire in Heaven* (1985), and *Song 'n' Dance for Harry Partch* (1999). In most pieces composed after 1985 Tenney simply indicated the precise intonation of each note in cents wherever necessary, although, for pragmatic reasons, the late *For Piano and . . .* (2005) and *Panacousticon* (2005) use 12TET to approximate harmonic-series intervals.

Tenney was not the first composer to use fine equal temperaments as a means to approximate selected just intervals. The most significant precursor was Ezra Sims, who used diatonic subsets of 72TET as such approximations beginning in the 1960s and systematically after 1971 (1991, 241). Tenney appears to have adopted the procedure independently.

15. James Tenney, conversation with the author, 2001, Valencia, CA. The same 5-cent intonational standard is cited in Tenney ([1996a], 395). As a guideline for the approximation of intervals in the harmonic series, it receives some support within the psychoacoustical literature. Studies of thresholds for hearing mistuned lower partials in harmonic complexes as separate tones set such thresholds as low as 8 cents for some subjects with stimulus durations of 1,610 milliseconds (Moore and Glasberg 1986). Furthermore, these thresholds fall with increasing stimulus duration (1,610 milliseconds was the longest reported).

Regarding the progressive narrowing of his intonational requirements, Tenney commented in 1985 that "in the first piece that I remember that uses the harmonic series, about 1972, I hardly used any special notation at all. I was using a very casual approximation of the harmonic series. I can't abide that anymore, and I'm almost embarrassed to look and see what I was doing in 1972. I was really careless about it" (1987b, 461).

16. In the psychoacoustical literature, the degree of resemblance to a tone is sometimes referred to as *tonality* or *tonalness*. Since these terms have other established meanings in music theory, in this book I have adopted David Huron's term *toneness* for this quality (2016, 33–38). In his notes, Tenney contemplated various terms for this attribute, including *fusion* (vs. *separation*), *monophonicity* (vs. *polyphonicity*), *singularity* (vs. *multiplicity*), *uniformity* (vs. *diversity*), and *integration* (vs. *differentiation*).

17. As a measure, this intersection ratio would require refinement in order for it to furnish a candidate gauge of toneness for incomplete harmonic complexes. For such complexes, the relationship between harmonicity and toneness can be complicated. For instance, the perceived toneness of a complex comprising successive odd-numbered harmonics (e.g., a clarinet tone, approximately) can be comparable to that of a complete complex. On the other hand, the pitch of certain complexes comprising only *selected* odd-numbered harmonics (such as the ninth and eleventh) is ambiguous (Roederer 2008, 53–55).

18. Tenney's own depictions of harmonic measures are selective with regard to the ratios included ([1979b] 2015, 253–54, 265).

19. Cf. Tenney ([1979b] 2015, 245, 253).

20. Pitch lattices enjoy a long history in Western music theory, dating at least as far back as 1739 in the work of Leonard Euler. Employed by many nineteenth-century theorists, today they are particularly associated with the theories of Hugo Riemann, who dubbed them *Tonnetze* (tone nets). Brief histories of such lattices are available in Cohn (1997, 1998). Tenney's writings cite more recent precursors, "including the 'duo-

denarium' of Alexander Ellis (in Helmholtz 1954 [1877], 463); the 'harmonic lattices' of Adriaan Fokker (1969); the 'harmonic dimensions' of [Christopher] Longuet-Higgins (1962a, 1962b), who also coined the term *harmonic space*; and the 'ratio lattices' of Ben Johnston (1971)" ([1993c/2003] 2015, 376). In particular, Tenney seems to have regarded the substantial original appendices that Ellis included with his English translation of Helmholtz's *On the Sensations of Tone* as especially important precursors, going so far as to reproduce Ellis's "duodenarium"—a two-dimensional lattice of key centers—in Tenney ([1979b] 2015, 268).

21. Negative exponents indicate multiplicative inversion (reciprocals). Any nonzero number raised to the exponent zero equals one.

22. For display purposes, the (3,5) plane in figure 7.7 is rotated clockwise about the 2-axis of the corresponding plane in figure 7.6. Thus, a step to the right in figure 7.7 corresponds to the *ordered pitch class interval* that contains the ascending just fifth (3/2), the ascending just twelfth (3/1), the descending just fourth (3/4), etc. Similarly, a step upward corresponds to the ordered pitch class interval that contains the ascending just major third (5/4), the ascending just major tenth (5/2), the descending just minor sixth (5/8), etc.

23. The correlate of Tenney's CDC-1 in the psychoacoustic literature is not entirely clear, but since *ab* represents the LCM not only of the dyad's two fundamental frequencies but also of its two waveform periods (in units of their GCD), *periodicity* theories of consonance are candidates (Boomsliter and Creel 1961; Palisca and Moore 2001; Stolzenburg 2015; Langner and Benson 2015). Such theories relate dissonance to increasing length of the "common long period" exhibited by the combination of waveforms or to the neural firing patterns associated with it. Accounting for the ability of neurophysiological mechanisms to rate the consonance of melodic intervals, however, remains an open problem for all theories of "consonance."

24. Appendix A discusses the logarithmic relationship between frequency ratios and pitch intervals.

25. In particular, for any positive real numbers a and b and any real number c, and regardless of the base of the logarithm, it is the case that $\log(ab) = \log(a) + \log(b)$ and $\log(a^c) = c \log(a)$.

26. Formally, a measure must satisfy a number of mathematical conditions in order to qualify as a metric. I supply a formal proof that HD is a metric in Tenney ([1979b] 2015, 453–54n19).

27. Tenney discussed quantitative measures of compactness in harmonic space based on *harmonic distance* and *generalized harmonic distance* functions in Tenney (1987b, 462; [1993b] 2015).

28. Care must be taken, however, in the interpretation of such a sum of harmonic distances. It may be that it should be understood as a *statistical* measure on the interval content of the set rather than a measure of any quality of the set apprehended as a whole (provided that it is so apprehensible). In a late essay entitled "On Crystal Growth in Harmonic Space" ([1993b] 2015), Tenney would investigate pitch sets for which the sum of harmonic distances over all intervals within the set was minimal given the cardinality of the set. He did not indicate, however, that such sums represented a measure of the harmonic complexity of the set as a whole; rather, prima facie they represented

a means to minimize the average complexity of the harmonic relationships between pitches in the set taken pairwise (in other words, of obtaining a collection of intervals that *on average* are maximally simple).

29. Figure 7.9 is based on Tenney's presentation notes for a colloquium held at Princeton University in February 1985 (JTF [unprocessed]). Tenney's exploration of non-Western scalar structures and tunings was fueled in part by field research that he conducted in Singapore, Java, Bali, Thailand, Hong Kong, and Japan during the autumn of a 1981–82 sabbatical year.

30. Here Tenney is referring to the pitch-class-projected version of harmonic space. He made further remarks regarding the "tonic phenomenon" in Tenney ([1983] 2015, 302).

31. Relative to its fundamental frequency, the partials of a harmonic series represent frequency ratios whose prime factorizations comprise only nonnegative powers of primes and whose ratio classes therefore comprise nonnegative powers of primes greater than two. All ratio classes in the first quadrant of figure 7.10 are of this sort and hence represent pitch classes residing within the harmonic series of any complex tone whose fundamental's pitch class is represented by ratio class 1/1. All other ratio classes in the plane contain at least one negative power of a prime factor greater than two and therefore do *not* correspond to any pitch class in a harmonic series whose fundamental's pitch class is represented by 1/1. Those in quadrant 3 (lower left) correspond to fundamentals whose harmonic series contain the pitch class corresponding to 1/1, while those in quadrants 2 and 4 correspond to pitch classes whose harmonic series neither contain 1/1 nor are contained within a harmonic series whose fundamental is 1/1.

32. In fact, Schoenberg's designations of "strong" root progressions correspond only to an extent with Tenney's. Schoenberg (1969, 6–9) describes progressions through a descending fifth or ascending fourth as "strong" due to the "great changes in constitution of the chord," wherein the root of the first chord is "degraded" to become the fifth of the second chord. Diatonic descending third progressions (through major or minor thirds, n.b.) are also "strong" in Schoenberg's view, degrading the root even further to become the third of the second chord. In contrast, descending fourth and ascending third progressions, according to Schoenberg, "promote the advancement of inferior tones," while in "superstrong" root progressions by step (up or down), "all the tones of the first chord are 'conquered,' i.e. eliminated entirely."

33. JTF 2010-050/001 (08). In composing with larger pitch-class collections—as in *Changes* (1985)—Tenney appears to have applied the following criterion:

> The tonic field of a tone extends upward and to the right in harmonic space, but the tonic pc can support some extensions to the left and below this region [if and only if] they're connected to it *above* the root itself. E.g., 6/5, 5/3 are still OK, as is 7/6.
>
> The important thing is to define what the tonic field *cannot* include without being shifted: 4/3, 8/5, 8/7, 16/9, 16/15, 32/21; i.e., ratios with 2^x in the numerator.
>
> But note that 5/3, 6/5 (or even 7/5) might also be taken as tonic unless it's assumed that such extensions may only be one level "deep." (JTF 1998-038/014 [09])

To choose a simple example, the root of the minor triad in figure 7.7(b) is C, because the root-determining effect of the negative-going G–C interval is stronger than the negative-going G–E-flat interval and because—absent the 8/5 A-flat—the E-flat is connected to the C only through the G "above" that C.

34. JTF 2010-050/001 (08).

35. JTF 2010-050/001 (08).

36. James Tenney, manuscript note, n.d., JTF (unprocessed).

37. Tenney's intersection/disjunction ratios and harmonic distance function are by no means the only proposed quantitative measures of harmonic relatedness to be found in either the music-theoretic or the psychoacoustical literature. While the logarithm appearing in the harmonic-distance function seems to originate with Tenney, the quantity ab as a measure of "dissonance" for dyads has a venerable history in the science of music. It is associated with the sixteenth- and seventeenth-century *coincidence theory* of consonance/dissonance, which related the perceived degree of consonance between two tones to the frequency with which their waveform peaks coincided; thus, for instance, two audible waveforms with periods of lengths 3 and 4 units would sound a just fourth, and their crests would align every 12 units, *assuming they began with crests aligned*. This theory was articulated as early as circa 1563 in the writings of Giovanni Benedetti (Palisca 1961, 104–10) and more influentially by Galileo Galilei and Marin Mersenne in the 1630s (Cohen 1984, 85–114). Despite early widespread acceptance, in this original form the theory proved untenable because it implied that adjudged consonance would depend on relative waveform phase, which it does not. More recent "long pattern" hypotheses avoid phase dependence by associating the product ab with the total period of the combined acoustical waveforms in units of the GCD of their individual periods (e.g., the sum of two waveforms with periods $a = 3$ and $b = 4$ would be a waveform with period $ab = 12$) (Boomsliter and Creel 1961; Palisca and Moore 2000; Stolzenburg 2015; Langner and Benson 2015). Various other functions of a and b can be found in the psychoacoustical literature as measures of consonance, as discussed in Schellenberg and Trehub (1994, 192–95). Among twentieth-century music theorists, Partch associated consonance with the relative period of the aggregate waveform ([1949] 1974, 151), and Tenney too refers to this "common long pattern," although he does not *explicitly* connect it to his harmonic distance function ([1979b] 2015, 256–57).

Other harmonic measures include Leonhard Euler's *gradus suavitatis* (Smith 1960), Ervin Wilson's *complexity function* (Chalmers 1993, 55–56), Clarence Barlow's *harmonicity function* (1987), Paul Erlich's *harmonic entropy* (Sethares 2005, 371–74), and Marc Sabat and Robin Hayward's degrees of tunability (2006), among others (Jedrzejewski 2006, 152–53).

38. This property interestingly compares with Tenney's conjecture that the tolerance range for categorical interval perception decreases with increasing frequency-ratio complexity (section 7.3).

8. Canons and the Harmonic Series (1972–79)

1. Tenney's colleagues on faculty in Santa Cruz would include a previous acquaintance, composer Gordon Mumma, while his students would include composer-performers Larry Polansky, Joe Hannan, and Doug Wieselman. Also studying there was percussionist William Winant, who would become a leading exponent of much new percussion music, Tenney's included. After Tenney moved to Toronto in 1976, his colleagues on faculty at York University would at various times include, among others, compos-

ers David Rosenboom and David Mott and musicologists Alan Lessem, David Lidov, and Austin Clarkson. He would participate in Toronto's lively new music scene, which included the Maple Sugar collective spearheaded by vocalist Jacqueline Humbert and Rosenboom (Humbert 1979). The community included former students from both CalArts (composer Michael Byron) and Santa Cruz (Polansky and Winant), as well as new students such as Wende Bartley, Gary Barwin, Miguel Frasconi, Mathew Patton, Tina Pearson, Bruce A. Russell, Jon Siddall, Eric de Visscher, and Gayle Young. The many other musicians and artists with whom he interacted notably in Toronto in the 1970s and 1980s included artist-filmmaker George Manupelli, pianist and sound artist Gordon Monahan, and composers Udo Kasemets and John Oswald.

2. Tenney's retrospectively critical view regarding intonational accuracy in his works of this period are described in section 7.3, note 13.

3. This second "clang" contains only pitch classes E, F, B-flat, and B and is voiced as a cyclical stacking of tempered fifths, tritones, and fourths: 7, 6, 5, 6, 7, 6, 5, 6, 7, 6, 5 (as intervals in semitones reading upward from the bass).

4. Tenney's structural use of this process in *Clang* predates its appearance in the work of composers such as Gérard Grisey (Rose 1996, 9–10).

5. Conlon Nancarrow, *Studies for Player Piano* (Columbia Masterworks, MS 7222, 1969, vinyl LP).

6. A reference score for *Spectral CANON* and a reproduction of its piano roll have both been published. The reference score is available in Byron (1975, 159–75) and the reproduction of the piano roll in Pearson and Monahan (1984). The reference score contains some inaccuracies in its latter half, as described in Wannamaker (2012, 62n42). I have previously published (in Wannamaker 2012) an analysis of *Spectral CANON* in considerable detail. Readers interested in a more extensive analysis of the work's structure and musical features are directed to that account.

7. James Tenney, conversation with the author, 2003, Valencia, CA.

8. Tenney at one time envisioned an electronically generated version of *Spectral CANON* that would include additional voices; it was never realized, however.

9. All logarithms appearing in this section use base 2. Thus the unit of pitch (or, here, duration) is always an "octave," since $\log_2(2/1) = 1$. In other words, the unit of pitch corresponds to a ratio of 2/1 in frequency (see appendix A).

10. Possible variations on these specifications suggest themselves, such as reversing the order of the voices' entrances or beginning in each voice with the retrograded series of decreasing durations instead of the forward series of increasing durations. In fact, Tenney composed three such *Spectral Variations* (1991/1998), which were realized by composer Ciarán Maher and premiered in 2007. The first of these variations can be heard online at http://www.dnk-amsterdam.com/media/music/02Tenney-SpactralVari-ationsNo1.mp3 (*sic*; accessed August 1, 2019).

11. The alignment between my gray curves and the score's noteheads is approximate due to changes of clef in the score and the nonlinear mapping of pitch onto musical staves. Some voice-glissando lines are bent for the same reasons.

12. This small intonational adjustment would be nil if the new bass entered a just rather than a tempered fifth below the preceding one, but Tenney pragmatically conformed each new bass pitch class to 12TET. Nonetheless, the (here approximate) presence of

a pitch class from the preceding harmony in the new one marks the progression as "downhill" in the sense of Tenney's containment theory (section 7.7.3). Questions of containment and intersection between successive harmonic series were some of Tenney's earliest concerns when he began a dedicated theoretical investigation of harmony in 1976, and he later remarked, "My entering into the theory of harmony coincides, chronologically, with that first *Harmonium*" (Tenney 1988b, 46).

13. Fiore (2018, 341) observes that this *Petrushka* bichord also appears in the first movement ("Emerson") of the *Concord* Sonata by Charles Ives (Block 1996, 56), which Tenney had studied and performed (section 2.3).

14. By the *GCD pitch* or *conceptual fundamental* of a pitch collection I mean the highest pitch of which all its members represent harmonics (section 7.6.1). Figure 8.10 invokes the simplifying approximation that the intervals between successive bass notes (fifths and fourths) are just rather than tempered, the difference being a normally imperceptible 2 cents. This assumption invokes Tenney's concept of interval "tolerance," wherein an interval sufficiently close but not identical to a simple just interval will be perceived as harmonically equivalent to that just interval (section 7.3). Under this assumption, milestone pitch sets in successive sections can be expressed as harmonics of a common fundamental pitch, as indicated in figure 8.10(a), which permits the assignment of GCD pitches for all available-pitch sets and computation of their intersection ratios with a harmonic series on that GCD pitch.

15. Section 7.6 discusses harmonicity as a gauge of toneness, and toneness as one sense of harmonic simplicity or *consonance*.

16. Tenney also provided the Coleman transcription with a more direct musical rendering in *Blues for Annie* (1975) for viola. The original 1927 Coleman recording for Gennett Records can be heard on Jaybird Coleman & The Birmingham Jug Band 1927–1930 (Document Records DOCD-5140, compact disc).

17. Examples of sine-wave speech can be heard at http://www.haskins.yale.edu/research/sws.html (accessed August 1, 2019). A *formant* is a peak in the power spectrum of an acoustical signal occurring at a resonant frequency of the originating acoustical system. Vocal formant frequencies vary independently of the vocal pitch as the shape of the vocal tract changes during speech or singing, permitting the production of different sonorants (vowels, semivowels, or voiced stops) with the same pitch (Parsons 1986, 104–6).

18. The initial *u* sound in "water" is transcribed in the previous measure.

19. Tenney's notes indicate that he began work on *Three Indigenous Songs* as early as 1975, and he apparently updated his working formant data during the course of composition. An early source was Peterson and Barney (1952), but it seems that in the late 1970s he preferred data from Fairbanks and Grubb (1961). Thus the frequency data in figure 8.11(b) correspond with Fairbanks and Grubb (1961) except for the entries in parentheses, which derive from Peterson and Barney (1952). The latter may have been invoked because they entailed a broader formant region within which harmonics might fall. Perhaps for a similar reason, the pitch associated with the asterisked 640 Hz figure is rounded up to E_5 when it is actually slightly closer to D-sharp$_5$.

20. It is unclear to me why the eighteenth harmonic (D-sharp$_7$), which falls squarely within the third formant's bandwidth, was not selected. It may be because this pitch

was present in the immediately preceding sound and a new pitch was considered appropriate for a new articulation.

21. Tenney revisited the project of speech synthesis by instrumental means in two subsequent works: *"Ain't I a Woman?"* (1992) is based on a text by Sojourner Truth, while *Song 'n' Dance for Harry Partch, 1. Song: "My technique"* (1999) is based on a recording of the composer's voice reading from the writings of Harry Partch.

9. Harmonic Spaces (1980–85)

1. *Harmonium #3* (1980) for three harps reached its final form before *Harmonium #2* (1977) for two guitars but after *Harmonium #4* (1978) and *Harmonium #5* (1978).

2. The title of this essay, "Reflections after *Bridge*," perhaps echoes that of Charles Ives's *Essays before a Sonata* (1920), which Ives had written to accompany his own preeminent statement for the piano: his Piano Sonata no. 2 (*Concord, Mass., 1840–60*) (1915).

3. Early notes for *Bridge* indicate a durational scheme based on the successive Fibonacci numbers 8, 13, and 21. Originally, both parts were to be 21 minutes long, with the first divided into sections of 8 and 13 minutes.

4. James Tenney, program note for *Bridge*, n.d., electronic file, JTF (unprocessed). By "aggregate density," Tenney here means vertical density (pitches per chord).

5. The precise tuning system for *Bridge* was among the last aspects of the composition to be fixed. As late as the spring of 1984 Tenney was describing it as "a slightly 'tempered' or quasi-just approximation of a '7-limit' just set" (depicted in Pearson and Monahan 1984, 1) using a subset of 72TET (Tenney, program note for *Bridge*). The excerpt of *Bridge* recorded on the cassette accompanying the special issue of *Musicworks* (Pearson and Monahan 1984) apparently uses this tempered tuning system (Belet 1990, 80). Sometime in 1984 Tenney settled on the tuning system indicated in the published score, which stipulates the use of precisely just-intoned 5-limit intervals.

6. Following Sabat (2008), the adjective *pythagorean* refers to a 3-limit interval (i.e., one whose associated frequency ratio involves no prime numbers greater than 3), while *ptolemaic* refers to a 5-limit interval (one whose associated ratio involves no primes greater than 5).

7. In *Bridge*, temporal gestalt duration and the number of notes per element are uniformly distributed on logarithmic scales (appendix A). As indicated in table 9.2, location in the cycle of fifths is not computed in part 1, section 1 and is a consequence only of the computed pitch value. Since all parameters except duration must be integer-valued, their computed values are truncated (rounded down) to integers.

8. Since all parameters except duration must be integer-valued, their computed values are truncated to the nearest integer, an operation that sometimes yields final values residing slightly below the gray-filled clang ranges in figure 9.13.

9. JTF 1998-038/018 (06).

10. James Tenney, program note for *Koan for String Quartet*, n.d., electronic file, JTF (unprocessed). Reprinted in the published score.

11. In a few instances in *Koan for String Quartet*, Tenney chose a frequency ratio that is not the simplest available within the given neighborhood. For instance, in measure 42, 81/80 is selected rather than 70/69, the latter being the simplest interval in the neighbor-

hood as determined by continued fraction expansion or Farey-sequence search. Such substitutions appear only near the very simple intervals of 3/2 and (especially) 1/1 that mark the endpoints of the fifth traversed by violin I's moving voice. The likely reason for these substitutions is to keep the sizes of the pitch steps in that voice more uniform. A property of the rational number system is that the simpler a rational number is, the better separated it tends to be from other comparably simple rational numbers (Hardy and Wright [1938] 1979, 30). Consider, for instance, the neighborhood immediately preceding one containing the simple rational 1/1. Within that neighborhood, the simplest rational will tend to reside near the end of the neighborhood that is farthest from 1/1. If that rational were selected to furnish the violin I pitch for that neighborhood, then a relatively large intervallic leap to the succeeding 1/1 would result. The aforementioned ratio substitutions appear calculated to ameliorate this intervallic unevenness. The resulting step sizes in the violin's moving voice range from 8 to 27 cents but average 16.7 cents with a standard deviation of 4.6 cents, as compared with the width of each neighborhood, which is also 16.7 cents (one-sixth of a semitone).

12. Appendix B provides a brief general introduction to the spectrographic analysis of audio signals.

10. Transition and Tradition (1986–94)

1. Since 1984 Pratt had been manager for artist Carolee Schneemann, Tenney's first wife, from whom he had separated in 1968 but with whom he remained friends. Pratt and Tenney met at a party for him that Pratt had helped Schneemann to organize. Schneemann maintained a close and mutually supportive friendship with the couple (Schneemann 2014).

2. James Tenney, program note for *Rune*, 1988, electronic file, JTF (unprocessed).

3. Courtesy of the John Cage Trust. The discussion preceding this passage concerns Cage's "number pieces," and the quoted remarks respond to an observation by the interviewer regarding the prevalence in them of tones relative to noises. Cage makes brief related remarks in "How to Get Started" (1989b, 19).

4. John Cage, "The Readymade Boomerang," 1989, courtesy of the John Cage Trust. The complete mesostic is published in Cage ([1990b] 1991, 24) and in De Visscher (1992, 53). Its continuation mentions the 1988 Miami premiere of *Critical Band* explicitly, along with the music of composer Pauline Oliveros, whom Cage identified as also working with harmony in ways that interested him.

5. The pitch interval corresponding to a critical bandwidth is similar at higher pitches but gradually increases for lower pitches, so that it would appear about twice as wide near the bottom of the figure.

6. The concept of a frequency set's *conceptual fundamental* is introduced in section 7.6.1. Strictly speaking, the conceptual fundamental in section 11 is A_2, but in table 10.1 the pitch A_1 is still indicated as the fundamental because it returns in section 12 and because the derivation of the frequency sets in sections 8–12 is clearer if A_1 is regarded as the fundamental throughout all of them.

7. *Flocking* was composed at the invitation of pianists Gertrud Schneider and Tomas Bächli. It would accompany their recording of Tenney's *Bridge* (1984) for commercial

release. A visual counterpoint to Tenney's music was later supplied by experimental filmmaker Stan Brakhage, a friend of Tenney's since youth, who adopted *Flocking* as soundtrack to his 1998 film of scratched imagery entitled "..." *Reel 5* (Smigel 2017a, 125).

8. James Tenney, BASIC program code for *Flocking*, 1993, electronic file, JTF (unprocessed).

9. The clangs in figure 10.4(c) are notional and serve a purely illustrative purpose. They do not literally appear in the music, although many similar clangs determined in the manner described can be found therein.

10. For *Flocking*, the bounds on pitch values for elements (the upper and lower dashed lines in figure 10.4[c]) were always set at least a tritone outside of the bounds on clang means (the edges of the gray-filled region). Thus, even if a clang mean was selected near one of those edges, the stipulated minimum width of one octave for the pitch distribution could still be observed. A similar concordance was imposed for dynamic and durational bounds. If the available parametric range for clang means had not been made narrower than that for individual element parameters, then, as the figure shows, following the 8-minute mark it would have been possible to select a clang mean for pitch that was so close to a limit of the keyboard that the distribution of element values would have to have been made narrower than the desired minimum of an octave. Preservation of a minimum parametric range at some or all hierarchical levels of formal organization had been a common feature in Tenney's composing algorithms since the 1960s (chapter 4, note 20).

11. Spectra and Diaphony (1994–2006)

1. Tenney's students of the 1990s in Toronto would include composers Louis Madrid Calleja, Allison Cameron, Peter Chin, Michael Dobinson, Graham Flett, Nic Gotham, John Gzowski, James Hullick, Mike Kane, Nicole Marchesseau, Andra McCartney, Ciarán Ó Meachair (Ciarán Maher), Marc Sabat, Jon Siddall, Chiyoko Szlavnics, Jesse Stewart, Paul Swoger-Ruston, Nadene Thériault-Copeland, Josh Thorpe, Andrew Timar, Garnet Willis, and the author. Upon returning to a faculty position at the California Institute of the Arts in 2000, he would join old colleagues such as Susan Allen, Stephen "Lucky" Mosko, and David Rosenboom and new ones that included composers Anne LeBaron, Michael Pisaro, and Mark Trayle. Tenney's students there would include G. Douglas Barrett, Raven Chacon, Eric K. M. Clark, Daniel Corral, Aaron Drake, Adam Fong, Joseph Kudirka, Travis Just, Catherine Lamb, Eric Lindley, Tashi Wada, Douglas Wadle, Michael Winter, and Harris Wulfson.

2. By definition, a probability mass function is normalized (scaled) so that its values sum to unity, but Tenney's code handled effective normalization at a later stage. Thus my reference to *probability weights* rather than probabilities.

3. However, this probabilistic promotion of adjacent pcs would only be applied by the stochastic feedback algorithm if their probabilities were not recuperating from previous suppression. In other words, avoidance of close pitch-class repetition within a voice was given priority over promoting dissonance between voices.

4. Bob Gilmore, essay in accompanying booklet, *James Tenney: Spectrum Pieces*, performed by the Barton Workshop, New World Records 80692, 2009, compact disc.

5. The sound pressure level from an omnidirectional source in an open space decreases by about 6 decibels with each doubling of the source distance, so that the loudnesses of identical omnidirectional sound sources at 20 and 60 meters from a listener differ by less than 10 decibels. Although musical instruments are by no means omnidirectional, their wide spatial distribution in *In a Large, . . .* still generally promotes dynamic balance at listening positions not close to a performer.

6. This F harmonic scale previously appeared in the *Spectrum* pieces of 1995, but therein it was filtered below F_4 to directly correspond with a harmonic series on F_0. The harmonic filtering procedure of the *Diaphonic* series thus represents an elaboration of that used in the *Spectrum* series insofar as the filtering is progressive rather than fixed. On the other hand, changes in dynamic and temporal density in the *Diaphonic* series outline relatively simpler forms than they do in the *Spectrum* series.

7. Figure 11.6 departs from Harry Partch's convention (adopted elsewhere in this book) of labeling ratio classes using a representative ratio in the range [1,2), as obtained by dividing each numerator by the largest power of two that does not exceed it (section 7.3). Here, each label instead assumes a denominator of one, which is not shown.

8. Tenney's sketches for *Arbor Vitae* render the tree structure as a projection of (3, 5, 7, 11) pc projection space (JTF, unprocessed; see section 7.7). In that projection, diagonals correspond to hyperplanes viewed "on edge." Following Winter (2008, 134), figure 11.6 simplifies Tenney's sketches by ordering ratio classes along each diagonal by magnitude. The (3,5) plane of pc projection space is still discernible as a distorted grid near the bottom of the figure, as is the (11,3) plane in the figure's frontal plane.

12. A Tradition of Experimentation

The title for this chapter is cribbed from Tenney (1984c), one of the most substantial and revealing interviews with Tenney.

1. The following artists have dedicated one or more works or parts of works to Tenney: John Luther Adams, Christian Asplund, Sandeep Baghwati, John Bergamo, Can Bilir, (filmmaker) Madison Brookshire, Michael Byron, Joshua Carro, Philip Corner, Steed Cowart, Greg Davis, Bryan Eubanks, Anthony Fiumara, Graham Flett, Peter Garland, Malcolm Goldstein, Georg Friedrich Haas, John Hails, Lou Harrison, Robert Hasegawa, Wayne Horvitz, Nathan Hubbard, Marc Jolibois (Traquers de Combs), Matthias Kaul, John King, Alison Knowles, Joseph Kudirka, Alvin Lucier, Thierry Madiot (Ziph), David Mahler, André O. Möller, Barbara Monk Feldman, Jordan Nobles, Pauline Oliveros, Matthew Patton, Larry Polansky, David Rosenboom, Marc Sabat, John Schneider, Philip Schulze, Elliott Sharp, Garrett Sholdice, John Siddall, Mark So, Jacob Sudol, Taylan Susam, Chiyoko Szlavnics, Jeffrey Treviño, Wolfgang von Schweinitz, Jeremy Wexler, Michael Winter, Christian Wolff, Gayle Young, and Ben Zimmerman. There surely are more of whom I am unaware. Around 2015, amid the pencil sketches of Tenney's *Harmonium #5* (1978) held by his estate, a small score to a previously unknown work by John Cage was discovered, apparently hidden there by Cage around 1978. It was never found by Tenney. Entitled *all sides of the small stone for erik satie (and secretly given to Jim Tenney as a koan)*, the score is in Cage's hand and signed "john 7/78." The work received its world premiere in Los Angeles in April 2016.

Appendix B. Spectrographic Analysis

1. The numerous spectrograms appearing in this book were all produced using the free, multiplatform audio playback and visualization environment Sonic Visualiser, developed at the Centre for Digital Music at Queen Mary, University of London. Although the program offers many advanced features of value to researchers, a novice launching it for the first time can nonetheless immediately begin making interesting and illuminating application of it. I recommend that readers of this book make use of it for listening to the analyzed examples of Tenney's music by adding a spectrogram layer that can be followed with the audio.

Sonic Visualiser homepage: https://www.sonicvisualiser.org (accessed August 1, 2019). Suggested initial selections in Sonic Visualiser are Open > *audio_file*, Layer > Add Spectrogram > . . . All Channels Mixed. Suggested initial spectrographic settings are Color = Green, Scale = dBV^2, Normalization = None, Window = 16384, Overlap = 75% (but reduce both for slower computers), Bins = All Bins, Frequency Scale = Log. The horizontal and vertical zoom wheels at the lower right of the spectrogram pane can be used to adjust the time and frequency ranges of the display.

References

The following acronym is used:

JTF   James Tenney Fonds (Inventory #F0428). Clara Thomas Archives and Special Collections, York University, Toronto, ON, Canada.

Adams, John Luther. 2013. Ojai Music Festival 2013: John Luther Adams at Ojai Talks Part 4: CalArts influence and James Tenney. https://www.youtube.com/watch?v=Kc7VcerG2jQ (accessed June 26, 2020).

Ames, Charles. 1987a. "Automated Composition in Retrospect: 1956–86." *Leonardo* 20(2): 169–85.

———. 1987b. "Tutorial on Automated Composition." In *Proceedings of the International Computer Music Conference*, 1–8. Urbana, IL: International Computer Music Association. http://hdl.handle.net/2027/spo.bbp2372.1987.001 (accessed June 26, 2020).

Anderson, Julian. 2000. "A Provisional History of Spectral Music." *Contemporary Music Review* 19(2): 7–22.

Archias, Elise. 2017. *The Concrete Body: Yvonne Rainer, Carolee Schneemann, Vito Acconci*. New Haven, CT: Yale University Press.

Arms, Jay M. 2013. "The Music of Malcolm Goldstein." Master's thesis, University of California, Santa Cruz. https://www.jayarms.com/uploads/1/2/3/7/123763579/the_music_of_malcolm_goldstein.pdf (accessed June 26, 2020).

Artaud, Antonin. 1958. *The Theater and Its Double*. New York: Grove Press.

Austin, Larry, Douglas Kahn, and Nilendra Gurusinghe. 2011. *Source: Music of the Avant-Garde, 1966–1973*. Berkeley: University of California Press.

Banes, Sally. 1983. *Democracy's Body: Judson Dance Theater, 1962–1964*. Ann Arbor, MI: UMI Research Press.

Barlow, Clarence. 1987. "Two Essays on Theory." *Computer Music Journal* 11(1): 44–60.

Belet, Brian. 1990. "An Examination of the Theories and Compositions of James Tenney, 1982–1985." PhD diss., University of Illinois, Urbana-Champaign. *Dissertation Abstracts International* 51(4): 1036 (UMI no. 9026136).

———. 2008. "Theoretical and Formal Continuity in James Tenney's Music." *Contemporary Music Review* 27(1): 23–45.

Bernstein, David W., and Christopher Hatch, eds. 2001. *Writings Through: John Cage's Music, Poetry, and Art*. Chicago: University of Chicago Press.

Bischoff, John, and Peter Garland. 1972. *Soundings* 1. Sylmar, CA: Soundings Press.

Block, Geoffrey H. 1996. *Ives: Concord Sonata, Piano Sonata No. 2 ("Concord, Mass., 1840–1860")*. Cambridge: Cambridge University Press.

Bonito Oliva, Achille, ed. 1990. *Ubi Fluxus ibi motus, 1990–1962*. Milan, Italy: Mazzotta.

Boomsliter, Paul, and Warren Creel. 1961. "The Long Pattern Hypothesis in Harmony and Hearing." *Journal of Music Theory* 5(1): 2–31.

Brakhage, Stan. 1982. *The Test of Time*. KAIR University of Colorado Radio. Transcriptions of twenty programs by Brett Kashmere. http://www.fredcamper.com/Brakhage/TestofTime.html (accessed June 26, 2020).

———. 1987. "James Tenney." *Perspectives of New Music* 25(1/2): 470.

———. 1993. "Fearful Symmetry: Stan Brakhage at Millennium, February 6th 1993." *Millennium Film Journal* 47–49 (Fall 2007 / Winter 2008): 118–26.

Brakhage, Stan, James Tenney, and Gregory Markopoulos. 1963. "Sound and Cinema." *Film Culture* 29 (Summer 1963): 81–102.

Braus, Ira. 1995. "Retracing One's Steps: An Overview of Pitch Circularity and Shepard Tones in European Music, 1550–1990." *Music Perception: An Interdisciplinary Journal* 12(3): 323–51.

Brecht, George. (1964) 1990. "Something about *Fluxus*." *Fluxus cc five ThReE*, Fluxus newspaper no. 4 (June): 1. Reprinted in Bonito Oliva 1990, 143–44.

———. (1973) 1978. Interview in French with Irmeline Lebeer, English translation by Henry Martin. In *An Introduction to George Brecht's "Book of the Tumbler on Fire,"* by Henry Martin, 83–90. Milan, Italy: Multipla.

Breitwieser, Sabine, ed. 2015. *Carolee Schneemann: Kinetic Painting*. Museum der Moderne, Salzburg. Munich, Germany: Prestel.

Byron, Michael. 1975. *Pieces: An Anthology*. Downsview, ON: Michael Byron.

Cage, John. (1952) 1961. "Composition: To Describe the Process of Composition Used in *Music of Changes* and *Imaginary Landscape No. 4*." In Cage 1961, 57–59.

———. (1954) 1961. "45' for a Speaker." In Cage 1961, 146–93.

———. (1955) 1961. "Experimental Music: Doctrine." In Cage 1961, 13–17.

———. (1957) 1961. "Experimental Music." In Cage 1961, 7–12.

———. (1958) 1961. "Composition as Process." In Cage 1961, 18–56.

———. (1959) 1961. "History of Experimental Music in the United States." In Cage 1961, 67–75.

———. 1961. *Silence: Lectures and Writings by John Cage*. Middletown, CT: Wesleyan University Press.

———. 1967. *A Year from Monday: New Lectures and Writings*. 1st ed. Middletown, CT: Wesleyan University Press.

———. (1989a) 2000. "An Autobiographical Statement." In *John Cage: Writer; Selected*

Texts, edited by Richard Kostelanetz, 237–47. New York: Cooper Square Press. https://johncage.org/autobiographical_statement.html (accessed June 26, 2020).

———. 1989b. "How to Get Started." Philadelphia, PA: Slought Foundation. http://slought .org/media/files/how_to_get_started.pdf (accessed June 26, 2020).

———. 1990a. Interview with Max Nyffeler. Swiss Radio. Unpublished. Audio file, JTF (unprocessed). Transcription by Breana Tavaglione, 2017. Also in the collection of the John Cage Trust at Bard College, Red Hook, NY.

———. (1990b) 1991. "Mesosticha." *MusikTexte* 40/41 (August): 23–27.

Cage, John, and Conlon Nancarrow. 1989. "Composer to Composer: Conlon Nancarrow and John Cage in Conversation, Moderated by Charles Amirkhanian." Telluride Institute, Telluride, CO, August 20. Recorded and transcribed by Laura Kuhn. http://johncagetrust.blogspot.com/2015/06/cage-and-nancarrow-1989.html (accessed June 26, 2020).

Chalmers, John C. 1993. *Divisions of the Tetrachord*. Hanover, NH: Frog Peak.

Chapman, David A. 2013. "Collaboration, Presence, and Community: The Philip Glass Ensemble in Downtown New York, 1966–1976." PhD diss., Washington University in St. Louis, St. Louis, MO. http://openscholarship.wustl.edu/etd/1098 (accessed June 26, 2020).

Cohen, H. Floris. 1984. *Quantifying Music: The Science of Music at the First Stage of the Scientific Revolution, 1580–1650*. New York: Springer.

Cohn, Richard. 1997. "Neo-Riemannian Operations, Parsimonious Trichords, and Their *Tonnetz* Representations." *Journal of Music Theory* 41(1): 1–66.

———. 1998. "Introduction to Neo-Riemannian Theory: A Survey and a Historical Perspective." *Journal of Music Theory* 42(2): 167–80.

Corner, Philip. 1995. *In and About and Round-About in the 60s: New York in Center*. Lebanon, NH: Frog Peak Music.

———. 2007. *FLUXstuff: a miscellany of documents (not only of "fluxus" per se, but of the larger scene of concerts, events, happenings from the 50s to the present), in the form of writings, articles, reviews, programs, letters, analyses, reminiscences, philosophizing, and the like*. Lebanon, NH: Frog Peak Music.

Corrin, Lisa G. 2016. "*Noise Bodies* and Noisy Women: A Conversation with Carolee Schneemann." In *A Feast of Astonishments: Charlotte Moorman and the Avant-Garde, 1960s–1980s*, edited by Lisa G. Corrin and Corinne Granof, 108–21. Evanston, IL: Northwestern University Press.

Cousineau, Marion, Josh H. McDermott, and Isabelle Peretz. 2012. "The Basis of Musical Consonance as Revealed by Congenital Amusia." *Proceedings of the National Academy of Sciences* 109(48): 19858–63. https://doi.org/10.1073/pnas.1207989109 (accessed June 26, 2020).

Cowell, Henry. (1930) 1996. *New Musical Resources*. Cambridge: Cambridge University Press.

Crane, Michael, and Mary Stofflet. 1984. *Correspondence Art: Source Book for the Network of International Postal Art Activity*. San Francisco: Contemporary Arts Press.

Cutler, Chris. (1994) 2004. "Plunderphonia." *Musicworks* 60 (Fall): 6–19. Reprinted in *Audio Culture: Readings in Modern Music*, edited by Christoph Cox and Daniel Warner, 138–56. New York: Continuum International Publishing Group.

Dean, Roger T., ed. 2009. *The Oxford Handbook of Computer Music*. Oxford: Oxford University Press.

Deutsch, Diana. 2013. *The Psychology of Music*. 3rd ed. London: Academic Press.

De Visscher, Eric. 1992. "John Cage and the Idea of Harmony." *Musicworks* 52 (Spring): 50–56.

Dibelius, Ulrich, Gisela Gronemeyer, Reinhard Oehlschlägel, and Ernstalbrecht Stiebler, eds. 1990. "Über James Tenney: Peter Garland, Daniel Wolf, Steve Reich, Jean-Claude Risset, Eric de Visscher, Gordon Monahan." Special issue, *MusikTexte* 37 (December).

Duckworth, William. 1999. *Talking Music: Conversations with John Cage, Philip Glass, Laurie Anderson, and Five Generations of American Experimental Composers*. New York: Da Capo Press.

Elder, Bruce R. 1997. *Body of Vision: Representations of the Body in Recent Film and Poetry*. Waterloo, ON: Wilfrid Laurier University Press.

Fairbanks, G., and P. Grubb. 1961. "A Psychophysical Investigation of Vowel Formants." *Journal of Speech and Hearing Research* 4:203–19.

Féron, François-Xavier. 2014. "Could the Endless Progressions in James Tenney's Music Be Viewed as Sonic Koans?" In *Proceedings ICMC|SMC|2014*, edited by Anastasia Georgaki and Georgios Kouroupetroglou, 103–8. September, Athens, Greece.

Filippone, Christine. 2011. "Schneemann, Carolee." In *Grove Art Online*. Oxford: Oxford University Press. https://doi.org/10.1093/gao/9781884446054.article.T2090898 (accessed June 26, 2020).

Fineberg, Joshua. 2000a. "Guide to the Basic Concepts and Techniques of Spectral Music." *Contemporary Music Review* 19:81–113.

———, ed. 2000b. "Spectral Music: History and Techniques." Special issue, *Contemporary Music Review* 19.

Fiore, Giacomo. 2018. "Tuning Theory and Practice in James Tenney's Works for Guitar." *Music Theory Spectrum* 40(2): 338–56.

Fletcher, Neville H., and Thomas D. Rossing. 2010. *The Physics of Musical Instruments*. 2nd ed. New York: Springer.

Fokker, Adriaan D. 1969. "Unison Vectors and Periodicity Blocks in the Three-Dimensional (3–5–7) Harmonic Lattice of Notes." *Proceedings of Koninklijke Nederlandsche Akademie van Wetenschappen* B72(3): 153–68.

Franklin, Joseph. 2006. *Settling Scores: A Life in the Margins of American Music*. Santa Fe, NM: Sunstone Press.

Gann, Kyle. 1991. "Cage's Choice." *Village Voice*, May 7, 1991, 78.

———. 1995. *The Music of Conlon Nancarrow*. New York: Cambridge University Press.

———. 1997. *American Music in the 20th Century*. New York: Schirmer Books.

Garland, Peter, ed. 1984. *The Music of James Tenney. Soundings* 13. Santa Fe, NM: Soundings Press.

———. 1990. "James Tenney: Some Historical Perspectives." In *A Celebration of American Music: Words and Music in Honor of H. Wiley Hitchcock*, edited by Richard Crawford, R. Allen Lott, and Carol J. Oja, 477–86. Ann Arbor: University of Michigan Press.

———. 2007. "Musik, Beat, Bier und Sex: An Jim Tenney erinnern." *MusikTexte* 112:50–60.

Gilmore, Bob. 2008. "James Tenney and the Poetics of Homage." *Contemporary Music Review* 27(1): 7–21.

———. 2014. "Five Maps of the Experimental World." In *Artistic Experimentation in Music: An Anthology*, edited by Darla Crispin and Bob Gilmore, 23–30. Leuven, Belgium: Leuven University Press.

Glover, Richard, and Bryn Harrison. 2013. *Overcoming Form: Reflections on Immersive Listening*. Huddersfield, UK: University of Huddersfield Press.

Goldstein, Malcolm. 1984. "Some Glimpses of James Tenney." In Garland 1984, 4–14.

———. 2006. Interview with Dan Warburton, April 28, 2006. *Paris Transatlantic*. http://www.paristransatlantic.com/magazine/interviews/goldstein.html (accessed June 26, 2020).

Gottschalk, Jennie. 2017. *Experimental Music Since 1970*. Reprint. New York: Bloomsbury Academic.

Hardy, Godfrey H., and Edward M. Wright. (1938) 1979. *An Introduction to the Theory of Numbers*. 5th ed. Oxford: Clarendon Press.

Harley, James. 2004. *Xenakis: His Life in Music*. New York: Routledge.

Hasegawa, Robert, ed. 2008. "The Music of James Tenney." Special issue, *Contemporary Music Review* 27(1).

Heller, Eric J. 2013. *Why You Hear What You Hear: An Experiential Approach to Sound, Music, and Psychoacoustics*. Princeton, NJ: Princeton University Press.

Helmholtz, Hermann von. (1877) 1954. *On the Sensations of Tone as a Physiological Basis for the Theory of Music*. Translated by Alexander J. Ellis. New York: Dover.

Higgins, Dick. 1979. "A Child's History of Fluxus." *Lightworks* 11/12 (Fall): 26–27. Reprinted in Bonito Oliva 1990, 172–74.

Higgins, Dick, Steve Clay, and Ken Friedman. 2018. *Intermedia, Fluxus and the Something Else Press: Selected Writings by Dick Higgins*. Catskill, NY: Siglio.

Hiller, Lejaren A. 1961. "These Electrons Go Round and Round and Come Out—Music." *IRE Student Quarterly* 8(1): 36–45.

———. 1963. "Electronic Music at the University of Illinois." *Journal of Music Theory* 7(1): 99–126.

———. 1987. "Jim Tenney at Illinois: A Reminiscence." *Perspectives of New Music* 25(1/2): 514–16.

Humbert, Jacqueline. 1979. "Something Called Maple Sugar." *Musicworks* 6 (Winter): 8.

Huron, David B. 2016. *Voice Leading: The Science behind the Musical Art*. Cambridge, MA: MIT Press.

Ives, Charles. 1920. *Essays before a Sonata*. New York: Knickerbocker Press.

James, David E., ed. 2005. *Stan Brakhage: Filmmaker*. Wide Angle Books. Philadelphia, PA: Temple University Press.

Jedrzejewski, Franck. 2006. *Mathematical Theory of Music*. Paris: IRCAM–Centre Pompidou.

Johnston, Ben. 1971. "Tonality Regained." *Proceedings of the American Society of University Composers* 6:113–19.

Juhasz, Alexandra. 2001. *Women of Vision: Histories in Feminist Film and Video*. Minneapolis: University of Minnesota Press.

Kahn, Douglas. 1993. "The Latest: Fluxus and Music." In *In the Spirit of Fluxus: Published on the Occasion of the Exhibition*, edited by Elizabeth Armstrong, Joan Rothfuss, and Simon Anderson, 100–121. Minneapolis: Walker Art Center.

———. 2012. "James Tenney at Bell Labs." In *Mainframe Experimentalism: Early Computing and the Foundations of the Digital Arts*, edited by Hannah Higgins and Douglas Kahn, 131–46. Berkeley: University of California Press.

———. 2013a. *Earth Sound, Earth Signal: Energies and Earth Magnitude in the Arts*. Berkeley: University of California Press.

———. 2013b. "Let Me Hear My Body Talk, My Body Talk." In *Relive: Media Art Histories*, edited by Sean Cubitt and Paul Thomas, 235–56. Cambridge, MA: MIT Press.

Koffka, Kurt. (1935) 1962. *Principles of Gestalt Psychology*. London: Routledge and Kegan Paul.

Köhler, Wolfgang. (1929) 1959. *Introduction to Gestalt Psychology*. New York: New American Library.

Kramer, Jonathan D. 1988. *The Time of Music*. New York: Schirmer Books.

Kubitza, Anette. 2009. "Flux-Proof or 'Sometimes No One Can Read Labels in the Dark': Carolee Schneemann and the Fluxus Paradox." *Women and Performance: A Journal of Feminist Theory* 19(3): 391–409.

Langner, Gerald, and Christina Benson. 2015. *The Neural Code of Pitch and Harmony*. Cambridge: Cambridge University Press.

LeBaron, Anne. 2006. "American Composers Remember György Ligeti (1923–2006): A Memorial from Anne LeBaron." *NewMusicBox*. https://nmbx.newmusicusa.org/American-Composers-Remember-Gyorgy-Ligeti-19232006/ (accessed June 26, 2020).

Lely, John, and James Saunders. 2012. *Word Events: Perspectives on Verbal Notation*. London: Continuum.

Lewis, George E. 2008. *A Power Stronger Than Itself: The AACM and American Experimental Music*. Chicago: University of Chicago Press.

Longuet-Higgins, H. Christopher. 1962a. "Letter to a Musical Friend." *Music Review* 23:244–48.

———. 1962b. "Second Letter to a Musical Friend." *Music Review* 23:271–80.

MacDonald, Malcolm. 2003. *Varèse: Astronomer in Sound*. London: Kahn and Averill.

MacDonald, Scott. 2005. *A Critical Cinema 4: Interviews with Independent Filmmakers*. Berkeley: University of California Press.

Marshall, Ingram. 1975. "New Music at Cal Arts: The First Four Years (1970–74)." *NumusWest* 2(1): 52–60.

Mathews, Max V. 1961. "An Acoustic Compiler for Music and Psychological Stimuli." *Bell System Technical Journal* 40(3): 677–94.

———. 1963. "The Digital Computer as a Musical Instrument." *Science* 142(3,592): 553–57.

———. 1968. "Lecture." Transcript of tape-recording, February 4, 1968. Experiments in Art and Technology records, 1966–93. Accession no. 940003. File 29, box 28. Special Collections, Getty Research Institute, Los Angeles.

———. 2003. "John Robinson Pierce." *Physics Today* 56(12): 88. https://doi.org/10.1063/1.1650249 (accessed June 26, 2020).

Mathews, Max V., Joan E. Miller, John R. Pierce, and James Tenney. 1965. "Computer Study of Violin Tones." Abstract in *Journal of the Acoustical Society of America* 38(5): 912–13.

McDermott, Josh H. 2014a. "Consonance and Dissonance." In *Music in the Social and Behavioral Sciences: An Encyclopedia*, edited by William Forde Thompson, 250–54. Los Angeles: SAGE.

———. 2014b. "Harmonicity." In *Music in the Social and Behavioral Sciences: An Encyclopedia*, edited by William Forde Thompson, 527–29. Los Angeles: SAGE.

McDermott, Josh H., Andriana J. Lehr, and Andrew J. Oxenham. 2010. "Individual Differences Reveal the Basis of Consonance." *Current Biology* 20(11): 1035–41.

Micheyl, Christophe, and Andrew J. Oxenham. 2010. "Pitch, Harmonicity and Concurrent Sound Segregation: Psychoacoustical and Neurophysiological Findings." *Hearing Research* 266(1/2): 36–51.

Midgette, Anne. 2005. "Pioneer. Composer. Psychoacoustician?" *New York Times*, May 8, 2005.

Miller, Leta E. 2001. "Cage, Cunningham, and Collaborators: The Odyssey of *Variations V*." *Musical Quarterly* 85(3): 545–67.

Moore, Brian C. J. 2013. *An Introduction to the Psychology of Hearing*. 6th ed. Leiden, the Netherlands: Brill.

Moore, Brian C. J., and Brian R. Glasberg. 1986. "Thresholds for Hearing Mistuned Partials as Separate Tones in Harmonic Complexes." *Journal of the Acoustical Society of America* 80:479–83.

Moorman, Charlotte. (1973) 2003. "Interview with Charlotte Moorman on the Avant-Garde Festivals." Interview by Stephen Varble. In *Critical Mass: Happenings, Fluxus, Performance, Intermedia and Rutgers University 1958–1972*, edited by Geoffrey Hendricks, 173–80. New Brunswick, NJ: Rutgers University Press.

Mosko, Stephen, and James Tenney. 2004. Interview with Martin Herman, Amy Knoles, and Glenn Zucman. *Border Patrol, #2 (Mapping Music)*. Green Valley, CA. December 9. Audio file, JTF (unprocessed). Transcription by Lucien Ye, 2017. https://glenn.zucman.com/blog/border-patrol (accessed June 26, 2020).

Mumma, Gordon (chair), Allen Kaprow, James Tenney, Christian Wolff, Alvin Curran, and Maryanne Amacher. (1995) 2001. "Cage's Influence: A Panel Discussion." In Bernstein and Hatch 2001, 167–89.

Neumann, John von. 1951. "Various Techniques Used in Connection with Random Digits." In *Monte Carlo Method*, edited by A. S. Householder, G. E. Forsythe, and H. H. Germond, 36–38. National Bureau of Standards Applied Mathematics Series 12. Washington, DC: United States Government Printing Office.

Novak, David. 2013. *Japanoise: Music at the Edge of Circulation*. Durham, NC: Duke University Press.

Nyman, Michael. 1999. *Experimental Music: Cage and Beyond*. 2nd ed. Cambridge: Cambridge University Press.

Oja, Carol J. 2001. "Rudhyar, Dane." In *Grove Music Online*. Oxford: Oxford University Press. https://doi.org/10.1093/gmo/9781561592630.article.24082 (accessed June 26, 2020).

Oswald, John. 1986. "Plunderphonics, or Audio Piracy as a Compositional Prerogative." *Musicworks* 34 (Spring): 5–8. https://econtact.ca/16_4/oswald_plunderphonics.html (accessed June 26, 2020).

———. 1989[?]. "Plunderphonics: An Interview with Transproducer John Oswald."

Interview by Norman Igma. http://www.plunderphonics.com/xhtml/xinterviews.html (accessed June 26, 2020).

Ouellette, Fernand. 1968. *Edgard Varèse*. New York: Orion Press.

Palisca, Claude V. 1961. "Scientific Empiricism in Musical Thought." In *Seventeenth Century Science and the Arts*, edited by Hedley Howell Rhys, 91–137. Princeton, NJ: Princeton University Press.

Palisca, Claude V., and Brian C. J. Moore. 2001. "Consonance." In *The New Grove Dictionary of Music and Musicians*, edited by Stanley Sadie. Oxford: Oxford University Press.

Parncutt, Richard, and Graham Hair. 2011. "Consonance and Dissonance in Music Theory and Psychology: Disentangling Dissonant Dichotomies." *Journal of Interdisciplinary Music Studies* 5(2): 119–66.

Parsons, Thomas. 1986. *Voice and Speech Processing*. New York: McGraw-Hill.

Partch, Harry. (1949) 1974. *Genesis of a Music*. 2nd ed. New York: Da Capo Press.

Patterson, Benjamin, Philip Corner, Alison Knowles, and Tomas Schmit. 1965. *The Four Suits: Benjamin Patterson, Philip Corner, Alison Knowles, Tomas Schmit*. New York: Something Else Press.

Patterson, David W. 2012. "'Political' or 'Social'? John Cage and the Remolding of Mao Tse-Tung." In *Cage & Consequences*, edited by Julia H. Schröder and Volker Straebel, 51–65. Hofheim, Germany: Wolke.

Pearson, Tina, and Gordon Monahan, eds. 1984. "James Tenney." Special issue, *Musicworks* 27 (Spring).

Penrose, Lionel S., and Roger Penrose. 1958. "Impossible Object, a Special Type of Visual Illusion." *British Journal of Psychology* 49(1): 31–33.

Perkis, Tim. n.d. CD review, *James Tenney: Selected Works 1961–1969*. CD 1007 Artifact Recordings. http://www.perkis.com/wpc/w_tenney.html (accessed June 26, 2020).

Peterson, Gordon, and Harold L. Barney. 1952. "Control Methods Used in a Study of the Vowels." *Journal of the Acoustical Society of America* 24: 175–84.

Piekut, Benjamin. 2011. *Experimentalism Otherwise: The New York Avant-Garde and Its Limits*. Berkeley: University of California Press.

———, ed. 2014. *Tomorrow Is the Question: New Directions in Experimental Music Studies*. Ann Arbor: University of Michigan Press.

———. 2018. "On and Off the Grid: Music for and around Judson Dance Theater." In *Judson Dance Theater: The Work Is Never Done*, edited by Ana Janevski and Thomas J. Lax, 68–75. New York: Museum of Modern Art.

Plomp, R. Rainer, and Willem J. M. Levelt. 1965. "Tonal Consonance and Critical Bandwidth." *Journal of the Acoustical Society of America* 38(4): 548–60.

Polansky, Larry. 1984. "The Early Works of James Tenney." In Garland 1984, 114–297.

———. 2007. "A Few Words about James Tenney." *Musicworks* 90 (Spring 2007): 10–13.

Polansky, Larry, Alex Barnett, and Michael Winter. 2011. "A Few More Words about James Tenney: Dissonant Counterpoint and Statistical Feedback." *Journal of Mathematics and Music* 5(2): 63–82.

Polansky, Larry, and David Rosenboom, eds. 1987. "A Tribute to James Tenney." Special issue, *Perspectives of New Music* 25(1/2): 436–591.

Pritchett, James. 1996. *The Music of John Cage*. Cambridge: Cambridge University Press.

Pritchett, James (chair), James Tenney, Andrew Culver, and Frances White. (1995)

2001. "Cage and the Computer: A Panel Discussion." In Bernstein and Hatch 2001, 190–209.

Reich, Steve. (1968) 2002. "Music as a Gradual Process." In *Writings on Music, 1965–2000*, edited by Steve Reich and Paul Hillier, 34–36. Oxford: Oxford University Press.

———. 1987. "Tenney." *Perspectives of New Music* 25(1/2): 547–48.

———. 1988. "Texture-Space-Survival." *Perspectives of New Music* 26(2): 272–80.

Reich, Wilhelm. 1960. *Selected Writings : An Introduction to Orgonomy*. New York: Farrar, Straus and Cudahy.

———. 1971. *The Function of the Orgasm: Sex-Economic Problems of Biological Energy*. New York: World Pub.

Reich, Wilhelm, and William Steig. 1948. *Listen, Little Man!* Noonday, 271. New York: Noonday Press.

Reilly, Maura. 2010. "Painting: What It Became." In *Carolee Schneemann: Within and beyond the Premises*, edited by Brian Wallace, 82–119. New Paltz, NY: Samuel Dorsky Museum of Art.

Remez, Robert E., Philip E. Rubin, David B. Pisoni, and Thomas D. Carrell. 1981. "Speech Perception without Traditional Speech Cues." *Science* 212: 947–50.

Risset, Jean-Claude. 1987. "About James Tenney, Composer, Performer, and Theorist." *Perspectives of New Music* 25(1/2): 549–61.

Roads, Curtis. 1996. *The Computer Music Tutorial*. Cambridge, MA: MIT Press.

Roads, Curtis, and Max Mathews. 1980. "Interview with Max Mathews." *Computer Music Journal* 4(4): 15–22.

Robinson, Julia. 2009. "From Abstraction to Model: George Brecht's Events and the Conceptual Turn in Art of the 1960s." *October* 127 (Winter): 77–108.

Roederer, Juan G. 2008. *The Physics and Psychophysics of Music: An Introduction*. 4th ed. New York: Springer.

Rose, François. 1996. "Introduction to the Pitch Organization of French Spectral Music." *Perspectives of New Music* 34(2): 6–39.

Rothenberg, Jerome. 1972. *Shaking the Pumpkin: Traditional Poetry of the Indian North Americas*. Garden City, NY: Doubleday.

Rothfuss, Joan. 2014. *Topless Cellist: The Improbable Life of Charlotte Moorman*. Cambridge, MA: MIT Press.

Sabat, Marc. 2008. "Three Crystal Growth Algorithms in 23-limit Constrained Harmonic Space." *Contemporary Music Review* 27(1): 57–78.

Sabat, Marc, and Robin Hayward. 2006. "Towards an Expanded Definition of Consonance: Tunable Intervals on Horn, Tuba and Trombone." Plainsound Music Edition. http://www.marcsabat.com/pdfs/tuneable-brass.pdf (accessed June 26, 2020).

Sainer, Arthur. 1997. *The New Radical Theater Notebook*. Rev. ed. New York: Applause Books.

Schellenberg, E. Glenn, and Sandra Trehub. 1994. "Frequency Ratios and the Perception of Tone Patterns." *Psychonomic Bulletin and Review* 1(2): 191–201.

Schneemann, Carolee. 1979. *More Than Meat Joy: Complete Performance Works and Selected Writings*. Edited by Bruce R. McPherson. New Paltz, NY: Documentext.

———. 1990. "Fluxus." In Bonito Oliva 1990, 89.

———. 1991. "The Obscene Body/Politic." *Art Journal* 50(4): 28–35.

———. 2003. *Imaging Her Erotics: Essays, Interviews, Projects*. Cambridge, MA: MIT Press.

———. 2005. "It Is Painting." In James 2005, 78–87.

———. 2009. "Oral History Interview with Carolee Schneemann, 2009 March 1." Interview with Judith Olch Richards, March 1, 2009, Springtown, NY, transcript. Archives of American Art, Smithsonian Institution. https://www.aaa.si.edu/collections/interviews/oral-history-interview-carolee-schneemann-15672 (accessed June 26, 2020).

———. 2010. *Correspondence Course: An Epistolary History of Carolee Schneemann and Her Circle*. Edited by Kristine Stiles. Durham, NC: Duke University Press.

———. 2014. "Notes on Fuseology: Carolee Schneemann Remembers James Tenney." Interview with Robert Enright. *Border Crossings* 33(4): 38–44. http://bordercrossings mag.com/article/notes-on-fuseology (accessed June 26, 2020).

———. 2016. "Carolee Schneemann with Jarrett Earnest." Interview with Jarrett Earnest. *Brooklyn Rail*, December 6. http://brooklynrail.org/2016/12/art/carolee-schneemann -with-jarrett-earnest (accessed June 26, 2020).

———. 2018. *Carolee Schneemann: Uncollected Texts*. Edited by Branden W. Joseph. Brooklyn: Primary Information.

Schoenberg, Arnold. 1969. *Structural Functions of Harmony*. New York: W. W. Norton.

———. 1975. *Style and Idea: Selected Writings of Arnold Schoenberg*. Edited by Leonard Stein. London: Faber and Faber.

———. 1978. *Theory of Harmony*. Translated by Roy E. Carter. Berkeley: University of California Press.

Seeger, Charles. 1930. "On Dissonant Counterpoint." *Modern Music* 7(4): 25–31.

———. (1931) 1994. "Manual of Dissonant Counterpoint." In *Studies in Musicology II: 1929–1979*, edited by Ann M. Pescatello, 163–228. Berkeley: University of California Press.

Sethares, William A. 2005. *Tuning, Timbre, Spectrum, Scale*. 2nd ed. London: Springer.

Shannon, Claude E. 1948. "A Mathematical Theory of Communication." *Bell System Technical Journal* 27(3): 379–423, 623–56.

Shapira Lots, Inbal, and Lewi Stone. 2008. "Perception of Musical Consonance and Dissonance: An Outcome of Neural Synchronization." *Journal of the Royal Society Interface* 5(29): 1429–34. https://doi.org/10.1098/rsif.2008.0143 (accessed June 26, 2020).

Shepard, Roger N. 1964. "Circularity in Judgments of Relative Pitch." *Journal of the Acoustical Society of America* 36: 2346–53.

Sims, Ezra. 1991. "Reflections on This and That (Perhaps a Polemic)." *Perspectives of New Music* 29(1): 236–57.

Sinclair, James B. 1999. *A Descriptive Catalogue of the Music of Charles Ives*. New Haven, CT: Yale University Press. Revised 2012 at https://elischolar.library.yale.edu/ivescatalogue/1 (accessed June 26, 2020).

Smigel, Eric. 2012. "Metaphors on Vision: James Tenney and Stan Brakhage, 1951–1964." *American Music* 30(1): 61–100.

———. 2017a. "Sights and Sounds of the Moving Mind: The Visionary Soundtracks of Stan Brakhage." In *The Music and Sound of Experimental Film*, edited by Holly Rogers and Jeremy Barham, 109–28. New York: Oxford University Press.

———. 2017b. "'To Behold with Wonder': Theory, Theater, and the Collaboration of

James Tenney and Carolee Schneemann." *Journal of the Society for American Music* 11(1): 1–24.

Smith, Charles S. 1960. "Leonhard Euler's *Tentamen Novae Theoriae Musicae*: A Translation and Commentary by Charles Samuel Smith." PhD diss., University of Indiana, Bloomington.

Spilker, John D. 2011. "The Origins of 'Dissonant Counterpoint': Henry Cowell's Unpublished Notebook." *Journal of the Society for American Music* 5(4): 481–533.

———. 2013. "Dissonant Counterpoint." *Grove Music Online*. Oxford: Oxford University Press. https://doi.org/10.1093/gmo/9781561592630.article.A2240654 (accessed June 26, 2020).

Stainsby, Thomas, and Ian Cross. 2009. "The Perception of Pitch." In *The Oxford Handbook of Music Psychology*, edited by Susan Hallam, Ian Cross, and Michael Thaut, 47–58. Oxford: Oxford University Press.

Stiles, Kristine. 1993. "Between Water and Stone." *In the Spirit of Fluxus: Published on the Occasion of the Exhibition*, edited by Elizabeth Armstrong, Joan Rothfuss, and Simon Anderson, 62–99. Minneapolis: Walker Arts Center.

Straus, Joseph N. 2016. *Introduction to Post-tonal Theory*. 4th ed. New York: W. W. Norton.

Stolzenburg, Frieder. 2015. "Harmony Perception by Periodicity Detection." *Journal of Mathematics and Music* 9(3): 215–38.

Stumpf, Carl. 1898. "Konsonanz und Dissonanz." *Beiträge zur Akustik und Musikwissenschaft*, 1:1–108. Leipzig: J.A. Barth.

Swed, Mark. 1993. "Cage and Counting: The Number Pieces." In *Rolywholyover: A Circus*, by John Cage and Russell Ferguson Los Angeles: Museum of Contemporary Art.

———. 2002. "A Piano Piece's Nuts and Bolts." *Los Angeles Times*, June 23, 2002.

Tenney, James. (1961) 2015. "Meta\Hodos." In Tenney 2015, 13–96.

———. 1962. "Discriminability of Differences in the Rise Time of a Tone." Abstract in *Journal of the Acoustical Society of America* 34(5): 739.

———. 1963. "Sound-Generation by Means of a Digital Computer." *Journal of Music Theory* 7(1): 25–70.

———. (1964) 2015. "Computer Music Experiences, 1961–1964." In Tenney 2015, 97–127.

———. (1965) 2015. "The Physical Correlates of Timbre." In Tenney 2015, 128–31.

———. (1966a) 2015. "Excerpts from 'An Experimental Investigation of Timbre.'" In Tenney 2015, 132–49.

———. (1966b) 2015. "Some Notes on the Music of Charles Ives." Essay in booklet accompanying *Charles Ives: Songs*, performed by Ted Puffer and James Tenney, Folkways Records FM 3344 and FM 3355.

———. 1968a. "Background—fragments of an unkept diary." Unpublished. JTF 2010-050/012 (01).

———. 1968b. "Computer Music." Transcript of tape-recording, February 5. Experiments in Art and Technology records, 1966–93. Accession no. 940003. File 32, box 28. Special Collections, Getty Research Institute, Los Angeles.

———. (1970) 2015. "Form in Twentieth-Century Music." In Tenney 2015, 150–65.

———. (1975a) 2015. "META Meta\Hodos." In Tenney 2015, 166–79.

———. 1975b. "Postal Pieces." *Percussionist* 12(3): 100–108.

———. 1975c. Radio documentation by Peter Kuhn and David Freedman of KUSP Radio,

Santa Cruz, CA. Audio file, JTF (unprocessed). Transcription by Breana Tavaglione, 2017.

———. 1976. "Morning Concert: Composer Jim Tenney." Interview with Charles Amirkhanian. Radio broadcast KPFA, Berkeley, CA, January 12. Transcription by Lucien Ye, 2017. https://archive.org/details/MC_1976_01_12 (accessed June 26, 2020).

———. (1977a) 2015. "The Chronological Development of Carl Ruggles' Melodic Style." In Tenney 2015, 180–200.

———. 1977b. "Conlon Nancarrow's Studies for Player Piano." In *Conlon Nancarrow, Selected Studies for Player Piano, Soundings* 4, ed. Peter Garland, 41–64. Berkeley, CA: Soundings Press. Also issued as liner notes to *Conlon Nancarrow: Complete Studies for Player Piano*, 1750 Arch Records S-1768/1777/1786/1798. Expanded and updated as liner notes to *Conlon Nancarrow: Studies for Player Piano, Vols. 1–5* (1988–91), Wergo Records WERGO 6907-2 (1999).

———. 1978a. "Gayle Young Interviews James Tenney." Interview by Gayle Young. *Only Paper Today* 5(5): 16.

———. 1978b. "In Retrospect." Program notes for two concerts in New York City produced by Steve Reich, December. Unpublished. JTF 2010-050/012 (01).

———. (1979a) 2015. "Introduction to 'Contributions to a Quantitative Theory of Harmony.'" In Tenney 2015, 234–39.

———. (1979b) 2015. "The Structure of Harmonic Series Aggregates." In Tenney 2015, 240–79.

———. (1983) 2015. "John Cage and the Theory of Harmony." In Tenney 2015, 280–304.

———. 1984a. "*Bridge*." Interview with Gordon Monahan and Tina Pearson. *Musicworks* 27 (Spring): 10–13.

———. (1984b) 2015. "Reflections after *Bridge*." In Tenney 2015, 305–8.

———. 1984c. "A Tradition of Experimentation: James Tenney in Conversation with Udo Kasemets and *Musicworks*." *Musicworks* 27:2–9, 20.

———. (1987a) 2015. "About *Changes: Sixty-Four Studies for Six Harps*." In Tenney 2015, 327–49.

———. 1987b. "An Interview with James Tenney." Interview with Brian Belet, December 1985, Toronto, Canada. *Perspectives of New Music* 25(1/2): 459–66.

———. 1987c. "Warren Burt Interviews James Tenney during the Philadelphia New Music America Festival, 1987." Transcription by Lucien Ye, 2017. https://soundcloud.com/innovadotmu/james-tenney (accessed June 26, 2020).

———. 1988a. *A History of 'Consonance' and 'Dissonance.'* New York: Excelsior. http://www.plainsound.org/Jtwork.html (accessed June 26, 2020).

———. 1988b. "James Tenney with Gayle Young." Interview by Gayle Young, June 10 and 12, Toronto, Canada. Interview no. 196a–d, transcript, *Oral History of American Music: Major Figures in American Music*, Yale University, New Haven, CT.

———. (1990) 2015. "Darmstadt Lecture." In Tenney 2015, 350–67.

———. 1991. "James Tenney: American Maverick." Interview with Peter Garland. *Ear* 15 (March): 31–34.

———. 1993a. "James Tenney." Telephone interview with Nicole Gagné, August 6 and 12, 1992. In *Soundpieces 2: Interviews with American Composers*, ed. Nicole Gagné, 389–412. Metuchen, NJ: Scarecrow Press.

———. (1993b) 2015. "On Crystal Growth in Harmonic Space." In Tenney 2015, 383–93.

———. (1993c/2003) 2015. "The Several Dimensions of Pitch." In Tenney 2015, 368–82.

———. 1995a. "Encounters with Cage: From My Notes for the Mills College Cage Conference of November 1995." Unpublished. JTF (unprocessed).

———. 1995b. "Whatever Happened to the Future?" Fax interview with Johan Kolsteeg, February–April 1995. *Key Notes: Musical Life in the Netherlands* 29(2): 4–6.

———. 1996a (2015). "About *Diapason*." In Tenney 2015, 394–96.

———. 1996b. "James Tenney: Transparent to the Sounds of the Environment." Interview with Gayle Young. *Musicworks* 65:8–18.

———. 1996c. "James Tenney with Libby Van Cleve." Interview by Libby Van Cleve, May 20, Toronto, Canada. Interview no. 196e–g, transcript, *Oral History of American Music: Major Figures in American Music*, Yale University, New Haven, CT.

———. 1996d. "just randeming: james tenney in conversation." Interview by Ciarán Maher, Fall 1995, Toronto, Canada. Unpublished. JTF 2010-050/009 (01).

———. 1997. "Hermits of Re-tuning." Interview with Dennis Bathory-Kitsz, Toronto, Canada. *Kalvos and Damian's New Music Bazaar, Show #115*, WGDR/WGDH Community Radio, Plainfield, VT, August 2, 1997. Transcript published at http://econtact.ca/10_2/TenneyJa_KD.html (accessed June 26, 2020).

———. 2000a. "A Different View of the Larger Picture: James Tenney on Intention, Harmony and Phenomenology." Interview with Ciarán Maher. *Musicworks* 77:25–29.

———. 2000b. "The Future of Music (revisited 2000)." Unpublished. JTF (unprocessed).

———. 2000c. Interview with Bruce Russell, May 3. Unpublished. Audio file, JTF (unprocessed). Transcription by Breana Tavaglione, 2017.

———. 2000d. Interview with host Larry Lake on CBC radio program *Two New Hours*, July 9. Unpublished. Audio file, JTF (unprocessed). Transcription by Lucien Ye, 2017.

———. 2000e. "Invisible Boundaries: James Tenney on His Cultural and Compositional Diversity." Interview with Gayle Young. *Musicworks* 77:20–24.

———. 2000f. "James Tenney Interviewed by Douglas Kahn." Interview by Douglas Kahn, Toronto, February 1999. *Leonardo Electronic Almanac* 8(11). http://www.leonardo.info/LEA/Tenney2001/tenneyinterview.html (accessed June 26, 2020).

———. 2001. Interview with Bonnie Barnett. Radio interview. Trilogy, KXLU Radio, Los Angeles, June 17. Unpublished. Audio file, JTF (unprocessed). Transcription by Lucien Ye, 2017.

———. (2003a) 2005. "Brakhage Memoir." In James 2005, 57–60.

———. 2003b. Interview by David Patterson, March 13. Unpublished. JTF 2010-050/009 (13).

——— 2003c. "Tenney Plays Cage: Inside Cage's Prepared-Piano Masterpiece, with One of His Most Renowned Artistic Heirs." Interview with Gayle Young. *Musicworks* 86:36–45.

———. 2004a. *Interim* interview with Ron Magliozzi. June 29. Electronic file, JTF (unprocessed).

———. 2004b. Interview with Philip Blackburn, St. John's, NL. American Mavericks, Minnesota Public Radio. Transcription by Alexandra Moreno Gonzalez, 2017. https://soundcloud.com/innovadotmu/james-tenney-1 (accessed June 26, 2020).

———. 2005a. *Interim* interview. January 10. Electronic file, JTF (unprocessed). Transcription by Lucien Ye, 2017.

———. 2005b. "James Tenney: Postcards from the Edge—Making Connections." Interview with Frank J. Oteri, May 8–11. *NewMusicBox*. https://nmbx.newmusicusa.org/james-tenney-postcards-from-the-edge/ (accessed June 26, 2020).

———. 2005c. Telephone interview with Austin Clarkson, February 3. Transcript. JTF 2010-050/005 (14).

———. 2007. "James Tenney Remembers: Excerpts from the Last Interviews." Interview with Eric Smigel and Veronika Krausas, July 31–August 4, 2006, Valencia, CA. *Tempo* 61(241): 22–33.

———. 2008. "Interview with James Tenney." Interview with Donnacha Dennehy, March 2, 2006, Dublin, Ireland. *Contemporary Music Review* 27(1): 79–89.

———. 2015. *From Scratch: Writings in Music Theory*. Edited by Larry Polansky, Lauren Pratt, Robert Wannamaker, and Michael Winter. Urbana: University of Illinois Press.

Tenney, James, with Larry Polansky. (1978) 2015. "Hierarchical Temporal Gestalt Perception in Music: A Metric Space Model." In Tenney 2015, 201–33.

Thompson, D'Arcy W. (1917) 1992. *On Growth and Form*. Cambridge: Cambridge University Press.

Varèse, Edgard, and Chou Wen-chung. 1966. "The Liberation of Sound." *Perspectives of New Music* 5(1): 11–19.

Varèse, Louise. 1972. *Varèse: A Looking-Glass Diary*. New York: Norton.

Wannamaker, Robert. 2008a. "North American Spectralism: The Music of James Tenney." In *Spectral World Musics: Proceedings of the Istanbul International Spectral Music Conference, Nov. 18–23, 2003*, ed. Robert Reigle and Paul Whitehead, 348–67. Istanbul, Turkey: Pan Yayincilik.

———. 2008b. "The Spectral Music of James Tenney." *Contemporary Music Review* 27(1): 91–130.

———. 2012. "Rhythmicon Relationships, Farey Sequences and James Tenney's *Spectral CANON for CONLON Nancarrow*." *Music Theory Spectrum* 34(2): 48–70.

Webern, Anton, and Willi Reich. 1963. *The Path to the New Music*. Bryn Mawr, PA: Theodore Presser.

Wertheimer, Max. (1923) 1938. "Untersuchungen zur Lehre von der Gestalt II." In *Psycologische Forschung* 4:301–50. English translation published as "Laws of Organization in Perceptual Forms." In *A Source Book of Gestalt Psychology*, ed. Willis D. Ellis, 71–88. London: Routledge and Kegan Paul.

Winter, Michael. 2008. "On James Tenney's *Arbor Vitae* for String Quartet." *Contemporary Music Review* 27(1): 131–50.

Wood, Patte, and John R. Pierce. 1991. "Recollections with John Robinson Pierce." *Computer Music Journal* 15(4): 17–28.

Xenakis, Iannis. 1958. "In Search of a Stochastic Music." *Gravesaner Blätter* 11–12:98–111, 112–22.

Young, Gayle. 2006. In "Tenney remembrances." Electronic file, JTF (unprocessed).

Zavagna, Paolo, Giovanni Dinello, Alvise Mazzucato, Simone Sacchi, and Dario Sevieri. 2015. "The Remake of James Tenney's *Analog #1: Noise Study*, a Didactic Experience." *Revue d'Esthétique Musicale LIEN: L'Enseignement des Musiques Électroacoustiques* 7:59–83.

Index

5-limit. *See under n*-limit
7-limit. *See under n*-limit

Adams, John Luther, 1, 88, 283n3, 298n1
aggregate: Cagean, 13, 115; pitch-class, 26–29. *See also* harmonic series aggregate
algorithmic composition, 2, 4, 31, 54, 63–68; dissonant counterpoint algorithm, 24, 237–41, 246–50; in electronic music, 5–6, 50–51, 76–82; in instrumental music, 9–10, 194–95, 231–35, 246–58; PLF subroutine, 77, 279n32; poetry, 7, 89
amplitude modulation (AM, tremolo), 61–63, 70, 77, 99, 276–77n15
Annual Avant Garde Festivals of New York, 6–7, 51, 84, 87
Artaud, Antonin, 94–96
available-pitch procedure, 113, 172–75, 187–88, 227–29, 244–45

bandwidth, 268–69
Barlow, Clarence, 177, 292n37
Bartók, Béla, 19–20, 73, 279n28
beating (acoustical), 126, 128–29, 173, 225; and tuning 146, 222, 286n25. *See also* roughness, sensory
Bell Telephone Laboratories ("Bell Labs"), 5–6, 13–14, 48–52, 56, 58, 60–62
Benedetti, Giovanni, 292n37
Bennington College, 3, 23–25, 31, 137
Berg, Alban, 20, 86

Brakhage, Stan, 3, 19–22, 41, 54–55, 96; collaborations with Tenney, 3, 19–20, 272nn2–5, 295n18, 296–97n8
Brecht, George, 7, 85, 87, 89–92
Brown, Earle, 55, 86, 87

Cage, John, 1–2, 259–60, 298n1; *Concert for Piano and Orchestra*, 98; and Fluxus, 7, 90–92; and harmony, 13–14, 138–39, 225–27; influence on Tenney, 6, 10–14, 49, 54–58, 123, 199–202; interactions with Tenney, 54–55, 237; *Music of Changes*, 6, 10–11, 52, 58, 112–13, 115; *Sonatas and Interludes for Prepared Piano*, 3, 20–21, 25, 54–55, 88; *Williams Mix*, 35; works performed by Tenney, 6, 55, 87–88
CalArts. *See* California Institute of the Arts
California Institute of the Arts (CalArts), 94, 110–11, 125, 169, 237; Tenney's students and colleagues at, 283n3, 297n1
Carrillo, Julián, 287
CDC. *See* consonance/dissonance concept
center frequency, 268–69
chance operations, 6, 10–11, 13, 37, 56, 112–13
Chou Wen-chung, 22–23, 25, 286n28
clang. *See under* temporal gestalt unit
cohesion (gestalt), 44–45, 53, 206
Coleman, Jaybird, 189, 294n16
collage, 25, 35–41, 93–94
combination tone, 128; defined, 286n23
compactness. *See under* harmony, theory of
compound polyphony, 6, 25, 47, 68

conceptual fundamental (GCD pitch), 187, 218; defined, 152, 294n14; octave progressions in, 172–75, 229–31, 247–48

connectedness. *See under* harmony, theory of

consonance/dissonance, 138, 144, 200; measures of, 151–55, 158–59, 165–68; theories of, 147–51, 155–57, 290n23, 292n37

consonance/dissonance concept (CDC), 147–51, 155–58, 168

contour perception, 246, 284–85n14

Corner, Philip, 6, 55, 83–87, 98, 283n2

cosmology, 236

Cowell, Henry, 88, 23–24, 42, 87, 238–39

Crawford (Seeger), Ruth, 10, 23–24, 88, 238, 247

critical bandwidth, 148, 227–30

Darmstädter Ferienkurse, 2, 177, 237

density: temporal, 71, 213; vertical, 65, 67, 99, 202

difference tone. *See* combination tone

disjunction ratio, 153, 165–68. *See also* intersection ratio

dissonance. *See* consonance/dissonance

dissonant counterpoint, 4, 24, 237–41, 247–48

dissonant counterpoint algorithm. *See under* algorithmic composition

element. *See under* temporal gestalt unit

Ellis, Alexander, 289–90n20

embodiment, 15–17, 93–98, 282n21

entropy, 236

envelope: amplitude 63, 73–74, 119; generation, 33–34, 59–61; stochastic determination, 65, 77–79; swell, 117; and timbre, 13, 81

equal temperaments, fine, xv, 146, 173–74, 232, 287n3, 288–89n14

Erbe, Tom, 119, 278n25, 284n13

ergodicity. *See under* form

Escher, M. C., 285n15

evolution, 16–17, 142–43, 246

Fechner's law, 261–63

feedback, acoustical, 33, 97. *See also* statistical feedback

Feldman, Morton, 55, 87

filter, 33, 59, 62, 77–80, 103

Fluxus, 7, 84–86, 89–92

Flynt, Henry, 84, 280n8

Folkways Records, 87

form, 66–67, 116–17, 136, 225, 231; ergodic, 56–58, 68, 81, 115, 117; extrinsically limited, 109; golden ratio proportion, 73, 117, 234, 248, 279n28; as an object of perception, 12–13, 81; and process, 52–54, 112–16; state, shape and structure, 46; theory of, 5, 41–47 (*see also* Tenney, James— writings: *Meta/Hodos*)

formant, 33, 59, 62, 77–78; defined, 294n19; in speech, 189–91

frequency modulation (FM, vibrato), 60–63, 77, 103, 107, 276–77n15

frequency ratio: complexity, 144, 148; correspondence with pitch interval, 142, 261–63; superparticular, 129, 168. *See also* harmonic perception

fusion, harmonic. *See under* harmonic perception

Gaburo, Kenneth, 31, 273n2

Garland, Peter, 15–16, 86, 88, 101

GCD frequency, 152. *See also* conceptual fundamental

GCD pitch, 152. *See also* conceptual fundamental

generalized harmonic distance. *See under* harmony, theory of

Gershwin, George, 18–20

gestalt psychology, 5, 43, 49, 53–54

Gilmore, Bob, 1, 88, 244

Ginsberg, Allen, 84, 96

Glass, Philip, 87, 110, 283n1

glissando, 267; gradual, 127–31, 217; harmonic, 176–82; rapid (contour), 75–76, 101–09, 118–24

golden section, 73, 117, 234, 248, 279n28

Goldstein, Malcolm, 6, 55, 84, 86–87, 98, 127

Grisey, Gérard, 172, 293n4

grouping, perceptual, 5, 13, 42–46, 66–68, 121

Guevara, Ernesto ("Che"), 102

Guttman, Newman, 275n2

Hába, Alois, 287n3

harmonic distance. *See under* harmony, theory of

harmonic perception, 137–44; harmonic fusion, 9, 139–41, 171, 188, 223; toneness, 147, 149–51, 170–71, 187–88, 218

harmony, theory of, 193; compactness, 160–61, 196, 205; connectedness, 160, 196, 252–57; containment, 162–65, 197, 253; generalized harmonic distance, 159; harmonic distance, 139–40, 155–60, 165–68, 193; harmonic period, 152–53; harmonic relations, 8, 135, 139–40; harmonic space, 9–10, 136–37, 155–68, 193–95; octave equivalence, 139, 156, 159, 287–88n5; pitch-class projection space, 156–62; polarity, 139, 162–65; proximity 139, 155, 160; rootedness, 139, 162–65; tolerance, interval, 139, 144–46

harmonic series, 8–10, 136–38; compositions referencing, 2, 169–72 (*see also* Tenney, James— compositions: *Clang, Spectral CANON for CONLON Nancarrow, Harmonium #1, Three Indigenous Songs, Critical Band, In a Large . . ., Diaphonic* Study); and containment, 162–63; definition and properties, 140–44, 150, 267–68, 288n9; history of Tenney's interest in, 136–38, 155, 170–72; rhythmic analogs, 9 (*see also* Tenney, James—compositions: *Spectral CANON for CONLON Nancarrow*)

harmonic series aggregate, 151–53, 137, 165, 201
harmonic spectrum. *See under* spectrum
harmonicity, 149–53, 168; as formal parameter, 170–72, 175, 177, 187–88, 217–18
Harrison, Lou, 88, 183, 238
Helmholtz, Hermann von, 148–49
Higgins, Dick, 83–84, 90, 283n3
Hiller, Lejaren, 4, 31–35, 48–49, 56–57, 137; *ILLIAC Suite*, 63–64

indeterminacy, 56, 90, 100, 118; subjective (listener indeterminacy), 116, 126 (*see also* Tenney, James—compositions: *For Ann [rising]*). *See also* available-pitch procedure
information theory, 31, 49, 56–57, 236
inharmonic spectrum. *See under* spectrum
interpolation, 60, 70–71, 79; cosine, 117, 233
intersection ratio, 139–40, 151–55, 168, 187–88, 218–21. *See also* disjunction ratio
Ives, Charles: compound (complex) polyphony, 47, 68, 202; dedications to, 114; *Essays before a Sonata*, 88, 295n2; influence on Tenney, 20, 36, 47, 88, 202, 238, 285n16; Piano Sonata No. 2 "Concord, Mass., 1840–60," 24–25, 87; quotation technique, 4, 35; Tenney as performer, 6, 86–88; *Three Places in New England*, 285n16

jazz, 287n1
Joplin, Scott, 87–88
Joyce, James, 55
JTF (James Tenney Fonds), xv
Judson Dance Theater, 6, 84, 91, 98
just intonation, 137, 144–46, 164; approximations to, 146, 288–89nn14–15; defined, 142. *See also* Partch, Harry

Knowles, Alison, 84–85, 90, 93, 283n3, 285n18; *A House of Dust*, 7, 89
Koffka, Kurt, 42–43, 53
Köhler, Wolfgang, 42–43, 274n14
Klangfarbenmelodie, 29, 225

lattice. *See* harmony, theory of: harmonic space
Lennon, John, 94
Lewin, David, 275n2
Ligeti, György, 1
logarithmic relationship, 142, 261–64
Lucier, Alvin, 87

Maciunas, George, 84, 89–90, 280–81n8
Mathews, Max, 5, 48, 50, 59, 62–63
Meta†Hodos. See under Tenney, James—writings
metric, 158–59, 290n26
Miller, Joan, 59
minimalism, 2, 88, 92, 114
minor triad, 144, 160–61, 228n10
modulation, signal; timbre, relevance to, 13, 62–

63. *See also* amplitude modulation; frequency modulation
Moles, Abraham, 263
Monk, Thelonious, 287n1
Moorman, Charlotte, 6–7, 84
monophonic, 45–45, 54, 68, 239; definition of, 47
morphology, 13, 46, 115, 130
motivic development, 12, 26–29
Mumma, Gordon, 87, 176, 292n1
Murail, Tristan, 172

Nancarrow, Conlon, 75, 86, 88, 176, 225
Neumann, John von, 64
neural plasticity, 17, 146–47
n-limit, 295nn5–6; 5-limit, 156; 7-limit, 196
noise, broadband: definition, 268–69; generation, 5, 58, 61, 276–77n15; as musical material, 63, 99–100, 134, 150 (*see also* Tenney, James—compositions: *Analog #1 [Noise Study]; Fabric for Che; Phases*)
noise music, 7, 101
Nowak, Lionel, 23, 189

octatonic scale 172–74, 186, 198
octave equivalence. *See under* harmony, theory of
Oldenburg, Claes, 93, 273n5
Ono, Yoko, 89, 90
Oswald, John, 40–41, 292–93n1

Partch, Harry, 4–5, 31–32, 86; dedications to, 88, 136, 171; theories, 42, 144–46, 156, 167, 200–201
Pierce, John R., 48, 274–75nn1–2
pitch-class repetition, avoidance of close, 26, 238–41, 247
pitch-class projection space. *See under* harmony, theory of
pitch perception, 137, 155, 246
player piano, 50, 57, 176–83, 239
plunderphonics, 2, 40–41, 273n10. *See also* Oswald, John
Polansky, Larry, 1, 178, 274n19, 292n1
polyharmony: polychord, 186, 255, 197–98, 294n13; polymodality, 206; polytonality, 255
polyphony, 5–6, 47, 67–68, 200–203, 240
polyrhythm, 104–7, 167–68, 176, 180–83
Polytechnic Institute of Brooklyn ("Brooklyn Polytechnic"), 6, 84, 102, 110
Pratt, Lauren, 224
Presley, Elvis, 4. *See also* Tenney, James—compositions: *Collage #1 ("Blue Suede")*
process, 52–54, 92, 112–14
distribution, probability, 64–65
pseudo-random number generator (PRNG), 59, 64–65, 70, 76

quarter tone, 146, 173, 231–32, 287n3
Quatuor Bozzini, 222, 251

Radulescu, Horatiu, 172
ragtime, 136
Rainer, Yvonne, 16, 280n1
Rameau, Jean-Philippe, 155
ratio class, definition of, 156
ratio. *See* frequency ratio
rational number system, 167
Reich, Steve, 110, 112–14, 283n1, 283–84n5
Reich, Wilhelm, 54, 94, 96–97
Risset, Jean-Claude, 48, 118
rootedness. *See under* harmony, theory of
Rothenberg, Jerome, 189
roughness, sensory, 147–51, 227–29
Rudhyar, Dane, 23, 86, 88, 238
Ruggles, Carl, 4, 23–24, 86–88, 238–39, 249

Satie, Erik, 19–20, 55, 87. *See also* Tenney,
  James—compositions: *Quiet Fan for Erik Satie*
scales, harmonic, 172–73, 186, 247
Schaeffer, Pierre, 42
Schneemann, Carolee, xiii, 3, 31, 83–85, 91–98,
  110; collage, 4, 36, 274n14; correspondence
  with, 111, 115; dedications to, 34–37, 41; films, 7,
  93, 96; and form, 52; kinetic theater, 7, 93–95;
  Meat Joy, 7, 93–96, 280–81n8; meeting Tenney,
  22–23
Schoenberg, Arnold, 11, 17, 22, 42, 86; and form,
  12–13, 113–14; and harmony, 135, 155, 164, 226;
  influence, 19–21, 239, 272n4; *Klangfarbenmelodie*, 29
scordatura, 146, 258
Seeger, Charles, 24, 238–39, 247
segment. *See under* temporal gestalt unit
segmentation, formal, 45–46, 65–67, 120–21
segregation (gestalt), 43–45, 53, 120, 206, 233
sequence. *See under* temporal gestalt unit
serialism, 12, 21, 86, 239
Shannon, Claude, 275n9
shape. *See under* form
Shepard, Roger, 119
Shepard tone, 119, 121, 284n9, 285n15
Sims, Ezra, 288–89n14
smoothness, sensory. *See* roughness, sensory
spectral music, 2, 172, 287n4
spectrography, xiii, 265–69, 299n1
spectrum, 265–69; harmonic, 267; inharmonic,
  131–33, 141, 150, 268
speech, musical transcription of, 9, 171, 189–92,
  225
state. *See under* form
statistical feedback, 238–41, 247, 256–57
stochastic techniques, 10, 57–58, 63–68, 194–95,
  239–41. *See also* chance operations; indeterminacy; Tenney, James—compositions: *Analog
  #1 (Noise Study)*, *Phases*, *Bridge*, *Flocking*, *Diaphonic Study*, *Arbor Vitae*
Stockhausen, Karlheinz, 42, 84, 87, 263

Stravinsky, Igor, 11, 135; *Petrushka* chord, 186, 197,
  294n13
structure. *See under* form
Stumpf, Carl, 150–51, 168
swell form, 73, 76, 116–17, 131, 184

tape-delay system, 33, 113, 170
tape-echo. *See* tape-delay system
tape music, 13, 32–41, 49, 101–7, 284n8
Taubman, Dorothy, 110
Taylor, Paul, 272n9
temporal density, 71, 213
temporal gestalt unit, 43–44, 47, 66–68, 120–21;
  clang, 44–47, 49, 66–68; element, 43–46, 66–
  68; sequence, 44–45; segment, 44, 67, 208–9
Tenney, James: as performer, 1, 24–25, 55, 84,
  86–88, 93–94, 201; students of, 283n3, 292–
  93n1; tributes to, 1, 298n1
—compositions: *A House of Dust*, 7, 89; *Ain't I
  a Woman?*, 171, 225, 295n21; *Analog #1 (Noise
  Study)*, 5–6, 50, 56–57, 68–76, 109, 115; *Arbor
  Vitae*, 10, 194, 250–58; *A Rose Is a Rose Is a
  Round*, 117, 124, 136; *August Harp*, 125; *Band*,
  194; *Beast*, 24, 117, 124, 149, 225; *Bridge*, 9, 88,
  194, 199–216; *Cellogram*, 24, 117, 125; *Chamber
  Music*, 85, 89, 91, 98; *Changes: 64 Studies for
  6 Harps*, 162, 194, 239, 251, 287n1; *Chorales*
  series, 24, 111, 172; *Choreogram*, 7, 85, 91,
  97–101; *Chromatic Canon*, 88, 194; *Clang*, 9,
  111, 113, 146, 170–76; *Cognate Canons*, 225;
  Collage #1 ("Blue Suede"), 4, 34–41, 52, 88; *Collage #2 ("Viet Flakes")*, 7, 85, 93, 102; *Critical
  Band*, 9, 171, 225–31; *Dialogue*, 50, 57, 117, 239;
  Diapason, 171, 241; *Diaphonic Study*, 10, 171,
  237, 239–41, 246–50; *Diaphonic Toccata*, 171,
  237, 239, 241, 247; *Diaphonic Trio*, 171, 237,
  239, 241, 247; *Entrance/Exit Music*, 7, 50, 89,
  91–92; *Ergodos I*, 50, 57, 92, 98; *Ergodos II*, 6,
  50, 56–59, 92, 98, 113; *Ergodos III*, 58, 225, 231;
  Essay (After a Sonata), 88; *Fabric for Che*, 7,
  101–09, 115, 276–77n15; *Five Stochastic Studies*,
  50–51, 63; *Flocking*, 9, 225, 231–36, 287n3; *For
  Ann (rising)*, 7–8, 92–3, 110–11, 118–26; *Form
  2*, 171; *For Piano and . . .*, 289n14; *Glissade*, 170,
  171, 194, 217, 288n14; *Harmonium #1*, 9, 16, 171,
  183–88, 293–94n12; *Harmonium #2*, 295n1;
  Harmonium #3, 9, 194, 193–99; *Harmonium
  #4*, 295n1; *Harmonium #5*, 295n1; *Harmonium
  #6*, 194, 188n14; *Harmonium #7*, 194; *Having
  Never Written a Note for Percussion*, 8, 95,
  114, 131–34, 286n20; *Hey When I Sing These
  4 Songs Hey Look What Happens*, 136, 189,
  287n2; *Improvisation*, 23; *Improvisations for
  Medea*, 35; *In a large, open space*, 10, 241–46,
  247; *In a large, reverberant space*, 241–46; *Instrumental Responses*, 50; *Interim*, 19–21; *In the
  Aeolian Mode*, 111; *Koan*, 8, 111, 116–17, 127–31,

216–17; *Koan for String Quartet*, 9, 117, 130, 216–23; *Last Spring in Toronto*, 225, 231, 236; *Listen . . . !*, 94; *Maximusic*, 91, 93, 98, 125, 131; *Metabolic Music*, 101; *Monody*, 24; *Music for Player Piano*, 50, 52, 57; *(night)*, 124; *Orchestral Study #1 (The "Creation Field")*, 235–36; *Panacousticon*, 171, 288–89n14; *Phases*, 5–6, 50, 54, 76–82, 96–97; *Pika-Don*, 225; political works, 7, 9, 85, 101–09, 225; *Postal Pieces*, 8, 91–93, 124–34, 216; *Prelude and Toccata*, 239, 247; *Quiet Fan for Erik Satie*, 111, 117, 136; *Quintext: Five Textures*, 111, 136, 170, 288n14; *Radio Piece*, 50; *Rune*, 224–25, 232; *Saxony*, 113, 170–71; *Seeds*, 3, 23, 25–30, 225; *Seegersongs*, 237, 239, 241, 247; *Septet*, 171; *Sonata for Ten Wind Instruments*, 24, 88; *Song 'n' Dance for Harry Partch*, 171, 288–89n14; soundtracks, 7, 19–21, 92–93, 272n3, 273–74n12, 296–97n7; *Spectral CANON for CONLON Nancarrow*, 9, 88, 113–14, 170, 176–83; *Spectrum* series, 237, 241; *Stochastic (String) Quartet*, 50, 57; *String Complement*, 50, 98; *Swell Piece*, 92–93, 117, 125; *Swell Piece #2*, 30, 75, 116, 125; *Swell Piece #3*, 125; *Symphony*, 146, 171; *Tableaux Vivants*, 194, 239, 251; *Thermocouple #1*, 7, 95, 97; *Thermocouple #2*, 7, 95; *The Road to Ubud*, 225, 239; *Thirteen Ways of Looking at a Blackbird*, 23; *Three Harmonic Studies*, 146, 171; *Three Indigenous Songs*, 9, 171, 189–92; *Three New Seeds*, 225; *Three Pieces for Drum Quartet*, 111, 170; *Three Pieces for Mechanical Drum*, 170; *Three Rags for Pianoforte*, 136; *Three Theater Pieces*, 85, 91, 97–98 (see also *Thermocouple #1*; *Thermocouple #2*); *To Weave (a meditation)*, 24, 117, 236, 239, 247; *Two Koans and a Canon*, 288n14; *Voice(s)*, 171, 194, 244, 288–89n14; *Water on the Mountain . . . Fire in Heaven*, 162, 194, 288–89n14
—writings: *A History of 'Consonance' and 'Dissonance,'* 147, 193; "John Cage and the Theory of Harmony," 139; *Meta/Hodos*, 5–6, 13, 25, 41–47, 53–54, 65–66, 120, 202, 231; "META Meta/Hodos," 47, 278n21
texture, 12, 17, 47, 116, 169–70

theater, 7, 85, 91–96
thematic development, 12
Thompson, D'Arcy Wentworth, 51–54, 76, 96
timbre (tone color), 136, 148–49, 267; duality with harmony, 141–43, 172, 195; origins of interest in, 3–4, 13–14, 20, 34, 58, 115; research, 5, 49, 62–63, 99, 138, 277n16. See also *Klangfarbenmelodie*; Tenney, James—compositions: *Seeds*
tolerance, interval. *See under* harmony, theory of
toneness. *See under* harmonic perception
Tone Roads Chamber Ensemble, 6, 51, 55, 86–87, 110
Tone Roads West, 88
tonnetz. See harmony, theory of: harmonic space
tremolo. *See* amplitude modulation
Truth, Sojourner, 225, 295n21

unit generator (UGEN), 58–62
University of California, Santa Cruz, 169, 183, 292n1
University of Denver, 20
University of Illinois, 4, 31–35, 41, 49, 56, 137

Varèse, Edgard, 1, 62, 86–88; dedications to, 76, 81–82, 88; and dissonance, 95–96, 238–39; and form, 51–52, 54, 112–13; influence on Tenney, 3–4, 25, 32, 34–35, 75–76; *Ionisation*, 21, 70, 76; *Poème électronique*, 34, 101; studies with, 3, 21–23, 51; and technology, 4, 32, 51–52
vertical density, 65, 67, 99, 202
vibrato. *See* frequency modulation
Vietnam War, 7, 85, 93, 97, 102
von Huene, Stephen, 170

Webern, Anton, 3, 19–21, 26–27, 86–87, 239; *Six Bagatelles*, Op. 9, 25, 29, 42
Wertheimer, Max, 42–43
Winter, Michael, 239, 251, 297n1

Xenakis, Iannis, 42, 63–64

Yale University, 6, 84, 111
York University, 169, 292n1
Young, La Monte, 90, 92

ROBERT WANNAMAKER is Associate Dean
for Academic and Special Projects in the Herb
Alpert School of Music at the California Institute
of the Arts. He is a composer, improviser, music
theorist, mathematician, and educator.

The University of Illinois Press
is a founding member of the
Association of University Presses.

———————————————

Text designed by Jim Proefrock
Composed in 11.25/14 Adobe Minion Pro
with ScalaSans display
at the University of Illinois Press
Manufactured by Versa Press, Inc.

University of Illinois Press
1325 South Oak Street
Champaign, IL 61820-6903
www.press.uillinois.edu